CORPORATION OF THE CITY OF BURLINGTON

STAND BY

BURLINGTON - ONTARIO

Floral bed at Central Branch of the Burlington Public Library, marking the 125th Anniversary of the incorporation of Burlington as a village in 1873.

Claire Emery Machan

From Pathway to Skyway Revisited

The Story of Burlington

Canadian Cataloguing in Publication Data

Burlington Historical Society
    From pathway to skyway revisited: the story of Burlington

Includes bibliographical references.

ISBN 0-9691040-1-4

1. Burlington (Ont.) – History.   I. Burlington
Historical Society.   II. Title.

FC3099.B87M32 1997   971.3'533   C97-901163-9
F1059.5.B9M32 1997

Published by
The Burlington Historical Society
Burlington, Ontario
1131 Carol Street
Burlington, Ontario L7S 1Z9
Telephone (905) 631-1097

Produced by
Ampersand Printing
123 Woolwich Street
Guelph, Ontario N1H 3V1
Telephone (519) 836-8800
Fax (519) 836-7204

David Craig

*The Burlington Historical Society thanks the artist, David Craig, for giving the Society
permission to copy his print, Yesterday, Today and Tomorrow, for the cover of From
Pathway to Skyway Revisited. Mr. Craig is a Metro artist who has recently completed
the exciting illustrations for the Canadian Tire Corporation's 75th Anniversary book,
Our Store. He has also been a designer/artist for the popular Bradford Exchange
commemorative plates on World War II. Mr. Craig's realistic art can also be seen in the
new Hockey Hall of Fame in Toronto. In his spare time, he lectures at the Onatrio
College of Art, a school of which he is a graduate.*

To ALL those men and women who, from the early 1800s to the present day, have worked for what they believed was the good of the area which now lies in the City of Burlington - and who have made it one of the finest places in Canada to live.

Contributors

To the artist David Craig who kindly permitted us the use of his eminently suitable print, Burlington Yesterday, Today and Tomorrow for our book cover, the Burlington Historical Society is greatly indebted. Mr. Craig's original painting hangs in the Council Chambers of the Burlington City Hall, while a larger version of the print is at the entrance to the Intensive Care Wing of Joseph Brant Memorial Hospital.

We also offer our sincere thanks to the following groups and individuals who have assisted us with the book project:

Frank Armstrong, Les Armstrong, Mary Becker, John Bauld, Laurie Branch, Bob Chambers, Suzanne Craven, Dave Davidson, Bob Freeman, Bruce Filman, Dr. Jim Galloway, Jane Irwin, Muriel Kempling, Elizabeth Mangnall, Mary Munro, Barbara Penfold, Karen Pettit, Gery Puley, Lois Unsworth Reynolds, Joyce Savoline, Karen Skidmore, Paddy Torsney, W.R. Warren, and Bill Whiskin.

Other Sources

Archives of Ontario
Burlington Historical Society members
Burlington Hydro-Electric Commission
Burlington Museums personnel
The Burlington Post
Burlington Public Library
Canada Centre for Inland Waters
The Canadian Champion
City of Burlington City Clerk's Office
    (Parks and Recreation Dept.)
Hamilton Public Library
The Hamilton Spectator (Burlington News)
Joncor Publishing Inc.
LaSalle Park Pavilion Fundraising Committee
Leaver Mushroom Company Ltd.
Royal Canadian Naval Association of Burlington
Voortman Limited

Acknowledgments

1967

The authors are grateful for help given by the following: Miss Ida Reddy and the staff of the Burlington Public Library, employees of the town in almost every department, members of the Centennial Committee, business and professional men and industrialists, Mrs. M. Easter and Bruce Lindley of the Board of Education administrative offices, and M.M. Robinson whose enthusiasm got the authors started.

Special gratitude must be given to those who helped prepare the book for publication: W.J. McCulloch who spent many hours with black pencil in hand, cutting the book down to size; Emerson Lavender who reviewed manuscripts; Mr. J. Richardson who proofread; and Leo Podetz who proofread and coordinated the Burlington end of the publication.

The authors are also greatly indebted to the many residents of Burlington and district who patiently answered questions and recounted stories of the old days. Some made available space in their homes in which the writers were able to work. Others lent valuable books, papers and pictures for months on end, trusting the authors to keep them safe. Still others helped with research and did typing. This cooperation and interest speeded the work and encouraged the writers. The many names of these people cannot all be listed - but *they* know who they are, and will, we hope, accept the thanks of everyone involved in the publication of this volume.

Barbara Ford and Claire Emery

1996

Once again I must express gratitude for the same cooperation from so many people, as Barbara and I had when writing the original book. The staff and facilities of the Reference Department of Central Library were vital to my research, and Kimberley Short and Chief Librarian Wendy Schick aided me in writing the library chapter. Volunteers at Information Burlington answered my many queries. City employees were helpful, especially Annie Budz, Records Coordinator, who lent booklets of information. Fire Chief, Terry Edwards, and Inspector Dan Okuloski of the police department gave me accounts of the workings of their bailiwicks. Mary Dillon and Laurie Branch provided input, and Scott McCammon of the Chamber of Commerce reported on the Chamber's work.

Tanya Jarvis, a McMaster University student helped with research and computerization. Ruth and John Borthwick worked on the church and education chapters. I made contacts, by phone and in person, with people who were knowledgeable about city organizations, clubs and societies; their eagerness to share information was encouraging. Artist Gery Puley spent time with fellow artists for data on their part of the cultural community.

I am most grateful to the Historical Society for undertaking the publication of this book and especially to the book committee who researched, proofread and edited: Ruth and John Borthwick, Mary Fraser, Peggy Armstrong, Florence Meares and Katherine Clifton. This group was assisted by Charles Davis, a computer consultant, Jane Irwin who proofread, Catherine Demers, Edna Phillips, and Glen Machan for layout and proofreading.

Claire Emery Machan

Introduction

1967

The authors of this history spent 15 months solving an intricate jigsaw puzzle. It began with a myriad of disjointed facts and stories from the days of the Mohawk Indians, United Empire Loyalists and the nucleus of a community that grew around Brant's Block. The puzzle began to take shape as copious notes were compiled about people and their lives in Wellington Square, Aldershot, Kilbride and Nelson Township centres such as Appleby, and Zimmerman which exist today only in people's memories.

Interviews with long-time residents and members of Burlington's pioneer families proved fascinating, and the hours spent culling stories and facts from old diaries, yellowed documents and hand-written council minutes, began to give us a clear picture of our town.

Pieces of the jigsaw puzzle were finally fitted together with the story of amalgamation in 1958, but history books never have an absolute ending and up-to-date facts about Burlington were being added, even as chapters were sent to the publishers.

Through research and editing, we have endeavoured to make this volume historically accurate as far as possible with the information available to us. For the sake of brevity, it was not possible to use all the material we collected and it must also be noted that the spelling of some names and places has changed through the years.

We realize that the first chapter may be of interest mainly to geography buffs and certain sections of the book will have more meaning to one family than to another, but the human interest stories and anecdotes that have passed down through the generations could have happened in any community.

We are deeply grateful to all the Burlington residents who searched their memories (and their family albums) for us, who lent us treasured documents, patiently answered our endless questions and checked our notes for accuracy. Thanks also to our husbands and children. Without their cooperation, this book would never have been written.

The people about whom we wrote seem very real to us and we feel nostalgia for a friendly small-town atmosphere that we sincerely hope has been transmitted in these pages.

Barbara Ford and Claire Emery

1996

When I told Barbara Ford I had been asked to update this book, her comment was "lucky you". I soon realized she may have been sarcastic. It was no easy task. The changes in the past 30 years have been tremendous. For one thing, Burlington has become a city and in more than name only. Some of the more visible growth has been in housing, schools, business and industry, places of worship and infrastructure.

When Barbara and I researched the original book there wasn't much information readily available. By 1996, there was too much. I had to try to record the most significant events and developments - my choices were subjective and may be disputed by some who were more closely involved. I fully expect to hear comments such as, "That's not the way it REALLY happened", or "The year's wrong" .. or the day .. or the month, or "I certainly don't remember THAT", or "Why didn't you mention such and such".

For an apology, I quote a comment by Robert Fulford in The Globe and Mail, Wednesday, May 1, 1996: "Time... when it converts people and events into history, erases differences, discards details, conflates categories that people once thought crucial - and often gets things wrong."

Claire Emery Machan

Preface

1967

On the occasion of the celebration of the one hundredth anniversary of Confederation in Canada, the Confederation Centennial Committee of Burlington commissioned Mrs. Barbara Ford and Mrs. Claire Emery to write the history of Burlington.

The many hours of diligent research spent in preparation for this publication has given us a most complete story of our community that every citizen now and in the future will find both informative and interesting.

I would personally like to thank the many residents who made available historical records, information and pictures, without which this book could not have been written.

To the members of the Centennial Committee for their assistance in editing the manuscript, Mr. W. J. McCulloch and Mr. Emerson Lavender, my sincere gratitude.

Between these covers history comes to life to acquaint the reader with Burlington in the past and, as the title depicts, it is truly a history of Burlington "From Pathway to Skyway".

James H. Parker, Chairman,
Confederation Centennial Committee of Burlington

1996

"Without words, without writing and without books, there would be no history." *Herman Hesse (1877-1962)*

The original *From Pathway to Skyway* was commissioned by the Burlington Centennial Committee to mark the occasion of Canada's 100th birthday in 1967; now 30 years later, the Burlington Historical Society has published a revised and updated version of the earlier book and titled it

From Pathway to Skyway Revisited. It has been written for the 1998 celebration of the 125th anniversary of our incorporation as the Village of Burlington.

From Pathway to Skyway Revisited has been a two-year labour of love by the Burlington Historical Society Book Committee. Its members, Peggy Armstrong, Ruth and John Borthwick, Katherine Clifton, Mary Fraser and Florence Meares have devoted hours to interviewing, researching, proof-reading and picture collecting and evaluating. Their efforts would have come to naught without the willing co-operation of local groups, individuals and institutions. For all contributions we are grateful. To tie various elements of our work together, we were fortunate to have the talents of Claire Emery Machan, one of the two original authors. With diligence and expertise and insisting on factual accuracy, Claire has written a detailed history of Burlington's last 30 years to add to the original book, now revised. Brava, Claire, and thank you from the Burlington Historical Society.

The Society would welcome any written information which would rectify in future editions any inadvertent omission of credit or factual errors.

Ruth Borthwick, President,
Burlington Historical Society

Contents

1

"Know Ye the Land. . .?" — *Byron*

Histories should start at the beginning. If this is true, then Burlington's story should begin millions of years ago when this area was all below the sea. Fossils found in the bedrock deep in the earth are of salt water organisms which indicate the truth of this theory.

Gradually this part of the continent arched above the sea and the water flowed off, cutting streams and valleys as it went. The Dundas Valley running west from the tip of Lake Ontario is one of the longest pre-glacial valleys in our vicinity.

Erosion by the water during this period ate into the softer rock and left the hard rock standing. The Niagara Escarpment is believed to be the result of this erosion.

About 250,000,000 years after the land appeared above the sea, its progress was set back by the great glaciers which began to cover it. The glaciers came and went, melted and froze again until at last they began to retreat permanently, some 10,000 years ago. Most of the physical features of Burlington today are the result of the Wisconsin Glacier and its recession.

It was in Pleistocene time when this great ice pack extended over all Southern Ontario and down into Ohio. As the dripping edges melted, they once more uncovered our area. Inland lakes were formed from the melted water and the largest of these were Lake Algonquin, covering Lake Huron and Georgian Bay, and Lake Iroquois covering Lake Ontario and extending down the Mohawk Valley to Syracuse and Rome, New York. These two glacial lakes were long-lived and their beaches and bluffs can still be seen today.

The glacier changed the drainage of the Great Lakes, and the St. Lawrence Valley was dammed early in the advance and re-opened late in the recession of the glacier. The water in the lakes rose until it found an opening and spilled down the Mississippi or east through the Mohawk Valley.

When the glacial dam in the St. Lawrence lowland withdrew, it meant the end of Lake Iroquois as its water began to flow down through the Hudson valley. Finally the present Lake Ontario was left, the rim of its water a full 115 feet below the level of Lake Iroquois.

The narrow belt of land along the shore of Lake Ontario formerly covered by Lake Iroquois water has been called the Iroquois Plain. It

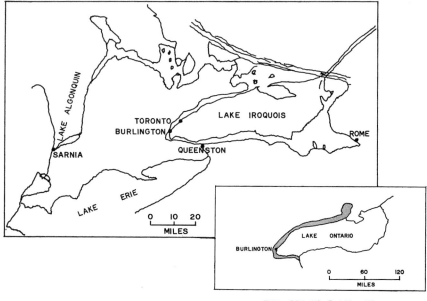

THE IROQUOIS PLAIN –

extends around the western part of Lake Ontario from the Niagara River to the Trent River, its width varying from a few hundred yards to about 8 miles. The City of Burlington is located near the southwestern end of the Hamilton-Toronto section of the Plain.

The shoreline of Lake Iroquois is marked by the great gravel bar which separates Coote's Paradise from Hamilton Harbour, and parallels the harbour and Lake Ontario shorelines into the gravel ridge in Aldershot.

The presence of the Iroquois Plain was instrumental in the settlement of our area; its physical properties supplied the early inhabitants with not only the basic necessities of life but also the means to create a thriving community.

Between the lake and the gravel ridge lies a well-drained, gently sloping, sand plain which varies in width from a mile and a half in the Willow Cove district in west Burlington to just under two miles in central Burlington. These sands were worked and re-worked by the water of Lake Iroquois until they became medium and fine textured. This fertile sandy loam soil formed the basis for the agricultural economy which was the area's first sustenance. The moderate climate influenced by the lake, giving a long frost-free growing season, and the presence of the Niagara Escarpment which deflects winds and causes the development of clouds and precipitation, have also contributed to the success of farming.

The Iroquois Plain was the first settled area in Ontario, probably due to its proximity to Lake Ontario and the avenues of transportation it provided. The attractiveness of the lake plain landscape encouraged settlement and the easy grades leading up from the lake ports made possible the spread of the growing population into the interior.

The Iroquois Bar separating Coote's Paradise from Hamilton Harbour was a natural bridge for first, road, and more recently, rail traffic. The Burlington Bar (Beach Strip) was also an important transportation route.

The old sand bars of Lake Iroquois and off-shore aprons of sand held a plentiful water supply for the first wells and the Iroquois Gravel Ridge supplied road-building material. The shale and clay inherited from Lake Iroquois have been used for brick and tile from the time of the first solid homes.

As well as providing natural resources, the shrinking Lake Iroquois and pre-glacial erosion gave the area interesting physical features which add to the beauty of the landscape. The Niagara Escarpment rises majestically 400 feet over the Iroquois Plain at Aldershot. Just northwest of Burlington, the escarpment alters from its general east/west direction and assumes a more north/south trend.

Most of the stream valleys in the Burlington area are deep, indicating that the process of down cutting has been going on since Lake Iroquois began to recede. There are no major streams here and the only one of any size is the Grindstone Creek which flows down the escarpment through Waterdown and the Hendrie Valley into Hamilton Harbour. The Twelve Mile Creek flows down through what was upper Nelson Township and empties into the lake at Bronte. The source of these creeks is back in the Beverly swamp.

Allen Creek flows through town and down into the lake just west of Brant Street. East of Brant and west of Torrance Avenue Rambo Creek discharges its water into the lake. Other similar-sized creeks flow down the escarpment at intervals all across town. Relatively short and water-filled only for a part of the year, many of them have created ravines which provide desirable residential settings.

2
Before the White Man

A history of the people of Burlington must include the first settlers, the native Canadian Indians. They came here when the land was unspoiled and left it in the same condition.

Burlington has been called "The Garden of Canada" and other descriptive phrases alluding to its beauty, but how much lovelier it must have been when the Indians pulled salmon out of the creeks and moved quietly among the stands of oak, white pine, ash, basswood and maple which came down to the water's edge. The only sounds were wind and rain in the trees, bird and animal calls and the ever changing voice of water.

The setting between lake and bay with the rising escarpment towards the rear made this area not only a place of beauty but, more important to the Indians, a strategic location. They camped at the beach and used trails up to their villages to the north. This was an important stopping place on the great lakes waterway, providing a sheltered harbour before entering the Niagara River, or, if going east, pushing across Lake Ontario.

Our knowledge of the Indian has been gleaned from descriptions left by early explorers and travellers and by discoveries made by archaeologists. Unfortunately, the Indians themselves did not write history books for our use. This fact not only has left historians groping in the dark for the early story of Canada but also has left the Indian the victim of misunderstandings. Indian public relations with the white man were, for the most part, very elementary.

Early explorers in this part of Ontario found three Indian nations, the Algonquins, the Hurons, and the Iroquois.

The latter two were inclined to the cultivation of the soil and tended to remain on the same land until, with no crop rotation, the soil was exhausted. They shared a similar language and culture but no love for each other.

At the beginning of the 17th century the Hurons lived in a narrow stretch of land along the north shore of the St. Lawrence River as far as Quebec and an area south of Georgian Bay. To the southwest were the Petuns or Tobacco Nation, friends and relatives of the Hurons. Southeast of the Petuns, west of Lake Ontario along the northeast shore of Lake Erie, the Niagara Peninsula and inland, was the Neutral Nation. This area included what is now Burlington. These Indians were on good terms with the Hurons and Iroquois who found it expedient to tolerate the Neutrals.

On the west bank of the Niagara River was the limestone quarry of the Neutrals which provided flint for arrows and spear heads used by Indians in a large part of the country. As long as flint was vital, other Indian nations respected the Neutrals.

The Algonquian territory spread above Lakes Huron and Superior, along the Ottawa River and across northern Quebec to Labrador. The Algonquins were numerous and their language was spoken by Indians from eastern Canada to the prairies except for a portion of eastern Ontario where Iroquois was the tongue of the Hurons, Tobacco and Neutral Indians.

Of the three Nations in eastern Canada, the Iroquois were the most fierce and probably the cleverest. Before America was discovered by the Europeans, three Iroquois tribes, the Mohawks, Senecas and the Onondagas had united, and early in the 16th century two other tribes, the Oneidas and Cayugas joined them to become the Five Nations. The legend goes that Hiawatha was one of the instigators of this union. In 1712, the Tuscaroras came from what is now North Carolina and the Six Nations were born.

The Iroquois were noted not only as warriors but also for their agriculture, their laws and their oratorical ability. The United States Senate and House of Representatives resemble the Six Nations council and were supposedly patterned after it.

It was not surprising then, that the Iroquois Nation, mighty in battle and with a relatively high level of development, eventually dominated the other Indian nations of this part of North America. They came to control a huge section of what is now southern Ontario and northern United States. Once the English and Dutch immigrants provided the Indians with steel, flint was no longer indispensable and the Iroquois were free to sever friendly relations with the Neutrals and to expand their territory.

In their 1609 campaign against the Iroquois, the Algonquins and Hurons allied themselves with the French. The English took on the Iroquois as allies, an attachment which persisted throughout the American Revolution and the War of 1812.

In constant wars between 1648 and 1650, the Iroquois vanquished first the Hurons and later the Neutrals. Only a handful of Hurons escaped. The few Neutrals and Tobacco Indians who were able to flee were absorbed by other tribes. The Algonquins withdrew northwest and were able to survive. The Iroquois were then free to travel unhindered from Hudson Bay to the Carolinas and controlled the routes of trade. They settled along the Mohawk Valley, the Allegheny River, in the rich Ohio country, the Upper reaches of the St. Lawrence and the eastern entrance to Lake Ontario as well as on land along the Great Lakes.

INDIAN SETTLEMENTS IN NORTH BURLINGTON

The accounts left by early French missionaries give a picture of some of the Indian settlements in Halton Region. Father Jerome Lalemant, a Jesuit missionary, wrote of a trip made by two Jesuits. They arrived in November, 1640 at the first village of the Neutral Nation named Kandoucho, which was reportedly located on Lake Medad. An old Jesuit map of this area shows an Indian village at about the site of Lake Medad. Unfortunately for the missionaries, false stories had been spread as to their characters and their intentions. They found "that terror had gone before them and caused the doors of the cabins everywhere to be closed." They visited 18 villages of the Neutrals before returning to Huron country.

The Jesuits, perhaps prejudiced by the cool receptions they received from the Indians, did not leave a favourable picture of the Neutrals in their written accounts of their adventures. Another missionary, however, corroborated the Jesuits' impressions. Father Joseph de La Roche Daillon gave an account of a journey taken in 1626 to the country of the Neutrals which he said included both sides of Lake Ontario. "Their real business is hunting and war. Out of that they are very lazy and you see them, like beggars in France, when they have their fill, lying on their bellies in the sun."

Father Lalemant, comparing the Neutrals with the Hurons said, "They appear taller, stronger, and better proportioned...They cover the bare flesh with a skin, like all Savages; but with less modesty than the Hurons as to the breechcloth which many do not use at all." Although the Neutrals did not fight the Hurons or the Iroquois while they were in a position to be "neutral", they did make war with a western nation, according to Jesuit reports, and should not be considered altogether peaceable.

Many relics of the days of the Neutral Indians have been uncovered in the Lake Medad-Waterdown area. Flint arrowheads, stone axes, stone chisels, pottery, wampum, shell beads and stone pipes have been unearthed by the ploughs of farmers. Indian bone burial grounds or ossuaries, peculiar to the Neutral Indians, have been uncovered in the vicinity of Lake Medad. The Neutrals revered the bones of the dead and displayed them after the flesh around them had decomposed.

Lake Medad, named after farmer Medad Parsons, is high on the escarpment and has to this day an air of mystery about it. Although the lake is now leased by the Medad Heights Golf Course Ltd., it is not part of the course and the land around the lake basin is still wooded with hemlock, birch, and cedar. The 40-acre lake is pure spring water to a depth of about 20 feet. Below this is a dark ooze, and solid bottom is not reached for 80 feet. This gave rise to the belief that the lake was bottomless and that bodies lost in it never were given up. In recent years at least two scuba divers have gone into the lake and confirmed that the bed is in shelves and does exist at about 80 feet depth.

Another peculiarity of Lake Medad which adds to its mystery is that while known to be fed by several creeks, it appears to have no outlet yet always keeps the same level. It is believed to have an underground outlet to the bay or Lake Ontario.

Before the turn of this century, water-power for Waterdown mills began to fail and a canal was dug from Lake Medad to the Grindstone Creek to augment the water supply. The water from the lake rushed into the canal but when the lake level reached the level of the bottom of the canal, the flow ceased. The small springs and creeks were enough to keep the lake full but were not sufficient to stand any large drain. No trace of this canal can be found in the 1990s.

Along the eastern shore there is a rocky ledge near which the remains of an Indian village have been discovered. After the Iroquois had destroyed and scattered the Hurons, they turned their attention to the Neutral Nation, and this village soon disappeared. From the trees that are growing over the ash pits it has been estimated that the village met its fate nearly 300 years ago. On a gravelly slope above the camp there has been discovered a burying place, also another a few miles distant on the banks of the Twelve Mile Creek as it flows through Upper Burlington.

From about 1350 to 1400 A.D., on the present day Guelph Line, south of Campbellville, there was an Iroquois village whose inhabitants were primarily horticulturists. The Crawford Lake Conservation Authority has reconstructed a native village on this site, including palisades, longhouses and a sacred medicine garden.

EXPLORERS MEET

In 1669, a memorable meeting between white men occurred near Lake Medad. On September 24, Father Rene de Brehant de Galinee arrived at Tinawatawa, an important camp of the Neutrals northwest of Lake Medad, with a party which included Father Dollier de Casson and René Robert Cavalier, Sieur de La Salle. They found that a Frenchman had arrived the preceding day, one M. Louis Joliet, who was on his way back to Quebec.

Joliet was amazed to see the Frenchmen emerge from the trail through the woods to the east. Unknown to each other these two parties had been converging on the same point. La Salle and the Sulpicians had been coming up the St. Lawrence and along the shore of Lake Ontario from the east. They had landed where La Salle Park is now and had proceeded north to the Indian village, located near the present village of Westover.

Joliet left after meeting La Salle but apparently La Salle's party stayed on at the village for several days since La Salle was unwell. Finally, when Fathers Dollier and Galinee indicated that in two or three days they wished to push on using Joliet's route, La Salle told them that the state of his health

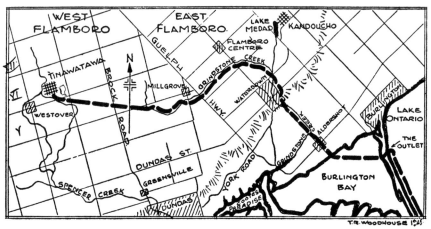

La Salle's route to meet Jolliet at Tinawatawa.

no longer permitted him to think of the journey he had undertaken to the west and that he intended to return to Montreal. The Sulpician missionaries left the village October 1, 1669.

Joliet and La Salle went on to make major discoveries in their journeys. In 1673, Joliet with Father Marquette descended the Mississippi as far as the junction of the Arkansas River and saw that it fell into the Gulf of Mexico. Nine years later La Salle completed exploration of the Mississippi and reached its mouth.

MISSISSAUGA PERIOD

By the end of the American Revolutionary War, when the first Loyalists began their entry into Upper Canada, the Neutral Indians were gone. The Iroquois, after defeating the Hurons, Algonquins and Neutrals had turned their attention to the French and for ten years battled the fur traders and settlers. The Indians finally realized they were fighting a losing battle and after enduring a winter of starvation due to French attacks on Mohawk supplies, they gave in. Peace descended on the lower Great Lakes region and the Mississauga Indians appeared in Halton County.

The Mississauga hunting ground was the entire area between Burlington Bay and the Humber River and extended north as far as Lake Simcoe, which was known to the Indians as "Lake of the Skies." The tract comprised about 80,000 acres and included what are now the counties of Halton, Peel, and part of York. The Mississaugas apparently descended from a more northerly location and are believed to be a tribe of the Algonquin Nation.

These Indians were peaceful, governed by three chiefs and Council of the Three Fires. There was a friendly relationship between the

Mississaugas and the Iroquois. In 1796, the former sold to the Six Nations Grand River Council a parcel of land adjacent to the Grand River Reserve. Later when the government was first negotiating with the Mississaugas for the purchase of land along Lake Ontario from Burlington Bay eastward, the Mississaugas adopted Joseph Brant, leader of the Six Nations, as their chief. The government, worried that Brant might become too powerful, set aside plans for the purchase at this time.

Brant's Indians were allowed to occupy land at Burlington Beach under an agreement that they did no hunting or fishing on Mississauga lands. John Graves Simcoe, the first governor of Upper Canada, also honoured the Mississauga land rights. Settlers were having to cross Indian territory more and more frequently on the journey from Newark, the old capital of Upper Canada, to York the new seat of government. Simcoe refused to force the Mississaugas to give up their land. The scattered houses erected in this territory were built with the sanction of the Indians. No roads were built; the Indians' trails were used instead.

The long term result of this wise policy was that when trouble brewed along the frontier with the Americans, the Mississaugas remained loyal to the British although the sympathies of their nation in the earlier part of the 18th century were not in this direction. The outcome of the War of 1812 might have been quite different had Simcoe and Brant alienated the Mississaugas.

Finally, in 1806, agreement was reached and the land of the Mississaugas between the Humber and Burlington Bay was purchased by the colonial government. The Indians gradually dispersed, some going with the Six Nations to their Grand River settlement and the majority joining the rest of the Algonquins to the east near Montreal.

Probably the most interesting evidence of Indian life in this area was unearthed by Samuel Thomas Jr. in 1892 on the old townsite of Wellington Square. Along with a medal weighing about two ounces, there was excavated a large skeleton presumably that of an Indian chief. It had two ivory rings through its nose and lay with a scalping knife, a tomahawk, pipe and hunting knife. The medal was presumed to be one bestowed at an important Indian council held at the mouth of the Niagara River in 1764. It was presented by Sir William Johnson to representative chiefs of Six Nations Tribes for bravery and loyalty to Britain during the Pontiac War. The medal bears the date, 1764, a relief of King George III and the words "Happy While United."

3
Joseph Brant: The Greatest Freeholder

The district's most illustrious settler was a Mohawk warrior, Joseph Brant, Thayendanegea. Chief of the Six Nations Indians during a most notable period in history, he earned a place in Canadian annals for his political and military astuteness.

His story is a thrilling one. Born in what is now the United States, he was one of the first United Empire Loyalists in the true sense of the word, one who preferred to remain loyal to the British crown and settle in Canada. Leading his people to the lush Grand River valley, he chose for his last home a splendid setting at the north end of Burlington Beach, a short distance from what was to become the townsite of Wellington Square.

Joseph Brant was born on the banks of the Ohio River in 1742. His father was a full-blooded Mohawk of the Wolf tribe. His grandfather, was one of the four Sachems who visited England in 1710 during the reign of Queen Anne, with Col. Peter Schuyler from the American colonies. When his father died Brant's mother married for a second time.

The Brants, events showed, had a partiality toward the white man. In 1748, Joseph's older sister, Mary or Molly, became at the age of 16, the morganatic wife of Sir William Johnson, General Superintendent of the Indian Department for the Crown. She remained as a devoted wife and chatelaine of Johnson Hall until the time of the revolt of the colonies when she fled to Canada and eventually settled her family at Kingston.

Joseph became a protégé of Sir William who watched over his military and academic training. At the age of 13, in 1755, Joseph was present with Sir William at the battle of Lake George. This was at the time of the Seven Years' War when Britain was seeking to break the chain of French forts stretching from the St. Lawrence to Louisiana. Four years later, Brant accompanied Sir William during the Niagara campaign and acquitted himself with bravery against the Iroquois' traditional enemies, the French.

Through the sponsorship of Sir William, Brant attended Moor Charity School for Indians at Lebanon, Connecticut, founded by Eleazer Wheelock. This later became Dartmouth College. Brant studied there for a few years before leaving to fight in the Pontiac Wars.

In 1765, Brant was again in the Mohawk Valley and in 1771, he translated the Gospel of St. Mark into Mohawk. A copy of his edition is in the Joseph Brant Museum in Burlington. About this time he married Christine, daughter of an Oneida chief. Leading a peaceful life, Brant acquired land, cattle, a share in a grist mill and generally enjoyed a comfortable existence.

Christine bore Joseph a son, Isaac, and a daughter, Christiana, before she died of tuberculosis. Christine's half sister became his second wife but she, too, died of tuberculosis within a year of the marriage, leaving no issue. Brant remained single for some time but toward the close of the American Revolution he married Catharine, eldest daughter of the head chief of the Turtle tribe, first in rank of the Mohawk nation. In her own right, she stood at the head of the Iroquois confederacy, clothed with the power to designate a successor to the chieftaincy.

Catharine Brant was of considerable beauty if descriptions of her are accurate. She was tall and graceful, possessing a proud manner and a sparkling personality, with which went a quick temper. She bore Brant seven children, Joseph, Jacob, John, Margaret, Catharine, Mary and Elizabeth.

In 1774, with revolt of the colonies imminent, the Six Nations Indians at the council of Johnson Hall plied Sir William Johnson with questions, attempting to clarify their position. A few hours after the conference, the exhausted Sir William died.

In the fall of 1775, in an attempt to learn the true political situation between the British, the American colonies and the Indians, Joseph Brant made his first visit to London, England. He was lionized, appeared at court and had his portrait, commissioned by the Earl of Warwick, painted by George Romney. This picture shows Brant not as typically Indian in appearance. His nose was small and his skin was not copper-coloured as others of his race. Indeed, this dignified, intelligent man was far from the Londoner's expectations of a savage redskin.

In 1775, the American colonies revolted against the motherland and the Mohawks at Canajoharie migrated with Col. Guy Johnson, Sir William Johnson's son-in-law, and the new Indian Superintendent, to Montreal. Joseph Brant, returning home from England in 1776, allied himself with Britain and thereafter took an active part in the war. His rank of Captain was the highest an Indian could attain.

Brant was a brilliant leader of his Indian warriors. With Fort Niagara, where they had relocated from Montreal, as their base, the Indians made commando-like raids into the Mohawk and Ohio valleys. The War of American Independence ended in 1783, but the issue was not ended for the Iroquois who had lost their ancestral lands. They felt the British had no right to cede the Mohawk Valley to Americans in the peace treaty and wanted the border placed south and east of the Ohio River instead of the dividing line through the Great Lakes. Added to this grievance, the Indians who stayed in the United States were faced with the encroachment on their lands of more and more settlers. This period of unrest below the American border was to result in spasmodic battles being fought for several years.

Chief Joseph Brant shown wearing his gorget. (portrait by Romney, 1775.)   *– Courtesy Joseph Brant Museum*

Brant acted as a peacemaker and is credited with preventing a general Indian uprising.

Throughout the American Revolution and the intermittent Indian fighting which followed, Brant, although fierce in battle, was never cruel or sadistic. He endeavoured to keep his warriors from committing excesses and stories written by his detractors alluding to his atrocities were proved to be lies. In 1821, his son, John, provided evidence to try to right the wrong done to his father's name by people such as the poet Thomas Campbell, in his "Gertrude of Wyoming."

It is little wonder that Brant and his warriors expected and deserved the same compensation as the white Loyalists. They had lost as much during the war and had fought with great effectiveness for the British cause. The Treaty of Paris, restoring peace between Great Britain and the United States in 1783, made no provision for the loyal Indians. Mother England had had a lapse of memory but Joseph Brant reminded her of promises made.

Governor Sir Frederick Haldimand, in 1784, granted the Six Nations Indians a large piece of land stretching six miles on either side of the Grand

Joseph Brant's gorget, on display at the Joseph Brant Museum.
– courtesy Joseph Brant Museum

River from its source to its mouth in Lake Erie and another tract at the Bay of Quinte, where a group of Iroquois settled under John Desoronto.

Joseph Brant received for himself a large sum of money as indemnity for the loss of his property. This he used to help his people start life on the Grand River. He bought nails, farm implements and stock and built a sawmill. The Indians were given supplies and provisions as were the other Loyalists and it was not long before they were well settled in their new home.

There was a difference, however, in the British treatment of the Indian Loyalists and the white Loyalists. The latter were given outright grants of land as well as monetary compensation and their children, when of age, were eligible for a further land grant. The Indian lands were so entailed that they could not be sold or leased without Crown consent. Governor Simcoe gave as his excuse for this differentiation, the fear that the Indians would be cheated by "land jobbers." Eventually their affairs became so legally entangled that the true value of their property was never realized. It cannot be said that the treatment given such loyal allies was other than shabby.

In 1785, Brant went to London again, this time to try to secure the deed to the Grand River land, promised by Sir Frederick Haldimand. Although in this effort he was unsuccessful, the visit was a personal social triumph for Brant. He visited the homes of the aristocracy, became a friend of the Duke of Northumberland, and went on several outings with the Prince of Wales. The Baroness Riedesel found Brant's manners "polished, and he expresses himself with great fluency." Brant was presented to King George III and Queen Charlotte and when the king offered the royal hand to be kissed, as was the custom, Brant is said to have refused it. He was, he said, a king among his own people; it was beneath his dignity to bow to anyone. He would, however, be pleased to kiss the hand of the Queen.

Brant returned to Upper Canada disappointed with the outcome of his mission, but continued to act as liaison between the Indians and the Government. He was appointed by the Indian Council as agent for the Six Nations in negotiations, and, in 1796, was given a formal power of attorney to handle land sales with the Crown. Before this, when the Indians first received their lands, they encouraged white settlers to become established on them and gave them unofficial land titles. There were only 2,000 Indians on the huge Grand River tract, which was more than large enough for their needs. Brant felt white settlers as good farmers and merchants would provide an example to the Indians. The proceeds of the land sales were to be used for the purchase of farm stock and implements, with the remainder put into a trust fund to support the Indians while they were adapting to a new way of life.

The Government tried to discourage these settlers and not honour the land titles but many of them had been allies of the Iroquois during the American Revolution and were people of integrity. Finally, in 1798, the government agreed to ratify the arrangements made with the Indians. Individual Indians, however, continued to sell parcels of land and many squatters entered the tract. Brant's services as a land agent continued to be sought and he never gave up trying to secure an unconditional deed to the Grand River property.

Brant's willingness and ability to accept the white man's way of life were most remarkable for his race and for his time. He used to the utmost advantage the opportunities he was given in his association as a youth with Sir William Johnson.

Yet, for all his adoption of white ways, he was an Indian in much of his thinking. In a letter written after one of his visits to England he commented, "you ask me then, whether civilization is favourable to human happiness...There are degrees of civilization from cannibals to the most polite of European nations...I was born of Indian parents and lived among those whom you are pleased to call savages; I was since sent to live among the white people... After all this experience, I am obliged to give my opinion in favour of mine own people...Among us we have no prisons; we have no pompous parade of courts; we have no written laws; and yet judges are as highly revered amongst us as they are with you and their decisions are as much regarded. Daring wickedness is here never suffered to triumph over helpless innocence. The estates of widows and orphans are never devoured by enterprising sharpers..."

One of the shadows in Brant's life was the death of his oldest son, Isaac, a wild young man, who was jealous of his father and of his step-sisters and brothers. He was of a violent disposition and had killed an American deserter. At Burlington Heights, in 1795, Isaac drew a knife and attacked his father. Brant, in defending himself, wounded his son on the head. Later Isaac tore off the bandage and, developing blood poisoning, died. Brant insisted he be placed on trial and was acquitted by both the white man's court and the Six Nations Council. Governor Simcoe said of the affair, "I consider it as a fortunate circumstance that in attempting to assassinate his own father, this dangerous young man fell the victim of his own atrocity."

Brant, although generally honoured and respected by white men, never forsook his own people. With his own holdings in the Grand River tract, with compensation from the Crown and his pension as a Captain in the army, Brant, after the American Revolutionary War, could have settled quietly and pursued the life of a country gentleman at Burlington Beach. He chose, instead, to act as intermediary between the Indians and the American and British governments. Those in authority listened to him and showed him the respect they were unwilling to give the average red man.

Due to his moderating influence, differences were often reconciled. He was firm in his dealings with the white man and would never back down when he felt Indian rights were being ignored.

Whatever Brant's motivations, and there were some who implied they were selfish, the Indians in Upper Canada had a devoted father in their Chief who on his deathbed whispered, "Have pity on the poor Indians...If you can get any influence with the great, endeavour to do them all the good you can."

BRANT AT BURLINGTON

The deed to Brant's property on Burlington Bay was registered in 1798 which, perhaps significantly, was the year that the white settlers at the Grand River had their deeds formally recognized. The descriptions of the property stated that it "contains by admeasurement 3,450 acres...being composed of a certain tract situate at the head of Lake Ontario...in the Home district of our province...together with the woods and water thereon lying...in the limit of the land heretofore purchased from the Mississauga."

It is almost certain that Brant owned land before 1798 and it is possible he was unofficially given it shortly after the Grand River property was bestowed in 1784. The Indians historically had had an encampment at the Beach, and Kayser and Wade, travelling through the district in 1769, on a mission for Sir William Johnson, mentioned "a great number of huts" at about this spot. Brant certainly would have been familiar with the area and, after the capital of Upper Canada was transferred to York from

Newark, would have passed this way on his journeys from the Grand River to York.

In a letter written in June, 1797, it was mentioned that at Brant's House at "The Beach" on the shore of Lake Ontario 160 Indians were successfully vaccinated for smallpox. Two years earlier Mrs. John Graves Simcoe sailed to the north shore of Burlington Bay where she and her party camped. "Captain Brant called on horse-back", she wrote in her diary, "on his way to Niagara but left his sons and attendants here till the wind proves fair for them to proceed." It was necessary for the Brant boys to share the Simcoe accommodation, which was a tent. The attendants found shelter under some boards. Surely, if Brant had had any kind of home of his own at the beach, he would have left his party there.

A drawing of Brant's home which was included in the John Ross Robertson edition of Mrs. Simcoe's diary was not painted by Mrs. Simcoe as many of the illustrations were. It was a painting by M. Fisher and mistakenly attributed to Mrs. Simcoe. It cannot thus be used as proof the house was finished before the Simcoes left Canada in 1796.

Certainly the Brants were still well-established at the Grand River as late as 1792 when Patrick Campbell described the household there. "Tea was on the table when we came in, served up in the handsomest China plate and every other furniture in proportion. After tea was over we were entertained with the music of an elegant hand organ...Next day dinner was just going on the table in the same elegant style as the preceding night, when I returned to Captain Brant's house, the servants dressed in their best apparel. Two slaves attended the table, the one in scarlet, the other in coloured clothes with silver buckles in their shoes and ruffles and every other part of their apparel in proportion."

When Brant built his house at Burlington Beach, he used logs from the Thousand Islands in the St. Lawrence, since the type of red cedar he wanted did not grow here. It was designed after the home of Sir William Johnson and a description of the house was set down by James Buchanan, British Consul at New York, in the summer of 1819. From the shores of Lake Ontario five miles away, he saw the Brant House "which had a very noble and commanding aspect...Driving up to the door we alighted. The outer door leading into the spacious hall was open; we entered and seeing no person about proceeded into the parlour...It was a room well-furnished, with a carpet and pier and chimney glasses, mahogany tables, fashionable chairs, a guitar and a neat hanging book-case in which among other volumes were perceived a Church of England Prayer Book translated into the Mohawk tongue."

After Joseph Brant's death on November 24, 1807, his widow and children returned to the Grand River. John and his sister Elizabeth by 1819 were living again in Burlington. In that year Elizabeth was described by a visitor to the Brant home as " a charming noble-looking Indian girl dressed partly in native and partly in English costume." Another visitor said, "She would not disgrace the circles of European fashion; her face and person are fine and graceful; she speaks English correctly with eloquence; she retains so much of her dress as to identify her with her people over whom she affects no superiority but seems pleased to preserve all the ties and duties of relationship."

John Brant was also well known to the early settlers of Wellington Square. When the war of 1812 broke out, Captain John Brant, as chief of the Six Nations after his father's death, took the field with his warriors. He fought with distinction at Queenston, Beaver Dams, Chippewa, Lundy's Lane and Fort Erie. In 1832, he was returned as a member of the Provincial Parliament for the County of Haldimand. Many of his voters did not have a freehold qualification for county elections and his election was set aside when his opponent contested the result. This occurred just before an outbreak of cholera spread through the country. John, at that time only 38, fell a victim and died. Ironically, the fate of his opponent was the same.

Elizabeth Brant married William Johnson Kerr, her second cousin, who was the grandson of Molly Brant, Joseph's sister. Anna Jameson, describing men alighting from a coach in Oakville, in 1837, said, "One was introduced to me as Mr. Kerr, the possessor of large estates in the neighbourhood, partly acquired and partly inherited from his father-in-law, Brant, the famous chief of the Six Nations. Kerr himself has Indian blood in his veins. His son, a fine boy, is the present acknowledged chief of the Six Nations, in his mother's right, the hereditary chieftainship being transmitted through the female though passing over her."

William Johnson Kerr took an active part in the life of the community. In the war of 1812, he was commander at Queenston and Beaver Dams and rose to the rank of Lieut-Colonel. In July, 1818, he was at York, a member of the executive committee of the convention called to effect land reforms. About 1819, he was elected a member of the Assembly for Lincoln, representing the settlers whose lot he was trying to improve. In the fall of 1828, he was found in charge of dredging operations for the Burlington Canal across the beach strip.

Kerr was described as a Wellington Square lawyer. He was interested in politics and his political leanings, while somewhat left of centre, were not so extreme as those of William Lyon Mackenzie. A story is told of an attack Mr. Kerr made on Mr. Mackenzie in Hamilton. After a tempestuous political meeting in March, 1832, Mackenzie set up a table outside the Court House and took signatures to a petition. He later retired for the night in a nearby hotel only to be awakened by Mr. Kerr who enticed him outside where he was beaten up by ruffians. Kerr later paid a fine for his adventure.

Elizabeth Brant Kerr and William Johnson Kerr are both buried in St. Luke's churchyard. They died the same day in 1845, possibly of cholera. Nearby lies W.J. Simcoe Kerr, their son. John Brant was buried at what is now Brantford.

The burial of Joseph Brant took place at the Six Nation reserve on the Grand River and not in St. Luke's churchyard as traditionally told. At the time of the chief's death, St. Luke's was not in existence and its site was part of the forest, a good distance from the Brant house. The story of Brant being carried by relays of Indians to the Grand River in 1850 likely originated at the time of his death when his wife and devoted followers wanted his grave to be located where they were living. Mrs. Brant returned to the Grand River after her husband's passing and remained there until her death thirty years later. It is inconceivable that a chief of Brant's stature would have been interred in a lonely place in the bush, and not in an honoured grave close by his own people.

In volume II, page 518, of Stone's *Life of Joseph* Brant there is a reference that in 1816 Lieut. Francis Hall of the British Service, who travelled in the United States and Canada that year, visited the Mohawk village on the Grand River. Writing of Brant, Hall is quoted at the time as saying, "His grave is to be seen under the walls of the Church."

In November, 1850, the editor and publisher of *The Hamilton Spectator*, Robert Smiley, was in Brantford to witness with a distinguished gathering the placing of the remains of Joseph and John Brant in the vault in which they lie today by the side of His Majesty's Chapel of the Mohawks. Smiley wrote a story of the occasion and in the lead stated, "The removal of the remains of the distinguished chief, Thayendanegea, and of his scarcely less illustrious son, from the frail and dilapidated graves, which they had inhabited, to a substantial and capacious stone vault in the churchyard of the Mohawk...was indeed a ceremony deserving the attention of the hundreds and thousands who took part in it." No mention at all of any trek from Burlington! This puts to rest the romanticism about Brant's body lying at Wellington Square from 1807 to 1850.

This, then, was the saga of Joseph Brant and his distinguished son and daughter. Today, Burlington is left with only a replica of his home, the graves of some of Brant's loved ones, and a few street names, "Brant", "John" and "Elizabeth", in memory of them.

Even the contours of his beloved beach have been changed with time, and Brant's Pond on which his house fronted was reclaimed years ago. Yet, gracing the property, is a modern and growing hospital which bears the name of Joseph Brant, fitting tribute by the modern age to Burlington's greatest freeholder.

4
Brant Park

Not too much is known about the Brant home in the years immediately following the chief's death in 1807. John Brant was only 13 when his father died and his sister Elizabeth, younger still. By 1819 John and Elizabeth were living at the head of the lake when James Buchanan visited them and recounted this conversation: "Having enquired of the Princess (Elizabeth) about her mother, she told us she generally remained with her other sons and daughters who were living on the Grand River." John's contested election to the Assembly in 1832 was as a representative for Haldimand county which suggests that by then he, too, was at the Grand River. By this time his sister had married and was possibly using the homestead.

Certainly there is proof that in 1837 Elizabeth, her husband, William Johnson Kerr, and their children were living in the old mansion of her father. W.L. Stone, biographer of Joseph Brant, is the authority for such a statement, which discounts the possibility the family was living at Port Nelson as another writer indicated.

Elizabeth inherited land in 1832 from her brother John who left her in his will, "all my land situate in Wellington Square, at the head of Lake Ontario, adjoining Flamborough East and other lands." When her mother died in 1837, Elizabeth fell heir to 700 more acres of land.

The Kerrs died in 1845 leaving four children, Walter, Joseph B., W.J. Simcoe and Catharine or Kate, all of whom shared equally in their parents' estate. Simcoe, born in 1837, became a Wellington Square lawyer like his father and shared his interest in politics. He was graduated from Osgoode Hall in 1862 and in 1867 was defeated in his bid for a Conservative seat in the Ontario legislature. He was the Master of Burlington Lodge A.F.& A.M., No. 165, in 1869 and again in 1871.

For some years it would seem that the Kerrs were not living in the old house at the Beach, although it was still in possession of the family. George Thomson, light-house keeper at the canal, mentions "the bank (of the lake) on Mr. Kerr's property" and relates that he walked from the canal as far as "Brant's farm yard." Another time he speaks of a "walk through Kerr's woods round by the stone road and down by the Square." He also mentions walking back home on another occasion "by Kerr's lane." He notes on October 2, 1860, that "Mr. Henry, the new tenant on Kerr's farm, commenced plowing with three new plows on the forenoon of the 19th

October." It is thus quite possible that the Brant house and farm were rented for a period around this time.

Mr. Thomson mentions many of his neighbours but not Simcoe Kerr until January 19, 1869, when he wrote in his diary: "Mr. Simcoe Kerr commenced to sell off his household furniture." Then on December 17, 1869, Mr. Thomson wrote: "Mr. Simcoe Kerr moving into his old homestead." From this date, until July, 1873, when the two men had a "civil growl", Mr. Thomson saw Mr. Kerr at least monthly, and sometimes more often, lending him books, calling at his home, meeting his friends and generally knowing him well. This suggests that the "old homestead" unquestionably was the historic Brant home. Simcoe Kerr married in 1870, indicating he was setting up housekeeping in the family home just prior to his marriage. His wife was Kate Hunter, daughter of Dr. John W. Hunter of Hamilton. The couple had no children.

Simcoe Kerr died February 18, 1875. A year later his sister Kate, who married John Osborne of this area, died. A newspaper headline read, "The Last Line" and went on to state that Kate was the "last connecting link between our times and the days of Brant."

The Brant home somewhere about this time was incorporated into the Brant House, a summer resort. Twenty acres of pleasure gardens, croquet lawns, a bowling green, bathing "machines", ice cream parlours and a dancing hall were some of its attractions. In the 1877 Halton Atlas a large page is devoted to a detailed sketch of this building. The proprietor was J. Morris, "late steward of the Hamilton Club".

The structure was probably built after Simcoe Kerr's death since diarist Thomson who walked through this section several times a week, did not ever mention it up to that time. A drawing of the "Brant House" was given to the town of Burlington by the town of Oakville and hangs in the lobby of the Public Administration Building.

From the late 1870s, this area became a fashionable resort and it was during this period that places like the Ocean House at the beach were built. The three-story Brant House with its verandah along two sides, its many gables and its interior which was a series of individual motel-like apartments, became a popular spot for vacationers.

Benjamin Eager, the lumber king, had bought a large tract of forest along what is now Maple Avenue. After removing the timber, he tried in 1874 to sell off "villa lots" north of the old outlet. He eventually acquired the Brant property which later was sold to a contractor, A.B. Coleman. In the winter of 1899 Mr. Coleman commenced to promote the Hotel Brant, a commodious structure to be built adjacent to the Brant House. Mr. Coleman's son is certain that the last load of bricks came across the ice of the bay from the brick yards at Kenilworth Avenue in Hamilton in April, 1902. The hotel opened on July 2nd.

Brant Hotel, built in 1900.   *– courtesy Joseph Brant Museum*

The Hotel Brant would rival in comfort any resort of today. For its time it was very modern with such improvements as elevators, electric light, sanitary plumbing and heating by hot water and hot air. The dining room was one of the finest in Canada, covering an area of nearly 8,000 square feet and opening upon spacious verandahs. There was music during meals and for dancing. Rates were $2.50 per day and upwards.

At one time the maitre d'hotel, a native of Jamaica, with his coloured waiters, worked in Kingston, Jamaica, in the winter and Hotel Brant in the summer.

The old hotel registers contained names of notables who visited the hotel, such as William Jennings Bryan. The registers were lost in a fire at Indian Point.

There is some confusion in the names of the Brant House and Brant Hotel. Burlingtonians began to call the hotel, the Brant House and this name became quite widely used. The older building, a series of attached apartments, was then known as the Annex.

Several cottages were erected to the south of the Annex and these were rented to summer visitors. Later they were winterized and rented all year long.

A.B. Coleman was a self-educated Englishman who, as a boy, worked for 50 cents a day. He taught himself to make and read blueprints, to prepare estimates and understand the building business. He built a number of houses in Burlington, some of which still remain. At the age of 21 he owned a planing mill on Ontario Street, and later built a larger one which burned down in 1898.

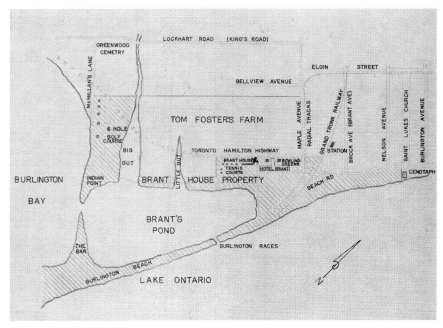

Brant Park (about 1915) as recalled by Brant Coleman.

After Mr. Coleman built the Brant Hotel he moved his family to Toronto where he engaged in construction work. He maintained an office in Toronto until his death and commuted three days a week. A.B. Coleman built Shea's Hippodrome, University of Toronto's Convocation Hall, three of the Toronto Exhibition buildings, Fort Erie Race Track, Brampton Home for the Aged and Westminster Hospital, London.

The Coleman family returned to Burlington June 4, 1909, just in time for a son, Brant, to be born in the old Brant House. By this time A.B. Coleman was developing Indian Point on land he had purchased from the Johnstons. He had built a walk along the Foster fence line over to the point, crossing the Big Gut inlet with a foot bridge. Then he built a road along the edge of Brant's Pond with a small vehicle bridge. This was the first convenient access to Indian Point since, previously, vehicles had to go via Maple Avenue, Sand Road and down McMillan's Lane. The contours of the whole area are different today with the filling in of Brant's Pond.

With a road to the point ready, Mr. Coleman built five very large cottages, four of them still standing in 1996. These he rented for the summer season at "pretty fancy prices" to people like the Mellons and DuPonts.

In August, 1917, the Brant Hotel buildings and land were purchased by the Federal government and the hotel remodelled for use as a soldiers' hospital. The verandahs facing the lake were enclosed for wards. A

The original Brant Inn (destroyed by fire, 1925.)

residence for the nurses and a canteen for the men were built. A long ward was constructed to the south, connected to the main building by a large corridor. The old Brant House Annex and "cottages" were occupied by hospital staff. In the 1930s, the remaining veterans were transferred to Toronto and the Brant buildings demolished.

The Brant Hotel did not serve hard liquor and to satisfy his thirsty patrons, Mr. Coleman bought a piece of land across the way and opened a Country Club, a male haunt, which after 1917 was closed and remodelled to become known as the Brant Inn, a quaint building with shingled outside walls, very warm and inviting. It was operated as a dance spot with rooms and dining facilities until 1925 when it was destroyed by fire.

Mr. Coleman reconstructed the Inn, first the annex to the east, then the main brick building which opened in 1927. Testrail Bros., a Toronto music distributing company, were lessees until 1928 when the Brant Inn Ltd. of Hamilton purchased the property. When this company ran into difficulties, Mr. Coleman found himself once more the owner.

John Murray Anderson, Clifford Kendall, and Cec Roberts of Roberts' Restaurant, Hamilton, began renting the Inn in September, 1934. By January, 1937, Messrs. Anderson and Kendall became sole tenants and at the time of A.B. Coleman's death bought the Brant Inn. They remodelled the premises and added the Lido Deck for dancing. In April, 1954, John Murray Anderson became the sole owner and remained so until his retirement in December, 1964.

Over the years the biggest stars in "show biz" were featured at the Brant Inn; Sophie Tucker, Ella Fitzgerald, Liberace, Lena Horne, Mart Kenney, Eddie Duchin, Ben Bernie, Benny Goodman, Guy Lombardo and Ted Lewis were some of the luminaries who played there. In the summer of 1959, the Miss Canada Pageant was held at the Brant Inn.

It seemed the end of an era when John Murray Anderson, in 1964, bowed from the scene he had graced so well. New owners carried on, however, adapting the facilities to please a new generation of diners and dancers until closing in January, 1969. It was demolished in April of that year.

The site received approval from the Ontario Municipal Board for zoning that would allow an apartment/hotel complex of up to 32 storeys. Construction was delayed due to problems with the CNR right-of-way and with financing. The city, believing the project was not suitable for the area, froze development in the spring of 1976. Eventually the site was purchased by the city in co-operation with Halton Region Conservation Authority and is a part of Beachway Park.

While the original Brant Annex was standing, a small boy and his mother were guests at the hotel. So impressed was the lad with the history of the area, that in later years he decided a replica of Joseph Brant's home should be erected. By then he was the Hon. T.B. McQuesten, Minister of Highways of Ontario. A horticulturist and student of history, Mr. McQuesten insisted the Brant Park area should be preserved.

The erection of this building was not without problems. It was in the depression years when historian Ronald Way and architect W.A. Somerville began work. The building was partially completed and remained empty until several Burlington residents, including William J. McCulloch and Mrs. W.A. Weaver, Regent of Thayendanegea Chapter I.O.D.E., prevailed upon the Hon. T.B. McQuesten during World War II to have the home finished. A heating plant was installed and the plank floors, which had buckled because of dampness, were replaced.

On a rainy May 23, 1942, the Joseph Brant Museum was officially opened by Mr. McQuesten. In May, 1943, T.A. Blakelock, M.P. for Halton, presented a flag on behalf of the Ontario government to the Thayendanegea Chapter IODE.

In one of the downstairs rooms, a few mementos of the Brant period were installed. An upstairs room was used by the I.O.D.E. and hospital groups. On the second floor and in the attic, rooms were assigned as living quarters for the curator, James Walmsley, and his family.

The Museum Board of Management was enlarged to include five Historical Society members: Earl Hartley, Irene Simpson, Walter Reeves, Vi Chornick and Mary Fraser. In 1965, an arrangement was concluded whereby the Town of Burlington leased the building from Joseph Brant Memorial Hospital for an indefinite period. This was the spark needed to

THE BRANT HOUSE BURLINGTON. A BEAUTIFUL SUMMER RESORT & EUROPEAN HOTEL SITUATED ON ONE OF THE CHOICEST SITES OVERLOOKING BURLINGTON BAY & LAKE ONTARIO. J. MORRIS. P

The Brant House, Burlington, 1877.   *– courtesy Joseph Brant Museum*

revitalize the museum. Town council voted a working budget and Earl Hartley, formerly chairman of the museum board, was appointed curator and a program of special displays was initiated.

The museum has made several acquisitions over the years. In 1968, it obtained Joseph Brant's silver-gilt gorget, a piece of throat armour. This had been presented by King George III in appreciation of Brant's contribution to the British cause during the American Revolutionary War. The cost was $13,000. The gorget was subsequently declared a National Treasure which cannot leave Canada. A sculpture, "Crooked Nose", by noted Indian Artist Joseph Jacobs was acquired in 1976. A pewter communion service, 130 years old at the time, was acquired from the Richardson family in 1985. It had been used by the first Baptist Church in Wellington Square, Calvary, which was at the corner of Ontario and Locust Street. Joseph Brant's ring, a miniature painting of Brant and some dishes from his home were purchased from Muriel Kerby, a descendant of Brant. An extensive collection of early clothing donated by Eileen Collard in 1967 led ultimately in 1997 to the establishment of the Eileen Collard Costume Gallery of Historical Costumes and Textiles..

Exhibits include a copy of Brant's 1786 Mohawk translation of the Church of England Book of Common Prayer. In 1974, the archive and book collection was named the Mary Fraser Reference Library to honour her on her retirement as Museum Board Chairman after ten years of service.

In 1992, to mark the 50th anniversary of the museum and the 250th anniversary of the birth of Joseph Brant, the first floor galleries were refurbished again. Volunteers prepared a commemorative signature quilt by selling $40 squares for purchasers to sign. The completed squares were joined to make an interesting record of community participation.

In May, 1994, the museum was closed for six weeks. Every item was catalogued and numbered. The event? The building was being moved a few hundred yards to the east, to the intersection of Lakeshore Rd. and North Shore Blvd. East. Although this was not the hoped-for extension, it did mean a brand new basement for storage and work space and included a parking lot of its own. It reopened appropriately on July 1.

With the erection to the south of the Ontario Provincial Police building and the Ontario Highways Department offices, and with the eventual completion of the enlarged hospital, the former Brant lands are in full use. The structures, one housing relics of the past, and the others providing services to meet today's demands, symbolize the emerging new Burlington.

5
The Beach

The beach strip, named Long Beach by surveyor Augustus Jones in 1791, was described by Anna Jameson in 1837 as "that very remarkable tongue or slip of land which divides Burlington Bay from Lake Ontario." The sand strip was formed many centuries ago by the action of winds and the waves. Marsh plants and bulrushes grew up on the bay margin and eventually trees flourished. At first an Indian trail crossed the strip but as the white man settled Upper Canada, orchards and gardens were planted and a dirt track was built.

At the southern end of the beach Governor Simcoe built in 1794 the King's Head Inn, a large two-storey frame house with two wings. It stood on the lake shore near Windermere cut-off. War between Great Britain and America was thought inevitable and King's Head Inn essentially was a "depot for stores and provisions, as well as a rendezvous for the militia and such other troops as it might have been found expedient to have stationed on the line of communication between York and Detroit and Niagara"...Innkeeper Bates paid rent of $1 per annum. Mrs. Simcoe stayed at the Inn in 1795 and described the beach as a "park covered with large spreading oaks."

An old map indicated that by 1798 several families were established at the north end of the strip, and by 1813 settlement was progressing with the construction of homes and storehouses. A shallow passage connected lake and bay near what was later Station 28 but this outlet became filled with silt and was good only for use by boats at times of high water.

In 1817, residents of Barton township complained of the "want of a cut through the beach to Lake Ontario. This concerns the district and the upper part of the province materially in as much as a safe and commodious harbour would then be found in the heart of the country of much importance to the government in time of war."

Residents of Saltfleet in a similar report pointed out that a "canal might easily be cut through the long beach which separates Burlington Bay from Lake Ontario - the present outlet only admitting small boats, and sometimes a canoe can scarcely pass." This inconvenience was borne out by a loyalist, Thomas Horner, who, in detailing his route from Albany to Oxford county in 1796 said they had to "draw their boats through a small outlet to the bay." The channel may have helped save British warships in 1813 but was of no advantage in the later development of the country.

The scow ferry crossing the canal before the bridge was built.
                                        – courtesy Joseph Brant Museum

In 1828, William Johnson Kerr, Joseph Brant's son-in-law, was in charge of dredging operations for a canal finally being cut through the beach, a canal which was completed in 1832. The location of this cut was south of the old channel and at the site of the present modern entrance to Hamilton Harbour.

The canal took many years to reach its present state. In 1826, the cut was much narrower and a small swinging bridge was erected by Nathan Goodall. The structure, light and strong, could be swung by one man; it remained until the canal was enlarged and completed in 1832 and scows were used to ferry traffic across.

In 1838, according to the Department of Transport's List of Lights, a lighthouse was built at the south bank of the canal. A lighthouse keeper was hired who kept the light burning during the navigation season for guidance of the sailing vessels. The first lighthouse was made of frame, unwisely as it turned out.

With the advent of the steam boats the lighthouse keeper was hard put to keep sparks from ships' stacks from igniting the building. Finally, on July 18, 1856, the winds showered sparks from the steamer *Ranger* onto the pier, setting fire to the lighthouse, the ferry house and the lightkeeper's two buildings, burning them to the ground.

A pier-end light had been installed by September, 1856, but it was not until June, 1858 that the first foundation stone was laid for the new stone lighthouse which may be seen today, although no longer in use, near the railway and traffic lift bridge. The Commissioner of Public Works reported in March 1859: "A permanent lighthouse of stone laid in hydraulic cement has been erected and completed in a creditable manner. In fitting up the lighting apparatus, it was adapted to the consumption of coal oil in order to test its merits for lighthouse purposes...so far as it is found satisfactory. It gives a brilliant and steady light." This structure was built by George Bent, of a large local family of builders.

At first there was no bridge over the canal. Scows were used to transport vehicles, animals and people from one side to the other. Later scows had wheels around which ropes wound and unwound to pull them back and forth across the canal. There were wooden "fences" at the sides. The tale is told of a small girl who fell over and was pulled to safety by a gentleman who reached out his umbrella. In the rescue the man lost the umbrella. When the ferry docked at the north side of the canal, he marched the dripping child home and requested reimbursement for his lost property. Children were not the only passengers to get a wetting. Accounts tell of horses jumping overboard, "their masters having a serious job in saving them."

Bad storms would ground the scow and in early spring and late fall chunks of piled-up ice would make the crossing impossible. On December 31, 1863, a Mrs. Green and her family were turned back from crossing the canal. They tried every day until January 3, when the water froze solid enough for them to cross on foot. Once it took three-quarters of an hour for a team to get across the gap. Often teams would line up at Baldry's tavern on the south side waiting their turn to cross.

During the winter the bay froze solid, as much as 22 inches thick and the shorter trip across the ice to Hamilton was made from early January to mid-March. Markers were sunk in the ice to mark the route around the mouth of the canal which did not stay frozen for long, probably due to the current. When it did freeze a "man-rope" would be stretched across by the lighthouse keeper to guide pedestrians. Paths across the bay to Hamilton were marked off by pine brush, the one from Brown's wharf at Aldershot being a well-travelled route. The winter season was much colder then, and on April 1, 1856, a horse and buggy crossed to the city. It wasn't until April 26 that year that the bay was clear of ice.

Accounts of loads ferried across in the scows (a large one and a small one at one period) record the rustic nature of the countryside in the mid-1800s. On April 15, 1862, 40 head of cattle were taken across and in June, 1874, when the district was more populous, 59 teams were ferried over in three hours.

In 1867, a large black iron bridge was swung over the canal to accommodate the Hamilton and Northwestern Railway whose line crossed the beach, with a station at what became Brock Ave. The ticket station was in a house on the southwest side of Burlington Ave. near Elgin Street. The building was later used as an office for Ontario Hydro. This railway put Hamilton in direct communication with Collingwood and Barrie. Previous to this, beach residents wishing to take "the cars" into Hamilton had to go to the Great Western, later the Grand Trunk, station at Freeman.

In 1897, the building of a radial electric railway line from Hamilton to Burlington was completed and a second bridge was built at the canal. It had wooden sidewalks and scant space beside the tracks for vehicles. In 1922, a bascule bridge, fabricated and erected by the Hamilton Bridge Works for the Department of Public Works of Canada, replaced the earlier structure.

The last scow used for ferrying people and vehicles had a useful existence after being discharged from active duty at the canal. Thomas Irwin, whose summer home was at Station 26, bought it and had it towed to his property on the bayside where it made a fine wharf.

In early days the beach was a naturalist's delight. The silence was broken by the calls of loons, crows, night hawks and canaries. Gannets, eagles and plovers rested there and in March, 1861, a large flock of swans, 122 white ones and 12 black, was sighted. The beach waters abounded with fish and game birds. Hauls of a thousand or more herring were common in the spring, selling at five shillings a hundred in 1854. Whitefish, bass and pike were plentiful, besides ducks and game birds. Early in the season, before the summer residents of the beach arrived, men from Wellington Square would come out to the beach to fish and shoot.

The beach pastoral era ended with the coming of the railway in 1876. Crowds from Hamilton and Dundas were visitors on languid summer days, especially week-ends and holidays. Wells' Tavern, the Sportsman's Arms, the Corey House, Dynes Hotel, Perry's Hotel, Martin's Pleasure Gardens and the Baldry Hotel were some of the oases for the visitors and summer residents. With the beginning of steamer service it was pleasant to sail to the beach and escape the city's heat. Special excursions and moonlight cruises began in the 1870s.

Before the Muskoka and Haliburton districts became popular, the beach attracted not only local people as summer residents but also visitors from the United States. By the turn of the century, it had become the fashionable resort for well-to-do Hamiltonians. Senator W.E. Sanford's wife built "Elsinore", a rest home for young mothers. The Royal Hamilton Yacht Club and the Ocean House with their ornamented framed facades were examples of society's favourite haunts. Landscaping was a challenge but earth was brought in to cover the sand in front of the homes to make lawns. Nasturtiums flourished in the sand and window boxes were popular.

Beach life centred around the entertainment "spots." On December 20, 1874, Baldry's hotel at the canal burned, the fire smouldering in its ashes for ten days according to a neighbour. On the same site, the Ocean House, built at a cost of $10,000, was ready to open by the following May. This three-storied resort faced the lake and boasted a dance hall, music salon, bowling alley, billiards parlour and boat livery. Across the road on the bay side the Royal Hamilton Yacht Club was built, its regattas sometimes drawing 20,000 people. Diversions such as band concerts, ball games, bazaars and garden parties took place mostly on the south side of the canal.

The radial line ran north close to the bay between the canal and Station 26, cutting across at this point to run parallel to the railroad, as far as the "Brant House hill" where it traversed Maple Avenue to "Ferguson's Curve" and down Elgin Street to the station on Brant Street. Buses today use the same beach "stations" as the electric radials did.

The first dwellings on the Burlington side of the canal were the Curtis, Parkins, and Hedley homes. Magistrate G.F. Jelfs lived between station 22 and 24 on the lakeside of the highway. Alexander Leitch had a home with three or four cottages which he rented at Station 24. Other well-known families who summered north of the canal were McGarrity, Grader, Irwin, Quarry, Powis, Newberry, Patterson, Stewart, Bizzie, Beatty, Leckenby, Balfour, Judd, Mundle, Yeates, Hutton, Wilson, Christie, Stewart, Philip, Newbigging, Jones, Malcolm, McPhail, Riddell, Main, Lumsden, Loosley, Dodson, and Sintzel.

About the turn of the century William Smith had an icehouse at the rear of his home near Station 28 on the bay side. Ice cut from the bay was bought by the summer trade on a cash and carry basis. For years Billy Smith skated down the lake shore to Toronto and back. Bob Curtis owned a refreshment booth at Station 22 on the bay near the canal. Curtis was a drover and well known throughout Halton County.

In 1908, cottages between the canal and Station 26 on the lakeshore had to be moved to the bay side to Morris (later Omaha) St. to make room for a line of towers carrying electric power lines.

Strolling along the boardwalk to the canal was a pleasant diversion before the automobile. Evenings brought the sound of music wafting over the water, and the bells of Hamilton and Burlington could be plainly heard at the beach. The perfume of the farm fields drifted across the bay in June, and in August the aroma of Aldershot melons was borne on the breeze.

Gradually the old way of life changed. Fire destroyed many of the buildings, often in a spectacular way. When the Ocean House burned, boys formed a bucket brigade to bring the water to the men. Witnesses told how mattresses were carefully carried from the second floor while panicky men were frantically leaning from the first floor windows tossing the china and glassware out.

The radial cars after 1897, and later the automobile, helped to bring about a transformation of the bucolic surroundings. The dirt road had given way to a paved highway by 1923 and swarms of visitors converging on the beaches each week-end put an end to the resort's exclusiveness. Family summer residences gradually were converted to permanent year round homes and the atmosphere no longer was the same. The "colony" disappeared for all time. The radial electric railway ceased operation in 1929 and the Hamilton Street Railway today operates the bus route across the beach to Burlington.

The original survey of Saltfleet township, made about 1788, did not include "Long Beach" as the sandstrip was called. This area was set aside as a military reserve but to some extent came under the jurisdiction of Saltfleet. Between 1840 and 1878, parcels of the beach were acquired by settlers but early in this period much of the land was Crown Land and the residents a law unto themselves. The beach north of the canal was in Nelson Township, Halton County, and south of the canal was in Saltfleet Township, Wentworth County.

For many years the beach was administered by a Commission, but records of Nelson Township and Wellington Square constantly refer to the sandstrip. Roads were the chief consideration.

An unsuccessful attempt was made by the City of Hamilton to annex the beach in 1907. Magistrate George Fredrick Jelfs of Hamilton, a summer beach resident, helped beat the attempt.

The beach commission was dissolved by Act of Legislation in 1956 and a part of the beach north of the canal was offered to Burlington. The town council under Mayor Ted Smith turned it down. All the lands south of the county line with some but not all of the beach strip lying within Burlington were annexed to Hamilton as of January 1, 1957.

Burlington continued to provide water to the area north of the canal as well as fire protection, and many children living there attended school in Burlington. The old pumping house on Lakeshore Rd. has been designated an historic site.

On May 25, 1964, the Ontario Municipal Board agreed that "the social welfare, education, religious and aesthetic habits of the residents should increasingly be bound up with those of Burlington." Annexation by Burlington of the north side of the Canal took effect January 1, 1965.

Canada Centre for Inland Waters, a $25 million Great Lakes water management and pollution research facility, opened May 5, 1968 on a 12 acre site at Pier 29 on the beach.

A beach strip park was proposed and in 1976 a Beach Strip Task Force was formed. Negotiation began with the C.N.R. for the strip of land between the former Brant Inn site and the first cottages on the lake. These 133 acres were acquired by Burlington. Gradually with the help of provincial grants, beach strip properties were purchased a few a year. These cottages were individually owned but the land was leased from the C.N.R. The five-year leases expired at differing times, necessitating gradual purchases of the various cottages. They were put into the possession of the Halton Region Conservation Authority for a park, Beachway, which would

The beach strip before the highway.

eventually stretch to the canal. The former Morris and McDonald Parks were included in Beachway.

A Burlington Beach Master Plan Proposed Strategic Review, prepared in 1995 by a consultant, recommended changes costing more than $20 million. It was ruled that cottage leases would be terminated as of December 31, 1998, and the buildings removed. Burlington Beach waterfront park was becoming a reality.

Picnickers at the beach.

6
A World of Ships

On the coat of arms of the City of Burlington is a three-masted, square-rigged clipper ship. This vessel is indicative of the important part played by ships in the city's history. Indeed, ships made possible much of Burlington's prosperity in the mid-nineteenth century.

The first craft used for express in Upper Canada were canoes but not the kind one thinks of today. These were large boats which carried an average of three tons. The largest could transport as many as 60 men or 50 barrels of flour. From this simple start the design of Canadian ships gradually progressed to multi-masted schooners. The earlier clumsier bateaux were found useful to load and unload cargoes when there were no proper docking facilities for sailing ships and the schooners had to anchor in deep water.

It is difficult now to think of Burlington as a port. Places such as Port Credit, Oakville, and Bronte at the mouths of good-sized creeks, and Dundas at the head of a smaller lake, had natural sheltered harbours. Docks were built at Port Nelson and Wellington Square to serve the growing local need for transportation facilities, lack of sheltered harbour or no. The schooner owners didn't care; they would stop anywhere for cargo.

At the foot of the Guelph Line was a sandy beach sloping gently into the water. Here the docks and warehouses of Port Nelson were built with two tall pines over 100 feet high serving as landmarks for sailors. About a mile and a half along the shore, three docks at Wellington Square pointed out into the lake . . . Bunton's, Baxter's and Torrance's. Around the north shore of the bay a sentinel oak proclaimed Alex Brown's wharf at what was sometimes called Port Flamborough, and today is known as La Salle Park.

The first cargo to be shipped from lake ports here was grain. The first settlers planted wheat in spaces between tree stumps and built up crops until there was a surplus. "Wheat was almost the only cash crop the Upper Canadian could grow, the only means by which he could get his hands on a little money," writes Prof. A.R.M. Lower, adding that by 1850 nearly 132 million bushels of wheat were being grown in Upper Canada. The Wellington Square area was one of the largest of the producers.

It must be remembered that this region was Canada's "west" and at that time Sarnia and Windsor were the farthest western points of settlement with nothing beyond but the wide, empty prairies, which had not yet proved they could become the breadbasket of Canada.

Between 1845 and 1865, wheat was the most important export of this area. At one time Port Nelson shipped more cargo than Hamilton. On busy days the Guelph Line from Fisher's Corners (now the Guelph Line and Queen Elizabeth Way) to the docks was an unbroken line of carts hauled by horses or oxen, waiting to unload. The same congestion occurred on Brant Street. According to Smith's 1844 Canadian Gazetteer, exports from Wellington Square included 34,921 bushels of wheat.

Two local farmers were proud of their records, one raising 200 bushels of wheat on seven acres in 1855. The other one raised 340 bushels on twelve acres in the same year. Farmers like these paid $4 to $5 per 100 bushels to have their grain threshed.

After reaching the lake the loads were dumped into bins and taken in little cars down small rails or tracks to the waiting vessels tied up at the dock. Every pound was scrupulously tallied to make sure the farmer got his due, and that the ship's captain was not short-changed. The docks were busy places and attracted small boys. In 1856, a young lad was suffocated in one of Baxter's wheat bins at the foot of Brant Street.

The manufacture of flour became an important local industry. A large steam flour mill was built in 1812 when James Gage laid out the townsite. In 1844, 10,922 barrels of flour were shipped from the "Square." Frequently

The schooner Azov.   *– courtesy Archives of Ontario*

200 teams in a single day would deliver their wheat to the flour mill. This mill, along with the village lots yet unsold, was purchased by Torrance and Co. of Montreal, which conducted a prosperous grain business.

Schooners came and went from here and from Port Nelson. In the middle 1850s and early 1860s several ships a day, some from as far away as Chicago, called to unload wheat to be ground into flour. Wheat was not the only cargo; boat-loads of empty flour barrels were delivered too. Occasionally, ships ran aground and on Sunday, November 30, 1856, crowds went from the "Square" to see the schooner *Ruby*, aground on the beach with a load of flour. In November, 1860, the schooner *Berlin* loaded with salt, drew the villagers to the lakeshore as she lay helpless. It took 17 days to unload and refloat her. In October, 1861, the schooner *Admiral* grounded north of the canal, and on October 31, 1863, the schooner *Peerless* hit the canal pier and sank in the channel.

The sight of these ships under sail coming in to the port of Wellington Square would be breath-taking today - it is understandable how, when listing and aground, they must have attracted sightseers of the time.

With the importance of ships in the life of Wellington Square, the development of ship building became a thriving industry along with grain export and flour making. One of the early ship builders was an American, Willet Green Miller, born in 1808. Deserting the American cause, he was headed for Hamilton in 1824 when a storm wrecked his boat on the beach. He decided to stay here and apprenticed himself to a local ship builder. He grew prosperous and rose to a partnership in the firm which became known as Bante and Miller. He built numerous sailing ships and steam-boats, one of which was the *Chief Justice Robinson* which boasted a protruding prow at the waterline for ramming the ice.

The *Highland Chief*, built by Mr. Miller in 1834, sailed on Lake Erie. In the fall of 1834, a violent storm that tossed vessels up on to the front streets of Buffalo wrecked the *Highland Chief*. Another of the Miller ships, the *Sir Robert Peel*, was driven ashore at Wellington Square in a snow storm. The demands of the trade forced vessels to sail very late in the season. Miller built his last ship, a small one, the *Kate*, at Oakville in 1866.

Willet Miller and his partner Bante must have had some association through business interests with another pair of entrepreneurs, Smith and Chisholm. Hiram Smith, born about 1805, and Andrew Chisholm bought land in 1833 at Wellington Square for a store site. The partners had shares in several boats built during the 1830s. Another Chisholm, William, built sailing vessels here and owned the first ship that sailed through the Burlington canal in 1826.

Some of the records of ships built here have been preserved. In April, 1861, it was recorded, "April 4, the new vessel at the Square has put her foremast into the step, her main mast yesterday...April 20, can see the new vessel at the Square bending sails...April 25, schooner *Charles Baxter*, launched at the Square, a large number attended."

Although the industry declined, many ships were owned by villagers of Wellington Square and Port Nelson. March 5, 1860, "Johnson exchanged a village lot in Port Nelson with a house for the schooner *Agnes*." (No mention of how big a house). In 1861, "Messrs. Irwin and Douglass of Port Nelson bought the schooner *Lively* for $850." The Halton Atlas lists in 1877 three ships owned in Burlington, the *Mary Jane* owned by Captain Daniel Henderson, a vessel of 22,000 bushels capacity, 345 tons register; the *Aizor* and the *Sweepstakes* each about 12,000 bushels capacity, 195 tons register, owned by John Waldie and William Bunton.

In 1868, on the Great Lakes, there were 56 steamers, 19 propeller craft and 64 tugs along with 266 sailing ships and 27 barges, double the amount of shipping as recorded for 1856.

Lumbering was another of Wellington Square's early enterprises depending on water transportation. Timber merchants had been established from the beginning of the 19th century in Quebec, the ship building centre of Canada. From there, lumbering spread inland. Square timber was shipped to England to replace imports from Baltic countries cut off during the Napoleonic War blockade. Square timber was much in demand because it economized cargo space, but it caused much harm...The outside portions of the trees were cut off in the forest, littering the ground. In no time clear creeks of Halton county were choked with sawdust, growing shallower until they could no longer support the varieties of fine fish that abounded when the country was first settled. Hardwood was much in demand, especially tall, straight red and white pines which were used for masts of sailing ships.

Burlington from the pier, showing narrow gauge tracks.   *– courtesy Joseph Brant Museum*

The Douglass Saw Mill, Port Nelson.   *– courtesy Joseph Brant Museum*

Canadian lumbermen soon realized it was less wasteful to cut a tree into planks instead of throwing away all but the centre core. Soon lumber mills were doing a brisk business and by 1846 there were 17 sawmills in Nelson township. Sawn lumber was shipped to Britain, but by the mid-1860s, the American market had opened up. The economy of British North America became based largely on forest products. Places like Kilbride, Lowville, and Zimmerman prospered, located as they were amid seemingly inexhaustible forests on creeks powering the mills.

At Wellington Square, Benjamin Eager was a successful lumber merchant. By the late 1860s, the sound of lumber being handled could be heard here and at Port Nelson. Just as the grain carts had lined up along the Guelph Line and Brant Street, so it was with the lumber wagons which formed a procession miles long to the lake-front wharves.

Teaming wood gave many men work, the wood being brought over the uneven roads in summer and over smooth ice in winter. On January 8, 1870, "Four teams with two saw logs each came over the ice on the north shore from Emery's to Eager's saw-mill." Mr. Eager owned at least some of his own transportation, as there is a record of his scow being damaged in the canal on December 5, 1870.

The lumber boom in the 1860s did not come any too soon. The Crimean War had created an inflated demand for grain and flour but at its end in 1856, a depression set in which was heightened by a poor harvest in 1857. Thanks to lumber, times improved somewhat and the economy was steady until the outbreak of the American Civil War in 1861. Then again, businessmen retrenched, fearful of what war so close to home could do to this country.

At the beach, in the spring of 1862, a battery of six guns was installed by a government which had not forgotten the naval engagement of 1813. Soon, however, anxieties were calmed by orders for timber pouring into Canada from the northern States. This was the start of the lumber "fever" in this district. Britain, and now the United States, gobbled up our forest output as fast as trees could be felled. At Wellington Square, the flour and grain business continued, but now lumber was "king."

After 1853, the locomotives devoured enormous quantities of wood. Other consumers of wood were the steamships. Before the steamers, the schooners had been the grain and lumber carriers. In 1816, there were 60 schooners on Lake Ontario alone.

The first steamers were paddle wheelers. In the quiet of the 1860s, the sound of the paddles of an approaching steamer could be heard for an hour before it came to the Burlington canal. Many of the first steamers were converted schooners, some with masts left on for use with sails in an emergency. They were used mostly for passenger and mail service. From 1846, steamboats to and from Hamilton usually stopped at Wellington Square.

An 1868 Detroit newspaper clipping announced: "Side wheel steamers have lost their former prestige...Propellers have been substituted...for the carrying trade they are the favourites." By the 1880s, schooners were disappearing and steamers were the only watercraft competing with the railways for the freight business.

These wood-devouring vessels had to be kept supplied with fuel. In the late 1840s, Alex Brown in East Flamborough built a wharf near today's site of La Salle Park and contracted with the Ontario Navigating Company of Toronto to provide its ships with cordwood. By the 1860s, Brown's wharf was the vessels' supply point with valuable timber from the slopes of the escarpment being taken aboard to satisfy the voracious appetites of the fleet.

The *Richelieu* and her sister ships, mighty consumers, provided lucrative employment for farmers and mill men in the winter months. In one season alone 5,000 cords were taken on by the steamers. The lumber wagons, drawn by great Clydesdales, came all the way from Puslinch township near Guelph. Port Nelson was another important port of supply for wood to feed the furnaces of the lake carriers.

But the end had come. Reforestation was unheard of and the lumbermen had simply denuded the country, chopping down every tree in sight. The early pioneers hated the sight of a tree and succeeding generations were happy to clear the forests and make money besides. Eventually, though, they were to realize how grievous the loss inflicted had been.

By the last decade of the 19th century, the best timber was gone. The mills in the north of Nelson township converted to grinding grist and once more mixed farming became the district's main occupation. Wellington Square found itself no longer a humming hive of activity. The forests were gone and the far West had taken over as the granary of the Dominion. A few factories had sprung up but now the railways were their commercial carriers. Ships still plied their way to Hamilton but ports like Burlington and Port Nelson, lacking harbours, were unable to accommodate the larger vessels.

The great grain, lumber and shipping days were ended and a new life centering around market gardening, manufacturing and quiet suburban living became Burlington's lot.

7
County Government

Before there was any local community, the first Lieutenant-Governor of Upper Canada, John Graves Simcoe, passed along the beach and gazed upon Lake Geneva. It may have reminded him of Yorkshire, England, and Bridlington Bay protected from the ocean by Smithnicks' Sand with Flamborough Head to the north.

On July 16, 1792, in a royal proclamation forming new divisions of Upper Canada, he designated the western riding of York as being "bounded on the south by Lake Geneva to be called Burlington Bay."

This name has been the cause of confusion for some historians. Bridlington or Burlington, whatever the derivation, Burlington it became - bay, beach, Indian encampment and small settlement at the north of the beach. As late as 1815, the area around the Brant home was still called Burlington in military reports on the Indians in the War of 1812. Joseph Brant's death in 1807 was documented as having taken place at Burlington. When the canal was dug it also took the name of Burlington.

What today is the northwestern entrance to Hamilton was known as Burlington "Heights" in the War of 1812. The land where it slopes down farther around the bay in the section now known as Aldershot was called Burlington "Plains." Writers in the early part of the 19th century sometimes did not distinguish between these localities, using the name "Burlington" in a general way, and leaving it up to readers to guess what they meant. The Burlington Board of Agriculture, formed in 1806, the Burlington Glass Works and the Burlington Hotel, popular in the mid-1800s, were all in Hamilton. It appears that the name, Burlington, was used in the early days, interchangeably with Head of the Lake, for Hamilton.

Some of the confusion was cleared up with the naming of the community to the east of Joseph Brant's home "Wellington Square". In February, 1810, a group of Niagara and West York petitioners described the settlement at the north end of the beach as having been parcelled out by Joseph Brant "into small irregular tracts and sold to individuals without any allowance or reserve for roads." Later the same year, James Gage began a more orderly settlement with the purchase from Catherine Brant and Augustus Jones, trustee under Brant's will, of 338 1/2 acres described in Gage's deed as the northeast angle of Brant's Military Tract." Thus Gage was the first "developer" of the town and in his time it became known as "Wellington Square".

Credit for choosing this name has often been given to Joseph Brant. That this was his recommendation is highly unlikely, however, since the Duke of Wellington was still relatively unknown at the time of Brant's death in 1807. He did not win fame until the 1815 Battle of Waterloo and at the time of Brant's last trip to England in 1785 was only 16. It became the popular practice locally after the Napoleonic Wars to name places in this area after Britain's heroic leaders - hence Nelson Village, Wellington Square, Bronte, etc.

Government came to Upper Canada after the Revolutionary War in the United States. Those loyal to the British crown made this their home. At first they lived under martial law with no courts of law as we have today. On July 24, 1788, Lord Dorchester, Governor-in-Chief of British North America, issued a proclamation dividing Upper Canada into four districts with judges, justices of the peace, sheriffs, clerks, and coroners. These districts were Lunenburg, Mecklenburg, Hesse and Nassau, which included the site of the present city of Burlington, although there were no white settlers here then.

The Crown Survey Act of 1792 commenced the laying out of townships. Prior to this time ownership had been established by staking out a claim and homesteading it. By this Act, townships were to be laid out in advance of the new settlers coming to the district and were a means of registering title to property, not for government. Once the principle of townships was established, surveying had to go ahead and Augustus Jones, deputy chief land surveyor for the district of Nassau, began his work in earnest.

Jones, brother of Mary Gage of Stoney Creek, was a Welsh surveyor who came to Canada after the American Revolution and settled at the south end of the Beach. Early records of this district are all based on the survey work done by Jones.

Surveying in those days was not the finely calculated science it is today. Robert Gourlay in his compilation of Upper Canada statistics recorded that "boundary lines in the wilderness are marked by blazing...their measuring chains cannot run very straight and their compass needles may be greatly diverted from the right direction by ferruginous substances...much dispute has arisen therefrom."

These disputes have come down "even unto the third and fourth generation," and to this day problems have arisen in the north Aldershot area when land has been changing hands. Early surveyors worked under the hardest conditions and did a remarkable job of charting the county, all things considered.

A surveyor's "bench mark" was X'd on the top of a large granite stone which stood on the Paul Fisher property on the Guelph Line. This stone was found near the corner of the Guelph Line and the Queen Elizabeth

Mrs. Mary S. Pettit, warden of Halton County, 1949. — courtesy Karen Pettit

Joyce Savoline, Chair of Halton Region from 1994 to the present. – courtesy Joyce Savoline

Way and when the highway was built, Mr. Fisher salvaged the stone and had it moved to his front lawn. The property became the site of Burlington Mall and the buildings demolished, the stone probably buried.

Nelson Township was laid out in one and one-quarter mile squares, 1,000 acres in each square with ten 100-acre farms in each. The base line, two and a half miles above Highway 5, is the boundary between the old and new surveys of Nelson. The new survey was planned on the principle that long narrow farms would need only a fraction as many roads. Abandoning the idea of square farms, the new ones were one and seven-eighths miles long but only seven-eighths of a mile wide. Nelson was set out as a township in 1806 (old survey), a year after Admiral Horatio Nelson's victory and death off Cape Trafalgar, and in 1819 (new survey). Flamborough, part of which now lies in Burlington, originally was called Geneva Township and was surveyed earlier than Nelson, becoming a township in 1799.

In 1792, a year after Upper and Lower Canada were designated, the population of Upper Canada had reached about 12,000 of which 10,000 were Loyalists. The courts serving the four large districts were forced to deal with more and more problems, many of them purely local in nature. The extent of these districts is seen in the size of Nassau which stretched from the Trent River in the east to Long Point on Lake Erie. The Provincial Act of 1792 continued the large districts but called them Eastern, Midland,

Western and Home (formerly Nassau). Each was governed by a Crown-appointed Governor. Nineteen counties were formed at this time as the basis of representation in the Legislative Assembly.

In 1798, at the second session of the second parliament of Upper Canada, eight large districts were designated with 23 counties and 158 townships. These counties each had a group of townships including any villages in the area. It was about this time that the township of Flamborough was divided into East and West, the two parts remaining in the Home district.

In 1816, the Gore District was formed, made up of land today in the Regions of Halton and Wentworth. Halton and Lincoln at one time met and Wentworth was created by taking part of Halton and part of Lincoln and adding other townships. Gore was named after Lt. Governor Sir Francis Gore, and Halton after Major Mathew Halton, secretary to Gore. Halton County at this time contained the townships of Beverley, Dumfries, East and West Flamborough, Nassagaweya, Esquesing, Trafalgar and Nelson in which lies part of the present town of Burlington. Gore was estimated to have 6,684 inhabitants in 1817.

The counties of Halton and Wentworth were reduced in 1832 but continued in a combination which included Brant County from 1851 to 1852. In 1852, Brant County broke away but Halton and Wentworth remained as one until the end of 1854.

The development of county government was a slow process. By the 1830s, the growth of urban communities was becoming extensive and governing power was transferred to bodies called "Boards of Police," elected by male resident householders. These boards appointed town officers, made assessments, purchased real property for town purposes and legislated in other ways. More extensive powers were granted to cities and towns which were incorporated by special acts. The power was vested in a mayor and common council.

In 1841, the District Councils Act was passed which established local municipal authorities. Inhabitants in each district elected councillors and a warden was appointed by the governor of the district who also decided on the clerk of the council from a list of three names submitted by the council. Later legislation provided that wardens, clerks, treasurers and surveyors would be appointed by the councils themselves.

In 1849, Robert Baldwin introduced an Act to "provide by one general law for the erection of municipal corporations and the establishment of regulations of police in and for several counties, cities, towns, townships and villages in Upper Canada." This Act, called the Baldwin Act, abolished the districts, and the counties became territorial divisions of the province for municipal as well as judicial purposes, thus providing the foundation of the government before regional government was enacted in 1974.

The county of Halton, 24 miles long and 15 miles wide, was eventually comprised of seven municipalities, the townships of Esquesing, and Nassagaweya, and the towns of Milton, Oakville, Georgetown, Burlington, and Acton. County council was composed of the reeve and deputy reeve from each of the seven municipalities, 14 members in all. The warden or council chairman, was elected annually by council members from among their numbers.

Burlington chose to remain a town long after her size permitted her to become a city. The advisability of this course proved to be wise. The town was closely involved in the government of the county and kept its hand on the spending pulse of council. County reforestation properties, the Emergency Measures (civil defence) Organization, agriculture, health unit, child welfare, operation of Halton Manor (a home for the aged), and administration of the Halton County Museum, are areas in which Burlington shared with the rest of Halton. The County provided adequate court facilities and maintained a county jail. All these services and institutions derived their funds from the municipalities.

Voting in county council was generally on the majority basis. In certain circumstances, however, a vote could be resolved by recorded vote with council members having voting power according to the population they represented. Burlington had a total of nine votes as compared with Nassagaweya which only had two.

Burlington always took its share of responsibility for administering the county as evidenced by the number of wardens who were residents of what is now Burlington; George Ghent, 1854; Robert Miller, 1855, 1857-1861 and 1864-1866; John Waldie, 1875-76; R.G. Baxter, 1886; P.D. Scott, 1890; W.G. Pettit, 1896; John C. Smith, 1901; James G. Wilson, 1903; M.C. Smith, 1910; John P. Griffin, 1912; Charles Readhead, 1917; E.A. Harris, 1922; W.A. Irving, 1923; E.M. Readhead, 1932; George Harris, 1934; L. Kerns, 1941; John Blair, 1942; Norman Craig, 1947; Mary S. Pettit, 1949; R. Shannon, 1955; Gordon Gallagher, 1964, and James Swanborough, 1972.

The popularity of Robert Miller has never been equalled. Born near Belfast, Ireland, he was a Zimmerman farmer who went into manufacturing in 1839. In 1850 he again took up farming and evinced a keen interest in local affairs. In 1867 he became clerk of the Sixth Division Court of the county as well as clerk and treasurer of Nelson township. He moved to Nelson Village to take up these duties and later settled in Burlington when he was made Collector of the Port in 1874.

REGIONAL GOVERNMENT

The Plunkett report on regional government recommended a county stretching from Burlington to Toronto Township. In 1967 Burlington town council opted out! Next came the Steeles Commission Hamilton Wentworth

Local Government Review, proposing uniting Burlington with Hamilton. The Citizens Committee for an Independent Burlington was formed and presented a brief to the commission stating that the majority of the town's residents preferred independence or a union with communities to the east.

In January, 1969, the Burlington *Gazette* printed a regional government petition opposing inclusion of Burlington with Hamilton in any form of regional government. Members of political parties, Jaycees, the Chamber of Commerce, Upper Burlington Citizens Forum and the Committee for an Independent Burlington circulated the petition. When it was presented to Municipal Affairs Minister D'Arcy McKeough in November there were 15,489 signatures. At the December, 1969, municipal elections, voters were 8-1 in favour of a Burlington/Halton/Peel region.

Finally, on Tuesday, January 23, 1973, a Halton regional government was announced. Anne MacArthur was the last warden of Halton County and Allan Masson, former Mayor of Oakville and former Halton Reeve, was appointed the first chair of the new region.

Burlington was to send the mayor and eight aldermen to regional council. Responsibilities were to be shared by the municipalities of Milton, Oakville, Burlington and Halton Hills and the region. The region was to be responsible for police, welfare, administration, roads, Halton Home for the Aged (later named Allendale), conservation authorities, planning and business development, Children's Aid Society, public health and child care assistance. Burlington's responsibilities included fire protection, waste management, parks and recreation, transit and traffic, planning and engineering, infrastructure maintenance, debt charges and capital, library, Museum Board, and the Arts Centre. The inaugural meeting of regional council was held at Central High School in mid-October, 1973, attended by Lieutenant-Governor Ross MacDonald, and cabinet ministers George Kerr, James Snow and John White. MPP Arthur Meen was official spokesman for the province. The regular working sessions of regional government began in 1974.

By 1996 some services were shared responsibilities: business development and tourism; parks and recreation; planning, growth and related services (both the region and the city of Burlington have official plans); roads; fire protection and museums (the region operates its own museum). Water supply, sewage and garbage disposal were taken over by the region which was also responsible for non-profit housing. The city collected taxes for the region and the school boards. In 1996, some restructuring of regional council was under way.

In January, 1996, "Greater Toronto: Report to the GTA (Greater Toronto Area) Task Force" was published. Commission chair was Dr. Anne Golden. This Golden Report, as it was known, suggested Halton become part of a giant Greater Toronto Area. The proposition was unanimously turned down by Burlington Council.

8
Politics - Federal and Provincial

Government at the provincial level, although it did not touch too intimately the individual lives of residents of the village of Wellington Square and the township of Nelson, materially shaped the affairs of the community at large. This was essentially true of the laws enacted by Governor Simcoe in his first parliament of Upper Canada.

In 1793, during the second session of that first parliament, an Act was passed to legalize many of the early marriages which had been performed by officers, and even army surgeons. The new Act also provided that if there were no ministers of the Church of England within 18 miles, one could be married by a Justice of the Peace who was to put up a notice in a public place prior to the marriage. If a minister did live within 18 miles and a justice of the peace officiated, the marriage was null and void. In 1798, the Act was extended to Church of Scotland, Lutheran, and Calvinist ministers provided one of the couple was a member of the church for six months before marriage. By 1831 ministers of other denominations were allowed to perform marriages.

In 1817, there were no churches or ministers in Wellington Square and only one Methodist minister in the whole of Nelson. East Flamborough was also bereft with no ministers or churches. This situation improved gradually, and by 1846 Rev. T. Greene was minister of the Church of England here (St. Luke's) and Rev. William King was a minister of the Church of Scotland in Nelson township. A free church (now Knox Presbyterian) was also listed at Wellington Square but was in the same charge as Waterdown, Nelson and Cumminsville.

Thus until St. Luke's was founded in 1834 the people of this region had to travel long distances to the nearest preacher or wait until he visited them. But at least their marriages were legal after the passage of the provincial legislation of 1793, and succeeding years.

The founding of militia was another important piece of legislation passed by the provincial government. At the same second session of the first legislature of 1793, the first Militia Act was passed. All males in the province between the ages of 15 and 50 (extended to 60 in 1794) had to bear arms. They were to have training of sorts and were to muster once a year, the date set in 1804 as June 4, the birthday of the reigning monarch George III. This muster also served as a census taking and at first the district of Nassau contributed 600 men to the militia.

The first militia in Nelson township was the 2nd Regiment York Militia organized in 1798. George Chisholm who settled on the north shore of Burlington Bay in 1794 was one of the officers. Another was Richard Cockerell, a tutor of John Brant. The same William Bates who had charge of the King's Head Inn in 1800 was another. Surveyor Augustus Jones belonged to the 1st Regiment of the West Riding of Lincoln in 1804. By 1821, there were two regiments of Gore militia, many of the officers of which had served in the war of 1812. By 1824, there were four regiments; by 1831, five.

In 1838, judging by the number who had enlisted, patriotism was running high because of the Mackenzie rebellion. Members of the 8th Gore regiment, Nelson township, came from many of the original families who settled the district. Some were Major Hiram Smith, Colonel George Chisholm, Lt.Col. Wm. McKay. Captains were: A.W.K. Chisholm, T. Cooper, James Wilson, W. O'Reilley, John Wetenhall, Joshua Ireland, John Lucas, John McGregor, J.F. Bastedo and J.A. Chisholm. Lieutenants were: Andrew Pettit, David Bastedo, J.S. McCollom, Wm. O'Reilly, A.G. McKay, Wm. Earls, W. Spence, James Langtry, Jacob Bastedo and James Panton.

The provincial government passed other significant laws at the second session in 1793. Slaves were no longer to be bought and sold but could be retained if already owned. Children of slaves were to be free at 25 years of age and, to close up a possible loophole in the Act, their names were to be registered not later than three months after birth. This Act did not greatly affect the area around here as there were few slave owners. Chief Joseph Brant was one. The Act did, however, make Upper Canada a haven for runaway slaves, some of whom came to Halton County to make their future homes.

There were no lawyers in the new province, but by 1794, with so many new laws being passed, it was necessary to appoint lawyers. A provincial law of that year provided for the appointment of 16 men to be licensed to practise law. The first legal documents were all handwritten and some of the signatures were mere "X"s indicating the inability to write. In lieu of seals, small bits of paper, about 1/2 inch square, sometimes torn from the corner of the document, were pasted to the document beside each signature with sealing wax. One of the early documents was an indenture between Honourable Peter Russell of York and John Fonger of Ancaster when the latter purchased land in the part of East Flamborough which was later called Aldershot. A copy of the original deed to the next transaction of this property is dated January 1, 1817. It is interesting to note that all the Fonger men could sign their names on the documents but only one of the four women could do so.

From 1792 to 1841, Upper and Lower Canada were each governed separately and the elected representatives of this area sat in the Legislative

Assembly at Toronto. Since there was no united Canada there was no need for two sets of elections, federal and provincial, such as we have now. Early representatives of this district included the names of John Wetenhall and Caleb Hopkins. Mr. Hopkins and his two brothers all settled in Nelson, Caleb buying land on what is now Highway 5 just east of the Guelph Line. He became a leading citizen and a Liberal member of the Assembly.

Political turmoil must have been at its height in Nelson Township toward the end of the 1830s. This was the time of the Mackenzie rebellion; William Lyon Mackenzie was a Scottish journalist who advocated popular government. He was elected to the Upper Canada Assembly in 1828 and became the first Mayor of the City of Toronto in 1834. In attacking the government by tongue and pen he became fanatical and eventually turned to violence. He robbed the Western Mail coach and took the cash of the passengers. According to a Tory account, one woman was robbed "of her all" meaning a suitcase. This gave rise to the ridiculous story that Mackenzie fled the country in female clothing.

In December, 1837, armed rebellion broke out at Montgomery's Tavern outside of Toronto. Mackenzie, defeated, with a price on his head fled along Dundas Street with young Alan Wilcox. They stopped near Streetsville where they were driven in a wagon westward toward the Sixteen Mile Creek. When they found the bridge over the creek guarded by troops they quickly left the wagon and hid in the woods. Stripping off their clothes they waded across icy water which was up to their necks. "In an hour and a half we were under the hospitable roof of one of the innumerable agriculture friends I could then count on in the country," Mackenzie recalled.

Mackenzie does not name this Nelson farmer who gave them dry clothes but said, "The sons and daughters of the Nelson farmer kept a silent watch outside in the cold while I and my companion slept." They took only a short rest and continued on, crossing the Twelve Mile Creek about midnight.

They passed by Wellington Square, and just before dawn reached the home of a magistrate known to Mackenzie. Asahel Davis warned him that his house had been searched twice by the troops, perhaps because, just awhile before, he had sheltered Dr. John Rolph, a Mackenzie supporter who was also fleeing with a price on his head. When the two refugees learned that large forces were looking for them, they decided to split up and Wilcox was left at the home of a friend of Mackenzie.

At daybreak it began to snow and to avoid leaving tracks for his pursuers to follow, Mackenzie called at the home of another Nelson farmer. Instead of hiding in the barn he hid in a tiny thatched peas rick where he watched soldiers search all the buildings around. When they had gone, the farmer brought Mackenzie food, and water to wash in. When darkness fell, a young lad led him to the home of a friend named King whose farm on what is now King Rd. was next to the Tory headquarters of John Chisholm's troops. The boy worked at Chisholm's but did not betray the rebel.

King fed Mackenzie and led him to the home of a friend who gave him a horse. Mackenzie reached Dundas that night and escaped to Navy Island in the Niagara River and later to the United States.

Christmas Day, 1837: Volunteers from Burlington and area, estimated at about 100, set out in sleighs for Chippewa to help put down the rebellion. Some of the names of the men include Tuck, Tansley, Birney, Easterbrook, Bastedo, Chisholm, Peart, Bridgman, Pettit, Blanchard, Ireland and many others.

It would appear that most of the leading citizens of this area were decidedly for or against the fiery Scot. Many men enlisted in 1837 and fought on the side of the Tory government. Few actually shouldered arms on Mackenzie's behalf, for example, Peter Fisher, supporter, "stayed home" that fateful summer of 1837 and built "Shady Cottage" at what became 801 Guelph Line and eventually the site of Burlington Mall. Mackenzie's Nelson sympathizers were legion, though, and if he was helped in his flight from Montgomery's Tavern by every farmer whose descendants claim he was, then he must have been a long time escaping from this region. Several years after the rebellion Mackenzie described his flight, and his account (which was used here) must be taken as the true story, if his memory did not fail him. He did not, however, mention by name all the Nelson farmers who helped him, which leaves each of today's "Mackenzie hid here" contenders equally justified in their claims.

In 1841, the two provinces of Upper and Lower Canada were united with one legislature, an elected Assembly with 42 representatives from both Upper and Lower Canada, and an upper house of not fewer than 20 Crown appointed members. This combination of Upper and Lower provinces was called Canada until, in 1867, it was enlarged to include Nova Scotia and New Brunswick, with other provinces joining in later years.

There appear to be no further successes for Nelson or Burlington candidates in elections in Halton for some time after Caleb Hopkins' day. The next candidate to run for office from this area was W.J. Simcoe Kerr, Joseph Brant's urbane grandson. He contested the first provincial election after confederation in 1867 as a Conservative but was beaten by William Barber, Reformer from Streetsville.

Barber subsequently gave too much support to Premier Sandfield MacDonald's Conservative government for the Halton Reform Association's liking and they withdrew their support. He later ran as an Independent Reformer and defeated the Reform candidate in the election of 1871.

From 1867 on, there were federal and provincial elections in Halton, most of them hotly contested. In January, 1874, John White, M.P. and

Reform candidate in the upcoming election, actually attended his opponent, D.B. Chisholm's meetings and commented thus on each: "Very rowdy meeting; large turnout Oakville toughs; meeting closed decidedly in my favour; numerous questions asked Mr. Chisholm, very evasively answered." The most amazing Chisholm meeting must have been the one where White said he "spoke two hours and demolished Chisholm." Demolished or not, Chisholm won the election by 23 votes. The Burlington vote went 50 to White and 51 to Chisholm, which can hardly be fairer.

This election was later contested - Chisholm was unseated. It was just one of many contested elections. The provincial election of 1875, won by the Reformers, was protested by the Conservatives and a cross-competition was then entered by the Reformers. The election of a Conservative in 1883 was protested on the grounds of undue influence. The Conservative winner of the federal election of 1888 was unseated for bribery. He was described by his opponent as "a very decent man but not worth a crack of the thumb in politics." A protest of the provincial election of 1898 succeeded again in having the Halton seat declared vacant.

Elections were fine fodder for newspapers. One journalistic utterance which was impartially pasted in the Reform Association minute book described a post-election parley: "On the night of the 17th (election night) after the result was known, Mr. McCraney (winning Reformer) addressed a number of his devotees in the back yard between the Wallace house and the stables adjoining the hotel. We don't know what constituted the platform on the occasion but to be consistent with the surroundings of the situation, we should infer it was a dunghill." The fact that their man had won probably made the Reformers magnanimous enough not to sue for slander!

In the provincial election of 1883, a Conservative, William Kerns of Burlington was elected. His grandfather had settled in Halton county early in the 19th century. He was a partner in a Burlington general store with John Waldie for twenty years. The political affiliations of the partners may have had some bearing on the eventual termination of their business relations.

In the federal election of August 22, 1888, Reformer John Waldie, of Burlington, won over Conservative David Henderson by 24 votes. As Reeve of Wellington Square in 1873, Waldie had been instrumental in having the village incorporated and its name changed to Burlington.

In March, 1891, with Henderson and Waldie once more rival candidates, it was Henderson over his opponent by 104 votes, but he didn't have long in the House of Commons since in December, 1891, he was unseated "for corrupt practices." The Reformers again called upon Waldie but he had had enough, apparently, and declined the nomination. Strange as it may seem, in the election of 1896, again the candidates were John Waldie

Hughes Cleaver, former Burlington   *John Waldie, reeve of Wellington*
M.P.   *Square and later a Burlington M.P.*

and David Henderson. Waldie lost by 84 votes. Denunciations for alleged "corrupt practices" and "bribery" were not as serious as they sounded. Henderson was well regarded and continued in politics for many years.

Until 1878, votes were cast orally as "the only bold, straight-forward manly way" of voting. Vote by ballot was first used in an Ontario by-election in 1874, and in the federal election of 1878. In a rural community it presented new problems. In the provincial election of 1902, John Barber of Georgetown defeated the Conservative, Dr. Nixon, after two recounts were made. Spoiled ballots were the cause of the appeal and at least one ballot was rejected because it was stained with tobacco juice!

By 1917, women had quietly entered the federal and provincial political scene, after being given the municipal franchise back in 1884. Possibly all along, behind the "bold straightforward manly" voting there had been some female influence. At any rate Halton Reformers welcomed the ladies and it was recorded that in Milton, June 15, 1917, "one of the best conventions ever held took place, there being over 200 women present." Individual female politicians, however, were not necessarily always accepted with open arms. In looking over a list of possible campaign speakers in September, 1926, it was thought inadvisable to have Miss Agnes McPhail speak here, after reading "some of her utterances at other points."

In the 1917 Federal elections E.H. Cleaver, a Burlington lawyer, was Liberal candidate. Mr. Cleaver's platform was, "Canada for Canadians."

William Kempling, former
Burlington M.P.
        – courtesy Muriel Kempling

Paddy Torsney, current Burlington
M.P.
        – courtesy Paddy Torsney

Unfortunately for the town's political prestige, Mr. Cleaver was defeated and the United Farmers of Ontario were swept into power. Robert King Anderson served Halton from 1917 to 1930, a Conservative for most of those years. E.H. Cleaver's defeat at the polls was later avenged by his son, Hughes, also a Liberal, who was elected in 1935 as the federal representative for Halton. Mr. Cleaver set a record for the riding by being elected again in 1940, 1945, and 1949. Mr. Cleaver was a member of parliament until 1953, when his law practice demanded his full attention. While on Parliament Hill, he was chairman for a decade of the Banking Commerce committee, the major parliamentary committee. He was also chairman of the War Expenditures Committee in the final two years of World War II and was chairman of the Government-owned railroad and T.C.A. committee. A Conservative, Miss Sybil Bennett, succeeded him at Ottawa.

In 1966, the Federal riding of Halton-Wentworth was added, then abolished ten years later. At that time a Burlington riding was formed from part of Halton-Wentworth. Bill Kempling (PC) was elected in 1979 and represented Burlington until retiring before the 1993 election. He died in May, 1996. Paddy Torsney (Lib) a resident of Aldershot won the seat. A part of Burlington to the east was in the Halton-Peel riding established in 1987. Garth Turner(PC) was elected in 1988 and Julian Reed (Lib) in 1993. The redistribution of 1996 moved Aldershot out of Burlington and into a new Wentworth-Burlington riding, taking effect in January, 1997. The riding includes Dundas, Ancaster and Flamborough.

In the provincial redistribution of 1966, Burlington was in Halton West including the township of Nassageweya and the town of Acton. In the redistribution of 1975, part of the city was Burlington South and the eastern part, Halton Burlington.

In 1959, Owen F. Mullin (Lib) ran against Stan Hall (C) for the Halton provincial seat and was defeated. Before the next election Mr. Hall died and George Kerr (C) filled the vacant seat. In the 1963 fall elections, Kerr defeated Owen Mullin by a comfortable majority. Kerr retired before the 1983 contest after a record 20 years in politics. Loyal voters were once more in evidence: Cam Jackson (C) was elected to Kerr's seat and in 1996 was still representing Burlington South.

The aforementioned Julian Reed won the Halton Burlington seat in 1975 and continued to be elected through to the 1984 election.

He ran federally in 1993 and won the Halton-Peel seat.

9
Nelson Township Council

The village of Wellington Square, (known as Burlington after 1873), for many years was governed as a part of Nelson township. It was considered, however, sufficiently a community to make a report on November 21, 1817, to Robert Gourlay, a Scottish immigrant collecting data on the townships of Upper Canada. John Brant, Augustus Bates, Asahel Davis, Thomas Ghent, Nicholas Kerns and Ralph and James Morden addressed Mr. Gourlay as "inhabitants of Wellington Square, being settlers on a tract of land granted to the late Captain Brant for his military services; and also being a part of the township of Nelson."

This dual nature of Wellington Square's existence, both as a community itself and as a part of Nelson, is seen in the township council on which Wellington Square was represented. For many years township bylaws and decisions governed "the Square" as well as the rest of the area, and a picture of the life in the village is reflected in the deliberations of the council.

Records of the first meetings in the township indicate they were public gatherings with "freeholders, householders and inhabitants" in attendance. On January 4, 1836, at the Inn of William Chisholm, Caleb Hopkins was appointed chairman; William McCay township clerk, a position he held for many years; and Peter Fisher, Francis Hamburg and James Cleaver, commissioners. It was decided that horned cattle, sheep and swine over 40 pounds weight could run loose, but horses, bulls, rams and boars, mercifully, had to be confined.

Successive meetings were held at John Mayhew's inn, John Peer's inn and for several years at Richard Hull's and Bright Naisbitt's inns.

The 1838 meeting elected commissioners George Dice, Joseph Ireland and Thomas Alton and elicited declarations of all overseers of highways that they would faithfully perform their duties.

On January 7, 1839, wardens were mentioned for the first time - Joseph Ireland, Peter Fisher and Thomas Atkinson. No commissioners were listed. Bylaws were not yet being passed, merely resolutions which had to be confirmed each year. Joseph Brant's son-in-law, William J. Kerr, chaired the 1841 meeting, and the next year district councillors Caleb Hopkins and John Miller were mentioned as well as town wardens George Ghent, Peter Simmerman and Peter Fisher. School commissioners appointed that year were Peter Fisher, Rev. Thomas Greene, Rev. William King, Rev. Anson Green, John Kinney, David McLeod and Thomas Douglas.

By 1843, with William Kerr still chairman, the livestock regulations were being tightened. Previously animals were not to run at large within a 1/4 mile of St. Ann's or Hannahsville and now Wellington Square could expect to see no more horses, horned cattle or hogs at large during the winter. Wardens that year were James Gage, John Wetenhall and David Pitcher.

In 1845, James Cleaver and Hiram Smith sought the councillorship title, with the latter winning. In 1847, John Miller was elected a member of the municipal council "by show of hands and no opposition." It appeared that township government was unexacting until 1850, with only yearly public meetings recorded.

In 1850, the leather bound minute book reveals: "according to the provisions of the (Baldwin) Act which provides for the establishment of township municipal councils and this, the Township of Nelson having been divided into five rural wards, the following persons were returned as duly elected councillors: Robert Douglas, Timothy Cooper, Andrew Gage, Titus G. Cummins and John Kenney." The first reeve chosen was Andrew Gage and his deputy was Robert Douglas. Assessors were George Crooks, William Panton, founder of Kilbride, and Robert Miller. Collectors were Vickers Peart and Walter O'Reilley.

From this time on, parliamentary procedures were followed with motions, committees of the whole, council meetings, bylaws and amendments to amendments. As the township was becoming more populated, so its government became more complicated.

The first bylaw of Nelson was passed in 1850: "Every dog to be assessed at 50 cents but every farmer can keep one dog free." Township records in succeeding years show that man's best friend was a considerable item in the township's annual expenditure. In 1871 "William Cartwright proved under oath the loss of one sheep by dogs...value $10." In February 1888, $11.33 was paid to J. Fothergill for the loss of one ram. The date, farmer's name, number of sheep killed and amount awarded to each were listed annually, totalling $96.10 for the year 1897, paid to 11 farmers... and many years were worse than this one.

Nor were dogs the only offenders in Nelson. A bylaw was passed in 1885 to prevent swine and geese from running at large in any village of the township. By 1888 a bylaw became necessary for restraining cattle, horses, sheep and poultry.

Nelson's second bylaw, also passed in 1850, provided a tax on showmen. It stated that "No person or persons shall be allowed to exhibit, practise or perform within this municipality any wax figures, wild animals, puppet shows, wire dancing, circus riding, or any idle act or feat which common showmen, circus riders or mountebanks or jugglers usually exhibit, practise or perform" without paying a tax on each performance.

The circus and showmen were some of the few forms of commercial amusement in the days before radio, television and the wide variety of entertainment which may be enjoyed today. These travelling performers, who usually set up their tents near well-known taverns, were eagerly awaited. One of the first to visit these parts must have been the Grand Caravan of Living Animals which stopped at Summer's Inn, Nelson, on July 19, 1828. For 25 cents, children half-price, one could see "a lion, lioness, tiger, jaguar, camel, leopard, catamount, ichneuman, jackal, black and gray wolves, llama, baboon, monkeys, ape and band of music." The impresario of the Grand Caravan neglected to add that some of the menagerie were stuffed.

Early council meetings had been held at local inns but the time came when a permanent structure was needed. In April, 1853, Stephen Atkinson offered a site and the sum of $30.00 to aid in the construction of a building. In due time the Nelson Township Hall was erected at the southeast corner of Dundas St. and Guelph Line.

Roads were probably the commonest item on the township council's agenda. In lieu of a works department, the upkeep of roads fell to the citizens themselves. Statute labour was the order of the day and pathmasters and fenceviewers had to be appointed regularly to see that the roads were kept navigable. New roads had to be opened and little-used ones closed. The location of bridges and culverts had to be decided and sometimes council would meet "on location" to view the site of a proposed road alteration.

Next to roads, the subjects most under discussion were taverns and "spirituous liquors." Robert Gourlay reported that before 1821 "dissipation with her fascinating train of expenses and vices had made but little progress on the shores of the lakes." By the 1830s, however, liquor, often of a poor quality, was consumed at every gathering and the number of taverns was out of all proportion to the population. For instance, in 1846, in Wellington Square with 400 inhabitants, there were four taverns, but only two churches. There were 10,000 members of temperance societies in Upper Canada by 1832 and, while the first ones only sought to stem the flow of liquor, later groups tried to stop it altogether.

Nelson township council took the former attitude and passed by-laws to regulate drinking places and liquor sales. Bylaw 110, passed in 1860, was one in a series of liquor laws. It stated that the number of houses of public entertainment in which spirituous or fermented liquor could be sold by retail was not to exceed 14, provided that not more than 4 of such houses (excluding the railway station) were in the village of Wellington Square, nor more than two in Port Nelson, three in Lowville, one at Cumminsville, one in Nelson village, one at Nelson Rocks, one at St. Ann's (later called Tansley) and one at the Middle Road.

At the first meeting of council each year one or more inspectors were to be appointed to inspect all houses of public entertainment and shops within the municipality, and grant licenses to those entitled to receive them. Their salaries were $1.50 for each day of inspection, not to exceed 10 days unless ordered by council.

Any person applying for a retail liquor license had to have "a fair character for sobriety and general good conduct. "A license for a house of public entertainment cost $30.00, for every shop license $80.00 and for a Temperance House it was only $2.00. Storekeepers and grocers were among those who could apply to sell wine, brandy and other spirituous liquors in quantities not less than one quart not to be drunk on the premises.

Inns or Temperance Houses had to be in a good state of repair with at least a dining or sitting room and four good clean beds in separate apartments over and above those occupied by the family and resident boarders, and there had to be, at a convenient distance, a barn and stable well secured for the keeping of horses, cattle, carriages, wagons, sleighs, etc., with good stabling for at least eight horses, with both the house and premises well supplied with pure wholesome water. "No tipling shall be allowed in any such house and it shall not be lawful for the keeper of any house to have on any part of the premises any faro table, roulette table, or any device for gambling."

Landlords were forbidden to sell or give liquors to any Indian man, woman or child, nor to any child, apprentice or servant without the consent of a parent or master or legal protector, nor to any person known to be an habitual drunkard.

The bylaw became effective April, 1860, and in December, Inspector Hugh Cotter of Port Nelson, reported to council, "I have endeavoured to do my duty without favour to any; 13 persons received from me certificates to keep houses of public entertainment and sell spirituous liquors viz: J.H. Baynes, Port Nelson; E. De Garmo, R.W. Bates, James Taylor, Wellington Square; Thomas Graham, railroad station; Robert Thompson, Cumminsville; C. Langford, Nelson Rocks; John Naisbit, Thomas Davidson, Guelph Line; H. McDade, Lowville; Thomas Heyden, Nelson; William Bunton, St. Ann's; Thomas Simons, Middle Road."

The following persons received certificates to keep Temperance Houses: James Irving, Port Nelson and William Zimmerman, Middleton.

"Much has been done," said the Inspector, "by your honourable body to reduce the amount of misery and crime arising from the too free use...of liquor, yet your Inspector finds much more remains to be done, which would condone to the welfare of our township...and that is a prohibitory Liquor Law altogether and believing that it is the duty of all township and county councils to move and exterminate forever from our land the worst

Your Vote and Influence are Respectfully solicited for

Wm. Bridgman

AS REEVE FOR 1919

Polling Day, Monday January 6th, 1919

Your Vote and Influence

ARE RESPECTFULLY SOLICITED FOR THE
ELECTION OF

WM. R. CLINE

AS COUNCILLOR

FOR NELSON TOWNSHIP FOR 1920

"IF ELECTED I WILL REPRESENT THE WHOLE TOWNSHIP"

VOTING JANUARY 5th, 1920.   (Gazette Print)

YOUR VOTE AND INFLUENCE

ARE RESPECTFULLY SOLICITED FOR

T. ATKINSON,

As Reeve for the Village of Burlington

FOR THE YEAR OF 1893.

If Elected I will endeavor to work for the best interests of the Village and to carry
out the wishes of the Electors, as I have endeavored to do in the past.

Your Vote and Influence

ARE RESPECTFULLY SOLICITED FOR

JAS. MORTIMER

AS REEVE

FOR THE VILLAGE OF BURLINGTON

FOR THE YEAR 1893.

Cards distributed by candidates seeking voters' support.

of foes (spirituous liquors) when sold by retail...it would greatly improve the morals of the people and many an unhappy home would be otherwise comfortable."

In 1861, two petitions were read, one praying that no license be granted for an inn at Kilbride and the other, that the number of inns on the Guelph Line be lessened. Other similar petitions were presented by other councillors asking that the number of taverns be limited. It is noted, however, on examining names on the petitions, that the same names appeared on petitions to limit taverns as also appeared on petitions of certain innkeepers applying for licenses! Council decided that there were enough inhabitants in the township to warrant nearly double the number of taverns instead of fewer. They therefore resolved that when a tavern keeper presented to council proper references of respectable municipal ratepayers, then that person should be considered "a sober, moral man and if the tavern is required, we do not see that this council can refuse such license."

The result of it all was that council concluded by granting ten licenses at that meeting. This whole rigmarole seemed to have gone on each time licenses were up for renewal.

In 1864, Nelson council found that plans had to be prepared of any unincorporated villages where the original owners of the land comprising the village "have not jointly laid out and surveyed the same...and whereas the village of Wellington Square...has been surveyed and laid out by three different parties, each having a separate survey." Since it was necessary that one complete plan of the village be made and deposited in the registry office, the ratepayers were assessed to pay the expense.

Of even more significance than the registering of Wellington Square's plan was the bylaw passed September 9, 1873, by the Halton County Council. This was to incorporate officially the village of Burlington. Wellington Square had come of age and was ready to change its name, elect its official council and make its own laws. After 1873, although some members of Nelson township council may have resided in Burlington, the village no longer was governed by the township council.

The first reeves of Nelson township were Andrew Gage, 1850; John Miller, 1851; George Ghent, 1852-1854; Robert Miller, 1855-67; W.J. Simcoe Kerr, 1868-71; John Waldie, 1872-73.

From 1873, reeves of Nelson did not directly represent the governing body of Burlington. These men, however, were residents of an area which is now a part of Burlington and their names should be remembered: Henry Foster 1874-79; George McKerlie, 1880-82; V.H. Peart, 1883-84; Edwin Dalton, 1885-86; P.D. Scott, 1887-90; W.G. Pettit, 1891-96, A.P. Alton, 1897-1900; J.F. Richardson, 1901-03; A. Dudley Alton, 1904-1907; W.G. Pettit, 1908; M.C.Smith, 1908-15. These reeves not only headed up the township council, but also sat on the county council as well, the same as all the reeves of the village, and later the town of Burlington. For the period from 1873 to 1914, there were reeves leading the councils of both Nelson Township and the village of Burlington. After 1914 when the village of Burlington became a town, the Burlington reeve was second in importance to the Mayor.

Nelson Township reeves after 1908 were J.P. Griffin, Charles Readhead, W.A.Irving, H.T. Foster, H.M. Pettit, E.M. Readhead, George W. Thorpe, John McNiven, Leslie Kerns, William J. Robertson, Mary S. Pettit, Charles Palmer, Russell Smale, George Brenhaltz, and Harold Adkins.

In 1958, Nelson Township and the Aldershot part of East Flamborough were amalgamated with the Town of Burlington.

Some of the Burlington reeves went on to become Mayor, for instance M.C.Smith was elected Mayor in 1915. Succeeding reeves included G.H. Richardson, Hughes Cleaver, Wm. Bridgman, E.A. Harris, F.D. Ghent, E. Holtby, J.W. Breckon, G.R. Harris, A.A. Allen, John Blair, N.R. Craig, E.W. Smith, H.D. Allen, R.H. Shannon, G.C. Atkinson, Wm. E. Hourigan, F.I. Ryckman, Gordon Gallagher, James Swanborough and Leslie Preston in 1973, just before Burlington became a city.

10
Local Autonomy

It was not until 1873, after incorporation as a village and the name change from Wellington Square to Burlington, that decisions of the village council became legal in regulating community affairs.

Halton county bylaw 76 reads: "Whereas the census returns of... Wellington Square...with its immediate neighbourhood...contains over 750 inhabitants whose residences are sufficiently near to form an incorporated village...And whereas a petition was signed by more than one hundred residents, freeholders and householders of the said village and neighbourhood," the area was "erected into an incorporated village apart from the township of Nelson by the name of Burlington."

The boundaries commenced "at the waters of Lake Ontario on the line between the lands of the heirs of the late Captain Joseph Brant and the lands of the late Augustus Bates, thence...northwesterly along the lands owned...by the Great Western Railway to the Hamilton and Nelson Road." This is now part of Plains Rd. The boundary on the southeast was the Guelph Line, down to the lake and back to the start. The town contained about 500 acres then, a contrast to the nearly 73 square miles within the 1995 municipal limits.

The first Burlington election was held in the Temperance Hall on Elizabeth Street. The first council was composed of John Waldie, Reeve, and Benjamin Eager, James Allen, George Murison and Charles Hales, councillors. Mr. Hales was succeeded by James Cotter. Villagers voted annually to elect a reeve and council, and election fever reached a pitch whenever something contentious had to be decided. New Year's Day was Election Day for many years.

In 1900, when 390 villagers voted, what was the total cost of holding the election?...$20.13.

On June 1, 1911, a bylaw was passed providing the village with three wards in place of the two it had had since 1886. Voters were divided according to the initials of their surnames. The ward system was not based on locality as it is today.

The Temperance Hall became the Town Hall and there Council debated the affairs of the village with as much solemnity as though it were Toronto they were governing. For their comfort on chilly nights a new furnace costing $130.17 was installed in 1900. Also that year, Council debated the need for a suitable flag for the village and the Ensign was bought for $11.50. In 1912, the Union Jack was the choice without there being a need for a flag debate.

Some council deliberations centred about problems as farcical as the occasional ones encountered today. In 1904, a communication was read by W.T. Jennings complaining that "his lot should be sixty feet instead of fifty-nine feet three inches." The appeal was dismissed.

Some decisions displayed the politicians at their best. In 1906, it was "moved by Councillor Little that the tree in front of Mrs. Busby's property be cut down, as it is a nuisance to life and property (i.e. if Mrs. Busby so wishes)"!

An historic entry in the minutes of June 14, 1907, read: "Moved by Councillor Young that this Council record its deep regret in the death of Mr. John Waldie, for many years an honoured resident and its first Reeve." (John Waldie was one of Burlington's greatest citizens, representing it in the Parliament at Ottawa and bestowing on it his philanthropy.)

Licensing was regulated by council. From 1903, a fee of $50 was charged "any persons selling...cigarettes or cigarette tobacco." In 1911 a bylaw was passed regulating the sale of milk in the village and appointing an inspector to enforce the law and inspect milk, cream, cows and dairies. In 1912, F.W. Parkin was granted a license for three pool tables at $60 for the year.

In 1896 a committee had been formed for the consolidation of bylaws. There were 186 bylaws on the books and of these only 46 were in force; some had been amended once, and others twice. Council was concerned because it could not keep abreast of all the regulations. Bylaw number 3107, passed June 13, 1966, is indicative of the multitude of decisions made in the intervening years.

Town salaries, then and now, showed a marked contrast. James Allen, clerk-treasurer, earned $200 in 1897, with an extra $10 for registering births, deaths and marriages. The auditors's salary in 1898 was reduced from $10 to $5. Ralph Young, appointed auditor in 1899, declined "owing to the meagreness of the renumeration offered." Assessor for 1897, J.H. Campbell received $41.02 for his services.

THE WATERWORKS STORY

Things were not always done in a strictly orthodox way. In the early 1900s, Council decided it should put in a waterworks. Tenders were called and it was found the cost might be nearly $50,000, an awesome sum for a small village to raise. A vote on whether or not the ratepayers wanted the waterworks was necessary.

Opposition came from the more conservative residents who, knowing that only property owners could vote on money matters, went to the registry office in Milton and checked the titles of those whom they knew would vote in favour of the waterworks. The names of those NOT eligible to vote were noted and given to the returning officer.

Reeve Max Smith heard about the list and sought the aid of Bill Brush, a colourful character who ran the Queen's Hotel (now the Queen's Head Inn) and raced horses at fall fairs. On election day Hotelkeeper Brush caused a sensation by driving his horse pellmell along Brant Street. He stood erect in the gig, cracking the whip all the way to the lakeshore. Then away he went up Locust Street.

People rushed to the window of the polling place to see what was going on. In the commotion the list of ineligible voters somehow disappeared, and no one could swear to the names on it. The bylaw passed and that's how Burlington got its 1909 waterworks.

Fountain, Brant Street, in memory of King Edward VII.

KING EDWARD FOUNTAIN

In 1910, King Edward VII died. Two years later Council moved "that the proposed style of fountain and drinking troughs recommended by the King Edward Memorial Committee be accepted and that the village bear the expense of installing on the proposed sites." In March, 1913, a fountain located on Lakeshore Road (then Water Street) near Brant, in line with the entrance of today's Royal Bank, was connected and three horse troughs installed. It was moved years later to what is now Spencer Smith Park on the lake bank, opposite the entrance to St. Luke's Church. Moved yet again on the occasion of the silver jubilee of Queen Elizabeth II, June 22, 1977, it was placed by the Optimist Club of Burlington in Civic Square.

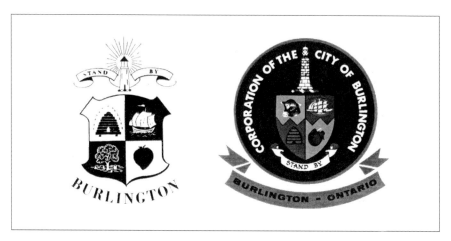

Former and current Burlington crests.

COAT-OF-ARMS

In 1913, Council decided to have a coat-of-arms and in June accepted the design of Miss Ariel Shapland (later Mrs. Hughes Cleaver). The old Burlington canal lighthouse appeared on the crest with the words "Stand By".

In 1963, Dr. G.P. Gilmour of McMaster University reported on the proposed revision of the crest. The apple representing fruit growing and the heifer symbolic of animal husbandry replaced the erstwhile apple trees and barrel, and the strawberry. The simplified beehive signifying industry avoided a resemblance to the beehive on Hamilton's crest. The lighthouse remained. The horizontal division of the shield suggests the three peaks, Flamborough Head, Mount Nemo and Rattlesnake Point. The new escutcheon was sketched by John Arculus, Toronto, an heraldic artist, and the finished device executed in ceramic by Joseph Gause, a Burlington artist. In 1973, it was slightly altered to reflect the town's change to city status in 1974. A donation of $500 by Miss Dorothy Stone made possible the official registration of the crest in the Register of All Arms and Bearings in Scotland by the Lord Lyon King of Arms. Stanley Arculus, a designer of Coats of Arms, made the minor changes necessary for registration, and in 1976 the city was officially notified of the registration. The crest is much admired by those passing the Civic Administration Building on Brant Street.

Over the years, the village has annexed bits and pieces of adjoining territory and by December, 1914, was large and populous enough to be declared a town by the Ontario Railway and Municipal Board. During the first busy year of town status, Council sometimes met twice a day.

In 1919, the Council was composed of Mayor Dr. T.W. Peart and Councillors Taylor, Kerns, Blair, Gray, Leitch and Page. Violent debates early in the new year culminated with the resignation of the mayor, deputy reeve and four councillors, leaving only Reeve Cleaver and Councillors Blair and Page. No mention of a new election is made in Council minutes but the entry of February 7, 1919, reads, "Present were Mayor Smith, Reeve Cleaver, Deputy Reeve Bridgeman and Councillors Allen, Jarvis, Blair, Page, Tufgar and Hobson."

By 1920, the town was showing signs of stretching out, and planning seemed in order. The Industrial Committee urged that immediate steps be taken to protect the residences of the town from unnecessary encroachment of commercial buildings. Certain streets were designated residential only. On November 21, 1921, Council decided to adopt a planning scheme and the town clerk was instructed to write to the government expert for some data.

For some time after 1907, the town clerk had his office in the Brant Street library and acted as librarian. Court was also held there as well as Council meetings. Three years after the town assumed full ownership of the library building under this shared accommodation arrangement, the library moved into headquarters on Elizabeth Street, in the former home of Dr. A.H. Speers. The move was timely since both the library and the town needed more space and the electors had just voted down a request from Council for $200,000 to build a new municipal building. The old town hall on Elizabeth Street was sold by the town to the Boy Scouts, and the police and fire services were located elsewhere. It was later demolished to make way for an apartment building.

This old building had been erected by the Sons of Temperance who sold it to the village in 1883 for $500. The only stipulation was that the Sons might still use the hall one night a week free.

THE TOWN BELL

A reminder of the Burlington of other days is the bell which stands alongside Central Library. When the bell tower was removed after the Boy Scouts took over the old town hall, the bell was preserved. Its history is interesting.

It was ordered by Council in 1894 to be used to summon volunteer firemen. It was later decided to use it as a town bell to be rung at 7 a.m., at noon, 1 p.m. and 6 p.m. To avoid confusion, the bell was pealed faster for fires and at a more leisurely rate when tolling the hour it was announcing.

James Powell was engaged to ring the bell for $50 a year. A succession of bell ringers followed and in later years the job was added to the duties of the town hall custodian. One of the last bellringers was Arthur Turcotte who lived at Elizabeth and Maria Streets.

Stolen and recovered, the town bell displayed by Detective Tom Oliver.

- courtesy Joseph Brant Museum

On June 2, 1916, with neighbouring municipalities adopting Daylight Saving Time, Council decided Burlington should keep in step and do the same, "commencing at 9 p.m. June 4." Bell ringing times were to be changed accordingly. Opposition to the idea arose and by Monday, June 26, the bell, at any rate, was back on Standard Time!

After being taken down in the fifties, the bell was stored at the Boy Scout camp on Twiss Road north of Lowville. One night it was stolen but the loss was discovered right away and the police notified. An officer on patrol that night noticed a car weighted down pretty heavily and forced it to stop. There was the bell!

It sat behind the Works Department building for some time until a fund was raised by the late William Gilbert, chairman of the library board for many years. With this financial assistance the bell was enshrined by the side of the library in 1962. When the new Central Library was built in 1970, the bell was moved once again to the building's front entrance.

TOWN HALL

Again the growth of Burlington made it necessary by the early 1960s to think of more commodious town offices. Did the town need a new building? Should it own one or rent space in a building which could be erected on the old cannery site at the foot of Brant Street? If a town hall were to be built, where should it be?...on the Guelph Line where many people believed the centre of town inevitably would be, or on Brant Street as proponents for "revitalization of the core area" argued that it should be? The Great Debate was on!

After prolonged deliberation, Council decided that the town had a future so promising it should own its own administration building. The town property on Brant Street was agreed on as the site. When the new

*Civic Administration
Building
Above: Old Town Hall and
Fire Hall*

civic structure was ready in November, 1964, it was the first time since the amalgamation of Aldershot and Nelson Township with the City of Burlington in 1958 that all municipal departments were under one roof.

Designer of the new building was George L. Schneider. The lens-shaped structure has a "floating" council chamber jutting out from the main eight-storey building, at the second-storey level. Eaglewood Construction Co. of Hamilton was in charge of the construction. The total cost was just over $857,000.

The official opening of the building celebrated the 50th anniversary of the declaration of Burlington as a town in 1915.

Officiating was the Hon. J.W. Spooner, Minister of Municipal Affairs for Ontario. The Mayor was presented with the new maple leaf Canadian flag, thought to be the first time the flag was presented to a municipality since approval by Parliament.

Mayor Owen Mullin, predicted that the new building would "make Burlingtonians out of the people of Burlington."

It is interesting to note that the population of the town in 1915 was 2,150 and in 1965 it had grown to 55,000.

M.C. Smith, mayor 1915-16, 1919.   *Mary Munro, first female mayor of*
Burlington, 1977, 1978.
- courtesy Mary Munro

In 1986, a 60,000 square foot addition was built to the tune of a further $8.4 million. Plans included an open civic square on Brant St. The structure is indeed a striking addition to the core area with its landscaping forming an oasis in the commercial setting.

The orderly development of any municipality is due in no small measure to the effectiveness of its public servants, elected or appointed. Over the years from 1873, countless men and women have guided Burlington's affairs. While only some can be mentioned, all have the satisfaction of knowing they played a valuable part in the community's growth.

The first reeve was John Waldie who was succeeded by William Kerns in 1879. Mr. Kerns served from that year to 1882 and again in 1899, and from 1900 to 1905. Other reeves were R.G. Baxter, 1883 to 1886; James Mortimer, 1893; Thomas Atkinson, 1892 and 1894; William Richardson, 1887, 1891, 1895, 1896, 1897; E.H. Cleaver, 1898; George Allen, 1906 to 1908; and M.C. Smith, 1909 to 1914.

From 1915 on, reeves were still the town's representatives on county council but no longer the chief administrators. The office of Mayor was created when the village became a town in January, 1915 ; the first one was M.C. Smith from 1915 to 1916 and again in 1919.

F.D. Ghent was mayor in 1917, C.F. Coleman in 1918 and T.W. Peart for part of 1919. Hughes Cleaver was reeve in 1918-1919 and mayor in 1920. He was succeeded by J.J. Hobson for the next two years. Mr. Hobson was later town clerk from 1930 to 1935.

 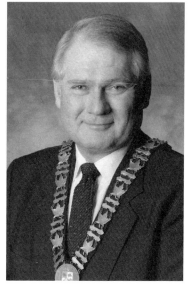

Roly Bird, mayor 1979-1991.   *Walter Mulkewich, mayor 1991-*
- courtesy City of Burlington   *1997.*
                                            - courtesy City of Burlington

Elgin Harris, publisher of the Burlington *Gazette,* was reeve in 1921-22, and mayor in 1923-24. James S. Allen was mayor from 1925 to 1928. Mayor for the years 1929-30 was Edmond Holtby, and Lloyd D. Dingle, Q.C., was a councillor in 1929-30 and mayor in 1931-32. J.O. Ryckman held the mayor's office in 1933 and F.W. Watson in 1934-35.

George Harris, son of Elgin Harris, was on Council in 1929, reeve in 1930-35, mayor from 1936 to 1939 and councillor again in 1951-52.

J. Gordon Blair, long time Director of Business Development, was a councillor in 1938-39 and mayor from 1940-1945. The mayor in 1946-47 was E.R. Leather, and N.R. Craig from 1948 to 1950. Previously Mr. Craig who served on the PUC, was a councillor in 1933, 1936 and 1944, and reeve from 1945 to 1947.

E.W. (Ted) Smith served as councillor from 1936 to 1944; deputy reeve from 1945 to 1947; reeve from 1948 to 1950, mayor from 1951 to 1956 and councillor again from 1958 to 1960, a total of 24 years of service to the town!

John Lockhart, for many years principal of Central Public School, was mayor from 1957 to 1961. In 1963, Edna Johnstone became the first woman to be elected to Burlington council. She served for two terms as a councillor. Owen Mullin was mayor from 1962 to 1965 and Lloyd Berryman was mayor in 1966 and 1967. George Harrington served from 1968 to 1976. Evelyn Burke, who led the campaign for Burlington Mall, became deputy reeve in 1968, the first woman to hold that post. In February, 1969 she

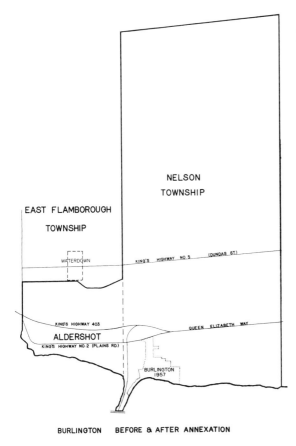

NELSON
TOWNSHIP

EAST FLAMBOROUGH

TOWNSHIP

WATERDOWN   KING'S   HIGHWAY   NO 5   (DUNDAS ST.)

KING'S HIGHWAY 403
ALDERSHOT   QUEEN   ELIZABETH   WAY
KING'S HIGHWAY NO. 2 (PLAINS RD.)

BURLINGTON
1957

BURLINGTON   BEFORE & AFTER ANNEXATION

succumbed to cancer. Mary Munro, mayor in 1977 and 1978, was the first female to take that office. Roly Bird set a record by being mayor from 1979 to 1991. Walter Mulkewich, who had served in many civic capacities, was mayor from 1992 until 1997.

Among the clerks who served the town have been Thomas Graham, G.T. Bastedo, W.G. Nelles, J.S. Allen, O.T. Springer, B.S. Hicks, Leonard Sykes, J.J. Hobson, M.M. Bush, and William K. Sims, from 1959 to 1973. Sims became Coordinator in 1973. After Roger Cloutier who served for one year, succeeding clerks have lengthy terms to their credit. Don Briault held the office from 1974 to 1981 and Helen MacRae from 1982 to 1996 when Ron Latham took over.

On January 1, 1974, Halton regional government was inaugurated. Responsibilities were shared, some continuing with the municipalities and some taken over by the region. Burlington's included fire protection, waste management, parks and recreation, transit and traffic, planning and engineering, infrastructure maintenance, debt charges and capital, library, Museums Board and the Art Centre. Eight aldermen and the Mayor represented Burlington on the regional council. By 1996, some of the responsibilities of the region and the city were being shared and a few taken over by the region, such as waste management and water supply.

The city's new official plan, "Future Focus" was completed in 1988 and updated in 1991. The plan replaced one adopted in 1969. Future Focus was designed to guide the physical development of the city until 2011. In September, 1994, city council approved a reorganization of the civic administration as an ongoing process over the next few years.

11
War of 1812

The treaty that ended the American Revolutionary War in 1783 failed to provide a foundation for a firm and lasting peace between England and her former colonies. Ill-feeling persisted between England and the new states and bickering over small issues eventually led to the War of 1812. Critical historians have differed since about the actual causes and winners of the war. In 1902 Woodrow Wilson in his "A History of the American People" said, "The grounds of the war were singularly uncertain..."

Another opinion on the war was expressed by Professor A.R.M. Lower in his book "From Colony to Nation": "It was the most satisfactory war on record, in that both sides won it. The Canadians and the Americans both report glorious victories. The British, who did most of the fighting, never heard of it and the one instrument which was responsible for the winning of that war, the Royal Navy, is never mentioned."

In order to try to sort out the events that reached the Burlington area during the War of 1812, it is necessary to go back to 1793, when the first Militia Act was passed at the second session of the first legislature of Upper Canada. It said that all males in the province from the ages of 15 to 50 must bear arms and that they must appear on demand once a year in the field, bringing a musket or fusil with six charges of powder and ball. This form of census taking, which kept track of the men in the area in case they were needed, actually turned out to be quite a social affair at the annual counting of heads.

When the Niagara District was set up, it extended to the Governor's Road (the present Highway 5) which, during the ensuing war, was the only land route for soldiers and their heavy cannon and artillery between Fort Tecumseh in Windsor and all points east. Men living in Ancaster, Barton and Saltfleet Township were enrolled in the 5th Regiment of Lincoln Militia and men in Nelson Township were enrolled in the 2nd Regiment of York Militia.

The Militia was not an effective instrument of war, as was realized by the British military authorities. When Major General Sir Isaac Brock became Administrator of Upper Canada in the fall of 1811, an effort was begun to infuse some form of military training. Brock knew well that a trial of arms with the United States would come sooner or later and in January, 1812, he organized the flank companies, consisting of one Captain, two Lieutenants, one Sergeant, a drummer and 35 other ranks. They included men of proven loyalty who would come out immediately in an emergency. The 5th Lincoln and 2nd York Militia each had two companies, and both were raised at the same time early in 1812.

The war with the U.S. broke out on June 18, 1812, and the flank companies lived up to Brock's expectations. They turned out immediately and were concentrated on the Niagara River line, stationed at Queenston. These soldiers had no equipment and no uniforms. Officers did have uniforms bought out of their own pockets, but the men were dressed simply in homespun, carrying blankets but in many cases no muskets.

Brock was able to outfit these companies from the stores at Fort George but all they received were the white cross-belts, a cartouche box and the bayonet on the brown brass flintlock musket.

Militia from Nelson Township took part in a daring manoeuvre proposed by Major General Brock. In August, 1812, he decided to strike at Fort Detroit, which had been conceded to the Americans at the close of the Revolutionary War. This was a very daring thing to do since Brock had very few troops on the Niagara Line and Detroit was a strong fortress.

Brock left York, however, on August 7, and came by boat to the head of the lake. He disembarked at Burlington Heights and rode overland to Long Point where he picked up 40 regulars and 260 militia, including Captain Samuel Hatt's special company of volunteers from the 5th Lincoln and 2nd York. Officers with Captain Hatt were Lieutenant Robert Land and Ensign William Chisholm, who served with 2nd York. To augment his small force, Brock counted on picking up the 41st Regiment who were concentrated along the Detroit area and he counted on the support of Tecumseh and his Indians. The American General Hull, who was terrified of an Indian massacre (although he had more guns than Brock and just as many men), surrendered Detroit without a shot being fired on August 16, 1812.

One result of this action was that Brock received a knighthood for it, but he never knew it. The dispatch about the capture of Fort Detroit reached London on October 6, and Brock was killed on October 13, at Queenston Heights. He was never addressed, while alive, as Sir Isaac.

Some men from this area who fought these battles were Richard Beasley from Burlington Heights; Jean Baptiste Rousseau who had been an interpreter for Joseph Brant; Captain George Chisholm who had settled on the north shore of Burlington Bay in 1794; Richard Cockerell, a tutor of John Brant; William Bates, a sergeant in the Queen's Rangers who had charge of the King's Head Inn on Burlington Beach, and Lieutenant-Colonel William Johnson Kerr, son-in-law of Joseph Brant.

In May, 1813, the Americans mounted a determined offensive in the Niagara area. As a result, Fort Erie was abandoned and Fort George fell to a combined assault by land and by sea. The senior British officer, Gen. John Vincent, was sent in retreat around the head of the lake to Burlington

Heights (Hamilton). In an effort to smash this force that had escaped, the Americans sent out companies of infantry, artillery and cavalry. To quote a plaque at Burlington Heights, commemorating the resulting Battle of Stoney Creek: "From these heights, Lieutenant-Colonel John Harvey set out with about 700 men on the night of June 5, 1813, to launch a surprise attack on an invading United States force of some 3,000 men camped at Stoney Creek. The rout of the troops commanded by Brigadier-General John Chandler under cover of darkness in the early hours of June 6, is generally credited with saving Upper Canada from being overrun by the enemy." Harvey was knighted in 1824 and served in high posts in the Maritimes after that.

Following the spectacular success of the British at Stoney Creek, Burlington Heights (the plateau between Dundurn Castle and the High Level Bridge in Hamilton) became the advanced base for the army operating in the Niagara Peninsula, taking over tactical importance from Fort George. The two areas in Upper Canada which had the greatest bearing on military advance from the spring of 1813 to the end of the war were Burlington Heights and Kingston where the dock yards were situated.

In July, 1813, American Commodore Isaac Chauncey decided to make an attempt on the Heights and destroy it. He sailed from Sackets Harbour and put in at Fort George on July 27, taking on board 150 regulars. He couldn't sail on that day because of a calm, but he did appear off the Burlington Beach strip on the evening of July 28, coming to anchor near the shore of what is now Burlington.

The following morning it was the duty of young Lieutenant - Colonel Winfield Scott's U.S. force to make a reconnaissance of the beach and examine defences on the Heights. The British heard of this movement and sent out urgent messages to Colonel William Claus of the Indian department to gather together as many Indians as he could from the Grand River area, and march at once to Burlington Heights.

After Joseph Brant's death in 1807, his son John gathered his warriors and they walked across country or travelled by water where possible in their birch canoes. The Indians were once again proving their loyalty to the British by assisting in the major battles of the war.

The garrison at Burlington Heights was very slim at that time with only about 150 men; but when the Indians arrived the next day with reinforcements from militia at Chipmans Corners (now St. Catharines), a formidable garrison was there to confront Lieut.-Col. Scott when he arrived. Scott reported back to Commodore Isaac Chauncey that there were seven guns overlooking the Bay, and also the distressing news that the channel leading into Burlington Bay was too shallow to bring in the large ships for a planned attack.

Chauncey's fleet consisted of two ships, one brig and eleven schooners. When Chauncey got this report, he had to weigh his chances. He could lower his long boats and have his soldiers row across to the Heights, but they would be under the fire of that formidable battery that Scott had reported, and his own guns from the fleet couldn't reach that far. Chauncey decided against such a suicidal course of action.

Again, the Americans could land, march around the bay and attack the battery on the Heights from the rear. This, however, would have left Chauncey's fleet unmanned outside Burlington Bay, and there was a British squadron lurking somewhere in the lake. After weighing these odds, Chauncey decided not to attack the Heights. Instead, he reassembled his force, pillaged Fort York, which they had previously burned out, and went back to Sackets Harbour.

The incident gave the local garrison such a scare that it never left itself with so few men again. The war brought great hardships to the people in Upper Canada with dislocation of their lives, their commerce interrupted and their farms and livestock neglected. It was not the same war at all as that encountered in the Maritimes and Quebec where privateering and profiteering were carried on.

The third incident involving this area in the War of 1812 was a naval action, later called the "Burlington Races." The British squadron on the lakes was commanded by Sir James Yeo, who arrived in Kingston in early summer of 1813 as senior naval officer of all ships of war on the Great Lakes. Opposing him on the American side was the same Commodore Isaac Chauncey who had created a fleet starting with only two ships, after being ordered by the Secretary of the U.S. navy to dominate Lake Ontario and Lake Erie.

Sir James' orders at the same time were to seek out and destroy the American squadron and also to keep the land army in supplies. He soon found he had his work cut out for him.

The two fleets met in action in September of 1813. Sir James had landed supplies at the head of the lake and returned to York. The next day the American squadron of 11 ships appeared off shore, and against this force Sir James mustered two corvettes, a brig, and three schooners. The Americans had more and heavier guns and, while staying out of range, battered the British squadron without having a shot fired near them in return.

Although Sir James was out-gunned and out-ranged, he put out to give battle off the present Canadian National Exhibition grounds at Toronto. Just after noon, Sir James broke off the action because his ship had suffered severely and a gale was coming up. Since the rest of the American ships were beginning to arrive, he decided to make a run for it to the head of the lake. British sailors later referred to this as the "Burlington Races."

About five o'clock in the afternoon, riding the high water that was raised by the storm that day, the British entered what is now Hamilton

Harbour, through a narrow channel near Brant House. Once inside the bay, Sir James' problem was to get out again, without Chauncey blocking him. Damages were repaired, and British casualties totalled five dead and 13 wounded.

Meanwhile, Chauncey had found shelter at Fort George. On October 2, he sent over a fast sailing schooner to see if Sir James was still at the head of the lake. The bay was empty. The British had sailed out again into the lake and headed for Kingston, where they licked their wounds and repaired their damaged ships.

During the War of 1812, Dundas Street (Highway 5) was an important artery of troop movement and a drill hall was located north of Nelson Village crossroads where the troops assembled. The 1st Halton Rifles drilled in one of the fields later belonging to the Ireland family. Capt. Ireland came to Canada with the British army, and served as Quartermaster in charge of the supply line along Dundas Street. Many a loyal soldier was given property after the war and some of them settled around Nelson. Two of these were Captain Ireland and Captain Joseph Birney.

The Six Nations Indians who had served the British cause received gifts of provisions for their part in the war. After truce was declared, many Indians stopped hereabouts on their way back to the Grand River, and an army officer's report stated that he was ordered "to accompany the Six Nations to their homes and in so doing, to lose no opportunity of annoying the enemy." After rewarding them with supplies, he "then caused the issue of provisions to cease at the Mohawk Village (except to the families of men killed in battle or disabled by wounds); the people there being more in condition of helping themselves than those who had fixed temporary wigwams in the neighbourhood of Burlington and Dundas."

These temporary wigwams had been erected in 1813 when the Indians had become worried about the course of the war. They abandoned their homes at the Grand River and came down to the head of the lake. A report of the day mentioned the "Indians encamped at the beach in the rear of Mrs. Brant's."

12
Impact of Two World Wars

In the waterfront park opposite the entrance to St. Luke's Church stood a statue of a World War I soldier facing the traffic on Lakeshore Road. When first erected, the monument stood in a setting of trees and park benches, farther back from the later-widened highway. Every year on Armistice Day, services were held there, and Tom Waumsley annually played the Last Post for many years.

The monument was unveiled by Lord Byng of Vimy, the Governor-General, on April 10, 1922, after long planning by the Memorial Committee of Burlington. Carved in stone beneath the statue are the 38 names of local men who fell in action and a list of places where they fought: places such as Ypres, Somme and Vimy Ridge. In honour of the men and women of Burlington and Nelson township who made the supreme sacrifice in World War II there is a plaque on the same cenotaph bearing 44 names. With the completion of the new City Hall, the monument was moved beside it.

During the first World War, 300 men volunteered from Burlington, and many of them drilled in a shed at Locust and Water (now Lakeshore Rd.) Streets. Recruiting took place at the Village Inn on the opposite corner.

The first Burlington contingent to go overseas left town on August 17, 1914, marching up Brant Street to the Freeman Station led by James Dick's bagpipes. This was the 20th Lorne Rifles Battalion. Following further training at Valcartier, Quebec, the contingent went overseas.

Many families in the town have treasured snapshots from the days of the Great War similar to the collection of R.J.M. (Bert) Allen. Included is a picture taken on Brant Street showing young boys curiously examining a tank of the Eaton Armoured Battery as it passed through Burlington.

A story, oft-told in town, concerns some troops quartered at Niagara who began a march to the Canadian National Exhibition grounds in Toronto. On the way, they camped overnight at Winona, went through Burlington the next day and camped north of Bronte. It took the regiment two weeks to complete the march; a battalion came through Burlington daily for a fortnight. Their system of communication was by heliograph or signalling glass and in Burlington the Methodist Church tower on Elizabeth Street was used.

The first battalion to reach town broke ranks on Ontario Street between Burlington Avenue and Locust Street. Camp cooks set up equipment and the men sat along the curbs to eat lunch. They were supposed to fall in

World War I soldier leaving by train for military duty. – courtesy Les Armstrong

again at 2 p.m. but the hotels on Brant Street looked too inviting to the thirsty men. The commanding officers had such difficulty getting them back into line that the next day, and every day thereafter, the regiments were marched through Burlington without a halt being made. George Bridle, a Burlington boy, was with the Bantam Battalion and got a big hand from bystanders.

They were welcomed at the Pettit farm halfway between Freeman and the Guelph Line, and the ladies of Burlington sent out pies and coffee. During the two weeks, 1200 pies were carried to the lunch stop by high school boys.

During World War I, women helped with Red Cross work and the Women's Institute assisted the Queen's Canadian Hospital Committee. This was a group of Burlington girls in their teens and twenties who met in the library to knit for the soldiers and make bandages.

In 1915, a Home Guard unit was formed and the men improved their marksmanship on an indoor rifle range. Burlington and Nelson councils approved expenses in aid of wives and families of enlisted men faced with rising living costs.

Early in 1918, when the peace seemed imminent, the Soldiers' Aid Commission asked council to form a branch in Burlington to help place returned soldiers in employment.

After peace was declared on November 11, Burlington council recorded a resolution of "our very great gratification upon the termination of the greatest war in the history of the world and of the overwhelming success of the allied armies." They expressed appreciation "to our Canadian boys, and the memory of those who have fought and fallen in the interests of democracy and the cause of right, who will not be forgotten."

Council then recommended a permanent monument and showed appreciation to the pastors of local churches for the public Thanksgiving services held at the Methodist Church on November 13.

An amusing incident occurred during the immediate post-war days. When news got around that the first local boy returning from the Front (his

Eaton Armoured Battery on Brant Street, 1917.
– courtesy Joseph Brant Museum

nickname was "Slick") was expected on the evening train, the townspeople made ready. The Citizens' Band assembled and a procession started off to the station at Freeman. The young veteran who had had his scraps with the local constable before joining the army, seeing the torch-lit parade coming up Brant Street, thought a posse was coming to get him. The welcoming committee had to reassure him and it was a startled young fellow who rode victoriously down Brant Street with Mayor M.C. Smith for a rousing welcome at Gore Park. It took the young man a week to regain his composure before resuming his old place in front of the pool hall.

As the rest of the servicemen gradually returned home, receptions were planned for them and a picnic and turkey dinner held. A military hospital had been established by the government at the Brant House during the war and the soldier inmates were not neglected.

Returned men soon formed a local branch of the Great War Veterans' Association, forerunner of the Canadian Legion. Several meeting places were used by the G.W.V.A., the first being a room over Kerns' store on Water Street.

Membership soon outgrew these quarters and the old Episcopal church building at the corner of Elizabeth and James Streets was bought. The building is the present headquarters for the Sea Cadets. Tom Waumsley was the first president of the Great War Veterans' Association.

In 1926, Canadian Legion, Post 60, received its charter. A chronicle of the town in 1927 mentions that "Military interests are represented by a Company of the Halton Rifles and a section of No. 14 Signal Company."

On September 10, 1939, Canada again was at war with Germany, and more than 600 men from Burlington joined the armed forces.

Thayendanegea Chapter, I.O.D.E called a meeting of representatives of

H.M.C.S. Burlington, *1941.*   *– courtesy Joseph Brant Museum*

all women's organizations in town to plan their war work and Mrs. W. Weaver was appointed chairman of the women's work for the Red Cross.

Victory Loan rallies held during the war saw Burlington meet its quotas substantially.

A unique ceremony was held on September 10, 1941, at Lakeside Park. A new navy minesweeper, *H.M.C.S. Burlington,* was dedicated as it lay anchored off the shore.

H.M.C.S. Burlington had left Dufferin shipyards that morning with her commanding officer, Lieut. Commander Fricker; Hon. Angus E. Macdonald, Minister for Naval Affairs; Hughes Cleaver, M.P. for Halton and several school children aboard, and arrived at Burlington by noon.

The landing party was welcomed by Mayor J. Gordon Blair, and the entire crew of the ship were declared honourary citizens of Burlington. School children sang a special song, "H.M.C.S. Burlington", written for the occasion by T. Reginald Sloan. The Hon. Angus Macdonald spoke, a guard of honour was inspected, gifts were presented by townspeople, and Rev. G.W. Tebbs dedicated the fine new ship in a solemn ceremony. It was a big day for Burlington.

Festivities continued at the Estaminet that night with all the town's dignitaries and ship's officers present and the toast to *H.M.C.S. Burlington* was proposed by W.J. McCulloch. Chairman John Wilkinson introduced his hard-working committee, Reeve John Blair, E.W. Smith, W.J. McCulloch, E.D. Lucas, M.M. Bush, Mrs. T.J. Hedley and Mrs. A.W. Milligan.

The townspeople? They spent the evening in happy street dancing and bingo.

H.M.C.S. Burlington was decommissioned and destroyed when the war was over. The ship's bell sat atop the Confederation monument in Gore Park on Lakeshore Rd. until 1996.

One of the most active organizations in town was the Burlington and Nelson District War Services Committee, inaugurated in September, 1942, with executive A.A. Allen, H.A. Cozens, and Mrs. T.J. Hedley. By May, 1946, 2,115 parcels had been mailed, as well as more than 300,000 cigarettes. This was a community project and all social and church groups participated. At one time there were more than 400 servicemen from Burlington and district overseas.

A parachute factory was built, and many people, mostly women, found work there. An aircraft accessories plant was opened, and ammunition boxes were turned out at Nicholsons.

An Air Cadet squadron was established to train boys who could take their places later as aircrew in the R.C.A.F. After the war, membership dwindled but No. 715 Mohawk Squadron was

War cenotaph, City Hall.
— Bob Chambers, photographer

later re-organized under the sponsorship of the Optimist Club. Meeting, by 1996, at the Optimist Hall on Prospect St., both boys and girls were eligible to join. Army Cadets were also formed and by 1996 members, both boys and girls, were meeting at the Legion Hall on Legion Rd.

During the war, many "old country" boys visited in local homes from the R.A.F. camp at Mount Hope. Several of them married Burlington girls who returned with them to Britain after the war.

Germany surrendered May 7, 1945, and the people of Burlington went wild. Bells rang, whistles blew and the town's churches were packed with grateful and prayerful people. When the war ended with Japan's surrender on September 2, it seemed like an anticlimax.

After the street parades and thankful prayers, Burlington waited for its servicemen to return and mourned the ones who would never come back.

Walter Cone was in charge of the welcoming committee who met the trains carrying returning ex-servicemen, no matter what hour they arrived.

After V.J. Day the town gave a rousing Welcome Home Dance for all district servicemen and women and their wives and sweethearts. A special welcome was extended to about 30 British war brides who were presented with boxes of Canadian apples.

Postponed peacetime projects were launched with enthusiasm and Burlington began to grow and prosper as never before in its long history.

The Canadian Legion was expanding with the demobilization of servicemen. In 1947, when Charles Gates was president of the local branch, a larger building was purchased. The membership increased from 65 to more than 200. Headquarters remained on Water Street at the foot of Elizabeth Street until the new hall was completed in 1959 on Legion Road. Mayfield School for Retarded Children was later built across the road on land donated by the Legion and the school became the veterans' main project. (By 1996 the building has become the home of Living Waters Church Inc.) Branch 60 was given the name of Vinton Memorial Branch in 1951, in tribute to the late N.R. Vinton, a former president.

13
Kilbride

In the early settlement of Nelson township, one thing was of primary importance for the growth of business and industry: water power. Beside the streams which fed the Twelve Mile Creek and snaked down across what is known as north Burlington, small villages grew up - small by today's standards, but from 1855 to 1870, comparatively thriving communities. Kilbride, Cumminsville, Willbrook, Lowville and, to the southeast, Zimmerman, were all on the Twelve Mile Creek and its tributaries. Flour mills were established first, and later, lumber and grist mills. Steam was developed for factories, and eventually each community became self-supporting with stores, blacksmith shops, churches and homes.

Kilbride, Cumminsville and Willbrook or Dakota were all within about a mile of each other and seven or eight miles from Milton. The first settlers had little time to leave written records behind, and few of their descendants are left to tell their stories. One of the first settlers in the area around Dakota was Thomas Simpson, a veteran of the Napoleonic Wars. In the reign of King George IV, he was given a Crown grant of 100 acres of forest. He built a log cabin there and began clearing land. He combined in his skills all the knowledge necessary for survival as a pioneer. He tanned deer skins and made shoes for his family. He carded and spun wool, wove and knit it into cloth mitts and socks, and with scissors and needles fashioned all his family's clothing. The Simpsons became successful farmers owning the first house in the vicinity. Mrs. Simpson was the first woman to sell produce on the Hamilton market, going all the way on horseback. It is also said that the Simpsons with their enthusiasm, encouraged the erection of the first church in the vicinity on the site of Nelson Presbyterian Church.

In 1830, the Hunt brothers, later of Carlisle, were said to have purchased 200 acres of land at what became the main corner of Kilbride for 12 shillings, six pence an acre. The George Harbottle home on a Crown land grant was once the local court house and Mr. Harbottle was the local magistrate who performed weddings in the homes. John Harris was also a local magistrate for many years.

The village of Kilbride was laid out by Francis Baker and William Panton sometime around 1850. Mr. Panton was born in Ireland in 1808 and emigrated to Canada in 1834. He settled on a farm in Nelson township and after spending some time in the Niagara district as Public Works Inspector, he joined Mr. Baker in a milling and lumbering business. Together they laid out a village and nostalgically christened it Kilbride after a town Panton remembered in County Wicklow, Ireland. Panton and Baker (now Kilbride) Streets were named in honour of these fathers of the village.

Lumbering gave Kilbride and neighbouring villages prosperity and when the forests were finally exhausted, this prosperity carried business along for awhile.

Kilbride's local emporium was the department store of T.L. White for many years. The original store burned down and was replaced by a bigger building. In the new store, a staff of five clerks in the grocery department alone, served the customers. Barrels held supplies of sugar, salt, molasses, syrups and oils. The meat shop was always filled with choice meats which Mr. White bought directly from the farms. The busy millinery department was at the back of the store and upstairs the tailoring department managed by Charles Thompson employed five men and eight women.

Kilbride, in the late 1870s, had a population of several hundred, with plenty of work for everyone. Up the creek to the north of the village stood a large woollen mill owned and operated by William Montgomery. There was a tin shop, a cooper shop, and a drug store owned by Dr. Beattie. This was later purchased for a harness shop and was eventually converted to a garage. Another general store was operated by Donald McGregor, then James Tweedle and John Harris. Just as, incongruously, the drug store became a harness shop, so this general store became a Gospel church and later a residence.

Blacksmiths kept busy were Charles Harris, John Greenlees, Bob Burton, Jack Small, A. Page and Bert Cartwright. Opposite T.L. White's store was the hotel owned by Frank Mills and later Charles Rasberry. After it burned down, a new building was erected on the site, not a hotel but a wagon-maker's shop operated by Joshua Worthington. During the First World War, this was purchased by Carey Brothers who equipped it as an evaporator for summer produce. William Mitchell owned a service station and refreshment booth and was loved by the village children for his generosity. Harvey Henderson was also happily remembered; he served as town constable for many years.

Kilbride Community Hall was Salem Church which in 1905 was moved to the village from Walker's Line and used for a time as a butcher shop. The community purchased the building for a recreation centre. It has since been replaced by a cement block building, the Ella Foote Centre located behind the school.

Mail came from Milton to Kilbride. Charles Rasberry was mail driver for 35 years, living in Kilbride and driving mail to Hamilton. It is said that he never missed a day or took a holiday in all those years, except the day of his marriage. Lowville was later brought into the route and deliveries were made by stagecoach. John Duncan, the chief driver, used four or five excellent road horses for the trip. The coach was always full of people, parcels and boxes, but it was a happy load, and drivers, including Frank Featherstone and Frank Robertson, were good natured and obliging.

Robert Rasberry, son of the early mail driver, owned one of the first automobiles in Kilbride, a 1911 model with a handsome brass front.

The history of Kilbride area was gathered by a church centennial committee of Kilbride United Church in 1960. Older residents of the district contributed their memories, and those of the late Mrs. Bertha Harbottle were of special assistance to committee members Gertie McArthur, Florence McDonald, Marion Cartwright, William Pickett, James Ayton and Laura Dixon.

Early records of the religious activity in the village are scant. The Cumminsville Bible Society, which began on May 9, 1854, drew residents of the area to its meetings, but even before this, in 1846, a Presbyterian church under the branch of the Free Church of Scotland began as a mission with Rev. W. McLean of Waterdown and Wellington Square in charge. Grounds for the now unused cemetery were purchased in 1848 from James Harris before Kilbride was laid out and were deeded to the Presbyterian Church of Cumminsville. A pastoral charge was formed in 1855 and, in 1856, the church was built east of Kilbride on property purchased from the Day estate. The manse stood beside the church which was closed in 1940 after 84 years of Christian service.

A few of the familiar names connected with this church are McClure, Corlett, Wilson, Fraser, Agnew, Labourne, Duncan, Pickett, Clugson, Hewson, Small, Turnbull, Nixon, Harris, and Dixon. After 1940, a number of families joined with the United Church in Kilbride while others joined Campbellville and Milton churches.

Four years after the founding of Kilbride Presbyterian Church, Kilbride Methodist (now United) Church was built in 1850 on land donated to the church by Mr. and Mrs. George Harbottle Sr. The deed is preserved at the church and, although faded, can still be read. The signatures include George and Rhoda Harbottle, William Galloway, Robert Simpson, Thomas Galloway, William Harris and witnesses John Mathews and Francis Baker. Robert Simpson made and donated the church's pulpit and William Bousfield, who owned and operated a saw mill in Tally Ho, supplied timber and siding.

By this time, services were being held in Bethel Chapel. In 1853 land on the south side of No. 5 Sideroad west of Cedar Springs Road had been deeded by John Prudham to the trustees. Mr. Prudham's homestead south of Kilbride had been a stopping place for itinerant ministers. It was quite usual for him and his wife, Elizabeth, to carry their children over the forest trail and across streams, over fallen logs to Collings Church in Lowville to

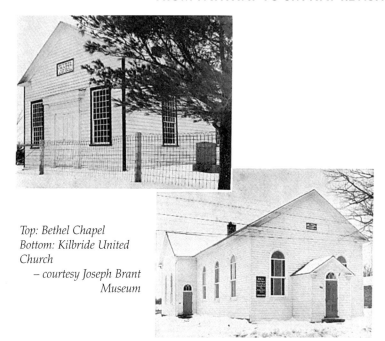

Top: Bethel Chapel
Bottom: Kilbride United
Church
*   – courtesy Joseph Brant*
Museum

attend service. Mr. Prudham and Mathias Canon, both of Nelson, along with Jonas Volick, Andrew Davidson and Richard Volick were the original trustees of the small church of the Methodist New Connexion called Bethel Chapel. The union of existing Methodist bodies caused Bethel to close about 1874 but a committee of trustees was appointed to care for the grounds and cemetery.

In 1995, ministers still conducted an annual service at Bethel which is believed to be the last church of the New Connexion still in existence. The historic place of worship has an unusual pulpit with doors on each side of the minister's bench. The antependium, though worn, retained its colour for many years and with its padded top and heavy fringe added dignity to the pulpit. The seats were sold, appropriately, for use in the Kilbride Community Hall which itself was a former church.

By 1876, Kilbride Methodist was on a circuit with Lowville, Salem, Bethesda (on the Trafalgar Town Line), Mountain, Nassagawaya and Davidson's. In the graveyard of Salem Church on Walkers Line lie Mr. and Mrs. Hamilton Bennett. Mr. Bennett was a local preacher who served for 50 years in the Lowville circuit. All seven appointments contributed to the salary of the minister and his assistant.

Sometime about 1878, the congregation of Kilbride Methodist Church decided to re-establish itself in a more central part of the village. Hall Gunby and Mr. Curliss, who had equipment for moving buildings, and the men of Kilbride went to work in "bees". James McNiven, George Harbottle and

George Bennett supplied oxen and the building was put on skids and hauled to its new foundation. The vestry was torn down and the present Sunday school was later erected. A gala re-opening ceremony was held for the church, and at the tea held the next evening donations were given that completely paid the church debt.

Kilbride School.

The cemetery still remains by the first site of the church and is another of the old burying grounds now maintained by the City of Burlington.

Over the years, countless devoted church and community workers have come and gone: Mrs. Charles Peer, who taught Sunday School girls at Kilbride United; superintendents Charles Peer, W.W. Forster, Frank McNiven, A.J. Harris and Charles Prudham, and local preachers George Harbottle and John Hollingsworth.

Dr. H.R. McDonald established his medical practice in 1923. Before the turn of the century, the medical practitioners were Dr. A.C. Jones and Dr. G.C. Carbert.

One of the first schools in Kilbride was in the frame home of John Harris who was the local magistrate for a number of years. A log schoolhouse once stood on the Coulson homestead, north of the village on No. 10 Sideroad. The earliest record shows that in July, 1855, William Panton and Francis Baker deeded lot 27 on the present Kilbride Street to the trustees of School Section No. 11 Nelson who later bought lots 28 and 29 as well.

Although there is no date on the building, the sturdy two-storey stone school was constructed in 1876 on lot 29 purchased that year. The school yard shared in the many trees planted throughout the village by Charles Rasberry and T.G. White.

The first teacher was W.R. Watson who taught until December, 1881. Although there were two classrooms in the school, the 1885 teacher, Mr. McCorrigan, had 90 pupils in his care. Attendance decreased at the turn of the century and one room was closed.

In 1902, summer vacation was in July only and in 1903, the first two weeks of August were added. There were other holidays such as on December 16, 1903, when the school was closed while the teacher went to the city to help buy Christmas presents for Sunday School pupils. Other closings were more essential. From November 14 to 20 in 1906, the closing was for repairs and from October 21 to November 18, 1918, Spanish influenza shut the doors.

Kilbride General Store.

On his appointment in 1938, Halton County's school inspector L.L. Skuce tried to interest trustees and ratepayers in the formation of school areas, in line with the re-organization into larger areas of administration throughout Ontario. There was much opposition, particularly in Kilbride. In 1943, Nelson Township Council voted in favour of including the 15 schools in the township school area.

Departures from former policy began to occur. Mrs. Jean Emerson was appointed the first music supervisor and the school board commenced supplying the pupils with work books and pencils. In September, 1945, home economics and manual training teachers were appointed to visit each school in the area. By January, 1949, the school population of the district had increased to such an extent that the upstairs classroom which had been closed for 50 years had to be re-opened.

Soon after the formation of the school area, a group of parents in the north of the township made an attempt to have a graded school built in the area. Many in Kilbride supported the graded school idea but wanted the school built in the village. Local township politics was at a fever pitch as trustees and councillors, for and against, were voted in and out. Eventually, in September, 1954, the new eight-roomed Fairview School was opened a mile and a half south of Lowville and four miles southeast of Kilbride.

Although the Board intended to close all the rural schools at this time, opposition was so strong from a group in Kilbride and the neighbouring Bell School Section that these two schools continued in operation and the parents were given the choice of sending their children to Fairview School by bus or allowing them to walk to the local school. The majority of parents who continued to send their children to the old stone school were those who, having attended it themselves, had an intense loyalty to it. The Board found it difficult to get qualified teachers for the Kilbride School and attendance decreased until in June, 1961, when it was closed, there were only 18 pupils.

Early in 1977, George and Helen Whyte purchased the old 1876 school from the city of Burlington. It had been empty since 1961. Plans by architect Trevor Garwood-Jones for gutting and rebuilding the interior gave the building a new lease on life. On November 6, the Whytes had an Open House to show off the renovations.

On January 1, 1958, Kilbride education came under the authority of the Burlington Board of Education. After this, the population continued to grow and shortly a second graded school was required in the northern part of the area. In December, 1959, the Board purchased three acres from Eric McArthur and plans were drawn up for a new six-roomed school. In September, 1960, the new school was opened with 190 pupils registering.

In her study of old school registers, Miss Florence Meares, first principal of the new Kilbride School, notes that whereas few children went on to high school when there was no public transportation, today with free school buses the desire for higher education has markedly increased.

14
Cumminsville-Dakota

In 1855, Nelson Township Council passed by-law No. 83 "to open and establish a line of road between the villages of Kilbride and Cumminsville". Indeed the village of Kilbride was really a continuation of Cumminsville which had been founded by Titus G. Cummins. Sidewalks eventually were laid parallel to the mud road from the upper end of Kilbride, south to Cumminsville and the Dakota grist mill.

On the corner at Cumminsville was a general store successively owned by a Mr. Hawkins, Robert Hay and Robert Thompson. The Temperance Hall, above the store, was a frequent rendezvous and was used as a polling place for Ward Four, Nelson Township. Here, too, was the office of the Montreal Telegraph Company, the only means of communication before the appearance of the telephone. Sandy Fraser was Morse operator and taught in the village school.

Sam Shouldice had a bakeshop, and on the opposite corner stood a large hotel owned by Robert Thompson. It, too, served as a polling division at one time. The inn was licensed and since there were no restrictions for many years on the serving of liquor during elections which lasted for several days, Thompson's must have been an exciting place to vote.

A grist mill was operated by Thomas Galloway. James Harvey was another miller. A saw and shingle mill was run by Abram King and later by Greenlees Bros. and by Thomas Dent. David Little had a turning and lathing shop, and furniture by him, although well over 100 years old, is still in an excellent state, treasured by the Rasberry family. By 1877, Schooley and McCay were making furniture.

After 1847, William Panton, founder of Kilbride, was first post-master of Cumminsville. Mail came from Hannahsville (Nelson Village) twice a week. There was the inevitable blacksmith shop, operated in 1877 by G.G. Greenlees. J.S. Jordon was a Cumminsville merchant, H. Leasley was the village tailor and Doctors McGregor and McClure looked after the health of the community. The twin villages of Kilbride and Cumminsville each led thriving commercial existences. In 1877 Cumminsville had 200 inhabitants, the same as Kilbride.

The Cumminsville Bible Society was founded May 9, 1854. Meetings were held in the Temperance Hall at first and members of the first families of the district were active, including James Tyner, William Wilson, Thomas Galloway, William Montgomery, John Mathews, Thomas Stokes, James

The Dakota Grist and Lumber Mill, destroyed by fire November 17, 1979.

Ingles, F. Small, A. Wilson, John Haggin, Robert Simpson, F. Baker, John Small, John Robb, James Molyneaux, John Duffis, Joseph Lynn, John Prudham, William Gunby, John Agnew, William Harris, Charles Stewart and Thomas Small. The Society alternated its meetings between Kilbride and Cumminsville, and one entry in the minute book read: "The roads were very muddy, the night very dark, the assembly very small."

Many residents of Cumminsville were employed in Dakota which lay immediately to the south. Here stood one of the first schools, Foster's, at the corner of No. 5 Sideroad and Cedar Springs Road. It was a log structure with benches on either side and a dirt floor. It was replaced in 1862 by Dakota Stone School, later named Cedar Springs, S.S. No. 10.

The old Dakota grist mill once served as a flour mill. In later years it was a saw and grist mill. Among the millers who operated there were Andrew Gage and Son, James Harvey, Daniel Smith, David Kirkwood, Thomas and Spencer Bennett, Charles Williams, Samuel Ecker, Clark Eaton, William Pegg and George Pegg and Son. Sadly, the mill was destroyed by fire on November 17, 1979.

Dakota originally had quite a number of residents. A place called "Willbrook" is mentioned as having been at this location. It would appear that these two names are for the same small village.

By far the largest business concern in the entire northern section of Nelson township was the Canada Powder Company at Dakota. Operations were begun about 1854 for the manufacture of gunpowder and the mills were constructed with great difficulty. The powder press had been shipped by boat to Burlington Beach and moved on greased rollers to Wellington Square; then it was drawn on a specially built sleigh by thirteen yoke of oxen to the factory site miles back from the waterfront, on top of the escarpment.

In 1862, the company was purchased by the Hamilton Powder

Company. By 1884, the mills were employing over 200 men, a large proportion of the male population of Kilbride, Cumminsville and Dakota.

In from the public road was the cooperage where the 25-pound kegs were made, a storehouse for empty kegs, the barn, and the manager's house where Edward Corlett lived. Over the Twelve Mile Creek which flowed through the mile-long valley of the mill property was a bridge. On the other bank of the creek were housed the boiler and engine used when the water power was insufficient. Here also stood five large frame buildings, widely separated among the trees in the lovely valley. Each building housed one of the processes needed in the manufacture of the powder and each was connected with the others by a narrow gauge, wooden-tracked railway, man propelled. A discreet distance away were the charcoal kilns fuelled with willow wood from the company's bush.

The mills were operated by water power for which there had been constructed two dams, one upstream, the upper dam, and the other one situated close to the mill buildings, the lower dam. Several acres of water were constantly available needing only the opening of the sluice gates to rush through the mill-race to set in motion the great water wheels in each building. The sluice gates were shut each night at closing time. By next morning water from the Twelve Mile Creek had formed a new pond for a fresh day's operation.

Gun and blasting powder were made of sulphur imported from Turkey, saltpetre brought from Chile, and charcoal. Sulphur and saltpetre shipments, transported by water, were teamed from Brown's Wharf in Aldershot, a distance of about 12 miles, to the Dakota powder plant.

When the C.P.R. was being constructed through the rocky terrain between North Bay and Port Arthur, the demand for blasting powder from Dakota mills was so great and so incessant that the factory operated 24 hours daily for several years.

Manager Edward Corlett, realizing the danger involved in the manufacture of explosives, stood for no carelessness. Women or boys were not employed. During the summer, men worked barefoot in the mills and were never permitted to wear shoes with anything but wooden pegs in the soles.

Each day at noon, in a field well away from the plant, a small brass cannon was used to test the strength of the powder. By such elementary quality control, the ingredients could be proportioned as well as assessed.

October 8, 1884, was a cloudy overcast autumn day. At noon the employees left as usual for their lunch break, only a skeleton staff remaining. At 12:45 noon a mighty explosion rent the air, its reverberations heard as far away as Owen Sound and St. Catharines. The ground shook as though by an earthquake as the powder mills vanished skywards. People in Hamilton heard the blast and witnessed the huge mushroom of smoke lifting above the earth to the northeast. Word soon spread that Dakota powder mills were no more.

Men rushed from every direction to the scene, some on horseback, others with wagon loads of helpers. Four men, Heatherington, Murray, Tibbles and Calder by name, were killed instantly and another died later of injuries. Andrew Coffee was blown to the treetops and landed in the Twelve Mile Creek, suffering no harm other than the loss of his false teeth which were found the following spring near the Lowville dam. A pall of shock and sadness descended over the countryside and relief organizations aided the bereaved families. A mass funeral service was held in St. George's Anglican Church, Lowville.

The cause of the disaster was never determined. The manager was in Cumminsville at the time of the explosion. No evidence of carelessness was discovered.

The mills were never rebuilt. Operations were transferred to the vicinity of Montreal, eventually becoming part of Canadian Industries Limited. The closing of the mills sounded the death knell for Willbrook-Dakota and Cumminsville. Men thrown out of work settled elsewhere and the countryside reverted to its former pastoral peace.

Edward Corlett stayed on at Dakota and bought the land from the powder company, building a profitable business from apple orchards. In 1885, land to the north of the powder mill site was purchased by W.D. Flatt who engaged in timber business on this tract of virgin pine. In 1905, Corlett sold his land to James Tweedle who was succeeded in ownership by

The entrance to Cedar Springs.

The memorial to W.D. Flatt at the Cedar Springs Gate.

Donald McGregor and Charles Prudham. In 1924, Mr. Prudham sold to Mr. Flatt who was charmed by the natural beauty of the surroundings and envisaged developing it with the land already owned by him as a resort community.

By 1926, the first rustic cabins were offered for sale. More followed and by 1932 the desired maximum of 80 was reached. With Mr. Flatt's relinquishing personal control, Cedar Springs Community Club came into being with a golf course, bowling green, swimming pool and ski slopes making it one of the most desirable private recreational resorts in Ontario.

Where the ill-fated powder mill once stood, a barn had been built and this became the Cedar Springs community hall. Following Mr. Flatt's death, imposing gates were built at the entrance to the property in memory of the founder whose enterprise had restored the valley to the lovely place it had been before tragedy struck in 1884.

15
Lowville

Southeast of Kilbride on the banks of the Twelve Mile Creek lies Lowville, the lowest point on the main road from Guelph to Lake Ontario. Some of the earliest arrivals there were John and Hannah Kenney, and Rev. Daniel Pickett, a saddlebag preacher who settled in 1822. Mr. Pickett's daughter later recalled how, as a girl, in 1824, sent to help the Kenneys get settled, she carried a glowing coal between two sticks to start the fire in the new neighbours' fireplace.

In later years, Mr. Pickett sold his farm to a Mr. Watkins, the father of T.C. Watkins, founder of the Right House, a former Hamilton retail store. The Bradts were also established at Lowville early in the 19th century. Albert Bradt traded a 200 acre farm in Caledonia for half as much property on the hills of Lowville, and $100. It was on "Bradt's Mountain," at Lowville, that a signal tower was erected during World War I.

Squire James Cleaver, a farmer and land surveyor, bought land in Lowville and built a grist mill on the Twelve Mile Creek. Squire Cleaver was a strong temperance man and his barn was the first to be raised without whisky as an incentive. The mill, running 24 hours a day, provided plenty of work. Jabez Nicholson was believed to be the last miller to make flour at the old mill. A chopping business was set up later by George Robinson. Another important sawmill was that of John Readhead on Walkers Line south of Lowville.

A Mrs. Foster emigrated to Canada from Ireland in 1832. Her husband died aboard the ship and was buried at sea. She landed in the new world with her eight sons and two daughters, and with little means to support them. Mrs. Foster first located land in Hamilton but being persuaded that a lakeport was no place to bring up a family of boys, she moved to Lowville. It is told that she would take a basket of butter on her head and walk to Hamilton to exchange it for groceries which she carried home in the same manner. Her son, Henry, was on Nelson Township Council for 18 years and her descendants still live in the community.

Like other hamlets on the banks of a stream, Lowville's development was linked with water power. Once the first people had established their farms and a mill was built, a few industries were started and small businesses emerged to meet the needs of the villagers. The village consisted of parts of the farms of T.E. Pickett, Joseph Featherstone and Squire Cleaver.

When the teaming of grain and lumber was an important means of

Lowville School
– courtesy
Muriel Goodbrand

livelihood, hotels were opened, nine between Burlington and Campbellville, and five in the Lowville area. McDaid's was at the foot of the hill, another was in Highville, the name given to the district above Lowville. Three more hotels were nearby.

Lowville had several industries at one time. The foundry owned by J. McLaren in the 1840s turned out everything in iron, from pots, griddles, muffin tins, and smoothing irons, to stoves and farm implements. This business was owned by John Johnson in the late 1870s. Across from the foundry was a tannery.

Back of the foundry on the banks of the creek was Mr. Rumple's furniture factory which supplied the neighbourhood with fine furniture, some of which is still extant. Mr. Rumple, a native of Prussia, had a main factory, with another building nearer the street for finishing and sales. Other businesses were a carpenter shop, a dressmaker, and a millinery shop run by a Miss Marsh of Dundas. This shop later became George Bradt's harness shop.

Sometime between 1853 and 1858, Andrew Pickett built the general store and it is believed the first post office was there. Mr. Pickett also had a cheese factory adjacent to the store, before leaving to make his home in the United States. His eldest daughter, Anna, born in Lowville, was the mother of Harry Hopkins, advisor to President Franklin D. Roosevelt.

Mr. Pickett leased the store to Oscar Mackay. In 1868, the telegraph office was installed there, bringing the villagers more in touch with the outside world. It is believed the first mail route to Burlington, which had been run by John Johnson, was afterwards taken over by the Mackays. About 1875, the store was purchased by Thomas Langton, and again the mail was linked with its proprietor who had the stage and mail route to Hamilton. The mail route to Burlington was discontinued and one was started to Milton.

At Highville, above Lowville, was located A.B. Culloden's general store, Miss Black's dressmaker shop and Klainka's tailor shop. Across the road was Emerson and McNair's blacksmith and carriage shop and J. Pembroke's shoe shop. A few years after Mr. Pembroke's death another shoe shop was operated by a Mr. Potchett in his home.

Lowville Park

The trade of the blacksmith was a vital one before the advent of the horseless carriage, and Lowville had its generous share of "smithies" over the years, including Burkholder and Smith, Alex Mitchell and George Ramshaw.

The post office was moved to this upper part of the village and was run by S. Nixon who did double duty as a school teacher. Later, a general store was built by Isaac Featherstone on the front of his farm. About 1907, the Nelson Telephone Company began operations with head office at Lowville.

About 1875, through the influence of Robert Coates, the village school-master, plank sidewalks were laid through the village, a new footbridge placed across the creek and steps built up the hill to the upper town.

Lowville General Store, 1997.

Village of Lowville, 1873.   *– courtesy Joseph Brant Museum*

The first schoolhouse was built near the present church corner. Later, a white frame school was built near the creek, to be replaced about 1888 by a stone school still standing in Lowville Park. The first school was called Barker's School House and was used for the first church services.

A story of an incident in the old school house during a church service was told by the late Mrs. C.A. Prudham, who chronicled much of Lowville's history. After the church services, the Bible was carefully wrapped in a white cloth and carried home by one of the parishioners, to be brought back the next Sunday. Once, when it was the turn of Mrs. John Thomas, she took the good book home and the next week brought the parcel back and placed it on the desk. When the minister unwrapped it for the service, in it was a block of wood. Mrs. Thomas sprang to her feet and pointing her finger at one of her sons, said, "George, this is your work!"

A number of young men of that generation became ministers. Rev. James Masson was ordained, and preached his first sermon in Barker's School House. From the first real church, built on the site of the later parsonage, went forth Rev. Joseph Colling, Rev. Thomas Colling, Rev. Solomon Cleaver, D.D., Rev. Joel Pitcher, and Rev. T. Webster Pickett.

After holding services in the school for some time, the Colling family decided to build a Methodist church. It was not long before "Collings' Church" opened its doors to worshippers. This church belonged to the Nelson circuit which was formed in 1832, embracing what is now Halton county and extending north to Erin and east to Toronto Township. *The Christian Guardian* of January 19, 1853, reported "The first missionary meeting of Nelson circuit was held Monday evening last in Collings' Church." There were only two circuit missionaries and meetings were held whatever day one of them arrived. In 1855, the old "Collings' Church" was

re-named Lowville Method-
ist Church and made a
pastoral charge along with
Davidson's. By the late
1860s, settlers were coming
into the area in greater
numbers and, by 1871, the
church was too small.

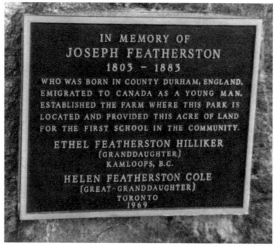

Once more, a member of
the Colling family, Thomas
Colling, donated the land
and a new church was
opened in 1873, with Rev.
Robert Bell, the first minister,
being paid $450 per year.
First Sunday School superintendent was John Foster.

Memorial plaque to Joseph Featherstone, Lowville Park.
– courtesy Muriel Goodbrand

In 1878 the circuit par-
sonage was moved to Lowville from Kilbride and again Thomas Colling
donated land on No. 5 Sideroad for a permanent parsonage. He made one
stipulation: the new building was not to obstruct the view from his home
of the church's front steps. The ornate ten-room parsonage was almost
completely built by parishioners who hauled stone and sand. When it
opened in 1884, an admission fee was charged to view the interior.

By 1887, Lowville and Zimmerman were the only two churches on the
circuit. Churches were usually packed to the doors for all services, and the
churchyards resembled market day, with every description of conveyance
on hand. A by-law had to be passed to allow churchgoers to erect sheds on
the road allowance in which to tie up their horses or oxen.

Among latter day changes to Lowville United Church have been the
construction of a modern split level parsonage on land donated by Eric
Gudgeon and the installation of an oil furnace in the church.

Across from the parsonage on No. 5 Sideroad is the church cemetery.
Family names on the gravestones include the Collings, Harbottles,
Featherstones, Gunbys, Readheads, Butts, Jays, and Coulsons.

A story told of this cemetery involves one of the first persons to be
buried there. He was a young man named Jackson who had come into the
district to work. Stricken with "hip disease" he died and was laid to rest in
the new cemetery, where his was the first grave. Some medical students
wanted the body but Jackson's friends would not agree to this. They dug
out the grave and filled it with large stones and earth before they were
satisfied that no one would molest the remains of their friend.

Some local preachers in this era were Hamilton Bennett, Sidney

Kenney and later, after the turn of the century, Elmer S. Sinclair, Charles Jay and Victor Butts who went to China as a missionary.

A Presbyterian Church was built but never used for worship. It was later converted to a dwelling.

St. George's Anglican is the oldest congregation in Lowville. Parishioners met first for Sunday School September 10, 1836. Later services were held in a frame house on what became the farm of Emanuel Coulson. From this small building, the congregation moved to DeForest Line School. It was there in 1856 that the first vestry meeting took place and the parish named St. George's. In June of the following year, Dr. George Dice donated a parcel of land at the Guelph Line and No. 10 Sideroad, two miles north of Lowville, for a church.

Little is known of this building except that it was frame and cost $800 for materials. A stone church was erected in 1896. This was substantially built, costing $4,000 and has needed no major repairs since it went up. The only replacement was part of the roof which was blown off in a big wind, March 21, 1913, an act of God and in no way attributed to the builders of the church.

St. George's has never had its own rector. Early in its history, about 1859, it was attached to Waterdown and Aldershot. In 1874, it joined Nassagaweya and Carlisle until the latter closed before the turn of the century.

The first rectory for St. George's was the home of Mr. and Mrs. Cowley who turned it over to the church. This was later sold and a farm house bought for the purpose. The third location of the rectory was in Campbellville where it remained in 1996.

The present stone St. George's is still the centre of Anglican worship for Lowville and the surrounding countryside and the cemetery is one of the loveliest in the community.

A beauty spot is Lowville Park which resounds in summer with the shouts of day campers and picnicking families, and in winter the festivities of a winter carnival. William Robertson, Reeve of Nelson Township from 1944 to 1946, headed a group of men, some of them prominent Burlington businessmen, who, in 1945, bought the land which became Lowville Park, at the foot of the hill on the Guelph Line. The land was covered with thick hawthorn brush which took 56 men and 11 tractors a whole day to clear out. With amalgamation of Nelson Township with Burlington in 1958, the town took over the park and built a new bridge and refreshment stand.

Now, during the summer especially, Lowville is no longer secluded in its valley. As visitors to the park come over the crest of the hill, the beauty of the scene below them is almost as impressive as it must have been when the first settlers arrived to make their new homes.

16
Zimmerman

Eva L. Bridgman (Mrs. Clarence Bridgman) compiled, in 1967, a history of Zimmerman, most of which is reproduced here, and which was of great assistance to the authors in researching this chapter.

Zimmerman, southeast of Lowville, at one time was a small centre catering to the needs of the farmers living nearby, its economy started by a mill, and its social life centred for the most part around the churches.

In the beautiful valley which lies between No. 1 and No. 2 Sideroads on Appleby Line, Henry P. Zimmerman (sometimes spelled with an 'S') had his sawmill and built a large stone house at the corner of the Appleby Line and No. 2 Sideroad.

As well as a general store, in the early years there were two sawmills and a grist mill, a school, a shoe shop, tailor, carpenter and blacksmith shops, and a woollen mill which was started but never finished. The post office was in the store and the mail driver would deliver the mail from Burlington. Two of the school pupils would fetch the letters for the children to take home after school.

With the coming of the automobile and the growth of towns and cities to within easy driving distance, the shops and stores began to lose business. In 1911, the grist mill burned down. The other old shops and mills were abandoned and either fell into ruins or were razed. The last time a general store operated was in the 1930s when Miss Frances E. Jones, of Toronto, bought the old Crawford home on Appleby Line near the bridge over the Twelve Mile Creek and ran a small shop for a few years. After she died, the store was eventually torn down and the house renovated. In later years, the house was abandoned and fell into such a state of disrepair that it was condemned and taken down. Thus the once thriving community has become only a memory today. Its importance as a lumbering centre is all but forgotten.

Five churches were once within driving distance of Zimmerman. Lowville United and Davidson's were both originally Wesleyan Methodist. Davidson's was a small frame church on the east side of the Appleby Line, north of the present church. The building was later used as a barn behind the parsonage but in 1907 it burned down. All that is left is a small deserted cemetery on the Appleby Line near No. 4 Sideroad.

Zimmerman Mills in 1865.
– courtesy The Canadian Champion

The other three churches, Mountain, Bethesda and Salem are also gone now but memories of Salem have persisted. This is the church most of the Zimmerman residents attended. It stood on Walkers Line at No. 2 Sideroad until it was purchased by Kilbride residents and taken away to be their Community Hall. The cemetery still stands by the church site on land donated by the Bridgman family and is still used for burials.

Salem Church earned a reputation for its camp meetings in the 1870s. These revivals were held at many churches in the summer and became very popular before the turn of the century and the invention of the automobile. Salem camp meetings were held at the farm of Burwell Bridgman. The "Evangelical Witness", a publication of the New Connexion Methodists, announced, "Notice is hereby given of a camp meeting to be held on Mr. Bridgman's farm near Salem Church, Nelson on September 11. Pasturage and stables for horses can be found in the vicinity at reasonable terms. No provision tent on the grounds and no provisions or groceries allowed to be sold on or near the ground on the Sabbath. Single tents $3.50, double $6.00 may be had by applying to Mr. Johnson, Zimmerman Post Office...horses fed for 25 cents a day."

These meetings lasted a week on end, Thursday to Thursday, and apart from the religious benefits, they also provided a good camping holiday. Fires lit many corners of the field at night and the sound of community singing echoed through the valley.

After the union of the Wesleyan and New Connexion Methodists, the Salem congregation joined Bethesda to become Zimmerman Methodist Church in 1882. Services were then held in an abandoned school which was also used for local boxing contests. This unique association was terminated when the congregation built its own church in 1891 at the cost of $2,900. Chairman of the building committee was Burwell Bridgman. The new church was nearer the centre of the community on the Appleby Line where, in 1996, it still stands, now Trinity Baptist. Lowville became a charge with Zimmerman, the parsonage being located in Lowville.

This brick church was renovated and modernized, but the tip-up, bucket seats remained there from the time it was built, in preference to pews. Zimmerman was rather isolated by urban standards. In 1966, Rev. Kenneth Griffiths, minister of the charge, said that, although the congregation was predominately rural, more urban residents were coming into the community.

In 1854, the ratepayers of School Section No. 8 secured a site and erected a schoolhouse on the bank of the creek near the 1996 site of the church. It was a one-storey frame building with a belfry in the front. The only playground was by the roadside or in the forest. There were no "conveniences".

Trinity Baptist Church, Appleby Line at No.2 Sideroad, formerly Zimmerman Methodist Church, built 1890.

By 1869, the population had increased until there were 80 children crowded into the small school. To meet the situation, a small frame building in the corner of Salem cemetery on Walkers Line was fitted up and the scholars on the Salem side of the creek went there while those on the other side stayed at Zimmerman on the Appleby Line. In 1872, a school to accommodate all the children was thought desirable. The trustees bought land from Johnson Zimmerman and during the winter the farmers drew gravel. In the spring of 1873, a two-storey concrete school was erected complete with belfry and bell to summon the children. Trustees Thomas Watson, James Zimmerman, and Nathanial Lamb kept construction costs down to $3,800 but farmers around were concerned about the rise in taxes to $70 on one hundred acres to help pay for the new school.

A reunion in 1895 brought former students from near and afar. Dr. Charles Campbell, who came from New York, was appointed chairman of the festivities, and Richard Watson, secretary. It was a day for reminiscences and walks amid the haunts of childhood. Even a baptism was performed when Pastor Reuben Zimmerman, of Toronto, baptized his brother Dr. Solomon Zimmerman in the creek at the foot of the hill, back of the old school house. It is said that in their enthusiasm, one of them nearly drowned.

In 1929, a committee was formed to have the old school house torn down and a new one erected. This one-storey brick building was used until a new graded school, Fairview, was built in School Area No.1.

For a time the Zimmerman school was kept open for those wishing to continue to send their children there, but in two years it was forced to close. It has been made into a residential duplex called the Fairview apartments.

This is all that remains of the Zimmerman of old, but residents for a few miles along the Appleby Line and across the sideroads still identify as a group, probably through church associations, and shared memories of the past. Some of the farmers have lived in the area for many years and three farms, those of the Bennetts, Bridgmans, and Campbells, were family-owned for well over 100 years.

17
Along Dundas Street – Nelson to Tansley

When Governor Simcoe conceived of a military highway in 1792 to link York with LaTranche (now London), he may have realized it would open up the interior of Upper Canada. Certainly, once the road was in use from York to Ancaster in about 1800, settlements were built up along it. The stage coach began to run along Dundas St. from Hamilton to Toronto in 1835, and hotels were opened to accommodate the travellers.

One of the early settlements was around the corner of the Guelph Line and Dundas St. and one of the first settlers there was Caleb Hopkins. Caleb and his three brothers settled in Nelson township but Ephriam Hopkins, who had also owned land in East Flamborough, moved on to Saltfleet. Caleb stayed in Nelson; his house is still standing in 1996, set back from the north side of Dundas St., a few houses east of the Guelph Line.

Like his father, Silas Hopkins, who owned land in Aldershot over-looking the bay, Caleb was interested in the area's development, and became a Liberal member of the Upper Canada Legislature in Toronto. One of his rivals for office was John Wetenhall, and both he and Hopkins were on Nelson Township Council in the first days of its existence.

As more settlers came to live near the Guelph Line/Dundas Street inter-section, the community became large enough to deserve a name of its own which Caleb Hopkins supplied. He called it Hannahsville in honour of his wife, Hannah. The 1877 Atlas stated that the name was changed to Nelson Village after the post office was established there. This, however, was in 1835, and as late as 1870 a registered plan of the area with small building lots mapped out still referred to the settlement as Hannahsville. Common usage dies hard and it was probably many years before the new name was accepted.

The early settlers came to Nelson with high hopes. An English day labourer, Thomas Hunt, settled in Nelson where he and his brothers had bought land. He wrote an encouraging letter home: "We are in a good country for poor folks," he said. "We have plenty of good fire and grog. We make our own sugar, our own soap and candles and bake good, light bread. We shall never want for water or timber. We have several adjoining houses, chiefly English people. We can raise up a good house in a little while at little expense...It is called the healthiest place in Upper Canada...They that think to work may do well."

Joseph Birney settled in Nelson after fighting in the War of 1812 and used his trade as a ship's carpenter to help build a bridge across the gap at

The Ireland House (built between 1835 and 1837), now a Burlington
Museum.   *– courtesy Joseph Brant Museum*

Burlington Heights. Colonel William Chisholm was another War of 1812 veteran who settled on a Nelson farm in 1816. He built up a large mercantile business as well as his farm and, in 1835, was made the first postmaster of Nelson P.O., the second in Ontario. The same year, he was made postmaster of Oakville where he moved in 1838.

Another prominent family in the area was the Irelands. Joseph Ireland, a native of Bowes, Yorkshire, England, petitioned for land in Upper Canada on December 14, 1819, after being in Upper Canada for about five months. His oldest brother, John, had emigrated and was listed on Captain Hatt's militia roll for York Company of Volunteers, part of the 5th Lincoln and 2nd York Militia. In 1820, Joseph Ireland bought 100 acres of land from Daniel Reilly, and by 1847, he had amassed 1043 acres. Between 1835 and 1837, on what is now Guelph Line, near the Dundas St. intersection, he built a stone house patterned on a typical country squire's home. It was designated as a heritage structure in 1977. The house was the residence of Joseph; his son, John; his grandson, George, and his great-granddaughter, Marie Ireland Bush.

In 1985, Marie died. She had hoped that the City would keep her home and its contents as a museum for the people of Burlington.

In 1986, the Ireland House was in danger of being sold, but the Historical Society convinced the city to buy it. Half the purchase price was to be raised from the public. This goal was achieved and in May, 1987, Ireland House was purchased by the city. Helen Caldwell, Marie's cousin and trustee of her estate, donated the furnishings and most of the contents to create a unique museum showing the life of a well-to-do Burlington farm family from 1835 to 1985. Ireland House Museum is administered by the Burlington Museums Board.

David R. Springer, son of a pioneer Hamilton family, moved from a farm in the Hamilton area to Nelson in 1835. He was a Justice of the Peace for 35

Nelson House, formerly located on the southeast corner of Dundas Street and Guelph Line.   *– courtesy Joseph Brant Museum*

years. He organized the first agricultural shows in Nelson and took an active part in the founding of the Provincial Agricultural Association in 1846.

According to the township records, there were three inns near the corners of Hannahsville. In 1836, a meeting of the inhabitants of the township was held at the inn of William Chisholm. The council met in B. Naisbitt's Inn in 1852, and for the same year, the Ward 2 voting was at Richard Hull's Inn, Hannahsville. Township council met in other inns as well until a proper township hall was built in 1853.

The hall, built on land donated by Stephen Atkinson, was 60 feet by 120 feet. Mr. Atkinson also donated what was a princely sum for those days, 30 pounds. Thereafter the hall was put to many uses, one of which was the agricultural shows. In January, 1897, the Literary Society was given permission to hold meetings in the township hall "providing they clean it up after and be responsible for damage."

There was, in the early days, a school house on the northeast corner of the Guelph Line and Dundas Street. No one today remembers the official name of the school but the children used to call it Ballykill Bay. Nelson's Anglican Church, St. John's, held its first service in the building, and Clarkson Freeman, according to the 1877 Atlas, "attended the common school a year under the instruction of Thomas Baxter of Nelson." Robert Kerr Chisholm, William Chisholm's son, also received his education in the common school in Nelson before moving to Oakville.

In August, 1872, Peter McCulloch sold an acre of land for S.S. No.5. The fine red brick school house was built a little to the north on the eastern side of the Guelph Line. The original trustees were William Davidson, John Gordon and William Richardson. The school was used until 1951 but then stood empty for many years before becoming the Academy Preschool.

In 1864, A.G. McCay was instructed by the Nelson township council to "procure plank and other material for a sidewalk from the town hall to the crossroad at the corner and to cause the same to be made." By this time, the population was probably about at its peak. The lumber fever was in full swing and the teamsters hauling wood down the Guelph Line to Port Nelson and Wellington Square swelled the town's business, and made it an important stopping place. An old map, dated 1855, shows the Guelph Line as a plank road for a portion of its length, mainly around the crossroad which was most heavily travelled. The wooden surface kept the dirt road from becoming a bog in wet weather.

By 1877, as well as the township hall and schoolhouse, there was a drill shed, three churches and a hotel, the Nelson House, whose proprietor was M.S. Atkinson. This hotel, on the southeast corner of the crossroad, was demolished in 1974. In 1877, R.D. Ireland and George McKerlie each owned sawmills, and McGowan and Smith and William Cartwright were both carriage-making firms. In 1877, the general store was run by Thomas Selby who also looked after a post office and telegraph office on the premises. The other corner also had a store at one time. The brick store on the northwest corner was owned by the Springers for some time but, about 1950, the building burned down. It was replaced by a variety store. There were blacksmiths over the years, too, and a man named Chamberlain, who owned a water pump repair shop. The children called him "Pumpy".

An 1858 sensation for Nelson was the Milton hanging of a pioneer Nelson farmer. A hero of the War of 1812, he became an alcoholic and shot his daughter. After serving a five-year prison term, he returned to Nelson and "threw himself headlong into a fresh career of dissipation." Finally in November, 1857, he shot two women with whom he was living and the newspapers proceeded to have a field day. A minute-by-minute account of the poor man's last hours was printed, including his speech on the gallows at 3 p.m., November 30, 1858, in which he warned, "Beware of bad company." Everyone in the county who could come was there to see the hanging. Before daybreak, sleighs and wagons were arriving and women appeared to outnumber men. It was said the people "laughed and jested as if they were come to a wedding instead of a hanging."

As the farming community near Nelson became more populous, the religious needs of the people were met with the erection of churches. The old Methodist church records were apparently destroyed with personal belongings, on the death of a former treasurer, David Springer. There were said to be two thriving Methodist congregations in the early part of the 19th century. One of these worshipped in a stone church at the foot of what is now Cedar Springs Road, built and donated by Charles Tuck. The church was later used as a home and has since been demolished.

The other branch built a frame church just forty feet west of the present Nelson United Church, a little west of the Guelph Line on Dundas Street.

In 1830, Moses McCay, a trustee, deeded to the trustees, for five pounds, the acre of land needed for the building. The trustees, including Mr. McCay himself, were David Pitcher, Isaac Van Norman, John Bastedo, David and Ebenezer Griffin and Justin W. Williams.

This frame church, which boasted a gallery, served until 1859 when the present church was built. During these years, the two congregations were friendly until, strangely, the Methodist Union of 1875. It was not long, however, before the local feeling of fellowship triumphed and the congregations banded together into one and closed the branch on the Cedar Springs Road at what had been known as Tuck's corner.

These Nelson churches had always been part of the Waterdown ministry, with the ministers living in Waterdown. In 1923, Nelson became a joint charge with Appleby. In June, 1959, when Appleby United Church's membership had grown large enough to have its own minister, Nelson United Church joined with Palermo.

The churches of Nelson all suffered a decline in membership, especially severe during the 1920s and 1930s. They managed to survive, however, and now, with the growth in residential building bringing houses closer to the Dundas highway or Highway 5, as it is known, the churches are thriving.

The history of St. John's Anglican Church on Highway 5, a little west of the Guelph Line, is closely tied with the Ireland family, for it was they who did much to stimulate early interest. The Ireland name is carved on many of the gravestones in the church's cemetery.

In 1835, the farmers around Nelson, who had to make the arduous journey down to St. Luke's in Wellington Square, decided they wanted a church of their own. William Spence, an Irish farmer who had settled at Nelson, obtained an introductory letter from the Archbishop of Dublin to Bishop Stuart of Quebec, there being no Niagara Diocese at the time. With this letter, Spence, Joseph Ireland, and John Wetenhall, went to see the bishop and were given permission to hold their own services.

The first service was on November 15, 1835, in the old schoolhouse called Ballykill Bay. The minister who served the St. Luke's congregation, Rev. F. Mack, came up to Nelson. In 1838, the group was ready to begin a building program. William McKay was named chairman of the building committee. Once more the Atkinson family donated three-quarters of an acre for a church and cemetery.

The contract was let to John Malcolm, William Grant and Alexander Brown for 348 pounds and the building was dedicated in 1842.

By this time, the rector of St. Luke's was Dr. Thomas Greene from Ireland, who continued to travel between the two churches. The pews in the new church were in the contemporary style with gates at each end. They were auctioned to the parishioners and sold for one pound each. Each family in the congregation then had its own pew for which it paid an annual rental. Six pews were free. One of the first donations to the church, a communion service of silver given in 1841 by the Stuart Mission Society, is still in use in 1996.

In 1890, St. John's at Nelson joined with Lowville and Nassagaweya after being attached to the Waterdown church for three years. During this period one of the ministers was a Rev. Seaman whose son, William, married Florence Ireland, the sister of George Ireland of the Guelph Line. The ceremony was performed in St. John's Church. The linking with Lowville and Nassagaweya was not too successful due to the long distance between the centres. It was 17 miles which was a considerable drive in the horse and buggy days. St. John's Church was closed about 1893.

In a year and a half, since there was a congregation once again wanting to use St. John's, a lay reader was procured and services were resumed. The attendance increased enough to justify a reunion with St. Luke's in 1895. By this time, the church building was in a bad state of repair, with windows broken, plaster broken and a leaking roof. The congregation went to work and made repairs in time for a new opening ceremony. In May, 1910, St. John's joined with Palermo and Omagh.

In 1922, St. John's was again in danger of being closed. Divinity students filled in for a while until the congregation once more joined with that of Grace Church, Waterdown. This union was later broken. Centennial celebrations were held in 1942. One of the guest speakers was Rev. William Seaman who had married into the Ireland family. With the population growth of the 1990s, this church is thriving once again.

St. Paul's Presbyterian Church, farther east along Highway 5, west of Walkers Line, was the oldest Presbyterian church in the area and one of the oldest congregations. In 1816, Rev. William Jenkins made visits from Scarborough to Hugh McLaren's barn and Bastedo's house where he conducted services. By 1819, Rev. William King was holding services in a house situated to the east of the subsequent site of the church. Within three years, this staunch group of British immigrants and Loyalists had built their small church. The congregation was the only one in the Nelson-Tansley district to have its own minister. This was partly due to circumstances and the fortuitous arrival of Mr. King. This energetic man of God purchased a farm soon after his arrival in Canada, and this became his headquarters. Since the farmers around could afford to pay a minister very little, the profits from the farm kept the King family supported for the next thirty years.

During this period, Mr. King started services in Waterdown and travelled into outlying areas, baptizing, marrying, and burying. In 1852, he retired, and died at the age of 69. He was buried at the rear of the church in the small cemetery which has been well maintained since about 1820.

The present St. Paul's Presbyterian Church, 2600 Headon Forest Drive.

The King farm was later owned by the Norton family and was the depot for Burlington's transportation system, the C.H. Norton Bus Lines. Laidlaw Transit now operates school buses and charters from this site.

The first elders of St. Paul's were Gilbert Bastedo, William McKerlie and Hugh Green, joined soon after by Neil Johnson. The congregation of St. Paul's outgrew the first little church which began to show signs of age. In February, 1868, at a cost of $1,500, a new brick church was completed, much of the construction work being done by the parishioners themselves. In 1877, on re-organization of charges after Presbyterian church union, St. Paul's joined with Kilbride.

In 1880, St. Paul's separated from the Kilbride circuit and became attached to Knox Church in Burlington until 1884. At this time St. Paul's "teamed" with another Knox, the one at the "Sixteen". Today still another Knox, in Waterdown, shares its minister with St. Paul's. The Tansley manse of St. Paul's, no longer needed, was torn down in 1964 to make room for railway expansion. A new St. Paul's Presbyterian church was dedicated October 3, 1993, on land just east of the old cemetery. Although on Highway 5, it fronts on Headon Forest Drive to serve the new subdivision. The old church became the rented home of First Methodist Church.

At Tansley, which is the area on Highway 5 just west of the city's eastern boundary, a community grew up around the waterpower of the Twelve Mile Creek. A mill was built which probably attracted the early settlers. In 1877, the mill was still operating but by the turn of the century it had been abandoned. The ruins remained in this valley until the last new four-lane bridge was built on Highway 5. The youth of Burlington enjoyed the "old swimming hole" at this spot.

The small village, like Hannahsville, had its own name, St. Ann's, a name which died hard. It is not known when the name was officially changed but it must have been between 1881 and 1890, according to local residents. Apparently there had been confusion with a St. Ann's near St. Catharines. The man who kept the post office at the Nelson St. Ann's, so they say, was a Mr. Tansley, so his name was used for the postal address.

By 1890, the postmaster was John Bunton. Like the Aldershot Sinclairs and the Burlington Pearts, the Bunton family passed the job along, first to Mrs. Bunton, after John's death, and then to Emma, a daughter. Another daughter, Beatrice, recalled that the postmaster's salary, based on revenue received, was $24 in 1901. By the time the post office closed to make way for rural delivery from Freeman, the sum was $100 a year.

At the turn of the century, the mail carrier lived in Zimmerman where he picked up the mail, then arrived at Tansley at 6 a.m. From there, he went to Nelson and on to Burlington Junction at Freeman. The mail was put on the early train about 7 a.m. The carrier would arrive back at Tansley with the incoming mail between 1 and 2 p.m.

The area was comparatively well populated into the latter decades of the 19th century, with a cluster of houses near the creek. A hall of the Grange of the Patrons of Husbandry was located on the west side of the Appleby Line just north of the intersection with Highway 5. It was a "tall" building of two storeys and dances were held upstairs. These granges were a type of farmers' cooperative society which bought goods in bulk for its members.

As well as serving as postmaster, John Bunton also ran a hotel for a few years in his eleven-room house, in the 1890s. There was a beverage room in the front downstairs, and after Mr. Bunton gave this up, the family continued to serve meals for a while and take overnight guests.

An amusing story is told of the days when John Bunton was postmaster and barkeeper. The Presbyterian minister thought the Bunton establishment was a dreadful, sinful place and he felt it unthinkable that the government should have the post office there. He wrote to the Postmaster General complaining that the atmosphere was so bad that he wouldn't set foot in the place himself - but had to send the hired girl instead!

St. Ann's was the stop on the stage coach route before the Trafalgar stop at the Sixteen Mile Creek. These creeks posed a transportation problem which was solved at the Twelve by a small bridge at the bottom of the river's bank. Residents of the area remembered how as children they used to sleighride down the west bank of the creek which was not so steep. The road wound down into the ravine and across a small iron bridge at the bottom.

When the first bridge was built is not certain, but an item in Nelson Township minutes notes work done on it in February, 1850, when "George Vanfleet was paid 26 pounds 10s., being the amount due him upon his contract for repairing the bridge across the Twelve Mile Creek on Dundas

Street." In November, 1850, William Bunton was paid 1 pound 8s. 7 1/2 d. for labour performed on the Twelve bridge. His son, John, who counted pathmaster among his many duties, was paid $63.23 for repairs to the bridge and hill at St. Ann's.

By the end of World War I, when many projects were being undertaken, the Ontario Department of Highways realized the old bridge was outmoded. The next year, the annual report of the Department of Public Highways included this item: "1919 the Tansley Bridge over the Twelve Mile Creek in Halton County on Dundas Street in the township of Nelson was erected at a cost of approximately $115,000. This bridge has a maximum height of 98 feet above the creek bed, concrete abutments, and four piers, has a steel superstructure 542.5 feet in length and concrete floor 20 feet in width." A new four-lane bridge was eventually built to replace this one, to accommodate the increasing traffic on Highway 5.

Over the years, there have been three schools at Tansley. The first has passed unrecorded into the limbo of the past but Beatrice Bunton had memories of a second and a third. The second school, S.S. No. 7, on the south side of the No. 5 Highway, just west of Appleby Line, was a large two-storey building made of stucco plastered over a wood frame, and marked to resemble blocks as was the fashion in those days. The boys used to pick pieces of the cement out. The large second floor room with a yellow blackboard was not being used by the turn of the century, except on rainy days when it was a good place to play at recess.

The third school was very familiar to Miss Bunton who taught there from 1923 to 1939. It was a one-room school made of brick and in Miss Bunton's time heated with a wood-burning Waterbury heater. This building is still standing but altered and enlarged to become Tansley School House, The Educational Day Care and Nursery, operated by the YMCA.

Among the early immigrants to Tansley were the Emersons. When they were sailing to America, their ship was wrecked in a wild storm off the east coast. The whole family perished except the father and young John who had three of his toes amputated due to freezing in the cold sea water. Father and son settled at St. Ann's.

A later generation of Emersons was noted for its ice cream. It was made in Emersons' farmhouse south of Dundas Street on what is now Orchard Road. Motorists used to line the long lane to the house to purchase the delicacy. In the early 1930s, the family bought a piece of land on Highway 5 and put up a small frame building to dispense the product. The ice cream was made in the basement in a big wooden tub-freezer turned by a gas engine. Thick cream was used with fresh fruit for flavouring. In 1948, Emerson Colling bought the business, and operated a variety store on the site.

The former S.S. #5 Nelson, now a day care centre, Guelph Line at Highway #5.

Jim Emerson ran a popular ice cream parlour in Burlington on Brant Street in the days of World War I.

A link with the past of the area was an old cemetery west of Colling's store, marked on the 1877 Atlas. When Highway 5 was widened, the few graves still marked were relocated to Greenwood Cemetery. The Collings store with new owners remained a variety store and truck stop, including a gas station. The name Tansley has been retained in the names of several 1996 housing developments in the area.

18
Appleby: The Disappearance of a Community

In the 1950s, Appleby was a hamlet at the intersection of Appleby Line and the QEW. There was a public school, a post office, a church, a house formerly a hotel, a blacksmith shop, the home of the veterinarian, the teacher's house and a community hall.

Appleby, however, was more than a hamlet. It was really the community made up of the four sections of land which went out from the post office, school and church. It is almost certain that Appleby received its name from the village in England, since several of its pioneers, Thomas Atkinson, Thomas Alton and the Fothergills came from Appleby in Westmorland, England.

One of the first settlers was a Miss Stringer in 1809 who obtained a Crown deed and settled on the farm at the corner of the Middle Rd. and Nelson-Trafalgar Town Line. When United Empire Loyalist Isaac Van Norman came in 1810 and built his home, there was only one other house between it and Burlington Heights.

In 1819, Thomas Alton came from England and the Breckons came in 1830. Other familiar names from the early days were Blanshard, Cline, Lucas, Dynes and Cotter. Most of the early Appleby settlers were from the British Isles, especially England, although some were Pennsylvania Dutch. One family who came to Appleby Line in more recent years were the Richardsons. Mrs. Joseph Richardson attended school in Appleby, England, and her family later studied at the public school here at Appleby.

One of the early roads in this area was an old Indian trail just below the ridge which was the ancient shoreline of Lake Ontario. In 1806, the Middle Road was surveyed and eventually built in 1838, later to become the modern Queen Elizabeth Way built in 1936.

Interest in the area was shown by the planning for the first railroad. Work began in 1817 on the Great Western Railroad (taken over by the Grand Trunk Railway – G.T.R. – in 1882) and took seven years to complete. This opened new vistas for trade and industry, plus faster mail service.

Appleby Post Office was established February 6, 1857 with Thomas Atkinson as first postmaster. Mail was carried from Wellington Square to Nelson and Zimmerman and then down the Appleby Line. It started as a twice-weekly delivery, and later the service was extended to three times a

The Village of Appleby, about 1946.

week. Previous to 1857, mail was available at Nelson, coming by stage coach in the winter and by boat in summer. The G.T.R. (later C.N.R.) set up a flag station on the Appleby Line in 1870 and in later years the Prescott family looked after the post office until the establishment of rural mail in 1915.

In the days when teaming of lumber and grain was carried on, blacksmiths performed a useful service; at one time there were four busy blacksmith shops in the area. The community also had sawmills or grist mills on practically every creek; taverns were built at many cross roads.

Early pioneers in the Appleby area lost no time in making provision for their religious and educational needs. Previous to 1846, there were two schools, one at the Nelson-Trafalgar town line and the other on the Edwin Blanshard farm. These both were replaced in 1846 when a school was built on the northeast corner of Appleby Line and the Middle Road. The brick building which was constructed in its place in 1863, and called S.S. No.3 Nelson, was torn down almost a century later to make way for the North Service Road.

The early Appleby School area extended from the lake shore north to the Upper Concession (Upper Middle Road) and from Walkers Line to the Nelson-Trafalgar town line. Children from the Trafalgar side of the line also attended this school.

In 1913 the new Strathcona School was built between the lake and Lower Concession (New Street) on Walkers Line. Children were directed to the school section in which they lived and a small fee was charged those attending Appleby School from outside the section.

There was great rivalry between the teachers of schools at Appleby and Bronte in seeing who would pass the most pupils at entrance examination time (the end of Grade 8 today).

First religious services in the community were Methodist meetings held at the home of Isaac Van Norman as early as 1824. Neighbours met at the call of a conch-shell horn which could be heard for five miles when the "saddlebag preacher" had arrived, regardless of day or hour. This sometimes caused problems on a working day when he ran the risk of his voice being drowned out by the buzz of the nearby sawmill on the Van Norman farm.

The Van Normans were a typical pioneering family who built their home out of bushland after acquiring a Crown deed to 200 acres in 1810. Isaac built a sawmill which was powered from a stream running through his farm. Neighbours brought their logs to him and took home lumber for their homes and farms.

The Van Norman daughter, Jane, was the first woman in Upper Canada to earn a Bachelor of Arts degree. She later taught in the Burlington Ladies' Academy, Hamilton, founded by her brother Daniel. She married Aaron D. Emory and religious services held in their home at Aldershot led to the founding of East Plains United Church. Descendants of this marriage still reside in Burlington.

Mr. Van Norman was eminently suited to become the lay preacher at Appleby, and he warmly welcomed the horse-riding ministers who usually visited every month. One of the first preachers to brave the wilds of this area was Rev. Egerton Ryerson who later became the founder of the public school system in Ontario.

Some years after services began in his home, Mr. Van Norman built a small frame church on his property, just opposite the old Mount Vernon Cemetery, not far from the one on Appleby Line. In one corner of the cemetery are buried the men who died of dysentery while building the tracks for the Great Western Railway in 1854.

Foreseeing the growth to come, a larger brick church was built in 1846 on the west side of Appleby Line just south of the Middle Road. The ladies gained quite a reputation for their chicken dinners, and when the railroad was built, people would come by train from Hamilton and Oakville to be met by local farmers who drove them in wagons to the church suppers.

The first Sunday school, an auxiliary to the Wesleyan Methodists, was started in 1839 in the log school on the Mathewman farm at Middle Road and the Town Line. It was called the Nelson Middle Road Sunday School Society; early officers were John Lucas, Aaron D. Emory, W. Van Norman, Benjamin Mathewman, James Teeple and John Breckon. A membership fee of two shillings and sixpence was subscribed by each pupil.

In 1906, when Rev. G.K. Bradshaw was pastor, a new larger church was erected on the Middle Road and this in turn had to be torn down when the QEW overpass and service roads were built in 1958. The congregation voted to rebuild in a more populated area, and the result was the modern Appleby United Church, constructed in the heart of the Shoreacres survey on Spruce Avenue.

Appleby Line, above and below the QEW, has become an industrial zone. How amazed would those early pioneers be, could they see their peaceful Appleby today!

19
Aldershot

Now part of the City of Burlington, Aldershot, although never an incorporated village, always had a strong sense of identity. Its boundaries were somewhat sketchy; even as late as 1965 Hamilton and Burlington were not sure of Aldershot's western border. In that year, a heavy piece of equipment went through the Valley Inn Bridge. The bordering municipalities debated which should pay for the damage. It was finally determined that the bridge was about 250 feet outside Burlington's boundary, and Hamilton and West Flamborough were left to argue it out.

Aldershot "on the Plain" attracted the earliest settlers to the bay region. David Fonger settled in 1783 on the Indian trail which ran from the boundary of the Mississauga Indian lands to Burlington Heights and called Centre Road by surveyor Augustus Jones. Fonger's land on Lot 5, concession 1, which later became the Emery and Gallagher farms, was purchased from Lt. Alex MacDonel. David Fonger Jr. settled in Aldershot in 1830. The Fonger family cemetery was on the site of St. Matthew's Church, across from their home.

Another of the first settlers was George Chisholm, a Scot who emigrated to New York in 1773. After the Revolutionary War, he settled in Niagara and in 1794 came to the shore of Burlington Bay.

In 1791, William Applegarth arrived from England and settled on a crown grant at "Oaklands". His farm stretched from east of the present LaSalle Park Rd. to west of Aldershot Plaza and down to the bay front. The first grist mill was built by William Applegarth in Hidden Valley in 1809 when salmon abounded in his stream. The mill was destroyed by fire in 1812 and re-built. The second shared the same fate as the first but a third mill lasted until it fell into decay.

One of the houses on the estate became a cheese factory and in later years was the home of the Crouchley family. A second large dwelling was erected at Oaklands by John Fuller, son of the first Anglican Bishop of Niagara, who had bought the Applegarth farm. In 1874, the gate house was put up at the entrance to the estate and later razed with other of the estate buildings to make way for Aldershot Plaza.

In 1806, Colonel Brown, an agent with the North Western Fur Traders Company in York, bought several hundred acres in Waterdown Heights. His grandson, Alex, married Sarah Applegarth, granddaughter of William. Her grandfather divided his estate, keeping Oaklands as the homestead; the land from Oaklands to St. Matthew's Church became known as the Brown property.

In the late 1840s, Brown built the wharf named after him and stacked cordwood there for the lake steamers to pick up. As early as 1828, Ebenezer Griffin, a Waterdown miller, used the bay to ship his flour on the first lap of its journey to wholesale houses in Montreal and Quebec. A generation later, Brown's wharf was handling the grist trade of his sons who sold not only to nearby markets but also to those in the distant Maritimes. Woollen goods were shipped from the Griffin carding mills, one of the first to be equipped with a double set carding machine. Stone from the quarries of Waterdown was another export. One of the last shipments from the wharf was 15,000 to 20,000 barrels of apples in 1897. As with any port, the presence of sailors made necessary a tavern and a bakery, and their proprietors did a big business while the boom was on.

Alex Brown, whose home was where LaSalle Park pavilion now stands, was, along with his father-in-law William Applegarth, a commissioner of the Burlington Beach canal project from 1823 to 1832.

Adam Fergusson settled in the Aldershot-Waterdown vicinity to the north in 1792, and in the 1840s the Gallagher family arrived there. It was not until 1879 that John Gallagher and his wife Mary Simpson, descendant of the Simpsons who first settled in the Kilbride district, moved to a dirt road, called Plains Road by then.

John Gallagher's eldest son, Richard, married and moved to Hamilton where he founded Canada Business College. A younger son, George, stayed on the farm with his father. The farm consisted of 100 acres when John Gallagher purchased it from David Fonger. He raised cattle and planted a fine apple orchard on the front of the property.

In 1910, his son George Gallagher purchased an additional 65 acres from the Johnson family where he raised cattle and pigs, later branching into market gardening and fruit farming. His sons, Howard, Gordon, Percy and Norman took their places in the management of the farm and planted more fruit trees. From 1925 to 1933, four apple orchards of some 2,250 trees were set out as well as 200 cherry trees and a large vineyard. On September 17, 1927, 250 growers from all over Ontario gathered at the farm to see the results of scientific apple growing. Melon growing became one of the farm's specialties. One week in August 1931, two thousand 20-quart baskets of melons were picked and packed daily for shipment to Winnipeg, Montreal and Toronto. The Gallaghers were responsible for developing the salmon-flesh cantaloupes, "Sugar-Salmon" which became the melon of choice for Aldershot market gardeners.

In 1961, the Department of Highways purchased 16 acres of the Gallagher farm to build Highway 403. In 1962, the C.N.R. purchased 30 acres of land, which included the cherry orchards and vineyard, to build additional railroad facilities. In 1963, Tridon Manufacturing Co. purchased the Courtland apple orchard for its factory site, later occupied by G.A. Love Foods Inc. Cuna Mutual Insurance Society (Cumis) purchased another of the apple orchards for its Canadian headquarters building, and close by Plains Rd., Percy Gallagher opened the White Oaks residential survey.

The Charles C. King property, "Crown Farm", ran from Campbell's Corners (King Rd. and Plains Rd.) to the bay. The homestead still stands on King Road opposite Greenwood Drive. A few years prior to Charles King's death in 1919, an acreage was sold to developer W.D. Flatt for a residential survey, and at this time the King family cemetery was moved to Greenwood Cemetery.

The Long family was related to the Kings through the marriage of George Long and Emma King in 1884. Longs operated a dairy on their land and later, Harry Long, who was Reeve of East Flamborough, turned to market gardening. The Longacres subdivision was carved from the Long farm.

The route down King Road, east along Greenwood and down to the beach, was once called the "sand strip". Old timers remembered a narrow gauge railway which ran along the strip from a quarry up beyond Campbell's Corners. During this time Greenwood Drive was the north shore road before the No. 2 Highway was put in.

The tip of land in west Aldershot, pointing southward into the bay, was a part of 40 acres of land purchased by Peter Carroll, a land surveyor and road builder. After his marriage in 1836, he began to build a baronial castle overlooking the bay. When completed, Rock Bay mansion was all he had dreamed of, and he and his wife, dubbed "Lady Carroll", lived there with servants to care for them. Carroll was one of the first to succeed in growing peaches outdoors in Ontario. Besides his farming interests, he was kept busy as a director of the Great Western Railway and a member of the board of Gore Bank. He was defeated in two attempts to be elected as a Tory member of the Assembly.

The Carrolls left no heirs and eventually the deserted mansion was destroyed by fire. On the estate today is Woodland Cemetery, and the name is carried on in Carroll's Point, the wooded peninsula at the end of the bay.

Charles Scheer lived at the gate house of the Carroll estate. He worked for the Wanzer Sewing Machine Company in Hamilton, and he and his wife also worked for the Carrolls. Scheer purchased two acres of land in west Aldershot, part of the Hendrie estate, and on this small plot went into market gardening. He bought more land farther east from the Schoan family. He was one of the first farmers to develop and grow the salmon-flesh cantaloupes for which Aldershot became famous. Two of the Scheer family homes are still standing in 1996, one at 192 Plains Rd. E. across from the former Emery's market, a second on the north side occupied by Ken Scheer's two sisters.

Early settlers were Peter Smoke and his family who moved to west Aldershot when Plains Road was a trail through the woods. Smoke carried grain in saddlebags to the Applegarth mill to be ground.

Jacob Filman came with his father Conrad and family to Ancaster from Pennsylvania in 1789 but settled in Barton Township when his son James was born. He moved with this son, who had become Capt. James Conrad Filman, about 1850, to a parcel of land stretching from Indian Point to Plains Rd., on the east side of King Road. Where King Road meets North Shore Blvd., James' son John built a large home, "Willowbank", in 1883. The intersection was known as Filman's Corners and the house later served as a dining establishment. It was destroyed by fire on February 25, 1963. A number of Filman family homes were surrounded by "Birdland" bungalows when a new survey was built.

The street names in "Birdland", Lark, Finch, Tanager, Oriole, etc., are quite in keeping with Joshua Filman's son Walter's love of feathered creatures. In a ravine just east of Shoreview Rd., the family had dammed up a creek to form a pond which was a bird sanctuary beloved by all.

Giles Gorton Unsworth in 1848 bought land west of the Applegarth farm, north of Plains Rd. His son Richard was a teacher in Nelson's S.S. No. 2, now Lakeshore School. A younger son, Albert, operated a small knitting business. The building stood on the north side of Plains Rd. just east of Unsworth Ave. Albert moved to Hamilton, but his son George stayed on in Aldershot, and in 1882 purchased an acre of land across from his father's home. He increased his holdings and, around the turn of the century, built small greenhouses. Between 1913 and 1940, six large greenhouses were constructed. The business prospered and many acres were eventually under glass. In the mid-1990s, two-thirds of the property was developed as a residential survey, Unsworth Green. Four large greenhouses remained in 1996, the company being operated by Bill and Lois (Unsworth) Reynolds, Catherine (Unsworth) Perkins and Eleanor Unsworth.

Aldershot Greenhouses Ltd., on Gallagher Rd. in Aldershot, was begun by Arie Van der Lugt in 1954 with one small greenhouse. The operation, which was taken over by his son Len, included, by 1996, six acres of pot chrysanthemums and roses under glass.

On the bay shore west of Holy Sepulchre Cemetery was a powder magazine in the latter part of the 19th century. Of solid brick, it was converted to a residence but was torn down in later years.

Robert Smiley came in 1855 and lived at the foot of the hill by Brown's wharf. The family lived on a rise of ground 300 yards from Plains Rd., across from the Aldershot Plaza. The house was later moved nearer the road. The farm, a 60-acre plot, in 1996 formed part of Hidden Valley Park. Robert Smiley was on the school board when S.S. No.1, East Flamborough was built at Smiley's Sideroad (now Lemonville Rd.), and he donated part of his farm as the school site. The school later served as a tavern and was eventually torn down. Robert's son, Joseph, was reeve of East Flamborough in 1911 and secretary-treasurer for nine years.

In 1881, Henry Blessinger, of German descent, bought 40 acres on the west side of Waterdown Rd. stretching from north of Aldershot Corners to the C.N.R. tracks. He drove to the market at Guelph to sell his produce and was one of the first farmers to employ workers from the Six Nations Reserve near Brantford as summer help.

With his son Roy, Henry Blessinger operated a coal business in the winter from the C.N.R. station. Henry's half-sister, Carolyn Fox, taught at Lemonville Rd. school and became the third wife of G.W.S. Johnson, the author of the song, "When You and I Were Young Maggie". Lemonville Rd. got its name from Thomas Lemon of Lynden who bought 86 acres, including the Smiley land, for a fruit and vegetable farm. Part of the farm later was sold to the Department of Highways for the building of Highway 403.

Aaron Emery came to Aldershot from Appleby where he was favourably known to the Van Norman family, being a staunch member of the Methodist group there. A widower, one of whose daughters became Mrs. Thomas Easterbrook, Aaron fell in love with Jane Van Norman, Isaac's daughter. She taught at Burlington Academy in Hamilton founded by her brother where, incidentally, one of Aaron's daughters was a student. After their marriage, Aaron and Jane purchased land from the Fongers, a part of which is now included in the White Oaks survey. Members of the family, W.A.Emery and his son, Russell, operated the farm and later the highway market. In 1930, Russell Emery became Warden of Wentworth County, an office held in 1908 by his father.

Russell and W.A.Emery participated in an experiment a few years after the Boer War ended. They, along with Walter and John Horne, decided to export apples to South Africa. They were to be sold to W.A.'s brother-in-law Jack Bell who owned a wholesale fruit business there. By the time the ship arrived, all the apples had been stolen.

In 1906, another shipment was sent, this time with Russell and his brother, Victor, along as crew members, to work their way on this expensive journey. The apples were accompanied by a cargo of 200 horses and mules, six passengers and a large shipment of bunker fuel from Dominion Tar and Chemical Co. of Hamilton. To make sure there were no deserters among the crew, there were two Hamilton policemen on watch. With all of this protection, the apples arrived safely. This venture was believed to be the first time Canadian apples had been exported.

Hornes were descended from the George Horne family who came from England in 1873 and settled on Plains Rd. The sons, Walter and John, developed a successful fruit farm. Walter was treasurer of East Plains Church for 42 years and built his home west of the former Busy Bee

Supermarket (first Loblaws, later Bingo Connection). The farm site of the Godwins' "Maplehurst", west of the Hornes', held 6,000 fruit trees. Part of it became the fairways of Burlington Golf Course; the Hornes' farm also contributed some of its acres to make the beautiful course possible.

When the Fuller estate was disposed of, about 1889, part of the farm was purchased by Otto Schoan, a descendant of William Schoan who had settled in the Waterdown area from Germany in 1861. These 20 acres Otto Schoan turned into a successful market garden where he developed the famous Hamilton Market hot pepper. He also specialized in early varieties of tomatoes and was once host to a delegation from New York Agricultural College who were interested in studying his agricultural methods.

The other section of the Fuller farm, including "Oaklands", was purchased by Thomas B. Townsend of Hamilton, an engineer who had helped to rebuild the High Level Bridge. Oaklands was one of the few houses which boasted plumbing. The Townsends did not occupy it at first, and vandals wrought a great deal of havoc before the owners moved in. Thomas Townsend's son was a Waterdown coal dealer who built his home on a hill overlooking Hidden Valley.

The family of Nathanial Scott lived at Oaklands in the original Applegarth home. Lily Scott, who took up market gardening after her husband's death, played an active part in local community affairs. She was one of the first women to attend local political meetings. Her son, R.L. Scott, returning from World War I, set up the Aldershot Distributing Co. and cold storage plant.

The Wyatt family, who founded St. Matthew's Church, came from England in 1845. Herberton House, 164 Townsend Ave. E. was the family home. Initially a lovely dwelling, the house was turned into a duplex and the circular staircase altered. The place was returned to its original elegance by the Scholes family who secured the original floor plan to guide their restoration efforts.

Capt. William Hall came from Burlington in 1878, forsaking the lake ships for a farm near the corner of Filmandale and Plains Rd. The Bell Motel was built on former Hall land.

Job's Lane was named for the family of John S. Job who settled in that vicinity in 1880. John R. Job farmed on land west of Campbell's corners. In 1928, son Walter established a feed mill on Plains Rd., becoming an expert on synthetic growth stimulants. He continued to farm as well. Job's Lane and the farm are now part of the Ikea property.

Campbell's Corners (King Rd and Plains Rd.) is a misnomer. At one time, at that spot, there was a sign, "Campbellville Village Inn", with an arrow pointing east. In time, the sign became broken and only the word "Campbell" was left. Bus drivers would call out, "Campbell's Corners", and the name stuck.

Easterbrook's hot dog stand, established 1930.

The Easterbrook family home, "Inverness" was near the northeast corner (since demolished). Thomas Easterbrook came to Aldershot in 1859 after coming to Canada in 1831 from England. His brother, William, had the toll gate at Campbell's Corners. Thomas was married twice and had two families. Among his descendants are Pearts, Smales, Lambsheads, Jobs and Smiths.

The Easterbrooks had two brickyards and two sawmills. Clay used for making bricks is still available. Another brickyard on the south side of the highway was owned by William Gibbs. His son, Tommy, was a non-conformist. He dressed strangely and lived in a hut on the bay shore. Boys skipped school to visit him and hear his stories. He earned a living by digging drains. It is related that when he started the day's work, he would toss the loaf of bread for his lunch ahead of him. Where it landed would mark the spot where he would cease from his morning's labours.

The western stretches of Aldershot once embraced the Hendrie farm. The old outlet from Cootes Paradise to the Bay was at the foot of the Hendrie property, not at the High Level Bridge. William Hendrie and Daniel C. Flatt were the first to raise Holstein cattle in Wentworth County. From there, the Hendries went on to raise purebred racing horses, among them, Martimas and Lyddite, winner of the first King's Plate in 1901.

Eddie White worked at the Hendrie stables as a boy before the turn of the century. He became their horse trainer and, in the 25 years of his career, gained a reputation as one of the best trainers in North America. He lived on Unsworth Rd. White's efforts were crowned with the achievements of Martimas, born in 1896, whose winnings totalled $52,000. The horse's ultimate achievement was overcoming 40-1 odds to win the Futurity Stakes in 1898. A stone to his memory was placed in the garden of the Hendrie summer residence at 1092 Unsworth Ave. N. but was moved to the Royal

Botanical Gardens. It stands behind the refurbished Hendrie Gates and a monument to the Hendries. The inscription on the stone reads: MARTIMAS, foaled 1896, died 1916. Winner of Futurity and other races. A Good Horse and a sire of good horses".

The Hendrie groundman's home, at 1064 Unsworth Ave. N., was enlarged and became the home of Leslie Laking, former director of the Royal Botanical Gardens. The Hendrie home was moved in two sections from Plains Rd., one half to Patricia Drive at the foot of Gorton Ave. and the other, to the west, on Patricia.

The Hendrie family founded Hendrie Cartage in Hamilton, and a son of William Sr., Sir John S. Hendrie, was mayor of Hamilton and Lieutenant-Governor of Ontario.

ROYAL BOTANICAL GARDENS

In September, 1931, 122 acres of Hendries' Valley Farm were presented by George M. Hendrie to the City of Hamilton as a park in memory of his father, William, and his four brothers. This land was turned over to the Royal Botanical Gardens to become Hendrie Park.

The ornate Hendrie Gates, designed by Fred J. Flatman, were dedicated in 1954, and are an outstanding contribution to the park at the sweeping highway curve.

At first, the gates led nowhere but soon became an important identification for Hendrie Park. A rose garden was established in the park in time for Canada's Centennial celebrations in 1967, and a trial garden became the second feature of Hendrie Park. The Turner Pavilion of 1974 and the Amy Memorial Pagoda two years later, along with forest trails, complemented the park's gardens.

The RBG headquarters began in the Rock Garden Lodge (formerly Bessie's Inn) adjacent to Hendrie Park. The first stage of the new headquarters was officially opened June 15, 1958, by Governor General Vincent Massey. In 1970, a greenhouse was attached.

A link between Hendrie Park and the headquarters building, a passageway under the highway, was constructed in 1964 and included a Fountain Court. A major extension to the headquarters building was completed in 1979 and included a foyer, auditorium, seminar and lecture rooms, a workshop and library. The completed building was opened by Lieutenant Governor Pauline McGibbon.

More was to come - a Mediterranean Greenhouse was added in 1986 and a glass-covered walkway including a new gift shop and restaurant was completed in 1994.

Leslie Laking was appointed horticulturalist of the Royal Botanical Gardens in 1946 and in 1953 he was appointed director. He served for the next 27 years, leading the gardens through a period of extensive develop-

Union Burying Grounds, Plains Road, established by United Empire Loyalist Families.

ment. His wife, Barbara, a trained horticulturalist, was a busy and valuable volunteer, providing a model for future volunteer services.

Halton County, the City of Burlington and the Region of Halton have all contributed financially to the RBG and sent representatives to the RBG Board. Since 1981, the Region of Halton has taken responsibility for this funding. The RBG is an important tourist attraction for the city and one of Canada's finest botanical parklands.

Adjacent to the Gardens is the Bayview Cemetery and Crematorium on Spring Garden Road. At its inception, it was thought the land would be part of Hamilton, so the story goes, and was called Hamilton Mausoleum and Crematory. James Blomfield, a stained glass artist of the early 20th century, produced windows for the headquarters building. When an extension was added in the early 1980s, one of the windows, which was to be covered, was taken to the Joseph Brant Museum. In 1995, a carillon was added on the height above the bay, complementing the deck, which had been established for viewing the beautiful scenery.

When Hamilton consisted of little more than a blacksmith shop and a few buildings, Daniel Freeman Sovereign settled in Aldershot on a crown grant as a United Empire Loyalist, at the time of the War of American Independence. His ancestors had emigrated to America about the middle of the 18th century. The original Sovereign homestead was torn down to make way for the QEW, but a later Sovereign dwelling was the home of Earl Sovereign on Plains Rd. E.

The Peart family came to Canada from England in 1817. A 120 acre farm on Plains Rd. passed through several Peart owners until the QEW was built and Plains Rd. widened. The beautiful family home was demolished for the overpass on Plains Rd. Another Peart, Willie, farmed across Plains Rd. His hobby was fine woodworking and it was he who fashioned the walnut pulpits of East and West Plains Churches. Ross Peart, a great-grandson of pioneer Vickers Peart, grew vegetables on Plains Rd. He was the first to stake up his tomato plants and used electric heat instead of manure.

West of his former home, at 1017 Plains Rd.E., a brick wall was built at the road to contain the Union Burying Grounds, established in 1848. Ten families started the small cemetery on land owned by Asahel Davis. These early settlers were Davis' sons Charles G. and Gilbert Davis, Tom Baxter, Joshua Kerns, Jacob Fisher, George and David Ghent, and Asahel and James Gage. Other well-known families came later: Cummings, Pearts, Fosters and Crosbys.

There are still old Aldershot families whose names should be remembered: Cutters, Hopcotts, Manns, Bowens, Vyses, Haywards and Bullocks.

LEISURE

Aldershot had its share of amusement parks on the bay. The earliest was the Bayview operated by George Midwinter and later by Matthew Ryan. The park, begun in the 1880s, flourished for many years. Situated at Rock Bay where the Carrolls once lived, it was reached from Hamilton by steamer. For many years the *Lillie*, the *Shamrock*, or the *Maggie Mason* made frequent trips each day in the summer with crowds of fun-seekers.

The park, on the embankment more than 90 feet above the bay, was reached by a small incline railway with two cars powered by a steam engine at the top of the bank. The more energetic could walk up one of the two stairways.

The merry-go-round was turned with a hand crank by an ex-sailor named Judd. There was a roller skating rink, and the Bayview Brass Band accompanied the skating and dancing in the days before "canned music". Track and field sports were held and there were swings for young lovers and the small fry.

The Bayview Hotel housed a winter and summer bar, a pool room, restaurant, candy store and ice cream parlour. There were four bedrooms in the large section of the hotel and two summer houses, one overlooking the bay for dining. The great days passed, the incline fell into decay and eventually the Bayview was forgotten. Wabasso Park to the east became the place to go.

The name Bayview is carried on in the name of a park located on King Rd. above Highway 403. Burlington Aldershot Lions Club pledged $25,000 to develop the park, built on a landfill site closed in 1972. In 1981, it was checked for leachade coming from disintegrating garbage.

The land for Wabasso was purchased from the Hamilton Parks Board of Management in 1912 and developed over a period of ten years. A

Waiting for The Macassa *on Wabasso Dock, pre-1920.*
– courtesy Joseph Brant Museum

pavilion was put up in 1918. A bathing house was constructed in 1922, an attractive functional building which later burned down. The remains suffered the ravages of time and were torn down. Several other buildings were constructed, along with a dock, roller coaster, and ferris wheel. Baseball diamonds, picnic facilities and pleasure walks were other attractions. Thousands would attend picnics and outings, arriving by car and boat. Tours and ferry services were offered by Canada Steamship Lines.

Wabasso Park's name was changed in 1923, when the Wentworth Historical Society erected a plaque to commemorate the landing of Sieur de LaSalle, the French explorer. In later years, LaSalle Park, once one of southern Ontario's finest picnic and recreational grounds, ceased to attract. The ferris wheel and roller coaster were taken down and the pavilion stood idle and forlorn. It was closed in 1991 and boarded up. In 1994, the main floor was rebuilt. Damaged by fire shortly after its grand opening in 1995, it was fully restored in 1996.

A First World War cannon was placed in the park to overlook Hamilton Harbour, a perch for children who also enjoyed splashing in the park's large wading pool. The cannon was relocated to the grounds of Dundurn Castle in Hamilton.

Plains Road, running through Aldershot, was once the Hamilton Nelson Toll Road. Toll gates were set up at the Valley Inn, at Unsworth's, at Easterbrook's and on Waterdown Rd. In the early days, when travel was by stage coach or horse drawn vehicle, hotels for weary travellers were

This tollgate once stood about one mile east of Aldershot. It was wrecked in 1902.

spotted at frequent intervals. Over the years, in Aldershot, they were Fenton's Valley Inn; the Bayview; Blain's on the south side of Plains Road near the Roman Catholic cemetery; one by Unsworth Ave.; James Kenney's Aldershot Hotel near the former rectory of East Plains Church (Mrs. Charles Forsyth was a later proprietor in 1898, at the time she drowned in the bay); Shorty Briggs' at the bay by LaSalle Park; the Red Light Hotel at Hall's Corners; and the Roderick Hotel on Waterdown Road near the Aldershot train station.

One of the first businessmen in Aldershot was Robert Sinclair, a custom shoemaker, who settled in 1856 at the southwest corner of LaSalle Park Rd. and Plains Rd., known as Aldershot Corners. Across on the southeast corner was a general store and post office and a blacksmith shop. Coal oil for the lamps used in those days was stored behind in the blacksmith shop. One day, a spark from the forge started a fire that destroyed all the buildings on the corner.

The post office at Aldershot opened in December, 1856 and the first postmaster was Alex Brown. One of the postmasters was listed as J. Roderick and in October, 1898, when George Sinclair, son of Robert, took on the task, it was the beginning of a family tradition. George's son, Bruce, was postmaster until 1956 when he joined the staff of the Burlington post office. When Bruce left, Jean, his sister, took over the work. The post office later moved to Longacres shopping plaza (begun in 1951 west of Campbell's Corners) where, like many postal outlets in the 1990s, it was relocated in a pharmacy, Big V Drug Store (now Shoppers Drug Mart).

About 1913, a new building was put up on the northeast corner as the Aldershot Post Office and general store. It was remodelled into a drug store and eventually occupied by Fred Huffman. In 1960, he sold it to Carl Rudolph who operated a variety store there. It later became Murray's Variety at No. 1 Plains Rd. E. The Royal Bank next door also began in this corner store, using a part of it a few days a week. The bank later built a small frame building, adjacent to the corner store, and the cash was transported back and forth between Hamilton and Aldershot. A new, modern bank on the same site replaced the frame one.

Across the road, a row of modern stores, just east of the southeast corner, was built about 1958 and extended the next year to include a drug store. The southwest corner, known as Joe's Place was a stage coach stop. The renovated building continued to house small businesses until January, 1964, when it burned down. The site became a part of the property of Aldershot Contractors Equipment, a firm founded by Robert A. Henderson. It later became JCB Construction and Materials Handling Equipment.

J. Cooke Concrete Blocks was purchased in the 1980s by Telephone City Gravel but the name remained in the Cooke Business Park, established east of Waterdown Rd., north of Plains Rd. Aldershot Cold Storage was another long-time facility built on Waterdown Rd.

Among Aldershot industries, the name Pollard is a striking example of entrepreneurial skill. In 1948, Norman Pollard, a craftsman from England, began a small manufacturing business in his own home, making storm windows. By 1996, N. Pollard and Sons Ltd., still a family business operated by Reginald Pollard, son of Norman, was turning out many types of windows and patio and entrance doors in a large factory on King Rd., using state-of-the art machinery.

There are no longer any farms in Aldershot and in the southern section land is becoming occupied by homes and high density residences. Harbard Square condominium towers, near Plains Rd. and Francis Rd., were erected in 1974, the name being changed with new ownership to Barkley Towers. In the mid-1980s, on Plains Rd. to the west, a 91 unit Wellington Square Co-operative housing project was opened. Plains Rd. is lined with commercial establishments, including several motels. The bucolic beauty that once was, has given way to the needs of a burgeoning population.

CHURCHES

Some of the Aldershot places of worship date back to the early days. The oldest congregation in the area is East Plains United Church on Plains Rd. E. It is believed services began in a log building. The second church was said to have been on the south side of Plains Rd. The third church was built in 1843 on land donated by Joseph Lyons. This was a frame building with a Sunday school building attached.

In 1858, Aaron Emery organized the Sunday school and was its super-intendent for 26 years. His wife, Jane, felt the school should not be stopped in the summer and, for three years, it was held all year round. In 1892, a brick church was built at a time when there were 77 members. This church was destroyed by fire in 1907. The pulpit, carved by W.E. Peart, and a china communion cup, used by the original congregation, were among the few items saved. The same year, a new church was erected at a cost of $9,967.

In 1956, when a sanctuary and Fellowship Hall were added, the 521 members displayed an example of ecumenical spirit when they accepted the invitation of Holy Rosary Church to use the parish hall for services while the construction was continuing. A Christian Education complex was completed in 1963 at a cost of $200,000. The rectory, just west of the church, no longer used by the minister, was torn down to make way for Downsview Plaza. The Aldershot library branch is in this small strip plaza.

Mr. and Mrs. Henry Wyatt, Anglicans who had settled in Aldershot in 1845, felt the need for a church closer than St. Luke's in Burlington. In 1849, the first gift for their new church came from Lord Bayning in England. The money was invested and bore interest for many years before it was used. Matthew Clark, brother-in-law of Mrs. Wyatt, made two donations which paid for most of the $158. cost of the frame church, completed in September 1861.

The name of the Church of St. Matthew-on-the-Plain may have been used to honour St. Matthew, since the church was dedicated the day after St. Matthew's feast day. On the other hand, the name of the generous donor, Matthew Clark, may have inspired the choice. Seats were placed around the walls until pews were installed years later. It was called Wyatt's Chapel of Ease at first. Until 1915, the church had no foundation, and a pot-bellied stove provided warmth and oil lamps the illumination. During 1915-16, a foundation was added, all labour being voluntary.

With the growth of Aldershot, St. Matthew's was faced with the task of meeting the needs of a larger congregation by the 1940s. Percy Gallagher, a local builder, supervised the men of the congregation who built an addition to the church itself, along with washrooms, furnace, vestry and a parish hall.

In the latest chapter in St. Matthew's story, the historic "white church" was torn down and a modern structure built at a cost of more than $150,000.

A contribution to the building program linked the past with the present. The farm of the Wyatts who donated the land for the first church was sold to John F. Read, a retired sea-captain. His daughter-in-law, Agnes Read, lived next to the church with her son and his wife. The Reads, in 1966, donated the land on which their house stood to make room for the larger church, requesting only that their home be moved to the east and located on land still next to the church.

West Plains United Church dates back to before 1876, when William

Church of St. Matthew– on– the– Plain, early 20th century.

Hendrie donated land for a church. The new one-room building on Plains Rd. W., called the Methodist Episcopal Church, seated 90. In 1883, when there were 25 members, the name was changed to West Plains Methodist and, with church union in 1925, to West Plains United.

The Hendrie estate donated more land and in 1930 the present large brick church was built. It was not, however, until September, 1954, that the church had its own minister. Previously, the same minister served East and West Plains. In December, 1962, sod was turned for the new Christian Education addition which was ready for use the next year. Only part of it is visible from the highway because the structure extends down the bank to the rear, overlooking the Hendrie Trails of the Royal Botanical Gardens.

Another historic Aldershot congregation is that of Holy Rosary. The Gothic style chapel at Holy Sepulchre Cemetery, built in 1889, was once the only Roman Catholic edifice in Aldershot. It was used for burial services and for annual services each November 2. Roman Catholics had to travel to Hamilton to attend services until 1947 when the first regular Masses were held for the 22 families in Aldershot. The year before, nine acres of the Bowen farm had been purchased in the area, and Holy Rosary School was erected on the corner of Gallagher Rd. and Plains Rd. E. The church services were held in the auditorium and Father Bernard W. Harrigan, former principal of Cathedral High School, Hamilton, the first pastor, lived in the old Bowen farmhouse.

In 1955, Holy Rosary Church was built to accommodate 430 people and the new rectory was blessed May 22, 1958. The chapel of Holy

Sepulchre Cemetery was used for services of St. Adalbert Czek Mission since 1975.

One of the relatively newer churches, opened in the spring of 1957, is Aldershot Presbyterian, set back from LaSalle Park Rd. Worship for Presbyterians in Aldershot had begun in May, 1953, when Glenview School was used for Sunday afternoon worship.

Park Avenue Church began in 1948 with cottage prayer meetings. In 1962, the 120 members worshipped for the first time in their new building, erected at a cost of $150,000. It housed a sanctuary seating 470, Sunday School rooms and office facilities, arranged around a central courtyard. It was later sold and became Park Avenue Manor, a nursing home. A new church, Park Bible Church on Kerns Rd. was dedicated January 15, 1989. On the site is Park Academy, an elementary school begun with 60 students in 1975 at the Park Ave. location. By 1996, it was accepting children for junior kindergarten to grade 8.

SCHOOLS

Education has not been neglected in Aldershot. The first school house, the Applegarth School, was built on the site of St. Matthew's cemetery in 1831. A second one was located farther east on property which now belongs to East Plains United Church. In 1868, it was decided to unite these institutions and two years later a one-room school, called the finest in a 40-mile radius of Hamilton, materialized. This school, at the northwest corner of Plains Rd. and Howard Rd., served the farming community for 43 years until 1913. William Stuart was principal for more than 30 years.

In 1912, the area was divided into East Flamborough S.S. No.1 Maplehurst and No.2 Fairfield. In September, 1912, the new Maplehurst School opened but three months later it burned down and classes had to be held in the basement of East Plains United Church. By spring 1913, Maplehurst was opened again, and that fall, the newly constructed Fairfield School in West Aldershot received its first students. The "twin" schools each contained four rooms, two unfinished, each school costing $25,000.

In 1923, the second two rooms were completed and utilized. The school population did not increase too rapidly and by 1935 there were only 135 pupils at Fairfield.

In 1945, a four-room addition was built on Fairfield School for $50,000, twice the cost of the original school. The addition was only partially finished inside and was not completed until 1948, at a further cost of $20,000.

At Maplehurst, also, a four-room addition was built in 1945. In 1958, four more rooms were added and another five in 1966. As building spread eastward, another school was necessary, this time Glenview on Townsend

Holy Rosary School.

Ave. behind St. Matthew's Church. By 1951, the new school was opened. Marble partitions, necessitated by a steel shortage at the time of construction, graced some of the washrooms.

Aldershot's first kindergarten teacher was Mrs.J. Horsley who came to Glenview in 1951. Students from Maplehurst attended kindergarten at Glenview until classes were begun at their own school.

In September, 1953, an eight-room addition to Glenview was ready for use and in 1955 the nine-room King's Road School on Greenwood Dr. (then Sand Rd.) was erected. After amalgamation of Aldershot with the Town of Burlington, Glenview witnessed another four-room addition in 1958 and, in the same year, King's Road had eight rooms added. Public school demand in Aldershot was met for the time being with the building of the six-room Woodview Public School on Flatt Rd. off Waterdown Rd. in 1962. In 1980, Woodview Mental Health Centre took over the building, moving there the following year. As well as a day treatment program for children aged six to nine, there is a residence in an addition on the rear.

William Stuart was principal of the old school at Plains and Howard Roads for over 30 years. Miss Freda Leathorn taught at Fairfield from 1926 until 1959. Miss Isobel McInnis, well known in musical circles, retired in 1962 after teaching for 40 years at Maplehurst. Under her guidance Maplehurst students excelled in choral work.

Prior to 1961, Aldershot students had attended Waterdown High School. In September, 1961, Aldershot High School, built on Fairwood Place W., was ready to receive 413 students in grades 9, 10, and 11. The two senior grades continued at Waterdown until the agreement with the Waterdown District High School Board was terminated.

Donald Thomas was the first principal of the school which held its first commencement in November, 1963, for the grade 12 graduates.

By 1964, the first grade 13 students were graduated and the school was becoming crowded. The following year, a 260-pupil addition was completed with commercial areas and shops. Aldershot High had become a composite school.

"May the search for truth be our guide", is the school motto. Communication with Aldershot, England, produced a copy of that town's crest. Its lion and crown were used in the high school crest with the addition of a maple leaf for a Canadian touch.

The school was the winner of the F.H. Gildea Memorial Trophy at the Hamilton and District Science Fair in 1965-66, after coming second the year before. In Southern Ontario Secondary School Association sports, Aldershot has won at golf, girls' track and field, girls' gymnastics and boys' senior basketball.

Community activities in Aldershot have been legion over the years. In 1919, the Aldershot Lawn Bowling Club was formed. The club flourished and teams competed in many tournaments. In 1931, quarters were built on Shadeland Ave. on land made available by George D. Filman. Eventually the site was no longer used for curling and became a residential development.

A garden club was formed in 1924, and a horticultural society in 1927. The Aldershot Women's Institute was organized March 21, 1930. The women did war work in World War II and supported many causes. In 1961, with the disappearance of the rural community, the Institute disbanded. Some of the members continued to hold meetings to finish the Tweedsmuir history of Aldershot they had begun. The finished volume is at Burlington Central Library.

A community council was formed in April, 1951, with Robert Pinhay the first president. It was in this same year that water mains were laid, hooking up to the Burlington water supply at Indian Point.

Several boys' ball teams were sponsored and a library established at St. Matthew's Church. The Teens Canteen was held at Fairfield School and a learn-to-swim program at Hidden Valley in the summer. The council's charter was taken over by the Aldershot Property Owners' Association after amalgamation.

Kiwanis and Lions Clubs were formed in 1959. Shortly after its inception, the Kiwanis Club bought a piece of swamp land on Townsend Ave. and developed it as Kiwanis Park. In September, 1960, town council approved construction of a new outdoor hockey rink at the park. In 1969, a roof was installed by the town over this open air arena. Both Kiwanis and

Lions Clubs gave large donations to the building fund of the Joseph Brant Memorial Hospital.

The Aldershot Senior Citizens Club was formed in 1962, with Joe Walmsley the first president and Roy Freckleton honourary president.

This, then, is Aldershot: large dairy and fruit farms giving way to market gardens; the smaller holdings in turn becoming residential subdivisions; a commercial strip developing along Plains Rd. and larger industries farther to the north. Since amalgamation with the town in 1958, the area has been linked more and more with Burlington, and, as services such as sewers and street lighting were added, the feeling of being a part of the city became even stronger. Yet it will be many years before the name Aldershot is forgotten and its residents cease identifying it as a place apart.

20
The Three Rs

The early pioneers could give little thought to formal education during the years when they were struggling to make a place for themselves in the untamed country. In families where the sons did seek education in order to enter a profession, they often had to travel long distances to find schools.

A biographical sketch of the David Springer family notes that before 1810 "the facilities for education were limited, there being no school nearer than Toronto or Fort Erie". Another man, Robert Miller, who was to become reeve of Nelson Township in later years, lived in Zimmerman as a young boy. His biography in the Halton County Atlas states, "Schools were not as free or as accessible then (about 1828) as now (1877) and he obtained his education in the Town of Dundas."

A history of Dundas mentions that in 1828 Manuel Overfield and James Durand of Dundas, Caleb Hopkins of Hannahsville and Abraham Nelles of Grimsby advertised in the *Gore Gazette* of Ancaster for a teacher of high school subjects. They subsequently hired Hugh McMahon, an excellent mathematician who also taught languages, and boys came from miles around to attend the high school which was set up in Mr. Overfield's home.

Another area high school located in Hamilton was called the Gore District School and one of its pupils was Reeve Robert Kerr Chisholm of Oakville who was born in Nelson Township in 1819 and attended early classes in the common (public) school at Nelson.

The difficulties of obtaining even an elementary education are recorded in the story of another Halton County man, John Warren of Esquesing who was seven years old in 1832. "His advantages for an education in the early part of his life were limited. For four years after coming to this country from Scotland, he was obliged to receive his education at home until, in 1836, a school was commenced in a little log house that had been used as a carpenter's shop, but had been cleared out for the purpose."

"A teacher was employed, a Mr. Charles Duncan from Nova Scotia, for three months of teaching in the winter for which each pupil was obliged to pay $1.50. He 'boarded round' with the parents of the youths who attended school. Young John attended this gentleman's school for five or six quarters during the winter months and in vacation tried his best to improve his mind by reading what books and literature it was possible to find. He served a good apprenticeship in learning how to swing the axe and the grain cradle and how to drive oxen. Those lessons were by necessity the rule, while school education was the exception."

An account of travels across Upper Canada in 1836 mentions the sad lack of interest in education: "Some schoolhouses built by the wayside were shut up for want of schoolmasters; and who that could earn a subsistence in any other way would be a schoolmaster in the wilds of Upper Canada? Ill fed, ill clothed, ill paid or not paid at all ... boarded at the houses of different farms in turn; some men, mostly Scottish or American, did teach, but were totally unfit for the office they had undertaken. There were no female teachers, except in the towns."

The formal education of girls outside the home was largely ignored in the early days, but United Empire Loyalist Isaac Van Norman was vitally interested in the education of all of his children. It was his son who "established a school for the education of young ladies, known in former years as the Burlington Academy. He subsequently went to New York where he carried on a ladies' school known as the Van Norman Institute."

School attendance was not compulsory and many children started classes when it became convenient for the family, or they attended only in the winter months when their help was not needed on the farm. It is written of one Nelson Township man born in 1849 that "owing to the death of his mother when he was but eight years of age, his education was very indifferently attended to until he was 16, when he entered the County Grammar School." Even though his education began when most boys of today are almost finished high school, this man persevered through university and later became a doctor in Toronto.

Another example of early education in this area is quoted from the Halton County Atlas of 1877: "Around 1840, one boy was sent to classes at an early age but because of the inefficient state of the common school, little or no progress was made. One day his father asked him how many rods there were in an acre of land and the boy couldn't answer. The father said, 'If this is all you have learned in seven years at school, I will teach you how to work on the farm instead'. The boy then commenced the pursuit of knowledge under difficulties by driving the team all day with one hand, with his book in the other hand."

"He was then a student in earnest and gave up all his boyhood sports and amusement for that of intense and close application to his books. During one year of self-teaching, he made greater progress than the seven years at school. One day he was resting under a shade tree after working in the hot corn fields. His father came along and said, 'Is this the way you work? I think you might as well go to school as you are no good on the farm'."

This boy was Clarkson Freeman, who was graduated as a medical doctor in 1853 and practised for a while in Lowville, later moving to Milton.

As the scattered communities that make up the city complex of

Burlington grew and prospered, more schools were built, but unfortunately reports of their activities were not preserved. There are records which show that an early school in the Aldershot area was called the Applegarth School, built by one of the early families in 1831. This was located on the site of what is now St. Matthew's Anglican Church cemetery on Plains Rd.

If settlers wanted schools, they had to build and maintain them and find a suitable teacher by themselves, since there were no taxes levied for educational purposes. Notes, taken at a meeting of ratepayers in 1835, report a discussion on the school situation in lower Nelson Township. There were no public schools in the Port Nelson/Wellington Square district at all, so the ratepayers decided to build one. Peter Fisher, a successful self-educated man himself, was appointed secretary to help draw up plans and raise the necessary funds. He offered one acre on the corner of his Guelph Line farm for the schoolgrounds and made up a subscription list. When the whole amount of 17 pounds had been raised, a log school was built in 1835 at the corner of Guelph Line and the Middle Rd. (Queen Elizabeth Way). Children from miles around walked to classes at Fishers Corners School.

Paul Fisher, whose father attended classes in the log school, said that the desks were placed along the walls on each side of the room with a stool for each child. Girls attended classes with the boys, but the teacher segregated them. Boys sat on one side facing the wall; the girls faced the opposite wall. When classes were being taught, each grade in its turn, the children stood at the front of the room while the teacher lectured.

In those days, Port Nelson was a busy and prosperous port and some crews from the lake boats spent the winters here. Since the men were mostly uneducated, they often enroled in Fishers Corners School to learn the "three 'r's" and also to pass the long winter days. When spring came and the navigation season opened, they were gone again.

By 1872, when taxes were being levied to pay for education and the area was divided into school sections, a brick school with arched windows was built at the same spot. This one was formally named S.S. No.4 Nelson Grove Academy because a bush had been left around it, but people still called it Fishers Corners School for many years. From an account in *The Burlington Gazette*, March 19, 1924: "About 4 o'clock on Tuesday afternoon, fire completely destroyed the school house at Fishers Corners...Owing to the illness of the teacher there was no school on Tuesday, and some of the pupils lost their books, etc. The trustees will take steps to replace the building at once." Insurance covered a portion of the cost.

A third and larger school was erected on the same site in 1925. The new pressed-brick edifice, still with one classroom (but with "north light"), had a "fine basement under the whole building". It served the Guelph Line area until the Q.E.W. overpass was built. A large oak tree on the site was the sole reminder of the schoolgrounds which existed there for more than a century.

S.S. #4, Nelson, Fishers Corners, about 1900.   *– courtesy Joseph Brant Museum*

Nearby Glenwood Public School replaced the old one in 1946.

During the years of activity at Fishers Corners, schools were being built in other parts of the township too. Smith's *Canadian Gazetteer* of 1846 lists 195 common schools in Gore District. Nelson Township had 15, East Flamborough had 7 and neighbouring Trafalgar had 18 schools. The village of Wellington Square had 400 inhabitants in 1846 but the *Gazetteer* lists no common school here at that time.

There is evidence, however, that a school did exist. The Ontario Archives have documents found in 1959 in a boarded-up cupboard at the home of R.A. Carlton at 3461 Lakeshore Rd. The papers had apparently been placed there not later than 1876, possibly by Hiram Smith, great-grandfather of Mrs. Carlton, Mrs. John Richardson and Mrs. Wm. Wright of Burlington. Mr. Smith was the first postmaster of Wellington Square in 1836, a partner in business with Andrew Chisholm, and later a school trustee.

One of the oldest papers is an account to cover the cost of tuition, pens and ink from September 28, 1842 to January 1, 1843, at the common school. There is a bill for repairs to the Wellington Square schoolhouse seats and many mysterious bills for "window glass and putty."

There is a petition for a school dated 1844, from the leading citizens of the village. The Honourable Dominic Daly, Provincial Secretary for Canada West, in reply to Rev. Thomas Greene, rector of St. Luke's Church, regretted that funds would not permit granting the request, since the amount disposable for the Gore District had already been allotted to the hiring of an assistant for the Palermo grammar school.

In the mid 1840s, Hiram Smith moved into his new farmhouse just east of Wellington Square. It is known that four children in his family were in school by 1850, since there was a bill for teaching "Misses Helen, Catherine, Isabell and Master Smith" from Miss Agnes McIlwrath, plus two shillings for ink, slate and pencils totalling one pound, 15 shillings.

In 1851, Hiram Smith was elected trustee at the annual meeting of the householders and ratepayers of School Section No. 2, Nelson Township, an office he held for many years. At the same meeting Richard Unsworth, Junior, pedagogue, was re-appointed schoolmaster "on the same terms as last year", proof that there were at least two teachers in this neighbourhood. Unsworth was paid one dollar per pupil plus part of the government grant. It was his duty to collect tuition fees in cash or in firewood, if money was scarce.

A year later, No.2 Nelson had a new teacher who signed the register, "Richard Trotter, Instructor." He graded each child's "Scholarship - Mental and Moral" as "Middling, Tolerably Good or Good." There were 47 scholars on the roll by 1853 and Mr. Unsworth had returned as a "duly qualified teacher holding a first class certificate."

With new qualifications, his salary was set at five pounds and two shillings or about $22 per quarter. A motion at the school board meeting in 1854 was carried, requiring that "each scholar shall pay the sum of two shillings and six pence per quarter for the ensuing year, balance to be made up by Government money and assessment on property in said section."

During the next few years, there was a succession of teachers at S.S. No.2 Nelson, some only staying for the six months of their contract, including Elizabeth Ryan, Harriet Bowes, Eliza Wilkins and Marion Brown. When Emily Hatton was hired in 1861, there were 61 children on the roll between the ages of 5 and 16, but the average roll call was 40 pupils with an attendance of 20, especially during harvest time.

Visits by the local superintendent were the only form of school inspection until 1871 and Rev. Thomas Greene was the township inspector around 1840. A brilliant graduate of Trinity College, he coached many district young men for entrance to University. The next inspector, appointed in 1861, was the Rev. Alexander McLean, pastor of Knox Presbyterian Church.

Hiram Smith's documents enable historians to reconstruct the early days of S.S. No.2 Nelson (the likely predecessor of Lakeshore Public School) from its misty beginning up to the end of 1862.

In 1871, Robert Little, principal of the Acton public school, became the first qualified inspector for Halton County, in accordance with a new statute of the Ontario Legislature. His report to Halton County council in 1875 showed there were 59 schoolhouses and he concluded that "Halton will compare favourably with any county in the Dominion." The total number of pupils enroled was 6,163 of whom there were 5,722 attending school; the number of teachers was 80.

A bylaw was passed by Nelson Township in 1871 saying that whenever the increased population of any school section warranted the employment of two teachers during the entire year, the money was to come from the Dog (tax) Fund, if the fund had enough in it. That same year Inspector Little reported that in three county schools two teachers were needed, the number of children attending these schools being 194, 124 and 206!

There are no records about the beginning of S.S. No.1 Nelson, but it is likely that it preceded, by a few years, the one on the lakeshore. It was a small frame building that housed the village school at Wellington Square and it stood at the corner of Brant and Caroline streets. Later used a residence, it was moved from Brant St. to 296 Appleby Line, and became a pleasant, well-tended home.

The needs of the village eventually outgrew the small school at Brant and Caroline and it was decided to build a larger one. On December 17, 1859, a Mr. Triller donated to the trustees of School Section No. 1, Nelson Township, one acre of land, the same property on which Burlington Central Public School now stands. A two-storey brick building was erected which served the community for 52 years.

In 1860, it was legislated that the expenses of common schools be met by direct taxation. The first standardized textbooks appeared and the term "public" came into use, displacing the name "common schools".

When Wellington Square became the incorporated village of Burlington in 1873, responsibility for maintaining its schools no longer lay with Nelson Township. Trustees were elected each year for a two-year term on a rotating basis. In 1897 O.T. Springer, H.S. Hurd and Ed. Weber were elected to the board and were joined by L. Lowe, P. Haney and J. Allen in 1898. That year, the board requested $2,500 from council for school expenses, and this was granted in quarterly payments of $600 or more.

In 1897, R.H. Watson, Alice G. Riach, Millie Allen and Barbara Lowe taught at Central and Frances Misener and Ora Taylor at East Burlington (Lakeshore School). There was a total of 417 students in both schools and the teachers' salaries ranged form $225 to $525. The rest of Nelson Township had 13 schools and 14 teachers.

The first Burlington Central Public School served until 1912. It was heated by wood-burning stoves, and sanitary facilities were primitive, to say the least. Principal Dan Smith was respected by all, and a teacher popular with the younger children was Mrs. Lomas.

Plans for secondary education were made in 1906 when the population of the town was 1,230. High tuition charges and travelling expenses to Hamilton meant that many Burlington students were quitting school after the eighth grade.

Elgin Harris was chairman of the school board, and Rev. James Kendall, F.W. Galloway, George Blair, J.J. Fields and William Tuck were trustees.

The old Central School, built 1860. *– courtesy Joseph Brant Museum*

Inspector F.H. Deacon addressed the board explaining that grants totalling $400 would be available if the village set up its own high school or continuation classes.

Debentures for $2,000 were issued to add two classrooms to the existing Central Public School. After a great deal of arguing with council, the money was made available, George Blair drew up plans for the building and the contract was let to Henry Garnham.

Needing two teachers, a principal and assistant, the board advertised and received more than 40 applications for the positions. D. Hicks of Port Dover, a University of Toronto graduate, became principal. Miss Garnet Freeman, daughter of Smith Freeman of Burlington, and a supply teacher at Central, was hired to teach languages.

That fall, thirty-four pupils were enrolled at the high school. The classes were divided into Form One and Form Two, now grades 9 and 10. In November six students decided that Mr. Hicks and Miss Freeman were pushing the work too heavily and dropped out of school. Mr. Hicks stayed only until the Christmas holidays when he departed, apparently due to a salary dispute.

By 1911, Central School building was almost bursting at the seams with both elementary and secondary students; on November 24 the school board petitioned council for a new building. A bylaw was approved to provide for the erection of a new school at a cost of $33,000.

Burlington Central High School, built 1922.

Trustees for 1912 were chairman E.H. Cleaver, W.C. Kerns, W.E. Tuck, W.R. Watson, B.A. Stephenson, J.T. Tuck and H.J. Blair.

The new building had eight classrooms, four on each floor with extra space in the basement. Materials were supplied locally. Burlington was very proud of its modern new school "an education institution unique, as it takes pupils from kindergarten to matriculation".

During the years of World War I, most town projects were postponed, so in April, 1918, Reeve Hughes Cleaver said at town council: "We do hereby express our approval of the formation of a High School District to be composed of the entire town of Burlington and all that part of the Township of Nelson known as the Old Survey, the building not to be constructed until the conclusion of the War".

The members of the school board ran into much opposition in 1919 when they decided they wanted a high school for Burlington alone, so they formed a high school board headed by Charles Potter and including Rev. D.Anderson, T.H.L. Bamford, Dr. R.J. Husband, W.J. Stinson and Mrs. W. Symington. Council was asked for $60,000 to buy a site and build a high school. A bylaw was passed in September, 1920, for this amount. The next day the board agreed to purchase from J.C. and M.C. Smith 4 1/2 acres just west of the public school grounds for $8,000.

Town council was asked to pay for the Smith site, but by then the 1921 council was in office and it refused the money. The school board then sought a ruling from the courts and the judge gave his verdict that once consent had been given by council, the next year's council could not rescind it. The board got the site it wanted and the Smiths got their money.

In January, 1922, council recommended "that the High School board proceed with the work of building a new high school as early as possible, to help relieve the unemployment situation which exists in the town of Burlington." The board found it needed a further $22,000 to complete and equip the building. Council turned thumbs down, but after lengthy and heated discussion, agreed to issue debentures - not for the exact amount asked but for $21,995!

From 1921 until the fall of 1922, when Central High School opened with D.A. Welsh as principal, classes were held in the Queen's Hotel, the public library and the Oddfellows Hall on Brant St. When the continuation classes were withdrawn, John A. Lockhart was engaged as principal of Central Public School and he continued for 26 years in this position until 1947, later serving as Mayor of Burlington. The number of high school students rose steadily from 72 in 1920 to 220 in 1925. By then, two classrooms in the public school were being used to take some of the overflow. In February 1927, the board applied to council for $31,000 to enlarge the high school. The matter was submitted to the electors and defeated. It was defeated a second time a few months later and at this stage there were 273 students enroled, with extra classes being held in the War Veterans' Hall, the library and the town hall on Elizabeth St.

Town opinion was split on the question because there were extra rooms in Central Public School and some contended these should be used, as well as rented rooms downtown, rather than spend taxpayers' money on new facilities. James MacFarlane Bates was appointed principal of Central High School in 1928 and in a short time he was engaged in a publicity campaign which led to the approval of an addition in 1929. Before long, Mr. Bates had engendered school spirit with a sports program, cadet corps, school colours and other extra-curricular activities.

The sum of $77,000, allotted to the enlarged school, was spent on an auditorium, a gym, seven classrooms, an office, teachers' room, two lunch rooms and cloakrooms. The students took several years of fundraising drives and concerts to provide the auditorium with furniture and a stage curtain. Further additions and alterations were made over the years, and in 1947, Burlington-Nelson District High School Area was formed, making the school the property of the township instead of the town.

By then, there were 400 high school students and a staff of 17 teachers under Mr.Bates. M.M. Robinson was chairman of the high school board. Some of the respected teachers of Burlington Central High were Miss Eva Newham (later Mrs. Paul Fisher), Miss Annie Haight, Miss Emma Eby (who retired in 1959) and Miss Edith Green. W.J.B. Kay was one of the institution's most successful and beloved staff members.

Fairfield Public School, formerly S.S. #2, East Flamborough.

Principal Bates, who retired in 1963, served with the RCAF during World War II and W.J.B. Kay was acting principal in his absence.

Norman R.Craig was an informed and highly effective chairman who contributed much to the advancement of education here, as did E. Holtby, for many years the secretary of the high school board.

Other schools were being built in nearby communities which were to become part of Burlington many years later. A school in the Aldershot settlement was erected in 1870. It stood on Plains Rd. opposite the present Zellers store. When Maplehurst School was opened in September, 1912, and Fairfield School in 1913, the old schoolhouse was sold. It served several commercial purposes before it was torn down.

Another school was S.S. No.14 located at the head of Maple Ave. Sometimes called the Plains School or "Miss Pattinson's School" it was erected by George Blair "who installed the blackboards, built the fence around the yard and dug the well, all for $2050." Miss Helen Pattinson taught there for 40 years. Located near the overpass on Plains Rd., this school shared the fate of Fishers Corners and Appleby Schools. When highway construction needed the property, it was demolished.

Two more schools, built in the 1800s were S.S. No.5 at Nelson Corners and S.S. No.7 at Tansley. Miss Beatrice Bunton taught at both schools between 1918 and 1939.

In the northern section the population was widely scattered. By 1877, there were, not one or two, but eleven schools dotted across Nelson Township from Fishers Corners and Appleby Schools in the south, to Limestone School and Bell's School near the northern boundary.

Burlington City Hall, 1997   *– courtesy City of Burlington*

Replica of Joseph Brant's house, now Joseph Brant Museum   - courtesy Joseph Brant Museum

The Colour Guard, Burlington Teen Tour Band   – courtesy City of Burlington

Waterfront Trail - Spencer Smith Park   *– courtesy City of Burlington*

Farmers' market   *– courtesy City of Burlington*

Royal Canadian Naval Association Monument, Spencer Smith Park   *– courtesy R.C.N.A.*

Memorial window, Knox Presbyterian Church – decorated for 150th anniversary of the church in 1995 – Tom White, photographer

Canada Centre for Inland Waters with Skyway Bridge in background   *– courtesy C.C.I.W.*

The twinned Skyway Bridge.   *– courtesy City of Burlington*

The Springer House (built about 1835), 2373 Dundas Street, Burlington.

Burlington Central Library, New Street, opened 1970.

Hendrie Gates, Royal Botanical Gardens.

Clowns at fundraiser, "Great Burlington Ride to Beat Cancer" 1984   – courtesy of Leo Podetz

Fire, May 19, 1995, at partially renovated LaSalle Park Pavilion
– courtesy LaSalle Park Pavilion Restoration Committee

Brant Street at Lakeshore Road, 1990s   *– courtesy City of Burlington*

School Section No.12 was the Limestone School, first a log cabin, and then a frame building which burned in 1933. The replacement school,when no longer in use, became a private residence at 3179 No.10 Sideroad.

About 1830, Absolom Bell emigrated from Scotland to Canada and located on a tract of forest land, the haunt of wolves and bears, three miles from Milton. Looking ahead to the future, he donated land for a school and the site was cleared of timber by Mr. Bell and his four sisters who later married the Messrs. Dixon, Cline, Cummings and Page. Some of the first pioneer settlers who arrived shortly after Absolom Bell were George Hume, William Cartwright, Mike Corrigan, Abram Bell, John Shields, James and Henry McMaster, John Turnbull, John Garbutt and William Nervel.

By 1958, the days of Bell's School were numbered although it was decided to continue lessons there until a new building was provided. The new Kilbride School, erected in 1960, drew students not only from Kilbride, but also from the rural districts of Mt. Nemo, Cedar Springs, Limestone, Bell's, Zimmerman and Lowville. Some of these schools had already been closed, such as the Lowville School, which is still a familiar stone building just inside Lowville park, used now by the Parks and Recreation Department during day camp sessions and for craft classes.

The new Kilbride School was officially opened on November 7, 1960, with the two-storey stone school erected in 1879, standing in one corner of its grounds.

A.S. Nicholson was chairman of the Burlington school board in 1918 when a new school was proposed for east Burlington to take the place of the old school on Water St. (likely the old S.S. No.2 of Hiram Smith's time) to help relieve congestion at Central. Council agreed to place the issue before the voters.

Electors went to the polls on July 22, 1918, and registered their disapproval of the expenditure when a war was being fought.

Armistice was declared on November 11, and on December 31, the voters were again asked to decide the question. The clerk didn't record the results of the ballot but, in 1919, council endorsed the school board's decision to tear down the old building on Water St. (Lakeshore Rd.) and erect the East End School west of the Guelph Line. The brick school had four rooms and by 1945 four more rooms had been built at the rear.

Following amalgamation in 1958, when the school area was no longer East Burlington, the Board of Education had the name changed to Lakeshore Public School.

Just prior to the outbreak of World War I, a red brick schoolhouse was finished on Walkers Line in School Section No 15. It contained one classroom and a teacher's room on the ground floor, with playrooms and utility areas in the basement. Strathcona School, built on part of Lawrie Smith's 200 acre farm, had a registration of 29 pupils in 1914. Prior to 1914, children living on the Lakeshore Rd. or near Walkers Line had attended either the Wellington Square village or Appleby schools. After 1911, J.T. Tuck represented the locality on the Burlington school board and when Burlington was incorporated as a town in 1914, this outside area faced the necessity of forming a new school section.

Two acres of land were purchased from W.L. Smith on Walkers Line and Section No. 15 was formed in the centre of the area. The first board of trustees were Messrs. W.D. Flatt, J.T. Tuck and Colin Smith. It was decided to name the school after Lord Strathcona because, a few years previously, when the neighbourhood was trying to raise money to build a hall for public meetings, Lord Strathcona was approached for a donation and gave so generously that the building was named Strathcona Hall. Later Mr. Smith called his property Strathcona Orchards, so the name seemed appropriate for the new school as well.

The original school formed the central part of the eventual structure which had the south wing added in 1948 and the north wing in 1955. With the development of new surveys, enrolment increased rapidly. In a half century there were three principals: Miss Mary A. Bate, Mr. George Green and Miss Edith L. Donkin, whose retirement in 1964 coincided with the school's 50th anniversary celebrations.

The first Home and School Association in the area was formed at Strathcona. In co-operation with the teaching staff, this group sponsored many activities in which pupils distinguished themselves. There was also an active Home and School Association at Fishers Corners and in other schools as well. In Burlington the Home and School Association was established in Central High School before one was formed in the public school; Mrs. Frank Galloway was the first president. The teen canteen was started in 1944. The foundation for the Home and School Council in Burlington had this dedicated beginning.

Industrial expansion was comparatively recent in Burlington at this time. Many people remembered when the emphasis was on agriculture and recalled fondly the annual school fairs of their youth. In large tents, children from the various schools displayed items they had made in manual training and domestic science classes. Since many of them lived on farms, there were also colourful displays of fruits and vegetables they had cultivated, and grave adjudication centred on the merits of their calves and chickens. The fair's weeks of preparation took place mostly in the fall when the apples, grapes and pears were ripe.

A team of horses would pull a wagon turned into a float decorated with sheaves of corn and pumpkins - and filled with as many children as it would hold.

The district agricultural representative at Milton supervised the fairs in different areas of the county and in this township there were several locations for fairgrounds. Burlington's fairgrounds were located first on Brant St. near the present Legion Hall, and later on Plains Rd. (Queen Elizabeth Way) east of Brant Street. Fairs were held on Highway 5, just west of the stop light at Guelph Line, and trotting races were held in the open pastures which were rented for the day from local farmers.

Economic problems of the depression years hit Halton County as hard as any other place. In January, 1933, at a conference of the Burlington Public School Board with teachers of the East End and Central Schools, the teachers agreed to accept a cut in their salaries. "Teachers receiving $2,000 and more were cut 10 per cent, those receiving $1,000 and more, seven and a half per cent and those under $1,000, five per cent".

During the war years, it was necessary to shorten the school terms at the high school. Boys from the farms had to work on the land and in orchards, in place of their older brothers and farm hands who had gone to war.

The memorial board at Central High has 343 names of former students who served their country in the military. Strathcona's's honour roll bears the names of 91 former pupils (both men and women) who served in the war from that area.

The prediction made that growing Burlington would be building one new public school a year for an unstated period was proved correct. Glenview School, in Aldershot, was built on Townsend Ave. in 1951. In the New St. and Roseland area, the Lawrie Smith School was constructed in 1952 and named after one of the community's most illustrious settlers.

John A. Lockhart, former principal of Central Public School and a mayor of Burlington, had a school named for him in 1953. The school served pupils from Burlington Beach as well as neighbouring blocks around Maple Ave.

As the northern section of Nelson Township continued to grow in population, one-room schools were gradually absorbed into Kilbride School, and Fairview School was erected in 1954 on No.5 Sideroad near Guelph Line.

Meanwhile Aldershot needed more classrooms and King's Road School was built in 1955 on Greenwood Drive. In that year, Clarksdale School on Mountainside Dr., was erected in a fast-growing subdivision north of the Queen Elizabeth Way. As Mountain Gardens built up between the Guelph Line and upper Brant St., Mountain Gardens School was erected in 1959; farther along Mountainside Dr, and to the north, Rolling Meadows School in 1960.

Burlington's core area continued to expand, and Wellington Square School was built in 1956 on Yorkshire Crescent. To the east along the lakeshore, Shore Acres survey needed a school to take the pressure off Strathcona, and one was built on Tuck Dr., just off Spruce Ave., and named after W.E. Breckon, for many years a Nelson township school board member.

When the township was annexed in 1958, children in the new subdivision of Elizabeth Gardens were provided with school facilities with the construction of Elizabeth Gardens School in 1959. It was the largest new school up to that time, with 16 classrooms. Since then, a further 14 classrooms were added.

The school fever spread to Roseland Heights and the Ravenswood district and in 1961, John T. Tuck School was built on Spruce Ave. to serve this area south of New St., honouring the name of another dedicated school trustee.

Woodview Public School was built on Flatt Rd. in 1962 with six classrooms, to further serve Aldershot students. The population explosion also continued in East Burlington where Pineland School was built in 1963. Extra rooms at Pineland, added the following year, made the new senior public school system possible, and Grade 7 and 8 students from neighbouring W.E. Breckon and Elizabeth Gardens were transferred there.

The first building for senior students only, Tecumseh Senior Public School, was built on Woodward Ave. in 1964. The latest in school design, triangular classrooms, was planned for Frontenac School on Pinedale Ave.

Between 1959 and 1966, Burlington Board of Education planned and built approximately 430 classrooms and other areas, costing about $5,925,000. Superintendent of public schools, Douglas S. Lawless, was appointed Assistant Director of Education in 1966. O.A. Gilmore was Superintendent of secondary schools. James. W. Singleton served as Director of Education until 1975 when Emerson Lavender took over. Walter Beevor succeeded Mr. Lavender in 1983. Robert Williams was Director from 1988 to 1996.

The elementary school system provided for central libraries, the unit and rotary systems, a program of Oral French for senior public students, Opportunity and Enrichment classes divided into schools across town. In 1966 there were Enrichment classes in grades 5 and 6 at Glenwood School and in grades 7 and 8 at Tecumseh. A hard-of-hearing class was at Lakeshore School.

Since 1967, the following schools were opened: Champlain, Mohawk Gardens and Pauline Johnson in 1967, General Brock High School (1968), Ryerson (1969), Lord Elgin High School and Tom Thomson (1970), Dr. Charles H. Best (1972), Paul A. Fisher (1974), Lester B. Pearson High school (1976), Sir Ernest MacMillan (1978), Bruce T. Lindley (1981), Brant Hills (1986) and C.H. Norton (1991).

As schools were opening, changes in population necessitated the closing of some schools: Woodview and Glenwood (1976), Elizabeth Gardens and Fairview (1984), John A. Lockhart and Wellington Square (1985), and Lawrie Smith and Strathcona (1987).

Until 1958, education in the Town of Burlington was under the jurisdiction of six school boards. Elementary school direction was vested in three boards: Burlington, Townships of Nelson and East Flamborough, and a Separate School Board. At the secondary school level, there were Burlington District High School Board and Waterdown High School Board. The first amalgamated board in 1958 had as its chairman, M.M. Robinson; vice-chairman, Roy Coulter; and trustees Ross Segsworth, Blair Ross, W.A. Nicholson, Phillip Metherell, G.E. Kerwin, A.L. Bailey and Mrs. Ellen Dawes. Bruce Lindley was business administrator.

The Board of Education for 1966 under chairman R.L. McLean, consisted of trustees from each of the town's eight wards, plus an appointee from the Separate School Board and one representing Halton County. Heading the administrative staff at the Board of Education building at 2050 Guelph Line was J.W. Singleton, Director of Education.

In 1957, Nelson High School on New St. opened its doors to 350 general and commercial students in grades 9, 10 and 11. With amalgamation imminent, and the township due to disappear, the name Nelson was retained for the new school, honouring at the same time Admiral Horatio Nelson.

Additions were made in the school in 1959 and again in 1964, making it a fully composite high school with academic, commercial and technical courses. By the end of the 1965-66 school year, the 69 teachers and 1,370 pupils had established a fine record of scholastic achievement. The school has won numerous honours and the staff and student body are proud of their top award winners in district and national science fairs and in athletics, their drama festivals and the senior concert band. Instrumental music as a curriculum subject began at Nelson. Because of the enthusiasm created, it was adopted at Central, and at Aldershot and M.M. Robinson Schools when they were built.

First principal of Nelson High School was O.A. Gilmore. Miss Edna Robinson was principal from 1963 to June, 1966 when she became an inspector of schools with the Ontario Department of Education. Miss Robinson, daughter of M.M. Robinson, was the first woman to head an Ontario composite high school.

Aldershot High School opened in September, 1961. The first principal was Donald W. Thomas, who became principal of M.M. Robinson High School on Upper Middle Rd. which was opened in September, 1963, with an initial enrolment of 1,092 and 54 teachers. The high school was named after Mr. Robinson in tribute to his long service in the cause of education.

Emerson Lavender was appointed principal of Burlington Central High School in 1963. An addition to the school in the 1960s was almost as large as the original building. Revolutionary changes in education altered the course of Central High from a single purpose school to a three-branch institution.

SEPARATE SCHOOLS

Roman Catholics in Burlington had no separate schools until 1948 when a four-room school was erected on Brant Street. A parcel of land, four and one-fifth acres, was purchased from William Bell and on May 7, 1947, a

Notre Dame Roman Catholic Secondary School.

meeting of freeholders and householders of St. John's Roman Catholic Church was held. Elected as the first board of trustees were Rev. J.C. Warren, chairman, John Marck, Austin Fitzpatrick, John Ryan, Ford Cosgriffe, Fred Keller, Wesley Coombes, Joseph Rigby and Maurice Hastings.

The sisters of St. Joseph provided the board with its first principal as they continued to do for each of the succeeding separate schools. They also supplied a teacher for Grade 1 pupils if one were available. In 1965, Kindergarten facilities were introduced to all separate schools in Burlington. When St. John's first opened, 75 per cent of the enrolment was in Grade 3 and younger, a forerunner of future growth patterns.

In 1951, Holy Rosary School on Plains Rd. at Gallagher Rd. was formed. The Rev. B.W. Harrigan, pastor of the newly-formed parish, directed the new board whose trustees included Robert Reed, Jack Pinnington and Vernon Granby. The school's first pupils were provided classroom space at St. Matthew's Anglican Church until Holy Rosary was opened with 94 pupils and three staff members. More rooms had to be provided for both St.John's and Holy Rosary schools by 1953, and a fourth expansion of five rooms in St. John's made it a 13-room school in 1955, and even larger with a 1960 expansion. (This school was razed, and in 1995 a new 16-room school was opened on the same site). A third school board was formed in Nelson Township in 1955, and trustees Elmer Fernandez, Jeff Kurtz and Ed Evans planned to build a new school but in the meantime leased space at St. John's.

A fourth board followed in 1959 to look after requirements east of the Guelph Line. Trustees John Visser, Ernest Hennessey and Doug Carrigan directed building of the six-room St. Raphael's School on New St. near

Trinity Christian School.

Walker's Line. St. Raphael's with 250 pupils and six teachers was opened in September, 1958. At the same time a three-room addition was built at Holy Rosary. With Burlington's northern section growing rapidly, another school, St. Gabriel's, was completed in 1959 on Parkway Dr. in the Rolling Meadows subdivision. It opened with eight rooms, 150 children and five teachers.

The individual boards disappeared in 1957, coinciding with annexation proceedings and were replaced by a new board. Since the town had eight wards in 1966 and the Separate School Act called for two trustees per ward, there were 16 school trustees sitting as members of the Burlington Separate School Board.

Additions were constructed at St. Raphael's and Holy Rosary in 1962. St. Joseph's on Drury Lane was the next separate school erected with its eight rooms initially holding 200 pupils. Carpeting of the rooms was an innovation.

Ascension School was completed on New St. near Appleby Line in 1965 with eight carpeted rooms and 270 pupils. The seventh school in the system, begun in 1965, was St. Francis Xavier on Francis Rd. A number of schools had additions and renovations over the years since 1965, including Ascension, Ecole St. Phillipe and St. Gabriel's. St. Joseph's School became the administrative building for the Halton Roman Catholic School Board. St. Francis Xavier School became bilingual in 1969 and was renamed St.Paul's, and in 1975, Ecole St. Phillipe also became bilingual.

New separate elementary schools built since 1967 include St. Patrick's (1970), Canadian Martyrs (1975), St. Mark's (1979), and St. Timothy's (1989). The first Burlington separate secondary schools were Assumption on Woodward Ave. (1980), and Notre Dame on Headon Forest Dr. (1989).

Other educational institutions were established. Three private Christian schools were opened: Park Academy (1975), and John Calvin and Trinity, both begun in the early 1960s. Pine School, an independent, non-profit school, was established in 1984 to help children who learn differently re-enter the school system. Several Montessori schools were opened for children up to age five or up to grade six. Developmentally delayed children attended their own school, Mayfield, which operated under the control of the Burlington Association for the Mentally Retarded (now the Burlington Association for Intellectually Handicapped). With changes in the Education Act, all children were integrated into mainstream classrooms.

A number of significant changes in education took place during the 1970s, '80s and '90s: integration of handicapped children into regular school classes, instructional assistants, French language instruction in elementary schools, French immersion programs, Junior Kindergarten, admittance of adults to daytime classes, the establishment of an adult high school (Lockhart) for those age 21 and over, increase in the use of school buses, increase in numbers of students bringing lunches to school, the introduction of cooperative training programs, the introduction of OAC levels, instruction on environmental issues and sex, heritage language programs and the intro-duction of "Rae Days" (school staff took unpaid days off to maintain salary levels and avoid layoffs).

None of these changes, though, had the same impact that the use of computers (introduced into Halton schools in the early 1980s) engendered. It was felt that despite the enormous cost of buying, servicing and upgrading enough computers for all schools, it was important to enable Burlington students to meet the challenges of the technological age.

As the end of the century approached, the local boards of education were faced with the loss of more provincial funding, meaning school closings, staff reductions, and the loss of some special programs. Enormous tax increases or drastic cuts faced the school trustees in an era of retrenchment.

21
The Garden of Canada: Agriculture

Upper Canada was still sparsely settled when the early immigrants began organizing agricultural societies, the earliest being in the Niagara district in 1793. Only a few were in existence before 1830. Halton Agricultural Society came into being in 1853, as did the four township societies of Nelson, Esquesing, Trafalgar and Nassagaweya. First officers of the Halton Society were Thomas Douglas, William Barker, D.R. Springer and Samuel Black.

The highlight of all agricultural society activities was the fall fair, and in the early days it was often the settler's only social contact with the outside world. Halton County Atlas of 1877 reported, "The Annual Fall Show attracts an immense crowd and is one of the great events of farm life. The Society also holds a show every spring for the exhibition of stallions of which Halton has some splendid specimens." Farmers exhibited their best livestock, grain and poultry, and their wives brought their finest butter, homemade bread, eggs, dressed poultry and preserves. Local stores and industries displayed merchandise, and tailors and shoemakers exhibited their best work in the handicraft sections.

Of Nelson Township in 1877, the Atlas says, "The soil of the township is generally good, the larger portion of the timber being hardwood. Considerable pine timber was found in the township, but has almost disappeared since the lumbermen commenced their operations. The land is rolling and in some parts very hilly or mountainous; spurs of the Burlington Heights running through its western and northerly parts. The Twelve Mile Creek flows through it, on which are several grist and lumber mills and factories.

"The township has an agricultural society which is well-supported by the farmers, and its exhibitions, particularly of stock and grain, are very fine". This description agrees with an earlier report in Smith's Canadian Gazetteer of 1846: "The Gore District consists of the Counties of Wentworth and Halton and contains some of the richest, best settled and most highly cultivated townships in Canada West."

Of Nelson Township it said, "In Nelson, 43,433 acres are taken up; 18,354 of which are under cultivation. This is an old and settled township containing good land, excellent farms and fine flourishing orchards."

Many farmers belonged to the Burlington and Nelson Agricultural Society which held its Fall Fair in a field on Brant St. south of Freeman. In the 1920s, much larger grounds, which boasted a splendid racetrack, were purchased on the Middle Road at Freeman.

Fruit being loaded at Freeman Station.   *– courtesy Dave Davidson*

A bright red apple is featured on Burlington's crest which is prominently displayed on the facade of the Civic Administration Building. The heraldic apple symbolizes the area's fruit growing industry in general, although apples have brought prosperity to Burlington since United Empire Loyalist days. The Ghent and Davis families, who were among the first settlers, paddled canoes across the Bay from Saltfleet Township in 1805, bearing with them young apple trees they had raised there from seed brought from the Carolinas. Pictures taken in 1902 show these same trees, gnarled with age.

One of the prominent fruit growers at the turn of the century was O.T. Springer, whose orchards and fine Gothic-style home were at the site of the present Brant St. shopping plaza. Where the house had stood, Bell's Cold Storage erected an apple warehouse which remained there for many years prior to the building of the plaza. Bell's orchard extended back to the Emerald Crescent area until the 1950s when the trees were gradually replaced by new houses.

Market gardens became established here and there from Aldershot to the fertile acres along Maple Ave. where many of the mailboxes read "Thorpe", a family originally from Aldershot.

Years ago, land on Maple Ave. could hardly be given away because of its sandy soil. Benjamin Eager bought it from the Brant estate and after cutting down the timber, offered the entire length of the road for $200 to one farmer who turned it down. He was in the grain-growing business and considered the sandy soil useless. It wasn't long, however, before farmers realized the value of the soil for various vegetable crops and the land on Maple Ave., in some cases, continued to support their succeeding generations.

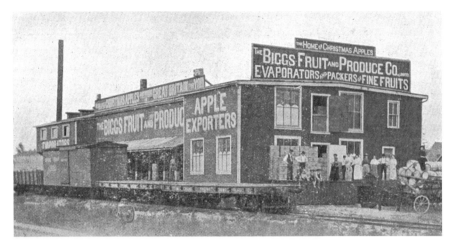

Biggs Fruit and Produce Company Limited.

According to "The Garden of Canada" printed in 1902, "most of the section was improved at an early date, but less than 25 years ago the lands along Maple Avenue were a wilderness of brush and pine stumps. These have now disappeared and are replaced with luxuriant orchards, hedges, lawns and beautiful homes, which testify to the remarkable suitability of the soil which is excellent, of great variety and well-drained."

The farms were eventually sold for future development and some leased back on a year-to-year basis. Much of the land on Maple Ave. became idle in the summer because construction of the Hager-Rambo Creek diversion project was expected. Rosart Properties, owner of property on the north end of Maple Ave., had rye planted to create a park-like appearance and keep down weeds. In November, 1975, a group of Maple Ave. farm families, the Lindleys, Pearts, Banks and Davidsons auctioned implements and equipment. Their farms had been sold several years before.

Local farmers were members of the Ontario Fruit and Vegetable Growers Association, including M.M. Robinson, Maple Ave., who was active in that association as well as on the Ontario Food Council. He served as vice-chairman of the Ontario Food Terminal. After serving in World War I, he bought a farm on Maple Ave. in 1920. Co-founder of the Hamilton Olympic Club, he managed the Canadian Olympic Track and Field Team in 1928 and the British Empire Games Track Team from 1932 to 1938. He was the founder of these games. For 25 years he worked at the Hamilton Spectator, serving as Sports Editor and City Editor. After his death in 1974, at the age of 86, he was inducted into the Sports Hall of Fame. In 1984, he was named to the Ontario Agricultural Hall of Fame for leadership in marketing fruits and vegetables, thus becoming the only person honoured by two Halls of Fame! A Burlington High School is named for M.M. Robinson.

Aldershot Greenhouses, Gallagher Road.

It is evident that local farming techniques and marketing have more than kept up with modern times. Colin and W.L. Smith won their share of prizes for apples at Toronto's Royal Winter Fair. W.E. Breckon counted among his many awards, that of World Wheat King for a sample of his white winter wheat.

The Burlington Horticultural Society was organized in March, 1889, by the fruit growers of Burlington and district. Officers in 1902 included George.E .Fisher, W.A. Emory, A.W. Peart, J.S. Freeman, W.F.W. Fisher, O.T. Springer, George N. Peer, W.V. Hopkins, Arthur Peer and Joseph Lindley. Local growers were also organized as the Burlington Fruit Growers Association. A 1902 publication proclaimed: "Unaided and alone, the Burlington fruit growers were pioneers in exporting perishable fruits in cold storage and continue their weekly shipments with gratifying results". He also reported, "The same morning they are picked, Burlington fruits are placed on the breakfast tables of Toronto hotels still wet with dew."

Leaf lettuce and green onion harvest.   *– courtesy Joseph Brant Museum*

George Fisher began shipping fruit overseas about 1897, and A.W. Peart's home, "The Maples", became the Burlington Experimental Station in 1896 under joint control of the Ontario Agricultural College and the Ontario Fruit Growers Association. The fruit growers sought to increase their practical and scientific knowledge of all aspects of the fruit industry and to determine the varieties of fruit best adapted to the area's soil and climate.

Each director of the Horticultural Society had supervision over a particular fruit and through the efforts of the society the fruit acreage of Burlington and district was doubled. Experimentation with more than 250 varieties of crops resulted in the hardiest samples of fruits and vegetables being produced.

For ten years, from 1892 to 1902, the Burlington Horticultural Society won first prize at the Industrial Exhibition at Toronto for the best collection of fruits. Other honours were garnered at the Chicago World's Fair in 1896, the Paris and Glasgow Expositions in 1900, and the Pan-American in Buffalo in 1901. It was no accident that the Burlington area became known as "The Garden of Canada".

Farmers at the turn of the century lacked mechanized vehicles but they still got their produce regularly to Hamilton market. They had to be there by five or six a.m. to get a stand, meaning that Nelson Township farmers had to leave home by three a.m. for the two-and-a-half-hour trip to Hamilton by horse and cart.

Until the 1920s, all local produce was marketed in Hamilton or through brokerage firms in various cities. In 1921, under the banner of "More profit to the grower... no increase to consumer", 30 growers in the area joined with others in the Niagara district to form a co-operative. In 1966, the Burlington District Fruit and Vegetable Growers Association was headed by Peter Lindley; its main function was to help growers work out problems of shipping and pricing.

The Burlington Horticultural Society in March, 1919, was re-organized under the leadership of Rev. G.W. Tebbs, with the object of beautifying the town and assisting citizens in procuring and planting shrubs, trees and flowers. At the first meeting, it was proposed to adopt the rose as Burlington's official flower and make the town famous for fine roses. This tradition is still carried on with the society's annual rose show and competition.

In 1920, town property along the lakefront from Nelson Ave. to Burlington Ave. was drained, graded, cleaned up and designated a park. Benches were donated by the Women's Institute, and members of the Horticultural society and property owners living opposite the park offered to keep the grass cut.

In 1924, Gore Park was created, and the following year, Brant Park, opposite the Brant Inn, adjacent to the C.N.R. tracks, was taken over. (Both these parks and Hydro Park at Brant St. and Elgin have disappeared with

Hand milking, a lost art.
— courtesy Joseph Brant Museum

redevelopment.) The Boy Scouts, nearly every Saturday morning, worked hard in doing their part to improve the town's appearance.

Spencer Smith was president of the Burlington Horticultural Society in 1933 when members cleaned up the shoreline below Lakeside Park. In April, 1942, the site was re-named Spencer Park. This valuable stretch of lakeshore was extensively reno-vated as Burlington's 1967 Canadian Centennial project, and called more formally, Spencer Smith Park.

In 1979, the society celebrated its diamond anniversary by planting two black walnut trees in Spencer Smith Park in memory of A.J. Bridgman, a former director of the Ontario Horticultural Association and past president of the Burlington society. In the fall of 1978, 7,000 daffodil bulbs, a gift from the Lincolnshire Bulb Growers of England, were planted in the lawn of Central Library. The next spring they were a spectacular sight.

The Horticultural Society maintained flower beds in Hydro Park, planted trees on many of the streets and was responsible for many years for the upkeep of all the town's parks.

Flower shows, held regularly in Burlington for many years before the war intervened, were revived between 1950 and 1953. The Garden Club of Burlington was organized in 1953 and, over the years, branches were started across the community.

Burlington has always had shady, tree-lined streets. To prepare for the city's first celebration of Arbour Day in the spring of 1975, an honour roll of trees was drawn up by the Tree Advisory sub-committee of council. (Two Burlington trees, a 67-foot maple on Unsworth Ave. and a 117-foot cotton-wood on Brant St. North were among 64 trees on the Ontario Forestry Association honour roll of Ontario trees.) Residents of Burlington were able to nominate city trees for great size or age, rare or unusual specimens or trees of historical significance. The project was sponsored by the Burlington Horticultural Society, supported by the city's Dept. of Recreation Services and the Royal Botanical Gardens. The final product, Dr.Peter Rice's books, a two-volume honour roll of trees, was presented to Central Library by the Horticultural Society in April, 1983.

The area of Burlington north of Highway 5 always was considered the prime agricultural district, largely for mixed farming, and although some of the finest fruit orchards were still found between Highway 5 and the Queen Elizabeth Way in 1966, housing developments were taking over acres of fruit trees. At that time, orchards of Chris Fothergill on Burloak, Arthur Kemp's Strathcona Orchards, as well as Fisher's Farms and Orchards on the

Marketing of the 1990s.

Guelph Line since the 1830s, and Waldale Orchards, with headquarters north of the Q.E.W. on Brant St., were all still in operation.

In the spring of 1966, the Chamber of Commerce encouraged a scenic tour of the town so that tourists and Sunday drivers might appreciate the beauty and richness of Burlington's agricultural districts.

Although few of the old farms remained in 1967, their founders were not forgotten. In October of that year, Nelson Township pioneers were honoured by the placement of a 12 ton commemorative boulder on the Board of Education property on the Guelph Line, a project sponsored by the Burlington Historical Society. To mark Canada's Centennial, Century Farms which had been operated by one family for at least 100 years were designated by plaques.

In 1996, Burlington agriculture had many specialties from the Leaver Mushroom Co. Ltd. to large greenhouse businesses. In 1882, George Leaver emigrated to Canada at the age of 19 from Henley-on-Thames, England. He became a successful grocer in Toronto. His son, Lloyd, an Ontario Agricultural College graduate, persuaded his father to buy 48 acres of land east of Burlington. This became a vegetable and fruit farm, Leaverleigh. For fertilizer, Lloyd picked up horse manure from a Mimico stable where he saw the owner growing mushrooms as a hobby. He and his father began to experiment with mushrooms and by 1929 the first profitable crop was produced. Eventually the market gardening, orchard fruits and turkey raising gave way to mushrooms. Land on the Guelph Line in north Burlington was purchased in 1956-57 and a large operation was carried on there for many years. The company is no longer owned by the Leaver family having been purchased first by Canada Malting and, in 1995, by Con-Agra, a large American food company. By this time, Leaver, based in Campbellville, was the largest mushroom company in Canada with five farms, two of them in Campbellville.

In 1995, Halton Region was the sixth largest producer of greenhouse flowers in Ontario. At one time there were several greenhouse operations in Burlington. In 1952, Cornelis (Casey) Van Staalduinen built greenhouses on Walkers Line and he and his wife Patricia built up an impressive business. When Fairview St. was extended, all 22 greenhouses were consolidated on the south side of Fairview. Their specialty was bedding plants which they supplied to city parks in Hamilton and Toronto and to the Royal Botanical Gardens. In 1988, they sold the property and for two years the business was continued in rented greenhouses at Unsworth and Son. A year after the death of his wife, Mr. Van Staalduinen retired but continued sowing seeds for Unsworth. Part of the Unsworth property has been developed as a residential subdivision but in 1996 there were still a number of greenhouses on Plains Rd.

In 1943, Jack Cockshutt began building greenhouses on New Street until he had 19 of them. His son, Stewart, who worked with him, bought the business in 1969. Stewart had horses and a barn behind his greenhouses. When the property was sold in 1992, he bought a farm in Rockwood to raise race horses. The greenhouse site has been developed as Roseland Green, a residential area.

Aldershot Greenhouses on Gallagher Road in Aldershot was begun by Arie Van der Lugt in 1954. From one small greenhouse, the operation which was taken over by his son Len included, by 1996, six acres of pot mums and roses under glass.

In 1936, Alistair and Marjorie Graham, from a gardening family on the Isle of Wight in England, purchased land on Lakeshore Rd. where there were a couple of old greenhouses. They began Roseland Greenhouses and, at the height of their business, had 12. In 1996, there were two greenhouses remaining and the business was a retail florist shop operated by the next generation, John and Judy Graham.

Bray Greenhouses was established on Lakeshore Rd. at Pine Cove Rd. In 1921, Alfred Bray bought seven acres of land in what was Port Nelson and erected his first greenhouse in 1934. Jack and Lynn Bray celebrated the 50th anniversary of the business in the spring of 1984. By 1996, the business was gone and private homes were on the site of the greenhouses.

In Aldershot, Unsworth greenhouses are being gradually replaced by an upscale housing development. (*See Aldershot chapter*)

Flowers were shipped to florists across Canada; tomatoes have been one of the most profitable crops, together with melons and all types of berries and fruits. Production reached its peak between 1920 and 1940. A bacterial wilt eventually tolled the death of melon growing. Farm statistics of 1991 show there were, in Burlington, despite residential and industrial encroachment, 112 farms encompassing 10,530 acres. Chickens and eggs, sheep (the first flock was begun by Thompsons on Walkers Line in 1914), hogs, cattle, horses and ponies were still raised. In the 1960s there were approximately 17 dairy farms in Burlington. By 1995 there were only two left, owned by Murray Harris, Appleby Line, and Keith Middlebrook, Walkers Line.

Potato and chicken farmers chose Burlington as home for their provincial head offices. The Ontario Potato Growers' Marketing Board moved to the city in 1976. Its staff is responsible for the interests of the province's 300 potato growers and their 60 million dollar industry.* Chicken Farmers of Ontario, in Burlington since 1965, is the organization representing Ontario's 1100 farmers who produce chicken meat, a 403 million dollar industry.*

A 1977 report revealed only one-half of one percent of Canada's land was classified as Class I farmland and that Halton's prime farmland was subject to the most intense urban pressure in Canada.

In April, 1974, a 50% Land Speculation Tax Act had been introduced which slowed development somewhat. It was later lowered to 20%. Selling land in the south Burlington area for housing, however, was still more profitable than farming. In 1996, a Capital Gains Tax is somewhat of a deterrent to land speculation.

A parkway belt to define the agricultural boundary was established in 1975 but, by 1996, only two portions remained: a strip running south of #1 Side Road at Guelph Line, slanting down to Brant St. and another west of Cedar Springs Rd. north of Highway 5 running down to the city boundary to the west.

Zoning of the rural area has changed over the years. The New Official Plan approved by the city council in June, 1994, laid out a rural area stretching roughly north of Highway 5 and Highway 403 to the city limits at Derry Road. Provision was made for three settlement areas, Kilbride, Mount Nemo and Lowville. Land use policies for the remainder of the area were devised to ensure strong protection for the natural environment and agriculture.

*(statistics as of 1997)

22
Industry and Manufacturing

Wellington Square was never noted as an industrial centre. Twelve Mile Creek had provided the first power for mills in the outlying areas but the Square itself was not so favoured in the early days. The only industry at first was in the arms of the settlers.

The same James Gage, who bought the 338 1/2 acres of Wellington Square from Joseph Brant's estate, built a saw mill, shingle factory, lath and stave mills in Wellington Square as well as flour and feed mills in Nelson Township. Gage continued to live on his farm in Stoney Creek and the businesses were managed by his sons. As the enterprises grew, he employed more and more men to whom he sold land to build houses. He was also able to sell them construction materials and flour.

Gage sold his Wellington Square holdings to Torrance and Co. from Montreal. On Mr. Torrance's death, Thomas Baxter sold his business in Lowville and came to Wellington Square to manage the estate.

Gradually a business community evolved and with it a few industries catering to, first, the grain and lumber trade and later, farming. In 1846, according to Smith's *Canadian Gazetteer*, there was a tannery here, a pottery, two wagon makers, a foundry and a steam grist mill.

Along with the Gage-Torrance enterprises, other business came to the Square. On either side of Gage's wharf appeared Bunton's and Baxter's wharves. Jonathan Galloway and Co. had its grain warehouse at the southwest corner of Brant and Water Streets, overhanging the bank of the lake, and Jonathan's son, Frederick, later was a partner in the firm of "Galloway and Baxter" grain brokers, across the street at the northeast corner of Water and Brant.

The 1877 Halton atlas bemoaned the lack of industry, "the manufacturing interest is but little represented which is to be regretted as the locality is especially well suited for this line of trade, the shipping facilities both by land and water being exceptionally good." The railway had given some impetus to industry when the Great Western came to town in 1854.

James Allen started a carriage factory in 1855 which, in 1877, turned out vehicles described as "hard to surpass in excellence of finish and durability". The company was later sold to Tuck and Webber.

Another of the early manufacturing interests was the "wire works" of Crooker Bros. and Co. This was purported to be, in 1877, "the only one of the kind on the continent of America and possibly of the globe, the wire turned out of this establishment being under a patent of which Messrs. Crooker are themselves the inventors." This was a process whereby after the wire was made, it was dipped to galvanize it for beauty and durability. The company went on to manufacture fancy "turned" baskets from the wire.

An early newspaper referred to a baby carriage factory whose product was much in demand in 1890.

W.J. Douglass ran a saw mill and planing mill toward the later part of the 1800s and Benjamin Eager had his lumber interests and mill. William Bunton had a brick shop at the foot of Brant Street. He owned a block of land from St. Luke's Church to Locust and from Water St. to about where Caroline St. is now, where he had other business interests. Any other industries at this time were far outside the limits of Wellington Square in the smaller centres along Twelve Mile Creek.

Toward the end of the 19th century, a few industries were established, mostly allied with farming and dependent on the railway for transportation. Flour mills and canning factories were needed by the local farmers to process the products of the field and orchard. In some cases these industries were built and managed by the farmers themselves.

The Burlington Box, Barrel and Basket Works was established in 1893 at Freeman by W.T. Glover, a fruit grower. All kinds of fruit containers were made including the imperial crate invented by Mr. Glover. By 1902, this was so much in demand that it was impossible to keep up with the orders. The raw material, the logs, were shipped in by rail and a 1902 publication claimed, "It is incomprehensible the quantity of timber used every season...elm and basswood mostly."

By 1908, the firm became known as the W.T. Glover Manufacturing Co. Ltd. with a nation-wide clientele. The officers in 1917, W.T. Glover, managing director; W.F. Fisher, president; and E.W. Lewis, secretary-treasurer, were described as "gentlemen of experienced methods and untiring energy". The Glover Basket Company became a branch of Oakville Specialities Ltd. owned by S.J. Zacks of Toronto in 1966. On the night of December 20, 1966, fire raged through the basket factory, burning it to the ground.

The Coleman Lumber Company was established by A.B. Coleman who, as a teenager, had been building homes in town. By the time he was 21 in 1886, he was the owner of a planing mill on Ontario St. which he operated there until his business demanded larger premises. In the winter of 1895, he built a large new mill, also on Ontario St. which was destroyed by fire June 21, 1898.

The following February, the Coleman Lumber Company's secretary-treasurer, James Harrison, opened a planing mill and lumber yard on Brant St. at Ontario St., extending back to John Street. By 1902, the planing mill was "fitted throughout with new machinery of the most improved make and is operated by electric power from Niagara Falls." The machinery was run by a first-class machinist, A. Coates.

Mr. Coates learned the business well because, by 1908, we find him proprietor of A. Coates and Son with offices, mill and yards on lower Brant Street. The company was described as "among the largest manufacturers and dealers in Burlington and Halton County." Their business was in builders' supplies but a specialty was fruit boxes of all kinds with "printing matter on the boxes as desired."

The lumber yard of James Harrison was bought by Allan S. Nicholson in 1911. Business mushroomed during World War I and in 1914 a new plant was built further along Ontario St. at Maple Avenue. In the 1920s, O.W. Rhynas Company operated the mill on Ontario Street. The Nicholson Company manufactured windows, doors, millwork and exported overseas. A second move, necessitated by the growth of the business, saw the company moved to a large site on the north side of the Q.E.W., between Walkers Line and Guelph Line. Warren A. Nicholson succeeded his father as president of the company. Al Nicholson and Dave Morton, cousins, took over after Warren and, by 1996, Al Nicholson was president of Nicholson Lumber, a large retail lumber and hardware operation at 4047 Fairview Street. The former property at Ontario and Maple is occupied by apartments.

John Kentner operated another lumber enterprise at the turn of the century. It was at Maria and Brant Streets. His lumber yard, planing mill,(which also turned out fruit containers), and stove wood yard, were all successful. He also ran a cider press "owing to the fact that there were large quantities of fallen apples unfit for foreign shipments from which cider is made for vinegar and other purposes."

On March 13, 1902, a meeting of village council was called by Reeve Kerns to discuss the advisability of encouraging the establishment of a company "either for milling, canning, or any other purpose that will bring trade to the village." In council minutes there was no further mention of a canning factory until the court of revision report in November, 1903, when the "Burlington Canning Co. was assessed the same as last year, $2,000". In 1905, council approved a radial line siding along John St., across Pine and Water Streets, to service P.C. Patriarche's coal yard and the Burlington Canning Co.

The cannery, taken over by Dominion Canners Co. (later Canadian Canners) in 1910, thrived on the same site at the foot of Brant St. until the early 1900s. At that time, the land was sold and the buildings taken down. The parent company amalgamated all its processing into a central plant no longer in Burlington. A branch of Canadian Canners was opened on Walker's Line in 1959, engaging in the manufacture of cans.

In Freeman, off the Middle Rd.(now the Q.E.W.) just west of Brant St. and adjacent to the railway, D.A. Hyslop opened a branch of his canning company in 1923. In 1925, the name was changed from D.A. Hyslop and Sons to Tip Top Canners. The premises, destroyed by fire in November, 1962, was rebuilt on the same site and the following year controlling interest was

Canadian Canners, founded 1903 as Burliongton Canning Company Limited.

purchased by Stuart House International. The company, which Hyslop started with the canning of asparagus, dealt in a wide variety of the area's fruits and vegetables as well as the production of soft drinks.

The coming of industry to town has not been an unmixed blessing. In 1906, council instructed the Reeve and two councillors to call on the president and directors of the cannery regarding smoke nuisance. The company was notified that unless it did something within a week to the satisfaction of the council, to prevent smoke from its chimney "committing a nuisance", council would pass a bylaw dealing with the smoke. It was not until 1953 that such a bylaw, No.1405, was passed, happily with the approval of most of the business interests in town.

One industry which Burlington has erroneously been given credit for fostering is the Burlington Glass Works which operated in Hamilton between 1875 and 1909 on the west side of Burlington Bay just behind the location of the Hamilton Yacht Club. This is another case where the name Burlington has been given to a company probably because of its proximity to the body of water known then as Burlington Bay and not referring to the Town of Burlington.

A 1914 letter on the office stationery of the new town's Publicity Commissioner boasted, "Progressive, Beautiful, Healthy Burlington -Good factory sites at the head of Lake Ontario, cheap electric power, fire protection, railways: Grand Trunk, Canadian Pacific, Canadian Northern, Radial Electric."

By 1917, a business promotion booklet described Burlington as one of the "Live Wire Towns of Halton County." The chief industries existing toward the end of World War I were listed as "lumber, saw and planing mills, canning factory, fruit packages, machine shops, carriages, wages, creamery, fruit growing, fruit evaporation, flour mill and mixed farming."

The 1917 booklet proudly advised "manufacturers or businessmen who are casting about for new localities... there is room for many various lines of industry that have not yet been overtaken." Although there was no town business promotion department at the time, the administration offered, "first class sites, with exemption from taxes" to manufacturers wishing to locate here.

Two chemical companies were established in town after the turn of the century. Max Smith, a fruit broker and later Mayor, founded, in 1909, the Niagara Brand Spray Co. Ltd. At this time, technology was rudimentary and few chemicals outside of sulphur were used in the manufacture of sprays for farm produce. Mr. Smith's products, simple as they were, filled a need in this predominantly farming area, and the business prospered up near Freeman station.

In the early 1930s, Mr. Smith sold his interest and the company operated as Niagara Brand Chemicals, Division of F.M.C. Machinery and Chemicals Ltd. The firm manufactured a diversity of products including weed, insect and fungus killers, paint removers and brush cleaners. It supplied sulphur for the rubber industry and was involved in the consumer package area for home and garden chemicals.

In 1913, a second chemical company, the Vera Chemical Co. built a plant for its four employees at Freeman. Rosin size to supply the requirements of Canadian paper mills was manufactured. In November, 1931, it was purchased by an American company and, in 1939, became Hercules Powder (Canada) Ltd. The plant, now Hercules Canada Inc. produces several major types of products and employed, in 1994, more than 60 employees at 942 Brant St.

At the close of World War I, the town began to seriously consider the need for industry and, in 1919, a new Industrial Reception Committee of town council was initiated. Several new industries did locate here during the decade before the depression years but not enough to affect the town's agricultural and residential nature.

The raw materials in the Iroquois Bar gave the impetus to two companies which started in the 1920s. The first sale of Howard sand and gravel was made in the spring of 1921 to a teamster who had heard that the Aldershot farm of Hiram Howard rested on sand. A load was dug for him from a hole in the middle of a cherry orchard and shovelled onto the man's horse-drawn dump wagon. Young John Howard assisted in the operation and remembers that the man returned for more and more loads along with others who heard of his source. As the Howard farm had not been too successful, the family gradually turned to the sand and gravel business. John Howard guided it from a hand-operated venture to one using small scale machinery. During World War II, a relatively modern gravel and sand crushing and washing plant was built. Later Howard Concrete and Materials Ltd. began to produce ready-mixed concrete with the most modern of equipment. By 1996, the company was Canada Building Materials, a subsidiary of St. Mary's Cement.

Jacob Cooke started in the hardwood flooring business in Burlington in the late 1920s. He began building homes and started making concrete blocks at his 3 New St. home. In 1940, he bought an Aldershot gravel pit and built a small block plant on St. Matthew's Ave. It became J. Cooke Concrete Blocks dealing in builders' supplies, manufactured from the stone of the Iroquois Bar. About 1980, the company, at 101 Masonry Ct., was purchased by TCB (Telephone City Gravel), with its head office in Brantford, materials coming from Aberfoyle, no longer Burlington. In 1996, the former name remains in the Cooke Business Park with a street, Cooke Blvd.

On the northern part of the Guelph Line, Nelson Crushed Stone (Nelson Aggregate Co.) has a large quarry operation.

The Burlington Brick Company once operated north of Freeman and the Dominion Sewer Pipe Co. started in Aldershot in 1928 on the finest red "sewer pipe" clay to be found in Canada. Canada Brick, a company with a 40 year history, moved into a beautiful new building in the mid-1990s on its Highway 5 property. It is a division of Jannock Ltd.

The end of World War II saw a few more companies locate here, such as N. Pollard and Son Ltd., Jones Tool and Machine Co. and Susan Shoes Ltd. which took over a wartime parachute factory. Even so, in January, 1957, within the small boundaries of Burlington, there were only about 14 plants. At the time of amalgamation, industrial growth was at an all-time low, a mere 3.83 per cent of the total assessment. In the process of amalgamation, such thriving industries in Nelson Township as Bonar and Bemis, International Harvester, Hendershot Paper and Butler Manufacturing were brought into the Town of Burlington.

The mayor at that time, John A. Lockhart, established an industrial and development committee and a former mayor of the town, Gordon Blair, was appointed its administrator. Under his guidance, the committee helped to establish the type of environment which would attract industry. Mr. Blair recalled that, in 1958, Burlington had only 58 acres of fully serviced land available for industrial development.

To keep Mr. Blair from "doing business from an empty wagon" the town purchased in 1958 from Studebaker of Canada Ltd. 180 acres on the Guelph Line north of the Q.E.W. for $600,000. This land, Progress Park, lies within easy reach of railways and roads, is 15 minutes from Hamilton Harbour, and 30 minutes from Lester B. Pearson International Airport.

Burlington in the early '50s was developing as a bedroom community for employees of Hamilton business and industry and for the Ford Motor

International Harvester Company of Canada, now Navistar International Corporation of Canada.   *– courtesy of Joseph Brant Museum*

plant in Oakville which was established in 1953. There had been industrial growth in Burlington; in 1958, 46 well-established industries were here. By the late 1960s, however, with Hamilton sites at a premium, Burlington began to develop its own pool of employment opportunity as more and more major industries moved here.

One of the first to move into Burlington following amalgamation was the Fuller Brush Company which moved here from Hamilton. Others followed such as the Steel Company of Canada which opened a research centre on Kerns Rd. in 1967. Other major industries to locate here in the mid 1960s were Midland Ross Corp., Fisher Ludlow, Cuna Insurance Society (which became The Cumis Group), Hoover Company Ltd., Delman Manufacturing Co., and British Motors (Leyland Motors). In March, 1970, Leyland's new building was selected one of the best designed buildings in Hamilton/Burlington in the past four years.

By mid-1962, there were 140 acres of prime, fully serviced industrial land ready in the city's first industrial park, Progress Park. To service additional development, sewer trunks and water mains were completed up Walkers and Appleby Lines as far as the Queen Elizabeth Way (QEW). This opened up a vast area for development on both sides of the QEW totalling approximately 4,000 acres between Guelph Line and Burloak Dr.

By the late 1960s, private companies had begun to assemble land for industry, mostly in the Fairview St./QEW corridor. A second municipal business park, Centennial Business Park, with 117 acres north of Fairview St., was established in 1974 and in ten years was nearly occupied.

The main business corridor stretched in 1995 from the Guelph Line to Burloak Drive, crossing Fairview at the south end then over the main CNR tracks northeast to Upper Middle Road. To the west it ran in pockets from the Guelph Line, following the CNR tracks and Highway 403 to No.6 Highway.

Increased transportation facilities and high Toronto housing costs enticed Toronto commuters here. At the same time, the high cost of doing business in Toronto led many businesses to relocate in Burlington. The result was a mix of housing needs and employment opportunities, which combined to produce healthy growth of the municipality.

Cookie production line at W. & H. Voortman Limited.
– courtesy Voortman Ltd.

In June, 1981, Wallace Barnes Ltd. (now Barnes Group Canada Inc.) of Hamilton built a new facility on Mainway and in late 1981, Strasser Alloy Steels, an alloy scrap metal recycling plant moved here from Oakville.

Political insecurity in Quebec led to the 1978-'79 influx of companies leaving that province and coming to Ontario. Some of the companies relocating in Burlington included Bailey Meter, Advanced Dynamics, Perkins Paper and Boehringer-Ingelheim.

The smell of W & H. Voortman Ltd.'s cookies has wafted on the Burlington breeze since 1956 when the company opened a building on King Rd. Brothers Bill and Harry Voortman, immigrants from Holland had begun baking in the back room of a house in Hamilton. In 1975, after two relocations in Burlington, a large plant was established at Appleby Line and North Service Rd. Voortman won the Business Achievement Award of the Burlington Chamber of Commerce and the Ontario Chamber of Commerce Achievement Award for 1987. Voortman's story is typical of that of many award-winning Burlington industries.

Conversion to metric had begun in 1971 causing great expense to manufacturers. A gradual process, bringing Canada in line with countries world-wide (except for the United States, our largest trading partner) it was hopefully to be completed in 1984.

CitiSite 5000 was a new concept of free-standing industrial condominiums on South Service Rd. at Appleby Line, constructed in 1988 by a team of Burlington architects and engineers. It met the need of small manufacturers for mid-sized buildings.

Burlington has been a favoured site for head offices. The packaging company, Bonar & Bemis (later Bonar Inc.) opened its national head office in 1973 with an addition to its McDowell Rd./Guelph Line facility. In September, 1972, Hoover Canada opened a new plant and head office on an

85 acre site on North Service Rd. By 1995, there were many head offices of manufacturing firms. Some were long-time Burlington industries such as Alchem (Nalco Canada Inc.), Fearmans Fresh Meats, and Westinghouse Canada. Other more recent arrivals included Boehringer Ingelheim (Canada)Ltd., a large pharmaceutical chemicals company; Tamrock Loaders (Eimco Jarvis Clark), trackless underground mining equipment; Hercules Canada, paper makers' chemicals; Degussa Canada Ltd., industrial chemicals and dental products ; Degussa Catalyst Ltd., automotive catalysts; Popsicle Industries, ingredients for frozen novelties; Shaklee Canada Inc., nutritional, household and personal care products; Stanley Tools; Thomson-Gordon Ltd., cellular rubber products, distribution and servicing of air compressors and accessories; Bull Moose Tube Ltd., steel tubing; Dover Industries, folding cartons; Robin Hood Multifoods, bakery mix formulas; Elsag Bailey Inc., industrial instrumentation and process control equipment; and Gentek Building Products Ltd., steel and vinyl siding.

One of the fields the Office of Business Development has been pursuing is the establishment of Burlington as a centre of excellence in knowledge-based and high-technology industries. To the major categories of metal fabricating, electrical and electronic components, chemicals, plastics and food processing was added a growing number of scientific and high technology corporations. By 1995, there were many such industries here. Some of the largest were: Gennum Corporation, Inverpower Controls Ltd., Westinghouse Canada Ltd., Antel Optronics Inc., CRS Robotics Corporation, General Electric Canada Inc., Dynovation Machine Systems Inc., Kingsbury Canada Inc., Siemens-BCL Magnetics, Asea Brown Boveri, Basic Technologies Corporation, Canadian Instrumentation and Research Ltd., Coulter Electronics of Canada Ltd., Elsag Bailey (Canada) Inc., Envirodata Ltd., Mettler-Toledo Inc., Quantum Inspecting and Testing Limited and Zenon Environmental Incorporated. High-tech companies provide employment for Burlington's high proportion of professional and technically-skilled personnel.

One of the high-tech companies, Evertz Microsystems, in the city since 1978, won an Emmy award for its development of equipment and computer software to read special bar codes on movie film to locate and edit film sequences.

The top ten largest employers of 1994-95 were Fearmans Fresh Meats (1,000 employees); Canada Centre for Inland Waters (650); The Cumis Group, financial services (563); Burlington Technologies, tool and die makers (429); Ball Packaging Products, manufacturers of steel and aluminum ends for cans (371); Elsag Bailey, manufacturer of instrumentation and process control equipment, (360); Boehringer Ingelheim (Canada) Ltd.,pharmaceuticals (355); GAN Canada (formerly Huron and Erie Group) insurance (327); and Westinghouse Canada Inc. Information Services Division, electronic

Maple Leaf Pork Company, formerly Fearmans.
– courtesy Maple Leaf Pork Co.

systems for airline communication, (230) (no longer in Burlington as of 1996).

Exports became an important focus of Burlington industries. In 1989, Canada signed a free trade agreement with the United States and three years later Mexico joined in the North American Free Trade Agreement (NAFTA). Increasingly the Pacific Rim markets became an important export target. To recognize and encourage Burlington companies, the Chamber of Commerce established an Export Merit Award.

One of the winners of this award in the mid-1990s was Aer-O-Flo Environmental which came to Burlington in 1985. It won a contract with China to construct municipal and sewage treatment plants in Tiaxin. Inverpower Controls exports 80-90% of design and assembly of high-power conversion systems and precision methods for heavy industry. Maple Leaf Foods, which bought Fearmans Fresh Meats in 1991, by 1995 exported pork to 37 countries in the world. At that time it was the largest food processing company in Canada.

One of many developments affecting manufacturing was the elimination of the 13.5% hidden manufacturers' federal sales tax, levied before marketing costs, which was replaced by a General Sales Tax.

In 1975, Gordon Blair resigned as Director of Business Development. Mary Dillon, his long-time assistant, took over as Manager of Business Development. She was the first woman appointed to head a business development office in Ontario. She retired in 1995.

By the 1990s, it has been very difficult to trace some industries. Old companies have been taken over by larger ones whose names have been adopted, as was the case of Howard Sand and Gravel, noted above. Names have also been changed to reflect more accurately a company's change in operations. Some Burlington companies have disappeared through relocation to other places or the dissolving of the business completely. This makes historical research in this area both a fascination and a challenge.

23
The Development of Business and Commerce

Prospective immigrants were encouraged to settle in Canada West by publications such as Smith's Canadian Gazetteer (1846). It warned, however, that land prices would be "generally rather high" in the Gore District, with "wild land" ranging from $6 to $15 an acre, and cleared farms from $25 to $50 an acre. On the other hand, the new country presented great opportunities for a man willing to take the chance.

The village of Wellington Square, "pleasantly situated on Lake Ontario," appealed to many settlers and, by 1846, the bustling community had its own physician and surgeon, a steam grist mill, a foundry, tannery, two stores, six grocery stores, a druggist, a pottery, four taverns (the principal one being Ontario House), a saddler, tinsmith, baker, two wagon makers, two blacksmiths and four tailors.

There were two churches in the village proper and daily postal service. A schooner was locally owned and large shipments of flour, timothy seed, wheat and butter were exported.

The English touch was evident in the advertisements of that day. The better hotels guaranteed London porters "always on hand", good stabling and covered stages leaving for distant points each morning. Tailors advertised west-of-England cloths, summer coatings and rich vestings.

According to an old diary, deliveries from butchers and bakers started about 1875. Diarist George Thomson, lighthouse keeper and ferryman at the canal, mentioned in 1870 the use of foreign 5 and 10 cent coins and quarters, there being no Canadian coinage and said that in Wellington Square, Walter Bastedo "gives American silver at its face value."

The Halton County Atlas appeared in 1877 with advertisements, one of which was a "Business Card" inserted by Alex Duffes and L.B. Allen. It read "Alex Duffes and Co. Junction of Great Western and Hamilton and North Western Railways, Wellington Square, Ontario. Wholesale and Retail Dealers in Grain, Seeds, Flour and Feed Etc. A choice lot of Groceries, Provisions, Boots and Shoes; also Salt in Bulk and Barrels ... Plaster, both Land and Calcined, Always on Hand. (The highest market price will be paid in cash for Grain, Wool and all kinds of farm produce.) Grain bought and sold on commission."

The business directory had expanded by 1889 when Wellington Square's population was 1,245 and it had become "Burlington, a station on the Toronto branch of the Grand Trunk Railway, at the crossing of the North Western Railway, about 18 miles southeast of Milton, the county seat and ten miles northeast of Hamilton, its nearest banking point."

The Canadian Express and the Great North Western Telegraph Companies were located here. F.R. Davidson was listed as appraiser for the Canada Permanent Loan and Savings Company and the Lion Provident Life and Live Stock Association had a branch office, as did Temperance and General Life Insurance company. F.R. Davies dealt in real estate, W.G. Nelles was postmaster and T.J. Greene and R.A. Pringle were in law practice. E. Thomas was the dentist, Charles Taylor the barber and E. Williamson the undertaker.

Women were also in business, such as Miss T.A. Cotter, music teacher; Miss M. Delongh and Mrs. Sarah Oakley, dressmakers; Miss H.L. Dunning, millinery; and Mrs. E. Virginia, a coloured lady whose late husband had been a barber. She had a confectionery store in the village.

Many prominent businessmen were Masons in Burlington Lodge No. 165 which was founded in 1864. They met first in a frame building at the corner of Brant and Pine, 367 Brant St. which once housed Dales Hardware. Charter officers were Francis Baker, James L. Gage, Chris Richardson, Fred Bray and Gilbert C. Bastedo. The lodge was unique in having had as one of its Worshipful Masters in the early days, W.J. Simcoe Kerr, grandson of Joseph Brant. Other meeting places were above Kerns' store at Water and John Streets, and most recently at 459 Brant Street. Brant Lodge was established in the 1960s, followed by Wellington Square Lodge. Two chapters of The Order of the Eastern Star were also founded.

Burlington's centre of business activity remained on the waterfront at the foot of Brant Street even after the dawning of the railway age. In 1810, James Gage purchased 338 1/2 acres from Joseph Brant's estate and built a wharf, warehouse, mills and factories at the foot of Brant Street. During the same period, Bunton's Wharf and Baxter's Wharf were located in the same area between Locust and Elizabeth Streets. Port Nelson, with its wharf at the foot of the Guelph Line, was an important grain shipping point.

Horses were stabled in the barns of the hotels or tied to hitching posts along the streets. A few of these posts survived until the late 1940s. Rings often were fastened in convenient trees as well.

In 1902, Charles F. Coleman doubled as a house and sign painter, paper hanger and as a successful florist, specializing in violets, roses, mums and carnations. Thomas Hood was manager and caterer at the Brant Hotel; James Harrison owned a planing mill on Brant Street and lived where the Riviera Motel now stands on Lakeshore Road; E.H. Cleaver, Solicitor of Supreme Court, Notary Public and Commissioner, dwelt in a turreted brick residence on Caroline Street facing Pearl Street.

George Allen, born in Wellington Square in 1843, was a hardware

John Waldie & Company, Water Street (Lakeshore Road) at John Street. — *courtesy Joseph Brant Museum*

dealer; John Ferguson sold coal and lumber; Byron S. Hicks was the jeweller and optician; William Brush was manager of the Queen's Hotel and F.B. Bennett managed the Traders' Bank of Canada on Brant Street near Water Street.

The building at the northeast corner of John St. and Lakeshore Rd. is one of the town's oldest commercial structures. Built by John Waldie, first Reeve of Burlington, well over a century ago, the store handled everything from groceries to dry goods and hardware. Waldie employed 14 clerks and on Saturday nights when the farmers came to town, the store and plank sidewalk outside thronged with shoppers. William E. Kerns was John Waldie's partner for 20 years before buying out the business when Waldie became a lumberman.

Later owners were Hicks and Bamford and Templins. In recent years the store served variously as a Brewer's Retail outlet and an automobile showroom. The building was extensively renovated in 1966 with three retail outlets on John Street being opened up.

The second floor was used as a dressmaking establishment, run by "Min" Johnson. At the rear was a hall with a stairway leading up from John Street. The Masons assembled there for many years, as did the World War Veterans Organization before they had a Legion Hall. The Burlington Citizens' Band held practices in the place on Wednesday nights.

A feature of this old building was a windlass, 13 feet in diameter, held together with square-headed nails, which was used to operate a hoist by which grain was hauled up. Gun racks found in the top floor gave rise to the romantic rumour that the building served as a fort. It may have housed militiamen during the Fenian Raids, or the 20th Halton Rifles (Burlington Company) may have gathered there, William Kerns having been Lieutenant-Colonel of the Rifles from 1888 to 1898.

Water St., east of Brant St., had several business establishments,

Max Smith and David Dick tour Brant Street near Water Street, 1906.

including the first two post offices. Clifton's tailor shop was later Farrauto's. Mr. and Mrs. W.A. Walker operated a millinery shop in this block and later owned a Red and White store.

Burlington's first movie house on Brant Street opposite Ontario Street was called the Crystal Theatre, later converted to commercial premises. Hume Theatre on Lakeshore Road later became the Roxy and then the Odeon. It closed in 1981 due to competition from the new multiple theatres. The site was formerly occupied by Dr. Watson and also served as a baby clinic. When the theatre was built, the clinic was moved to the basement of the library on Brant Street and later to the Maitland Young residence on the lakefront, in which Billy Kerns, son of the colonel, lived for years.

The former bus terminal at Lakeshore Road and John Street is another old building. At one time Richard Cole's bakery was located there and in 1912 it was the Bank of Hamilton branch, which was absorbed by the Bank of Commerce in 1925. In deference to its bus history, the building was later dubbed Coach's Corner.

A competitor of Kerns' store, for many years, was Taylor Bros. founded in 1906 on the site of the former McAlister Motors (later Discovery Ford). The firm boasted a $35,000 stock of dry goods, notions, ready-made clothing, furs and groceries. As Fred W. Taylor's ad read, "the store has carried into execution the latest ideas of mercantile endeavour."

The first bank to locate in Burlington was a private one owned by Richard Baxter and Company located on the southwest corner of Brant and Water Streets, one of the last buildings to be torn down in 1966 to make way for the Centennial park development. West of it was Galloway and Co., a grain warehouse which advertised, "Cash for Wheat."

A pier projected out from the foot of Brant St. and people recalled fishing from it. An incline track ran from the grain warehouse to the dock and this ingenious arrangement speeded up loading of the boats.

Eventually, parts of the warehouse were renovated to house a swap shop, Parkers' Cleaners and Virtue Motors which also owned the garage across the street at Locust and Water Streets. For several years after 1914 the property was the Ford Garage operated by Chas. Klainka. The office and garage were on Water St. with another garage and repair shop on Pine St. "with accommodation for 25 cars." An ad in 1917 said, "There is a continually-growing demand for automobiles and residents of this section generally are showing quickly their appreciation of the possibilities for pleasure and luxuriant comfort that the automobile possesses."

Before 1900, the northeast corner of Brant and Water Streets was occupied by Galloway and Baxter's store and after 1900 by the Traders Bank of Canada, "farmers' business solicited", with office hours from 10 a.m. to 3 p.m. and on Saturdays from 10 a.m. to 1 p.m. and from 7 to 9 p.m. (for the farmers' convenience). The business was absorbed by the Royal Bank of Canada in 1912 and the building torn down for a modern structure. In September, 1992, the Royal Bank moved all headquarters staff to a blue and gold (bank colours) five storey, 65,000 square foot building at the Q.E.W. and Burloak Dr. It was 80 years after the bank took over the Traders Bank at Brant and Lakeshore.

With the growth of the population, banking outlets proliferated. In November, 1972, Mayor George Harrington opened the first drive-in financial institution at Hamilton Trust and Savings Corp., Guelph Line north of New Street. By the late 1970s, drive-through banking was becoming popular, with the Royal Bank at the Guelph Line and Mainway another of the first to offer drive-in service. With the help of computer technology, banking services have become so varied that the old timers would shake their heads in wonder.

Burlington, "one of the live-wire towns on the new highway" had a population of 2,600 in 1917 and its merchants were described in an industrial promotion booklet as "progressive and successful". F.D. Ghent was mayor and G.H. Nicholson was reeve.

The businesses on lower Brant St. north of the Royal Bank included LePatourel's Drug Store in its second location in the same block over the years. A.E. Rusby's meat market, established in 1868 by his father, Leonard, advertised "the most reasonable prices with honest weights and measures always quoted." W.W. Currie, a former employee of Taylor Bros., stocked meats and oysters in season in his quality store, opened in 1915. Later it was Hucker's Dry Goods. Next to it was Tom Jocelyn's stationery and variety store which, until 1912, had been owned by J.M. Pollock. Tom Waumsley, who retired in 1966, was the proprietor for many years after the Jocelyns.

Bill Cardwell ran a tailor shop next to Fred Parkins pool room. Graham's Shoe Store, also in the first block north of Water St., 359 Brant St., was established in 1907 and became Mel Howden's Shoes in later years.

Roy M. Early owned a grocery store (formerly Billy Little's) with "the highest grade of goods at the most conservative prices" at the corner of Brant and Water Streets, later occupied by a Shell station. Lakeside Dairy was in the same block south of Burlington Cleaners. The old established business was taken

Interior of John T. Matthews Hardware Store, Brant Street, 1915.
– courtesy Joseph Brant Museum

over by A.W. Baker in 1915. "Doc" Noyes was the village's only barber for a long time. He advertised his shop which stood opposite James St. on Brant as a "Tonsorial Parlor".

E.W. Williamson, undertaker and furniture dealer, was in the first block on the west side of Brant St. immediately north of the old Burlington Gazette office. This business, dating from 1877, was owned by Mr. Williamson from 1901. On the opposite corner was Colton and Lorimer's Hardware and stove retail outlet. The partners bought it from James Allen in 1913. It was Main Hardware in the 1920s and, in 1934, was taken over by the Mills Hardware business of Hamilton. In the 1940s, Mills Hardware moved north to the site of a former A&P grocery store, the same building that had been owned by grocer Spencer Smith. Floyd Howell took over the business from Mills in 1958 and it became known as Howell Hardware. Dale's Hardware took over the building on the corner of Brant and Pine, which later became McDermott Hardware in the 1970s.

Farther along in the block to the north, on the east side, John T. Matthews also had a hardware store in 1909. It became Haswell's Home Furnishings at 421 Brant St. (later Brant Cycle and Sports). Jack Matthews had another hardware store at Freeman on the east side of Brant St. near Plains Rd. Adam Begg, a retired cobbler, lived in a cottage on the site of Burlington Pharmacy, 413 Brant St.

In 1917, Rae Bros. were agents for Gray-Dort and Chalmers cars. Their showroom was north of the Crystal Theatre on Brant, near what was the real estate office of Lloyd F. Utter, 445 Brant St. . Also on Brant St. was Shapland's shoe store just north of Ed Dickenson's candy store, later Watson's Jewellers.

"Polly" Brooking had a carriage works and shooting gallery next to Ed Corwin's real estate office in the next block north and N. Hubbert's grocery store was near Maria St.

Billy Campbell's meat market offered cash for hides and skins. It was established by J.C. Campbell in 1881, near the later office of Harvey McGrath Real Estate at 441 Brant St. A playground set up by the Lions Club was at the northeast corner of Brant and James Streets.

Another well-patronized butcher shop was located where Wellington Square Mall later stood. It had several owners, from R.W. Dingle to Albert England. "Hud" Sheppard was a popular butcher in the employ of "Dick" Dingle, whose sons became respected professional Burlington men. Frank H. Sheppard, tinsmith, was in the Odd Fellows block at Brant and Maria Streets.

Orman Bush, began his business career with his father in 1908. The Brant Street firm dealt in saddles, harnesses, blankets, valises and other travelling goods. Orman Bush opened his men's wear business in 1921 on Brant near James. Mel Bush, town clerk for many years, was of the same family. In 1965, the men's wear store moved to the Howell Hardware location on the retirement of Floyd Howell. With the construction of new commercial buildings, the store relocated to Sims Square and moved once more in May, 1995, to the east side of Brant Street. Win Howell, son of hardware merchant Floyd Howell, had worked with his father-in-law Orman Bush since 1948 and carries on the business into the 1990s.

In 1916, R.H. Wilson dealt in flour, feed and grain at Pine and John Streets. Phil C. Patriarche's Coal and Wood business on John Street was founded by George Allen about 1867. In later times, the business was owned by F.W. Watson and Son and Milne's Coal and Fuel. Clegg Glass Ltd. later occupied the premises, before relocating to Fairview St.

Remember Fischer's Garage in an old building on John St.? In 1988 the interior was gutted and transformed for a time into the home of Elizabeth Interiors which was later relocated to Brant St.

On the northeast corner of Maple Avenue and Ontario, not far from the core area, Halliday Homes was located. On Friday, October 24, 1974, in a spectacular fire, it burned to the ground. Sixty men and eight fire trucks were needed to contain it to one block. The company had been on that site since 1930. Relocating in 1976 to Highway 5 east of Appleby Line, the company had to dig its own reservoir for water, install its own services and protect a pioneer cemetery on the grounds. In the late 1970s, Goodfellow Inc.- Timber Specialties Ltd. took over Halliday Homes. Moving to the Campbellville area in 1994, the company is a huge complex just south of Highway 401.

Another lumber dealer, Nicholson Lumber Company, was opened at Brant and Ontario Streets in 1908. Becoming a retail store when it moved to a new location at New St. and Guelph Line, the company moved yet again to Fairview Street at Walkers Line in 1983.

Village Square, 1983 reproduction of the old fire hall.

At Locust and Elgin Streets, in 1970, Al Cummings opened A Different Drummer Books. In 1975, he moved to 513 Locust St., the former home of newspaper publisher Elgin Harris. The Canadian Booksellers Association presented A Different Drummer Books with the award, Bookseller of the Year, for 1983. Under the ownership of Richard Bachmann, the company's Books and Authors lecture series became the longest running one in Canada.

A fixture on Brant Street has been the Smith Funeral Home. The Williamson funeral business, which was located south of the Coronation Hotel, was purchased by Wilbert J. Smith in 1938. It was relocated across Brant St. and, in 1952, was expanded and remodelled. In 1978, a second storey was added. Donald S. Smith, son of Wilbert became sole owner. A second home was opened in the former Guelph Line fire hall.

The core area was revitalized by the charming Village Square complex between Elizabeth and Pearl Streets. Officially opened on September 27, 1978, it incorporated, as shops, old Burlington houses among newly built stores. The central building was a replica of the old town bell tower. Another phase, built in 1983, included the renovation of the old fire hall for shops and offices.

Several ideas were broached for downtown over the years, including a covered mall in the lower two blocks of Brant Street. Part of a five-year plan to rejuvenate downtown was the reconstruction and streetscaping of the older streets. On Sept. 18, 1982, the official opening ceremonies for phase I (Pine and Elizabeth streets) were held. This included new roads and sewers, ornamental street lights, patterned brick sidewalks with benches, shrubs and trees, and distinctive street signs. The project, including parts of Locust and Ontario Streets, was completed in the next few years.

In 1985, the Business Improvement Area (BIA) was awarded the Ontario Pride Award by the Provincial BIA for its work in restoring and promoting the core area. The BIA moved to new quarters on Lakeshore Rd. in the upper level of the tourist centre building in Spencer Smith Park, taking on tourist promotion. A few months later in May, 1985, a revised Visitor and Convention Bureau officially opened.

With the advent of condominium buildings, some included stores and offices on lower levels. Burlington Square project at Brant and Ghent was approved by the city in 1973 but financing caused problems. It was built as an apartment but converted to condos in 1983. There is still a retail section fronting on Brant St.

One of the largest residential/commercial buildings was Peter Lush's Upper Canada Place opened as an apartment building in 1977 on Locust St. with an indoor retail mall on Brant Street. Two years later a 6-theatre Cineplex Odeon was opened there. In 1990, several of the old Brant Street stores were torn down to be replaced, in 1995, by Wellington Terrace, a seniors' residence and commercial complex stretching between John and Pine at Brant Street. Across the street, Sims Square, a large office/retail complex, was built. The massive Harbourview Residences rose at the corner of Lakeshore and Locust, a condominium development with commercial and retail uses as well at street level.

The downtown area in 1995 was now considered to be comprised of 50 blocks. The Downtown Partnership, instituted by council in 1991, was headed by a group of concerned citizens, cultural representatives, business people, members of city council and members of the Downtown Business Improvement Area, whose purpose was to revitalize the retail and office sectors in the downtown. It also emphasized the importance of residential, institutional and cultural development in the area.

Lower Brant St. has taken on a whole new look with Sims Square, Upper Canada Place, and Wellington Terrace replacing old buildings and new shops and renovations - there is a new vitality and hopefully a return to the busy days of yesteryear.

In 1919, Mr. and Mrs. George Byrens opened the Estaminet on Water St. with only four tables and soon had earned a reputation as restaurateurs par excellence. The stately Mrs. Byrens operated the Estaminet until 1952 when Reginald Cooper bought it. After his retirement in 1963, his son Brian enlarged the premises and made other changes without in any sense removing the familiar homey atmosphere. It changed hands several times and by 1996 was called The Water Street Cooker. At the corner of Maple Avenue and Plains Road stood the Tien Kue Inn, located in another old home. It opened about the same time as the Skyway Bridge was finished, so was named Tien Kue, which means "Sky Bridge". After many successful years, it was demolished to make way for highway construction.

Overlooking the grounds of the Royal Botanical Gardens stood the Rendezvous Restaurant, home of Kentucky Fried Chicken, on the far western end of Plains Road. Operated for many years by the Swire family, this was a popular gathering place for young people in the 40s and 50s and on into the 90s. It has been sold and operates under the name, Louis' West Side Grill.

By 1996, the city had a wide selection of eating establishments from fast food outlets to large buffet-style restaurants and elegant dining places, offering a variety of cuisines.

Burlington had its good and bad times during the depression, in common with the rest of the country. Grocery prices in 1933 were low but so were wages. There was still money being spent for cars though, and a report of 1933 read, "Executives of the automobile industry report the biggest turnover in years ... on the sales floor and regrettably in the ditches".

In 1941, there were 65 stores in town. By 1956, these had increased to 104 due to the town's rapid growth. Up to 1940, the Burlington business district didn't extend much farther north than Maria and Brant Streets. Brant Plaza, Slessor Motors (later Acura on Brant) and St. John's Church occupied land on which Bell Orchards once produced the finest grades of apples. From the 1960s on, businesses have sprung up in all directions. Shopping districts mushroomed with the spread of Burlington to the east and north. First came the small, then the larger plazas to compete with downtown.

Skyway Plaza, opened in 1963, was refurbished in 1985 to become Lakeshore Shopping Village. Burlington Heights was opened in 1974 at Guelph Line and Upper Middle Road. Appleby Square, opened in 1980 at Fairview St. and Appleby Line, won the Mayor's Award for Design. A second phase, opened six years later, included a McDonald's Restaurant and a public library. There were White Oaks and Maplehurst in Aldershot, Tyandaga, and Headon, to name just a few, so that, by 1995, shoppers were offered a choice of more than 75 shopping centres as well as individual stores all over the city.

The plan for a huge indoor mall on Guelph Line was strongly opposed by some who hated to see fine farmland and the Fisher orchards overrun with concrete, and by others who feared the deterioration of downtown shopping. Evelyn Burke, who later became a city alderman, launched a petition in favour of the mall. Eventually it was built and Burlington Mall opened October 16, 1968. The mall included, after several expansions, Robinsons, The Bay, Eatons, Simpson-Sears and K-Mart. Simpson-Sears, becoming Sears, relocated to Mapleview Centre and Zellers took the place of Robinsons. A summer attraction, the Lions Farmers' Market, begun in 1959, moved to the mall parking lot in 1969. The Lions Club Carnival also moved there in the summer of 1982.

Appleby Mall, opened in 1970 at Appleby Line and New St., was another of the first enclosed malls built to serve the area to the east.

Ikea Canada, head office and retail store.

Mapleview Centre, at Maple Ave. and Fairview St., was opened in 1990, delayed for several years like so may other projects by the horrendous double digit interest rates of the early 1980s that inhibited borrowing. Mapleview opened with The Bay, Sears, relocated from Burlington Mall, and space for 200 stores.

A phenomenon of the late 1980s and 90s was the super store with a large floor space. The Brick Warehouse, a furniture and appliance giant, was opened in 1988. IKEA, a home furnishings outlet, opened a 185,000 square foot retail store and its Canadian head office (moved from Vancouver) on Plains Rd. near the QEW/Highway 403 interchange in 1991. On the North Service Rd., Leon's opened a furniture warehouse. In 1995, a "big box" book store, Chapters, opened on Fairview St.; it included a Starbucks coffee outlet, a chain migrating from the west coast.

On Fairview St., west of Brant St., a retail plaza was built in 1993 consisting of large stores - Michaels, craft supplies; Business Depot and Base Electronics. The 1986 Super Centre on Guelph Line, a Loblaw's enterprise, expanded in 1993 to include a Bulk Barn foods, and Winners clothing as well as smaller retail outlets. COSTCO (Price Costco Inc.) at Brant St.and North Service Rd.,opened in time for Christmas shoppers, in December, 1995, offering a new concept. Annual membership cards were made available for certain segments of the population who could then indulge in wholesale, warehouse shopping.

The Barn Fruit Market was opened on Fairview St. by G.A.Love Foods Inc. with headquarters on the North Service Rd.in the Aldershot area. G.A.Love received the first annual provincial Economic Renewal Award in 1994. Longo's Fruit Market, another popular produce outlet, also opened on Fairview St.

Other supermarkets include Miracle Mart, A&P, Fortino's, and Loeb. The metric system was introduced to Canada in 1971 but it was not until

Pizza making at Fortino's supermarket.
– courtesy The Burlington News, *a publication of* The Hamilton Spectator

1982 that stores began to convert their scales to metric, to be completed in the next two years. In the 1980s, Universal Pricing Codes, a series of bars printed on merchandise, were introduced in supermarkets and eventually in most retail outlets.

On January 1, 1991, the federal General Sales Tax was inaugurated, the hated GST.

In early 1985, stores were allowed to stay open Wednesday nights as well as Thursdays and Fridays. Big opposition to this came from small merchants but business was being lost to Oakville stores which were open Wednesday nights. In 1985, city council turned down Sunday shopping but eventually it was approved and has been widely accepted.

HOTELS/MOTELS

According to Fuller's Peel and Halton Directory for 1866 and 1867 there was a Burlington Hotel on Brant St. with Elias DeGarmo, proprietor. The hotel's advertisement read, "The travelling public will find this to be the best and most comfortable House in the Village. Good Sample Rooms for Commercial Travellers." The same publication carried an ad for the Lake View Hotel on Water St., "Joseph Henderson Prop. Farmers and others will find this a good house to stop at." The Raymond Hotel, (later named the Coronation House and then the Coronation Sports Bar and Grill), was presided over by Art Truman. In August, 1971, the old hotel sign saying "No liquor for persons under 21" was torn down at the request of the first legal 18-year-olds.

The Zimmerman House, 400 Brant St., was built as a tavern and owned by Peter Zimmerman. The three-storey brick hotel became known as the

*Royal Bank Offices, North
Service Road at Burloak Drive.*

Sherwood Inn. In the mid-1990s, the dining area was renovated and opened as Queen's Head Pub.

The Brant Inn, on the lake front at Maple Avenue, became one of Canada's best-known dance spots in the 1930s and 1940s, under the management of John Murray Anderson, one of the country's outstanding impresarios. It was torn down in April, 1969, to make way for a proposed hotel/marina complex. The development was deemed inappropriate for the surrounding area and the proposition was turned down. The site was acquired by the City of Burlington in cooperation with the Halton Region Conservation Authority for park use.

Farther east along the lakefront, the Pig and Whistle Inn was built in 1930 at what is now Burloak Drive, overlooking the lake. Built by a firm which had similar English-type inns in other towns, it was returned to the contractor, Hughes Cleaver, during the depression. The inn changed hands several times and was eventually extensively renovated.

The Holiday Inn opened on Guelph Line in May, 1973, #1514 in the large chain, with two storeys of the six storey building open. The first visitor, from Winnipeg, was given free accommodation. In 1980, a 14,000 square foot addition was added to the original 200 room hotel. It featured a Holidome, a glass enclosed six storey climate controlled courtyard, with pool, benches and trees.

In mid-July, 1982, in time for the tourist season, the 100-unit three storey no-frills Journey's End Motel opened on South Service Rd. and Cumberland Ave. (later called The Comfort Inn).

In February, 1972, council approved a tower/apartment/commercial development at the foot of Brant St. on the old cannery property. For years this project was beset with controversy. The Save the Lakeshore Committee went to the Ontario Municipal Board which turned the development down. Council fought back and after bylaw changes, the Anchorage was approved in 1977 with buildings set back from the lakeshore and an exit to Spencer Smith Park.

The Canadian economy, however, entered the picture and by 1982 developers were still seeking financing in a period of very high interest rates.

Central Square Properties, the owner, was searching for a big hotel chain which would operate the hotel. Finally the Bank of Nova Scotia, holder of the first mortgage, pulled the plug and called for an auction of the 5-acre property. But there were still no takers. The value of the land dropped.

Finally, in February, 1983, city council gave approval for Wellington Square Properties to erect a $6 million building, a 7-storey 124-room hotel with meeting rooms, pool and health facilities, restaurant and gift shop, a much more modest undertaking than the 18-storey, twin tower concept envisioned for The Anchorage. On June 18, 1985, the Venture Inn had its official opening.

Two weeks before this opening, Admiral Motor Inn opened on Billings Court near Walkers Line. A block away, on July 7, the Relax Inn (later the Travelodge) opened. The core area, Lakeshore Rd. east of Brant St., was a popular site for visitor accommodation and boasted the Ascot and Riviera on the Lake Motels. The Aldershot area along Plains Rd. was also a favourite spot for motels.

New housing, including multiple dwellings, have steadily increased the number of consumers, giving rise to a need for new business and industrial office accommodation to better serve them. In 1962, Peter Lush opened a realty business in a house at 466 Brant St. The company which became Lush Realty Corp., expanded over the years, and listed among its most visible projects Upper Canada Place on Brant St., Abbey Life building at Harvester Rd. and Guelph Line, and the Holiday Inn. Lush developed Interchange Business Park (site of Abbey Life) and the Hoover Business Park at the Walkers Line/QEW interchange (with a four storey Hoover office building).

John D. and Dominic Rosart's retail/commercial/residential development company, Rosart Properties Inc. has been active in the Maple community. The farms of Lindleys, Thorpes, Robinsons and Tregunnos along Maple Ave. were purchased, beginning in 1968. The area has been developed as residential, commercial and recreational properties.

Builder/developer Rudy Reimer, a successful Grimsby builder, constructed custom homes in Burlington before turning to the commercial/industrial field in the early 1970s. His office, service and recreational facilities adorn the QEW and dot other city thoroughfares. Occupants of his buildings include banks, law and insurance firms, the Chamber of Commerce and industrial offices for companies such as Domtar and Westinghouse.

CHAMBER OF COMMERCE

The Chamber of Commerce was organized in 1947, developing out of the Burlington Business Men's Association, founded in 1925. Former mayor, Gordon Blair, was the first president. That same year the Chamber provided the start-up financing for the Burlington District Girls and Boys Community

Band, which became the Teen Tour Band. By 1956, the organization had expanded into the Burlington-Nelson Chamber of Commerce. Following amalgamation in 1958, the name was changed to the Burlington Chamber of Commerce. At the first council meeting the Chamber presented Mayor John Lockhart with a chain of office.

First locations were on Elizabeth St., and Spencer Smith Park. Under the presidency of Roy A. Nicholson and the management of Leo Podetz, the Chamber prospered at its Brant Arts building offices. It was finally relocated to the Reimer building on Harvester Road. Following Leo Podetz as manager were Ebbe Marquardsen, Brent Hamre, David Job, Lydia Jones for eleven years and Scott McCammon who became Executive Director in 1993.

In conjunction with the city and other community organizations, the Chamber sponsored a day of summer fun and fitness activities in 1987. What was to become the first annual competition for the City of Burlington Challenge Cup was between teams from the business community.

The Chamber made contacts with the Chamber of Itabashi, Japan, and, in 1988, the two cities became twinned. The city's Mundialization Committee has responsibility for maintaining cultural and business relations. The city, the Visitors and Convention Bureau and the Chamber have also established a "sister city" relationship with Myrtle Beach, South Carolina.

Annual awards bestowed by the Chamber in conjunction with the city include the Burlington Outstanding Business Achievement Awards for small operations of up to 50 employees, and for larger companies. The Chamber's Environmental Award and the Export Merit Awards, both in two categories, are also presented at an annual dinner celebration. In cooperation with the Boards of Education, high schools and teachers, the Chamber works to maintain a close link between business and education. This has been done with programs such as Career Day, job shadowing, mentoring and guest speakers.

24

"Render Unto God": The Churches

No one can deny the influence of the church in any community, and in pioneer days the church served not only as a place of worship but also as a community centre for the only social life the settlers knew. Our ancestors' religious backgrounds, varied though they may have been, were well-established in the Gore district in the early years of the 19th century. According to the Halton County Atlas of 1877, th first church in this area was built in 1822 on the farm of Gilbert Bastedo for Presbyterian adherents. Rev. Mr. King, sent by the Synod of Ulster as a missionary to this part of the country, was the minister. The first Methodist Church was built soon afterwards at Nelson Village.

According to Robert Gorlay in "Sketches of Upper Canada", by 1817 "the most numerous of all denominations are the Methodists who are spread over the whole province". One of Burlington's modern churches, Appleby United, traces its history back to an early Methodist supporter, Isaac Van Norman, who began services in his home in 1824. In the early days, Rev.Egerton Ryerson was the circuit preacher here.

An early account of the saddlebag preachers, such as Rev. Ryerson, reads: "The preachers travelled to the farthest back settlements in the wildest places, under the most severe privations as to food, shelter and home comforts, preaching the gospel of Christ to the settlers. They travelled through swamps at the risk of their lives, to sing the good, old, Methodist hymns and pray for the poor backwoodsman and his family." No one was more welcome than the preacher who not only gave them religious consolation but also the latest news of the outside world.

Prior to 1834, people in Wellington Square, hungry for the Word, were ministered to by itinerant missionaries. St.Luke's was built in 1834 on bush land which had been set aside as English Church property. The first child baptized at St. Luke's Anglican Church was Martha Elizabeth Tassie, daughter of a stonecutter, on November 15, 1835 and the first marriage recorded was that of William Dalton, Nelson Township farmer and Elizabeth Sinclair on December 28, 1835. Elizabeth Brant, daughter of Chief Brant, solicited funds for the church building in England. She, her husband and son are buried in the churchyard. Nestled among the trees off Ontario St., St. Luke's historic past is graphically related on its tombstones.

Rev. Dr. Thomas Greene, who had been sent out by the Irish Mission Society in 1832, became the first rector in 1838 and remained until his death

An early view of St. Luke's Anglican Church, Elgin Street.

Knox Presbyterian Church, Elizabeth Street.
— courtesy Joseph Brant Museum

in 1878. St. Luke's has had distinguished clergymen in its pulpit, including Canon Frank Hovey and Rev. G.W. Tebbs, a colourful figure in the community. In 1840 the acacia trees associated with St. Luke's from the beginning were planted by Mrs. Greene, an ardent gardener; some of these trees were replaced years later in 1927. Her beautiful rose bushes brought from Ireland gave Roseland its name, the Greene home being situated in that general area.

Years later, when a church at Elizabeth and James Streets became too small for the Methodists, the building was purchased by St. Luke's and used as a Sunday School from 1889 to 1923. During the tenure of Rev. Tebbs in the 1920s the Memorial Parish Hall was built by St. Luke's and dedicated in memory of boys who fell in World War I.

Members of Knox Presbyterian Church still meet at the same site where the founders worshipped in 1845. Land was donated by Andrew and Martha Gage who had bought the property in 1810 from the trustees of Joseph Brant's estate. Inscribed on the deed dated April 18, 1845, are the names Isaac Buchanan, Gilbert Bastedo, John Bent Sr. and John T. Bastedo.

That summer a plain frame church was built at James and Elizabeth Streets and named after John Knox who founded the Presbyterian faith at the time of the Scottish Reformation in the 16th century. The first minister was Rev. William McLean. Thirty years later, the little church was becoming overcrowded and eventually a new sanctuary was built and dedicated on May 20, 1877. The original building was moved a few yards east and brick veneered for use as a Sunday School. The church entrance on Elizabeth St. was built in 1910 to accommodate the stained glass window given by Hon. Colin Campbell in memory of his mother. To celebrate its 150th anniversary, a new spire and spire lighting was added.

In 1852, a little group of Wellington Square residents formed a Methodist Society and on Sundays walked through the bush to Fishers Corners schoolhouse on Guelph Line where the Episcopal Methodists had been worshipping for some years. Before building their own church, the villagers also met in the Temperance Hall (later the Town Hall) with the first class organized by Dr. Van Norman. A site for Burlington Methodist Church was donated by David Torrance on Elizabeth St. and the church, which in 1947 became the Sea Cadet Hall, opened for services in 1858.

Burlington Methodist Church, later Trinity United Church, 1893- 1965.
– courtesy Joseph Brant Museum

The hall of the Iron Duke Sea Cadets has been a visible reminder of old Burlington. Tragically, on Nov. 11, 1980, shortly after the Remembrance Day parade to the Cenotaph, the interior was destroyed by fire. Insurance, a tag day and corporate donations enabled the building's restoration to be completed late in 1981. An extension was built on the rear in 1996.

As time went on, the Methodist congregation needed more accommodation. A new church, built in 1886, was destroyed by fire on Christmas Day, 1892. In 1893, a second was built on Elizabeth St. next door to the Town Hall which had been an earlier meeting place. When the Methodist Church across Canada joined in union with a portion of the Presbyterian Church and the Congregationalists in some areas, in 1925, to form the United Church of Canada, Burlington Methodist became Trinity United Church.

Port Nelson United Church at the corner of Rossmore Blvd. and South Drive, Roseland, was founded by some members of Trinity United Church. The new church was dedicated January 10, 1954, but a larger building to serve a growing congregation was dedicated in September, 1961. The original church was converted to a Christian education wing.

The trowel used in laying the cornerstone of Burlington Methodist Church in 1886 was put to use again in November, 1965, in connection with the new Wellington Square United Church on Caroline St. which combined the congregations of Trinity and St. Paul's (a former United Church congregation on Prospect St). Trinity was torn down to make way for an apartment building, Elizabeth Manor.

A Roman Catholic parish, St. John the Baptist, was established in 1849 but no church was built until 1861. The people were attended by Rev. John Cassidy from Dundas who also had under his care Waterdown, Milton and Oakville. Parishioners from Burlington had the opportunity of assisting at Mass only once a month, but hardy souls walked from here to Dundas, on Sunday mornings, to worship at St. Augustine's.

Before the church was built, those of the faith gathered at Napoleon Ogg's home on Pine St. whenever a priest would arrive for the monthly Mass. A parish house was erected in Oakville in 1858 and Burlington was joined to it as a mission. This church had few material comforts and parishioners worshipped on the bare ground with rough boards as pews. The Ogg family had donated a piece of their property at the corner of Pine and Elizabeth Streets and St. John's Church was erected in 1861. It remained a mission church attended from Oakville until 1925 when Rev. D.A. Ford was appointed as first resident pastor of the separate parish. Father Ford also served the Beach, Milton and Milton Heights churches. Later the Church of the Little Flower, Hamilton Beach, was the only mission.

Rev. (later Monsignor) J. Corbett Warren was appointed Pastor in 1945 and remained until his death 20 years later. In 1948, St. John's Separate School was built on Brant St. (It was taken down and rebuilt on the same site, opening in September, 1995.) By 1952, construction had started on the large, modern St. John's Church at the corner of Blairholm Ave. and Brant St.

The original St. John's at Pine and Elizabeth was taken over by St. Mary's Ukrainian Catholic Church congregation but, in 1975, it was demolished to make way for a high rise building. That year, a new Ukrainian church was completed on Martha St., Holy Protection of the Blessed Virgin Mary.

A good example of co-operation between local churches was the Wellington Square branch of the Bible Society, formed in 1849. The first preserved record of the annual meetings is for October, 1855, at the Temperance Hall. Executive members were Henry Foot, James Laing, John Bent, Daniel B. Chisholm and William Beeforth, with a committee of 17 prominent businessmen and clergymen in the community. The local branch had a depository for the sale of Bibles with more than 200 of them sold in 1854.

Later known as the Burlington branch of the Upper Canada Bible Society, it was a well-conducted organization and wives of the members regularly solicited donations for the work of the church around the world. The Bible Society made a valuable contribution to the religious life of the community.

Churches continued to be built and the Port Nelson area was served for years by the Wesleyan Methodist Chapel, built in 1862 at the corner of First Ave. and Guelph Line. The white frame church still stood in 1996, having served many different congregations over its life. For many years it was used by the Red Cross.

The first mention of Baptists in Wellington Square was in 1850 when an earnest few assembled for services in the home of James Cushie Bent. This property, originally part of Brant's Block, is at 507 Elizabeth St. while the first meeting place still stood at the bend of Rambo Creek in 1996.

In 1875, trustees of the Regular Baptist Church bought from Deacon John Bent the site for Calvary Baptist Church at the corner of Ontario and Locust Streets. Residents of the village joined the new church and a measure of prosperity followed. A branch mission

Holy Protection of B.V.M. Ukranian Catholic Church, Pine Street.

was started at Port Nelson and the new Mission House was crowded at the opening services.

A succession of pastors served during the early years of Calvary Baptist which was linked with churches in Waterdown and Bronte between 1906 and 1923. The church building was later taken over by St. Phillipe Roman Catholic parish, the first French-language parish in Burlington. Calvary, which became a member of the Fellowship of Evangelical Baptist Churches, was rebuilt on St. Frances Dr.

In 1930, when Calvary withdrew from the Convention of Ontario and Quebec, some members left the congregation. A Baptist Women's Mission Circle was kept active by Mrs. James Chapman and Mrs. E.R. Swift until the post-war years when Baptists were growing in number in Burlington and a new congregation within the Convention was needed. Assisted by the women's group, Rev. Dr. N.H. Parker held a meeting at the home of D.D. Dingle, Q.C. and services were begun at Trefoil Lodge in 1952. Knox Presbyterian Church offered use of its facilities for Sunday afternoons and mid-week Bible classes. In 1954, Burlington Baptist Church was erected at Bridgman and New Streets.

In 1920, the Lambshead and Almas families on East Plains Rd. began to

St. Philippe Roman Catholic Church, formerly Calvary Baptist, Locust and Ontario Streets.
– courtesy of Joseph Brant Museum

hold meetings in their homes; the group became known as the Freeman Mission. As attendance rose, a regular meeting place was needed and a house on East Plains Rd. near Brant St. was bought in 1921. Such enthusiasm was shown that, by 1928, the charter members voted to apply for membership in the Associated Gospel Churches of Canada and Gospel Chapel, Freeman, came into being. Acting pastor was A.N. Lambshead, who continued his thriving market garden business while studying for his ordination. He remained as pastor until 1947. Property on Brant St. was donated by Ellen Almas and 119 people were present for the cornerstone laying of the new church in 1929. In 1960, the name was changed to Brant Street Bible Church and in 1978, to Brant Bible Church when members dedicated a new church on Eaglesfield Dr. near Highway 5.

While the population of Burlington was, at the outset, predominantly British, some of the early settlers were Pennsylvania Dutch (Fishers, Engleharts, Ghents and Clines). Scottish and Irish immigrants came after 1820 and the 20th century saw groups of Germans, Italians and French entering the area.

Since 1920, there has been a noticeable increase in the number of Dutch who came to work on farms but later took up positions with local industries, in many instances. Starting in 1928, a few Dutch families from Burlington and surrounding districts worshipped in Hamilton wherever space was available - a church basement, a bricklayers' meeting hall and the Labour Temple. Some years later, they bought a former Baptist church building at Dundurn and Main streets in Hamilton and, from it, a number of branch churches originated. After World War I, many families from Holland settled on the land hereabouts and John Boersma, who later moved to Burlington, was one of those who often helped the new settlers.

A number of the newcomers began church meetings in the Burlington Lions Club Hall and, in 1953, bought the old Wesleyan Methodist Church at Guelph Line and First Ave. By 1959, they had built their own Christian Reformed Church on New Street. In 1964, members of the congregation assisted in the formation of Trinity Christian School on Walker's Line. A regular elementary school curriculum is followed and religious instruction given. This area had a second congregation of Dutch families at Ebenezer Canadian Christian Reformed Church on Dynes Rd. where Sunday morning services were in English and afternoon services in Dutch. In 1989, the building burned down and a new church was erected in 1991, the services then conducted in English.

The old Wesleyan Chapel on Guelph Line, which served the Dutch congregation so well, was also used by charter members of Port Nelson United Church in 1952 for Sunday School classes and church services, before their own facilities were built.

As the population spread eastward, another Anglican church was needed. In March, 1952, the first service of St. Christopher's Mission was held at Fishers Corners School. Property was purchased on the Guelph Line between Prospect St. and Woodward Ave. and the congregation moved into their new quarters, St. Christopher's Anglican Church, in February, 1955. As orchards and farms gave way to new subdivisions, the parish grew quickly.

Strathcona Presbyterian Church has served the eastern part of town since 1957, the congregation meeting first in the Scout Hall on Belvenia Rd. and then in Nelson High School. The church was officially recognized in 1959 with 118 charter members; the edifice on Walkers Line was built in 1961.

Trefoil Lodge was used again as a temporary church when Glad Tidings Assembly, a Pentecostal church, was founded in 1957. A permanent church on Mountainside Dr. opened in March, 1961, with a seating capacity for 200. By 1986, this was not large enough and a new church was built on Guelph Line.

A new Roman Catholic parish, St. Raphael's, was welcomed in 1958. At first, the parish extended from the Guelph Line to Appleby Line and north to Highway 5, with more than 200 families. Mass was attended at St. Raphael's Separate School on New St. until the new church building was opened in October, 1960, with accommodation for 775. Prior to 1958, Catholic families living in Elizabeth Gardens had attended church at St. Dominic's in Bronte, but with the establishment of St. Raphael's they were included in the new parish.

Ebenezer Canadian Reformed Church, Dynes Road.

The first Lutheran service to be held in Burlington was in October, 1959, at Glenwood Public School. Church land was purchased on Lakeshore Rd. between Pine Cove Rd. and Walker's Line in 1960 and the new congregation was called Holy Cross Lutheran Church, part of the Lutheran Church in America. The membership moved into its new home sanctuary in September, 1963.

The second Lutheran organization in Burlington was formed in October, 1960, at a meeting in the home of Mr. and Mrs. John Allan on Townsend Ave. Rev. Kenneth L. Zorn, under the auspices of the Ontario District of the Lutheran Church-Missouri Synod, began a new church called Prince of Peace Lutheran; the first chapel at 1199 Homewood Drive was purchased from Glad Tidings Pentecostal Church. A new, modern structure was later erected on Brant St. near Mount Forest Dr. and dedicated in the late autumn of 1966.

Following its opening, the building on Homewood Dr. was sold to Faith Gospel Church which had been meeting in Lawrie Smith School. Another religious body active in mission work was Burlington Alliance Church. It was founded in 1959 at Strathcona Public School and later moved to the Scout Hall on Belvenia Rd.; a place of worship was erected on New St. near Appleby Line in 1964.

Because of a generous gift of 35 Acres on Panin Rd. in Aldershot, the administration offices and homes for retired missionaries of the Christian and Missionary Alliance in Eastern Canada was situated in Burlington.

In March, 1960, St. Elizabeth's Anglican Church was founded as a Sunday School in Elizabeth Gardens School to serve the area east of Appleby Line. A stirring ceremony took place in May, 1961, when a 30-foot wooden cross in front of St. Christopher's Anglican Church was removed and carried along New St. by men of both congregations to mark the spot where the new sanctuary would rise. St. Elizabeth's Church on Bromley was dedicated January 25, 1962.

St. Stephen is a United Church located on Parkway Dr. north of Mountainside Park, established in 1960, after meeting in Clarksdale School.

Groups which met in area schools in the 1960s were the Christian Science Society at Glenwood School, and Pineland Presbyterian Church at Pineland Public School on Meadowhill Rd. The latter congregation, which was founded in 1964, built a church at 5270 New St., in 1969, Members of the Church of Jesus Christ of Latter Day Saints met in the Lions Hall until their church was built on Headon Dr. in 1976.

St. Gabriel's Roman Catholic Church on Parkway Dr. was founded in 1962 as a mission, served by priests of St. Stanislaus, a Hamilton Polish parish, until its own priest was appointed the following year. St. Gabriel's church was built in 1964. In the same general area is a new Anglican Church, St. Philip the Apostle at 1525 Mountain Grove. Dedication of the

St. Gabriel's Roman Catholic Church, Parkway Drive.

Halton Mosque, Fairview Street.

sanctuary took place January 31, 1965, following two years of meeting in area schools.

Since *Pathway to Skyway* was originally published in 1967, new places of worship have been built. Some of these are: Brant Hills Presbyterian Church, Brant St., (1980); St. Paul the Apostle Roman Catholic Church, Headon Rd, (1990); Tansley United Church, Walkers Line, (1991); The Halton Mosque, Fairview St., (1988); and Jehovah Witness Kingdom Hall on Mainway (1990). The Salvation Army, after worshipping for a year in the Optimist Club building, dedicated their new church on Prospect St. in 1968; an extension was added in 1983. The Chinmaya (Hindu) Mission Halton Region Centre, Appleby Place, spread from their original site in Newfoundland to Burlington in 1981, with 25 or more families attached by 1996.

In 1994, Living Waters Church congregation purchased Mayfield School on Legion Rd., having used the school for worship since 1991.

Crossroads Centre, very visible from Highway 403 at 1295 North Service Rd., had its origins in Pembroke in 1962. Broadcasting a radio program known as 100 Huntley St., its location in Toronto, the facility was moved to Burlington in 1992. Crossroads Christian Communications Inc. presented its 5000th telecast in August, 1996. Another significant change in church homes in recent years involved new congregations taking over a church building when the original congregation moved elsewhere. One example is the Sikh congregation that occupied Kingdom Hall on Queensway after the Jehovah Witness group left. The former Zimmerman United Church on Appleby Line became Trinity Baptist Church. In 1984, Faith Christian Reformed Church bought the Glad Tidings building on Mountainside Dr. when Glad Tidings built their new structure.

Many local congregations undertook major renovations. These included enlarging the sanctuary, increasing the number and sizes of the meeting rooms or making the building accessible to the disabled (aided by government grants) by the addition of an elevator and ramps. St. Raphael's Roman Catholic Church on New St. reversed the direction of the seating in the sanctuary so that the new main entrance to the church is now directly accessible to the parking lot at the rear of the church property. Among other churches to make renovations are St. John's Roman Catholic (Brant St.), St. George's Anglican (Lowville), Aldershot Presbyterian (La Salle Park Rd.), St. Stephen United (Parkway Dr.), St. Philip the Apostle Anglican (Mountain Grove Ave.), Port Nelson United (South Dr.), Nelson United (Highway 5), Prince of Peace Lutheran (Brant St.), St. John's Anglican (Highway 5), Appleby United (Spruce Ave.), Strathcona Presbyterian (Walkers Line), Holy Cross Lutheran (Lakeshore Rd.), St. Luke's Anglican (Ontario St.), East Plains United (Plains Rd.) and Burlington Baptist (New St.). In 1996, St. Christopher's Anglican Church on Guelph Line was starting to raze all church buildings, except the sanctuary, and replace them with a larger, multi-purpose addition.

All these many and varied changes to local religious buildings speak well of members who were not only financing expensive improvements at a time when economic conditions were much poorer than in the recent past, but were also helping the community beyond their doors with food drives, donations and other assistance to non-profit groups such as the Nelson Youth Centre and Neighbourhood Link. Helping beyond Burlington boundaries, some local churches have adopted families from war-torn countries or the third world.

In 1960, through the efforts of the Burlington Ministerial Association,(formed in 1950),the town was chosen by the Canadian Council of Churches and York University, for a sociological study of the community, under the direction of Professor Mann. The result was several recommendations including, first, the formation of the Interchurch Council composed of representatives, both lay and clergy, from all the Burlington churches. The second major recommendation of the Mann report was the establishment of COHR (Counselling and Human Relations). In 1968, the first office was opened in the home of Lionel Horncastle on the Guelph Line at Eileen Street. The churches were responsible for the initial funding and later, grants were obtained from the Provincial government and United Way. COHR quickly outgrew the small office and was moved to Fairview St. and, in 1994, to 460 Brant St. COHR developed into a wife assault, individual, marriage and family counselling organization. In 1976, the council started a branch of Telecare, a 24-hour distress telephone service and in 1993, The Hub, a drop-in centre and counselling service for adults and teens in Burlington Mall. Another community service was Runaway Kids, established in the mid-1970s, in which church members provided temporary homes for teens.

Only some of the many religions organizations have been included here. The history of others are interesting also, but to include all faiths would necessitate a book of its own. Suffice it to say, Burlington's residents enjoy the opportunity to worship as they wish, with a variety of choice to suit almost any religious affiliation.

25
Avenues of Transport

PART I - RAILWAYS

History of the railroads in this part of the country dates back to an 1832 meeting in London, Ontario, which petitioned the government to grant a charter to build a railway from Burlington Bay to London. Lack of sufficient capital in the province to finance such an undertaking delayed matters for more than a decade. By the 1840s, the situation had changed greatly and construction of the nation's railways proceeded rapidly in terms of mid-nineteenth century standards.

The first tracks laid through Wellington Square belonged to the Great Western Railroad. Begun in 1847, the railroad took seven years to complete and was finished here about 1854 with a line laid through the northern part of the village. There were also great celebrations when the G.W.R. laid the first tracks between Niagara and Windsor in 1854. The first through train passed between Toronto and Montreal in October, 1856, with the completion of another line, the Grand Trunk Railway.

The trains drew curious crowds at first. Diarist George Thomson mentions seeing a locomotive running on the Hamilton to Toronto railroad in November, 1854. Later he noted with dismay, no doubt due in part to facial injuries and a broken axle, that during a trip to Hamilton he was pitched out of his wagon by his horse taking fright at rail cars hauled by a locomotive.

The coming of the railroads opened up developments throughout the whole countryside and brought prosperity to many, although communities such as Wellington Square and Port Nelson, dependent on lake freight, did not welcome the advent of the railroad too warmly at first. Business fell into a humdrum rut until the onset of the "lumber fever" a few years later. In the late 1860s, the railway had begun to compete successfully with lake schooners and stagecoach lines which had monopolized passenger service along the lakefront. By 1870, almost all of the important stage routes had been abandoned.

Railroad tracks were laid across Burlington Beach in 1875 and this shuttle service greatly improved industrial transportation at the head of the lake. A newspaper clipping dated March 13, 1874, says, "Yesterday the Halton by-law granting $65,000 to the Hamilton and North Western Railway was carried by a majority of 257." (Burlington voted 82 for, and two against.)

The Halton County Atlas said of the complex railway facilities in 1877, "The Grand Trunk Railway runs through the northern extremity (of the

Grand Trunk Railway Station. *– courtesy Hamilton Public Library*

county) from east to west and the Great Western through the south. The Hamilton and North-Western Railway cuts it diagonally from Burlington to Georgetown and the Credit Valley Railway is partly constructed, which will divide it in the opposite direction."

The railway came none too soon, according to the Atlas: "Truth compels us to say that the roads are, as a general thing, only fit for travel in summer or when covered with snow. At other times the road is something to be remembered with anything but pleasure by the unfortunate traveller."

Speaking of railroads that passed through Burlington, the Atlas notes that, by 1877, "The railway advantages here are unusual as both the Great Western Railway and the Hamilton and Northern R.R. pass through the corporate limits, thus giving a railroad in all directions. These facilities being duly recognized, the village will doubtless rapidly increase its present population of 1,400. The last school census did indeed figure up to 1,600 but as the H. and N.W.R.R. employees were then working in the village, doubtless 1,400 is nearer the number of permanent residents."

In August, 1882, the Grand Trunk Railway acquired control of the Great Western Railway and became the competitive threat to the Canadian Pacific Railway still under construction.

A lucrative line, the Toronto, Hamilton and Buffalo Railway, began operation around the turn of the century. In 1895, Burlington's reeve and clerk were authorized to sign a petition to the Dominion Government asking for a grant of $3,200 for the proposed T.H.& B. Railway.

In 1897, 55 residents signed a petition to Nelson and Burlington councils asking "that some action be taken to further secure the safety of the travelling public at the G.T.R. crossing at Freeman" and the G.T.R. was duly "notified of the nuisance of their trains stopping on the public highway at the Freeman crossing and asked to stop it." In 1899, council corresponded with the railway committee of the Privy Council regarding the need for a gate at

Aldershot Station. – courtesy Bruce Filman

the Brant St. crossing of the G.T.R. "to ensure the safety of the travelling public."

Council records show another letter was sent to the Grand Trunk Railway in 1904 in which Reeve William Kerns requested the G.T.R. to have a morning train stop at Burlington Junction "to pick up passengers." It is not recorded how successful the reeve was in his plea.

The G.T.R. was granted the right, in 1916, to cross Brant St., with a switch to be used for the handling of fruit and car loads of perishable goods. Some of the early industries in town were built close to the railroad tracks since they were dependent on the railway to transport their raw materials and finished goods. The Canadian National Railway system acquired the Grand Trunk Railway in 1923.

There have been several railway stations in the Burlington area. For many years, the Hamilton and North Western station was located just north of the Brant Inn, above Lakeshore Rd. on the curve of the railroad line. The earliest mention of this station in the lighthouse keeper's dairy was in 1857: "William left for Wellington Square station...". There was also the station at Freeman which burned down April 1, 1904.

A temporary building was used until a new brick station was built. All switches were handled from the tower which was later used to operate the gates across Brant Street. Harry Blair was agent of the Freeman station at one time, which was known as Burlington Junction, later the C.N.R. station. With the advent of GO commuter trains, this building was no longer needed. Its historical value led to the formation of SOS, Save our Station, a group advocating the station's relocation and preservation.

In May, 1967, GO (Government of Ontario) commuter service to and from Toronto and areas farther east was initiated from the C.N.R. station. Three years later, its success led to a pick-up and commuter parking area at the Guelph Line/QEW intersection. This was retained as a parking area when a new GO station was built in 1980 on Fairview St. just east of Brant Street. C.N.R.passenger train service, taking the name VIA, switched from the old 'Freeman' station to a shared facility at the Brant St. GO station. In 1996, GO trains provided rush hour service to Burlington but as well there was a bus service taking passengers from the Guelph Line/QEW parking area to Oakville. C.N.R. freight trains provide industrial service.

Increasing passenger use of GO dictated a second station be built on Fairview east of Appleby Line. A third station was opened on Waterdown Rd. south of the North Service Road. GO service now extends as far as Hamilton.

An exciting event must be mentioned. On November 11, 1979, a freight train was derailed in Mississauga. A threat of escaping chlorine gas prompted the evacuation of 250,000 people from Mississauga and Oakville. Burlington hotels filled up and 400 people were accommodated in gyms at M.M. Robinson High School. The Red Cross and Halton Social Services volunteers made them as comfortable as possible. As any tragedy does, it pulled the communities and their people more closely together.

Today, the old steam locomotives are gone and diesel engines haul piggy-back carriers and refrigerated cars. It is a far cry from the pioneer days of the wood burners chugging their stoical way past the town.

PART II - RADIAL LINE

The electric cars of the radial line provided a vital link with Hamilton. Workers and shoppers used the cars daily, along with students attending classes in the city. The first official steps towards the construction of the line were taken in May, 1894, when the Legislative Assembly of Ontario passed an act to incorporate the Hamilton Radial Electric Railway Company. Then the fun began! The radial company wanted the right-of-way over certain streets and Burlington businessmen favoured various other routes through town. The Burlington Library has a copy of one of the petitions dated 1896 in which council and owners of property along Water Street asked for construction to begin along their choice of route while the Radial Company favoured Ontario Street.

W.G. Pettit was Reeve of Nelson Township in 1896 when bylaw 378 was passed "to grant certain privileges to the Hamilton Radial Electric Railway Company." It was authorized to survey, lay out, construct, maintain and operate a railway from Hamilton to Burlington (across the Beach Strip) and through Nelson Township. The route through each municipality had to have a favourable two-thirds vote of each council before the right-of-way could be approved. As though in anticipation of trouble, the bylaw stated that disputes between the company and council were to be settled by the County Judge of Halton who would act as arbitrator.

There were disputes over the right-of-way along Elgin St., New St. versus Water St. and opposition to the railway crossing Church Ave. (Elizabeth St.). When construction finally got under way in 1898, ratepayers objected to the freight shed started on Elgin St. and the company was given one week to remove equipment. When the company declined, council gave notice that it would "remove same to the public pound at the expense of the

A radial car at the Queen's Hotel, Elgin and Brant Streets.
                                    – courtesy Joseph Brant Museum

company by April 11." A special meeting of council was held April 6 to read a letter from the radial company regarding the proposed site for the station and freight shed.

Once the arguments were settled and the radial line in operation, riding the electric cars became part of the town's way of life. The route finally settled on was from Hamilton along Wilson St. and Birch Ave., then across the Beach. In Burlington it ran beside the hydro towers from the Brant Inn up Maple Ave. to what is now Elgin St., and on to Brant St. The station was located where the parking lot is on Brant St. opposite Elgin, and the line continued through Lions Club Park where the car barns were. By 1904, the radial cars were running along tracks from Burlington on the north side of New St. as far as Oakville. This section never paid its way as well as the heavily patronized leg to Hamilton, and these tracks were taken up when service on this part of the line was abandoned in 1925. An observer of the Burlington scene said at the time, "It might possibly have been more successful had it been extended to Port Credit from Oakville and thereby made a direct connection with Toronto."

The radial line was used not only for passenger service but also for transporting freight, such as a carload of stone which cost $2.50 to haul. Radial sidings were approved and a switch ran down John St. to the coal yard of P.C. Patriarche and the premises of the Burlington Canning Company. Early rules of the line provided for public waiting rooms, "passenger cars with all modern improvement for safety and comfort including lighting and heating and they shall each day (not including Sunday) run at least six passenger trains each way."

The rate for any distance less than three miles was five cents and for any greater distance, two cents per mile. For the return trip from Hamilton to Burlington it was 25 cents; 30 cents for a return trip from any point on the line east of Burlington (the Guelph Line was the town boundary). Speed was restricted to less than 15 miles per hour and "every

Go Station, Fairview Street.

car running over said railway shall after sunset carry a white light in front and a red light in rear conspicuously placed as a signal light, and every car or train shall be provided with a gong or bell, which shall be rung when approaching every public crossing."

Over the years, there were disputes over rates, schedules and trains stopping in front of driveways. At various stages, mention was made of other companies putting lines through different sections of the Province. At one time, Sir Adam Beck and the Ontario Hydro conceived the idea of an electric railway from Toronto to Niagara Falls. Nothing ever came of it.

The radial cars served Burlington from January, 1897, until January 1929, when the service was discontinued in favour of buses. A romantic era had ended. Old timers who had used both means of conveyance cast their votes in favour of the electric cars any day.

PART III - BUS SERVICE

In 1936, Cecil Norton, living on Dundas St., needed transportation to get his son to Central High School. There was no public transportation at that time. He purchased a seven-passenger Pierce-Arrow limousine and piled in his son Grant and some of his neighbourhood friends for the trips to school. By 1946, this service had become a business. Cecil Norton had bought an old army chassis and fitted it with a bus body so more students could be accommodated. In 1947, the school Board agreed to pay for this service so the Nortons purchased their first real bus, a Reo. This developed into Burlington's first public bus service and was continued by the Norton family for many years. On September 1, 1975, the city took over the local bus service from Norton Bus Lines which continued to supply school bus service.

The first bus station was on Lakeshore Rd. at John St. In January, 1972, a new bus terminal opened on Elizabeth St., used by Canada Coach Lines and Gray Coach Lines Ltd. as well as the local buses. An official ceremony, in

Burlington Transit Station, John Street.

September, for the city transit, featured free bus rides, doughnuts and coffee, all courtesy of Norton Bus Lines. Only two years later, the terminal was expanded and the exact fare system inaugurated. This station was demolished to make way for an apartment building. The third terminal was erected on John St. south of James St. As well as Burlington Transit, the terminal is used by Greyhound providing service to communities outside the city.

Later developments in bus service included the erection of bus shelters which were built at no cost to the city since advertising adorned their sides. In 1995, there were 151 of these. Dial-a-Bus was tried in areas west of Aldershot Plaza, Tyandaga, Brant Hills and Palmer Community where service was not as frequent, but was not adopted as bus service improved.

The Business Line was officially launched on September 17, 1991, at the Chamber of Commerce offices. The route, which stopped at both the Fairview and Appleby GO stations, ran early mornings and late afternoons. The half-hour schedule provided service to business and industrial sections from Guelph Line east.

Handi-Van service for the handicapped began in the 1970s and linked passengers to a commuter service to Hamilton and Toronto. Easier Access buses with a front steps lowering feature and other improvements such as air conditioning, developed in the 1990s, made travelling more accessible for the frail elderly and the disabled.

PART IV - ROADS AND SIDEWALKS

At the time of Confederation in 1867, Wellington Square was a rustic and almost entirely isolated village and its few streets were roughly paved with stones gathered from the beach. According to old accounts of council meetings, road building and repairing was the biggest headache the politicians had.

Authors of early days had many harsh words about the road conditions of Upper Canada between villages or clearings. A traveller writing in 1837 said, "The roads were so bad that no words can give you an idea of them. We often sank into mud-holes above the axle-tree; then over trunks of trees laid across swamps, called corduroy roads. A wheel here and there or broken shaft lying by the wayside told of former wrecks and disasters. In some places they had, in desperation, flung huge boughs of oak into the mud abyss, and covered them with clay and sod, the rich green foliage projecting on either side."

Passengers had to grasp an iron bar in the front of the wagon to keep from being flung out on the bumpy road. They were unable to get out and walk because the borders of the so-called roads were tangled, untrodden bush, infested with rattlesnakes and insects. Sometimes there was no road at all, merely a blazed path with the trees on either side as the only guide to the traveller.

No one moved very far during the wet spring or hot summer months unless it was absolutely necessary. Autumn was harvesting time and so it was not until routes were frozen and snow-covered during the winter that they were busy with sleighing parties or farmers selling their crops and gathering the coming year's provisions from a distant trading post.

Before the first settlers arrived, Indian trails wound through the forests which covered Burlington. These were later used by the pioneers as the first roads and some of the descendants of these recalled hearing of trails such as one leading from Dundas to Toronto. The pioneer, Isaac Van Norman, built his home at Appleby where the South Service Road is now, facing an Indian trail. He was so sure it would become the main road that even after the Middle Road was built he continued to use the trail and carried planks in his buggy to bridge the culverts.

Legend has it that an Indian trail lay close to the present Guelph Line. There is evidence of another trail from the bay northward. D.W. Smith, surveyor general, lists in 1782 "a sawmill-gristmill on a creek that empties into the head of Burlington Bay near the road leading from the said Bay to the Mohawks' village." Plains Road was also begun by Indians, and it wound its way to Burlington Heights, now part of Hamilton.

John Graves Simcoe, first Lieutenant-Governor of Upper Canada, was responsible for the building of "Governor's Road" or Dundas Street, today known as Highway 5. About 1793, a detachment of his Queen's Rangers cut the road westward from Burlington Bay to the Grand River, but the section from Burlington to York (Toronto) was not built until the lands owned by the Mississaugas were purchased in 1805.

Water transport was good so there was no need to hurry road building in these parts. When Dundas St.was opened, the route was blazed several miles back from the lake shore to avoid the difficulty of bridging the wide mouths of the many creeks and streams and for greater safety in transporting troops and supplies in time of war. Governor Simcoe's road proved the wisdom of such planning in the War of 1812.

The old Mississauga trail along the lake shore from York to the head of the lake was not blazed into a good road until later. The first mention of a lake shore road appeared in the *Upper Canada Gazette* in 1804 when the government called for tenders for the construction of roads and bridges from York to Burlington Bay. Four years later, the *Gazette* was urging the government to complete the section from the Credit River to the head of the lake.

On October 8, 1811, seven magistrates sitting at the Home District quarter sessions approved the first cross-country road in this area, from Burlington Beach to Dundas. An old map shows that the road came across the beach to the present North Shore Blvd., went west to what today is Shadeland Ave., from there to Plains Rd., west to Waterdown Rd., north until it intersected the Old York Rd. and proceeded from there to Dundas.

The first roads were not financed by legislative grants but were built by the Imperial government as military thoroughfares or at the expense of settlers or traders. The Northwest Company, for instance, contributed large sums of money towards improving Yonge St. in Toronto. Between 1825 and 1850, gravel or plank roads were built and designated toll roads. These were an improvement over log or corduroy roads, since the road bed was drained and bridged and steep hills reduced in grade. This type of highway was usually laid out in straight lines, surmounting obstacles instead of going around them. Plank roads were satisfactory at first, but variations in lumber and the condition of the road bed made constant and expensive repairs necessary, particularly after heavy frost. Joint-stock companies in charge of the toll highways were authorized to collect tolls and they agreed to keep the road bed in repair, which they seldom did. At least these roads had a better foundation than earlier ones. When troops built the first sections of the Governor's Road, they just chopped off the stumps close to the ground but when Col.G.T. Denison supervised construction of the road between Toronto and Burlington he took the more radical course of pulling the stumps out by the roots.

The first stage coach between York and Niagara began its run in 1826, charging 5 pounds for one passage; it took at least 17 hours to cover this route. During the coaching days, the most famous line of stages was William Weller's Royal Mail line of four-horse vehicles, bright red with the Royal coat-of-arms emblazoned on the side. Staging was an involved process since fresh relays of horses had to be provided at each 15 mile interval. It was not until 1842 that a daily line of stages operated across the province from east to west. The largest coaches could carry 16 passengers when the roads were good.

The statute labour law of 1793, the first of its kind, provided that every landholder might be required to work on the roads from two to twelve days as directed by the area pathmaster. This law was found to be unjust since landlords who owned an entire township were taxed no more than a person owning a few acres. After a few years, a scale was arranged according to assessment which varied from time to time. The work of opening roads was retarded for a time by the Clergy Reserves and by absentee landlords who at first were not required to perform road work. Later, when many of the main highways became toll roads maintained by private companies, municipalities were able to apply the statute labour laws to the less important roads.

When Caleb Hopkins was Nelson Township chairman in 1836, William McCay was township clerk, and commissioners were Peter Fisher, Francis Hamburgh and James Cleaver, much of their deliberations revolved around road business. There were 39 pathmasters in Nelson Township at that time, each assigned to his own immediate district.

They supervised the building and repairing of bridges, hauled stones and logs to fill swamps, had holes in the roads filled up, graded and gravelled when necessary, cut new roads through the township and sold the timber. Pathmasters also had to keep accounts for materials purchased by various men working on the roads. The law by that time provided that every male inhabitant of the township between the ages of 21 and 60 years was liable to two days' statute labour on the roads. Further, more days were exacted according to the assessment rate on the property; e.g. at more than $300 and not more than $500, three days' work, etc. If physically unable to work, an individual paid the pathmaster 75 cents for each day's labour not performed. One had to turn out when called on by the pathmaster, with three days' notice, to work in one's division. Fines and jail sentences were levied against those who refused to either work or pay for the labour.

Items such as these appeared in Nelson township minutes: "The road committee reported again...two culverts crossing the highway at Port Nelson and the creek are closed...We think there is sufficient statute labour...to complete the work." Many farmers in the area belonged to the Guelph Line Road Company.

As road construction improved, acts were passed in the legislature "to regulate travelling on Public Highways." These early traffic laws prohibited racing: "No person shall race with, or drive furiously, any horse or other animal or shout or use any blasphemous or indecent language." Signs were erected on any bridge exceeding 30 feet in length saying, "Any person or persons riding or driving on or over this bridge at a faster rate than a walk, will on conviction thereof, be subject to a fine."

People still used "shank's mare" a great deal and it was not uncommon for enthusiasts to walk from Burlington to Hamilton, or to Waterdown on a Sunday afternoon. The story is told of a woman who walked to Hamilton to shop for a hat. When she couldn't find what she wanted, she walked on to Dundas. It is not recorded if she had enough energy to walk home again. Another story is told by a member of the Fisher family about an incident which took place on July 1, 1868, the first anniversary of Confederation. Two brothers were sent out to the barn to grease the wagon wheels. Later the family drove as far as the Middle Road at Freeman where a wheel fell off. The boys had forgotten to replace a nut. They walked home, found it in the barn and returned to fix the wagon and continue on to Hamilton. They thought the trip worthwhile. The speaker at Dundurn Park that day was the Father of Confederation, Sir John A. MacDonald.

In 1894, the Good Roads Association came into existence in Ontario and it aroused great interest in improved methods of road construction. By 1898, the first automobiles made highway improvement a national necessity but it was almost 20 years before Burlington had its first paved roads.

Lakeshore Rd., as we know it today, has been changed and diverted over the years as the water rose or the lake bank eroded. The Halton County Atlas of 1877 shows streets in the Village of Burlington which no longer exist. South of Lakeshore Rd.(or Water St. as it was called then) another road is shown, called Front St. which also ran parallel to the lake. Green St., Market St., St. Paul St. and Guelph Line all extended to the vanished Front Street. Another road now under water was Port Street. It was between Beaver and Market Streets on the south side of Water Street. The only indication we have of these roads and the surrounding lost property which included a market square, are the painted guardrails at the end of Green and St.Paul Streets which prevent cars from driving on into the lake. At the foot of Guelph Line a parkette was established. Two inns were on the lakeside and a third, the Royal (because it was owned by a Mrs. Royal in later years) was located at the northeast corner of St. Paul and Water Streets. It became a private residence but a reminder plaque was placed beside its door reading: "Elijah Halstead, Innkeeper 1848". The other two inns disappeared with the rising water of Lake Ontario.

Several miles east along the lakeshore in the vicinity of Secord Lane there was, south of the present highway, another road which disappeared with erosion and the rising lake. When the original lakeshore road was washed away (some say it took a stagecoach with it in the dark of a stormy night) the present road came into being. Legend says that Laura Secord was given property in this area as a reward for her service to the Crown in the War of 1812.

The main north-south roads ending at Lakeshore Rd. are part of the old survey of Nelson township, Guelph Line (it led to Guelph), Walkers Line (named after the Walker farm), Appleby Line and the Town Line (Burloak Dr.) are all exactly 1 1/4 miles apart.

In 1912, the lake rose to such a level that it was found the lakeshore road near the Guelph Line was dangerous in spots and "unfit for public traffic and very expensive to maintain." The township blocked it off in places and gave land to owners of adjacent property in exchange for "a sufficient portion of land running through their properties for a new highway 66 feet wide." Considerable dissatisfaction resulted in some cases and arbitration and expropriation were necessary before the road could safely be rerouted.

Maxwell C. Smith, later to be the town's first mayor in 1914, was proud owner of the first car in Burlington. Bought in 1902, it was a single-cylinder Rambler, painted fire-engine red, and townsfolk looked on in awe as he chugged along Brant St. at 20 miles per hour. Local legend gives "Max" Smith credit for

Grading the Walker's Line.

the white lines which now divide the highways. It was said that people who were watching concrete being poured for the new Toronto-Hamilton Highway in 1914 wondered, "How are we going to stop cars from hitting each other when they go around the bend?" Smith simply said, "Paint a white line down the middle," so they did.

This was such a sensible idea that it has also been attributed to some others including W.D. Flatt. His enthusiastic use of the highway resulted in a speeding ticket in 1916 for exceeding the 20 mph speed limit. Howard Fairbrother remembered bringing a mechanical striper from the United States to Toronto to demonstrate it to Department of Highways officials. The white lines were in use on some roads in the States previous to World War I. They began to be used here on hills but it was not until 1930 that the lines began to be painted on all Ontario highways.

The appearance of the main highways changed very little until after World War I when, with the great increase in motor traffic, gas stations with their pumps began to replace blacksmith shops and watering troughs. One of the first concrete roads in Canada was the Toronto-Hamilton Highway (Highway 2), commenced in 1914 and formally opened November 24, 1917. The cost was $1,250,000 or approximately $33,000 per mile.

First mention of the section to be laid through Burlington along the lakeshore was made in January, 1913. At that time, council introduced a petition signed by property owners endorsing the government's plan and "praying that we take the necessary action to further the proposal and assume our share of the obligation." In 1914, council took the stand that the provincial government should build main highways, assisted by frontage taxes in the communities they passed through and "that the Lakeshore Road which connects the cities of Hamilton and Toronto and serves a population of over half a million people and which at present is in a deplorable condition, should be the first provincial highway constructed."

There was much contention about the route the new highway would take through Burlington. At the first meeting of Nelson Township council in 1915, it was noted that "we have learned with a great deal of surprise and regret" that the highway commission planned to run the new road down Brant St. instead of along the bay shore where the township wanted it.

On January 27, 1915, in Judge Monk's chambers in Hamilton, commission and township presented their cases about the route and a compromise was reached. Since the bay shore route was unsatisfactory to property owners near Freeman and in the northern parts of the township, and the Brant St. route was not favoured by Hamilton and part of East Flamborough, the route by the bay shore, up King's Rd. and along Plains Rd., approved by most of the municipalities, was the one decided on.

The cost was divided between the Province of Ontario, the municipalities of Toronto and Hamilton, and the townships and communities on the route. The lakeshore route was selected in place of Dundas St., a longer thoroughfare with numerous hills, or the Middle Road which at that time was not regarded as being of very great importance. Highway No.2, sometimes referred to as the "Father of all Canadian Highways", was taken over by the Ontario Department of Highways on April 14, 1925.

In 1973, Lakeshore Rd. (called Water St.until 1958) became a part of the Ontario-Quebec Heritage Highway System. Plans were made to widen Lakeshore Rd. between Stratheden and Gore but this meant tearing down 50 trees and bringing the street nearly to the doorsteps of neighbouring homes. A compromise was reached in 1974, with the widening of Lakeshore Rd. east of Brant St. only to Torrance. In the 1980s and '90s, turning lanes were added at major intersections to the east.

Completion of the Toronto-Hamilton Highway spurred development of macadamized roads and Burlington's council was urged by residents to build a permanent surface on New St. and Brant St. and effect improvement elsewhere as needed. An estimate of the cost of a concrete roadway on Brant St. from Water St. to Plains Rd. was finally obtained in 1922. The road across the beach strip was paved in 1923 and, by the end of the 1920s, work on town streets was completed. Houses were numbered in 1925 and street signs positioned in 1926.

July and August, 1966, saw the reconstruction of Brant St. from Lakeshore Rd. to Caroline St. with new sidewalks and road, street lights and underground services. On June 29, 1967, the new Lucolux lighting was switched on, making the street twice as bright as Broadway. New St. was widened to four lanes and given a sidewalk from Guelph Line east in the mid-1960s, the work carried out in stages over several years. Four lanes stretch from Mayzel Rd. right along to Burloak Dr.

The Middle Road, originally an Indian trail, was first known as the Iroquois Road. It was surveyed in 1806, and a rough corduroy track built.

The later route was established in 1838 by pioneers who dug the ditches and graded the road. Later a stock company gravelled it and tolls were charged. It took 35 to 40 years before a good quality road was built and named Nelson Gravel Road. In 1931, as the Middle Road, it became an alternate route to Hamilton midway between Dundas St. and Lakeshore Road.

Known now as the Queen Elizabeth Way, it was originally intended in 1934 to be a 40-foot pavement similar to the Lakeshore Road. The following year it was decided to make it a divided highway with a centre boulevard. The first section built was from Highway 27 to Niagara Falls and was officially opened to traffic on June 7, 1939. Dedication ceremonies were held at the Henley Bridge near St. Catharines and present were their Majesties King George VI and Queen Elizabeth, who were visiting Canada at the time. By 1956, the Q.E.W. connected Toronto with the Peace Bridge at Fort Erie and in September, 1960, the section between Toronto and Hamilton became a completely controlled-access highway.

Between 1970 and the 1980s, to combat the traffic congestion caused by the CNR tracks running across the city, underpasses were built for Brant St., and Guelph Line. A pedestrian walkway over the tracks at Drury Lane was opened to accommodate students attending a Drury Lane school.

Some bicycle lanes were established as a project for Burlington's Centennial. In 1982, a five-year plan for bikeways was announced by the city. Any new road construction or road widening was to include bikeways.

For easier access to the QEW, since the 1980s, interchanges were built at Brant St., Fairview St. and North Shore Blvd. To the east, interchanges were completed for Guelph Line, Walkers Line, Appleby Line and Burloak Drive.

Several provincial highways run through the city, the Queen Elizabeth Way (QEW), Highways 2 and 5 and the Hamilton-to-Toronto Highway 403. To the north of Burlington is the MacDonald Cartier Freeway, Highway 401.

Major Burlington arteries have been under construction, reconstruction, realignment and extension since the 1960s, notably Brant St., New St., Walkers Line, Guelph Line and Appleby Line. Fairview St., Harvester Rd., King Rd., Maple Ave., Mainway and Upper Middle Rd., were improved and, in some cases, extended.

Meanwhile Highway 403 construction continued apace into the 1990s from the QEW interchange on, to eventually connect with the 401, west of Highway 27 at the western edge of Toronto.

Burlington's location on routes leading to major cities such as Toronto, and to the United States, has given rise to numerous trucking companies, truck rental agencies and truck sales, servicing and repair businesses.

Governor Simcoe would never know the place were he able to return to appraise the changes that have occurred since he laid out the first roads in 1793.

What of cars using these roads? It was in 1903 when cars first required registration and licensing - $2. a tag. Early metal car license plates of 1925 were black with yellow figures. Drivers were required to have $1 licenses in 1927 but no examinations. Those over 16 filled out an application form and swore they had a minimum of 6 months' experience and had no disabilities. In January, 1986, photographs were required on drivers' licenses and ten years later "smart cards" containing information on a variety of things including insurance were being contemplated by the Ontario government.

The first parking meters were installed in the core area in 1958 and brought in $20,000 the first year. In 1975, non-leaded gasoline was introduced, and seatbelts became mandatory in 1976. That year, compulsory $100,000 third party automobile insurance was enacted. As a trial, in 1984, municipal vehicles were driven with headlights on in daylight. A few years later, it became mandatory that headlights on all new cars in Canada were to come on automatically with the ignition.

SIDEWALKS

In common with other Ontario towns, Burlington in the late 1800s had wooden plank sidewalks. As early as April 2, 1855, Nelson bylaw 75 was passed to assess certain portions of the township in the area affected, for laying a "plank sidewalk from William Bunton's brick shop on Water St...to the station of the Hamilton and Toronto railroad opposite the residence of Joshua Freeman, Esquire."

Sidewalks were an improvement over walking on the dusty or muddy road, but they required constant upkeep and council was often sued by people who had stepped through rotten planks, or who had been struck by loose boards flying up and hitting them. Burlington council had a Roads and Sidewalks committee whose duties were many and varied. For example, in one short period in 1896, they had to deal with and remove "if thought best", a certain pine tree on Guelph Line, put a crossing down "at once" on Brant St. in front of Hurd's gate, replace sidewalk sections on Water St. and lay new ones on Brant St. opposite the Queen's Hotel and on Guelph Line between Water and First Streets. Then they ordered stone to repair bridges on Water and Pearl Streets.

In 1899, walks were built north on Guelph Line to New St. and a section replaced near the Glover Basket Factory at Freeman. It was a never-ending job for village workers. Finally, in 1900, council decided to get estimates on the new type of granolithic sidewalks. Meanwhile they replaced walks in front of the post office; from George Allen's shop at Pine and Brant to Caroline, and sections in front of Dalton's and Rentons's.

On the matter of permanent sidewalks, council minutes record a letter from the Royal Artificial Stone and Paving Company of Guelph asking for the privilege of tendering for concrete walks if any were planned in 1902.

Council still hedged; although they discussed the matter of raising money by debentures for new walks, they went ahead grading James St. from Brant to John St. and repairing boulevards on Brant St, "the owners of the property to pay for the planks."

By June, as petitions had been received by council from several parties asking for concrete walks on Brant and Water Streets, a special meeting was called on the matter. Meanwhile, petitions poured in from residents in the downtown area wanting the modern walks in front of their properties. Tenders were called in August and then council had another problem. A Guelph firm put in the lowest bid, and the highest, 14 cents per square foot, was from a local man. One councillor moved that he be engaged to lay the walks so as "to employ Burlington labour as far as possible." A heated discussion ensued; council adjourned for a week to think it over and then the low tender of 11 1/2 cents per square foot was accepted. The Guelph firm was requested to charge for cement curbs as if the curb were an extra foot of sidewalk, and council arranged to borrow $1,500 to pay for the walks.

One of the first granolithic crossings was laid at Water and Elizabeth Streets. The entire plank walk from the Brant St. schoolhouse to the G.T.R. tracks was termed a menace and was completely removed to make room for a cement walk. A firm from Simcoe was hired in 1904 to build further walks and crossings as the petitions continued to pour in. Walks were laid on those streets where requests had been signed by taxpayers and, since everybody wasn't in favour of paying for the new-fangled cement walks, council threatened to make it a ruling "that on any streets where the sidewalks are worn out and parties refuse to sign for a granolithic walk, board walks be built and the cost be charged to the property fronting the walk."

A court of revision dealt with sidewalk disputes and, by 1915, most of the arguments were settled. By then, more pressing matters such as sewers, watermains and plans for paved streets claimed the attention of officialdom.

M.C. SMITH'S COUP

The Roads and Sidewalks committee also had to turn their attention to the waterfront on occasion. They decided in 1901 to build steps down the bank to the lakeshore on Pearl St. so that the public could have access to the lake, the cost not to exceed $15. The commissioner was told to hurry and build the steps "so the public can use them while the water is warm." The townspeople enjoyed the swimming right at their doorsteps so much that in July, 1908, council sternly resolved "that the clerk procure cards forbidding bathing in the lake along the shore of the Village of Burlington, unless bathers wear suitable bathing suits, on penalty of a fine of $5."

In May, 1906, estimates were sought for building a crib to protect the lake bank on Water St. that was threatening to collapse. In August, two councillors went to Toronto to inspect timber for a proposed breakwater at the foot of Burlington Ave. The pounding of the lake was becoming so severe that two years later, David Henderson, M.P., was urged to ask the Dominion Government to build a cement breakwater "along the shore of Lake Ontario in and adjoining our village boundary to protect the shore from being washed away."

The request brought no action. In 1909, Reeve M. C. Smith petitioned the Dominion government again, through the Hon. William Pugsley, Minister of Public Works, again with no encouraging results. Two years later, storms were still washing over the highway and Reeve Smith worried a great deal about it, knowing that the town couldn't afford to build a wall without financial help. He privately conferred with an engineer friend and had a complete set of plans for a proper revetment wall drawn up which he took with him to Ottawa.

The new Minister of Public Works was known to him and when he reached Ottawa he found he had met the minister's secretary in Winnipeg some years before.

The federal government had never spent money on local improvements except harbours and docks for ocean-going vessels. The young secretary was unaware of this. In the absence of the minister, the secretary told Smith the chief engineer would have to approve the plans first. When the engineer was confronted with what appeared to be official plans sent down from the office of the Minister of Public Works, he assumed they had been passed and he added his approval without questions. When the minister returned, Smith told him the chief engineer had approved the plans. The minister assumed they had been passed and he signed them too.

The subsequent government wall built along the waterfront was the only breakwater the federal government ever built for other than an ocean port. Sparks flew around Ottawa but the wall had been built by then and the government was committed. An addition was built at the foot of Brant St. in 1926. When Spencer Smith Park was landscaped in 1967, the wall was made higher and in 1985, $89,300 was set aside for the first phase of major repairs, a project undertaken over several years. At the same time the boat ramp was doubled in size and siltation control commenced.

PART V - SKYWAY BRIDGE

Burlington Bay Skyway, the largest bridge constructed by the Ontario Department of Highways up to that time, was officially opened by the Hon. Leslie Frost, Premier of Ontario, on October 30, 1958. Steady streams of cars and trucks used this vital span on the Queen Elizabeth Way, while under this traffic, passed lake and ocean vessels from seaports of the world.

The history of Burlington Beach dates back to the 1790s, when John Graves Simcoe, Lieutenant-Governor of Upper Canada, purchased the sandy strip for 100 pounds in goods from the Mississauga Indians to be used as a link in the military road from York (Toronto) to Newark (Niagara on the Lake). In later times, for decades, ships passed through a channel built in the 1830s and wagons crossed the channel on a scow or on a swing bridge. Then came the age of the automobile and speed. Until the opening of the Skyway, the Burlington Canal was the cause of traffic tie-ups whenever the swing bridge on the beach highway was raised for the passage of a ship.

The number of highway traffic interruptions increased until 1952 when a freighter demolished the northern leaf of a bascule bridge over the channel. It was replaced by a temporary structure and ship traffic was restricted to one half of the channel. Mile-long queues of vehicles on both sides of the channel were a common sight on weekends when as many as 30,000 cars a day passed this point which had a capacity of 900 cars an hour.

There was great interest as the concrete supports for the new Skyway bridge went up and the steel spans were eased into place. In 1958, Burlington was apprehensive lest the bridge would not be named after the town. Burlington Jaycees presented a petition to Highways Minister F.M. Cass recommending the name "Burlington". In September Premier Frost agreed that the bridge would be officially named the Burlington Bay Skyway. As time passed the bridge came to be known merely as "The Skyway".

Previously to 1792, Burlington Bay was known as Lake Geneva or Macassa Lake. The name Burlington Bay was proclaimed by Governor Simcoe in 1792. Then, by an Order-in-Council of August 1, 1919, passed by the provincial government, the name was again changed, this time to Hamilton Harbour. Yet it seems, residents of the north shore still say "Burlington Bay" while on the other side, Hamiltonians prefer "Hamilton Harbour".

When the Skyway was completed in 1958, the centre span was 120 feet above the harbour entrance; it was 4.37 miles long and had cost $19 million. At that time it was the longest bridge built in Canada, consisting of 75 spans resting on 76 piers.

Newspapers reported that plans for the bridge had been in progress since 1954 and the *Burlington Gazette* added, "Premier Frost at the opening put an end to 40 years of muttering, grumbling and cursing by simply cutting the ribbon to open the span."

A 10-booth toll plaza was established with a 15 cent fee for use of the bridge. It was estimated that the tolls brought in $3 million in 1973, their final year of operation; during the summer 60,000 cars a day used the span, which became the mother of all bottlenecks. The aforementioned muttering, grumbling and cursing had begun all over again.

In January, 1974, tolls were eliminated, allowing traffic to scoot across the bridge uninhibited. Even this, however, was not enough to handle the ever-increasing use of the bridge. Burlington and regional officials favoured a tunnel, the province a twin bridge which was estimated would cost $15 million less than a tunnel. Halton people responded that a tunnel would cost, over a 15 year period, $21 million less to maintain. A twin bridge, however, it was to be. In March, 1982, surveys began and the bridge was completed in 1985.

The structure was composed of a trapezoidal steel box-girder and reinforced concrete deck for the approach spans and a prestressed, cast-in-place segmental superstructure for the main spans. This was the first use of cast-in-place technology in Ontario. The contract for construction was won by Pigott Investments Ltd. for $38.8 million.

What's in a name? Plenty, the Jaycees and many Burlington people thought. The province announced it would rename the bridge the James N. Allan Skyway after a former cabinet minister. The Jaycees then presented a petition asking that the original name, Burlington Bay Skyway be retained. A compromise was reached and Burlington Bay, James N. Allan Skyway Bridge was agreed upon, a mouthful. Politics aside, however, to drivers, it's still "The Skyway".

The official opening ceremonies took place in the middle of the bridge on a beautiful, calm October day in 1985. The red ribbon was cut by the aforementioned James Allan who was 91 at the time. Ed Fulton, the new Liberal Minister of Transportation for Ontario was present along with 200 guests who enjoyed a reception afterwards at the Burlington Golf Club.

John Shragge, Communications Coordination Officer for the Historical Information on Provincial Highways, who arranged the ceremonies, recalled the first accident on that very day. The car of Al Wittenberg, head of Planning and Design for the Ministry of Transportation collided with the car of a radio reporter.

Burlington's first police car – a 1947 Ford.

26
Services to the Public

PART 1 - POSTAL SERVICE

Communication of any kind was a major problem in pioneer days when there was no government postal service at all. It was the receiver and not the sender who had to pay the charges for the delivery of a letter with the result that many letters were unclaimed because there was no money to pay for them. In "Halton's Pages of the Past", author Gwen Clarke notes that much heartache was caused these pioneers in a strange land, longing for news from home and unable to collect the letters that awaited payment of postage.

Emigrants sometimes went to the local post office, homesick and eager for news from their home country, mostly the British Isles, and on finding their letters would cost as much as five or six shillings, would turn away in despair. One post office in the early 1800s had 48 unclaimed letters on hand. A notice hung in the office saying that if the mail wasn't picked up and paid for by a certain date, it would all be sent to the dead letter office.

Letters from home were prepaid as far as the coast then were sent across Canada in several ways - by bateau on the St. Lawrence, by government schooner across Lake Ontario, by stagecoach on land and by courier or private messenger on foot or horseback until the mail finally reached the recipient.

By 1816, there were still only nine post offices served by mail coach in all of Upper Canada. Roads were bad beyond description.

When the mail coach, painted a bright red, reached the post office, the driver blew a blast on his horn and threw the mailbag to the ground. The postmaster took out what was addressed to his district, put in the outgoing mail and returned the bag to the driver.

A letter posted in England in autumn might, under favourable circumstances, reach York (Toronto) by the following spring. Eventually mail in Halton County was dispatched along the lake front five days a week. In December, 1836, Wellington Square postmaster Hiram Smith wrote to Thomas Stayner, Deputy Postmaster General in Quebec," There is required..a larger mail bag..as the mail is generally carried on horseback between this office and the office at Nelson. I think it should be made to sling over the carrier's shoulders and let the bag hang by his side." By 1846, Wellington Square had "post every day". Postmaster in Nelson was T. Cooper.

By the end of the 19th century, Nelson Township was dotted with post office stations at Burlington, Port Nelson, Freeman, Ash, Appleby, Tansley, Nelson, Zimmerman, Lowville and Kilbride. After 1910, rural mail delivery

Burlington Post Office, Brant Street, constructed 1937.
— courtesy Les Armstrong

was introduced and as a result, post offices in tiny communities were closed. Postal reform in 1898 brought about penny postage, a great relief to many who had been unable to afford the luxury of writing letters.

Burlington's post office was in the first block of Water St. east of Brant. Postmaster W. Peart presided over a tiny frame building which was a gathering place for people to stop and gossip.

An incident which was recalled with amusement concerned a villager who was often bad-tempered with the children. One day, he was in the tiny crowded post office, loudly arguing politics with his neighbours. The children sneaked up outside and closed the window on his coat-tail so that when he tried to walk away he was caught tight. "We made our own fun in those days," recalled Nellie Morrine.

Port Nelson's post office, in the early 1900s, was in the store at the corner of Water St. and Guelph Line. William Douglas and Hugh Cotter were responsible for its construction, and the building with a cut-off corner became a landmark. T. Bamford followed Hugh Cotter as postmaster of Port Nelson.

A story is told about John Waldie, who was a friend of Mr. Bamford's. In those days, a postmaster's salary was based on the number of stamps he sold, so it boosted Bamford's prestige and wages when Waldie bought $400 worth of stamps from him each year. Eventually, postal authorities requested Mr. Waldie to patronize his own post office in Burlington where his business was located.

By 1913, Burlington had a more commodious post office on Water St. and was on the verge of becoming a town with its population of more than 2,000. Council petitioned the federal government for a larger and more suitable building, but the outbreak of World War I caused postponement of all non-essential government projects.

By 1927, Audrey Peart was postmaster, succeeding his father, Vickers Henry. There were two other post offices at that time, one at Port Nelson run by George Brown and the other at Freeman under William Cannom.

Burlington finally got a new post office in 1937, an attractive stone building on Brant Street. Fred Ghent was appointed postmaster. When house-to-house delivery was begun in Burlington, it was made easier by the numbering of houses in 1925 and the erection of street signs in 1926.

The 1937 post office was built next door to the old library, a gift to the town by John Waldie; this library eventually became municipal offices. Both buildings were used as municipal offices after

Postal Outlet, Roseland Plaza.

1959 when the new post office was finished farther north on Brant St. After the amalgamation of Nelson Township, Aldershot and surrounding area, nearly 3500 homes were re-numbered to eliminate confusion for police, fire and postal services.

In 1942, mail delivery was reduced from twice a day, six days a week, to once a day. In 1947, when service men had returned after World War II and employees were plentiful, the twice a day delivery was resumed for awhile. In 1981, the Post Office Department became a Crown Corporation. Service has been reduced from six days to five with no Saturday delivery.

Strikes and threatened strikes of postal workers have plagued the public. A national strike in the summer of 1968 gave a boost to private courier services. Some Burlington students earned money that summer delivering company mail to businesses in Toronto (without some imaginative action such as this, the prolonged strike meant some businesses were faced with substantial losses or even bankruptcy). The Chamber of Commerce estimated the strike of 1975 cost 600 firms a total of $500,000. To meet competition, Canada Post introduced Priority Courier, Express Post and Custom Imports services, and purchased Purolator Courier.

One of the most important innovations in postal service was the postal code system. Introduced in Ottawa in 1970, it was to be in effect in Burlington in 1973. Postal workers were trained during the summer of '72 and that August the public was informed of their new numbers. Postal workers, however, members of the Canadian Union of Postal Workers, fearing the loss of jobs, boycotted the system and it was not until 1976, in time for Christmas mail, that postal codes were in use in Burlington.

In 1978, a new post office was opened on the Guelph Line near Upper Middle Rd. to serve the area above the QEW.

In 1996, there were 126 letter carriers and two rural routes. Suburban Services, with green community mail boxes, served a new area south of

Highway 5 which did not have door-to-door letter carriers. The Brant St. facility still served as the main post office but the designation "Postmaster" held by such as Wallace Kirkwood in 1966, eventually became a "Superintendent" for Burlington with a "Zone Manager" in Stoney Creek.

Few other postal employees could boast the record achieved by the Greer family. George retired as a rural mail carrier in 1965 after 35 years of service. His father William, a blacksmith, had delivered R.R. 1 mail from 1908, using a horse and cutter in the winter and a Model T in the summer for the 18-mile trip.

Even though postal operations have become more complex, Canada Post in Burlington still carries on a tradition of service handed down from the first building on Water Street.

PART II - FROM BUCKET TO SNORKEL: THE FIRE DEPARTMENT

The cry of "Fire" was a frightening sound to the early settlers who often lost, in a matter of minutes, homes that had taken weeks of back-breaking work to build. Since many homes were constructed of wooden planks or logs, there was little anyone could do to stop a fire once it started, unless there was a bucket brigade.

Of course, fire within proper bounds was a valued aid to the pioneers, not only for domestic purposes, but for burning off patches of land for farming purposes.

In the late 1890s, when villages in this area were flourishing, and dwellings were being built close together, there was often the danger of the flames leaping from house to house. A story is told about the day the Kilbride hotel burned in 1875. The home of Rev. D.C. Clappison of the Methodist Church was situated temporarily in the house next to the hotel. The parsonage was in grave danger of catching fire because the wind was blowing that way. Folks rushed to save the furniture. Mr. Clappison calmly told them not to trouble themselves because the parsonage would not catch fire. The people stood and prayed with him and, miraculously, the wind changed direction and the parsonage stood untouched. It was an impressive demonstration of faith.

During the 1800s, the Burlington Volunteer Fire Brigade was formed and the first horse-drawn apparatus bought in 1893. It is recorded that the engineer in 1895 was H. Lowe who was paid $21 per month for his services.

A bell had just been erected at the town hall which did duty as police office, "lock-up" and fire station. Inscription on the bell (which now stands outside Central Library) reads "Erected by Burlington Council in 1894. Commissioners: George Blair, George Renton, O.S. Colbrain, P.N. Ogg, James Allen, Clerk and Treasurer; and Thomas Atkinson, Reeve".

In 1895, Councillor Campbell moved that the first person ringing the bell in case of fire "receive a gift of $2", but the motion was defeated. Council did buy a clock for $10 for the bell tower.

Accounts paid to firemen and helpers were important items for council. "Mrs. John Henley and James Parkin were paid the sum of 35 cents each for watching ruins of a fire on Brant St. as directed by Chief Hatton". Bills of five dollars each were paid for services at a Zimmerman fire and at the Ocean House, a popular resort hotel at the canal.

In the early days, there seemed to be a constant turnover of chiefs. Fire Chief Hatton resigned in 1896 and L. Hennings was appointed in his place. The lieutenant was Alfred Wills and members were John Little, John F. Cline, George Galbraith and C. Blanchard. A few months later, Chief Hennings quit and John Tudor took his place with Richard Coleman his assistant.

In 1897, it was recorded that "Mr. Ogg moved that the Burlington Fire Committee purchase four coats, six pair boots, six hats, five pair gloves, one pole hook with chain attached, one roof ladder, one ladder suitable for fire purposes, one lamp and table for fire hall, one steel bar four feet long, said items to be purchased in the cheapest market." They were, too, since the bill for boots, coats, and hats came to only $26.40. Council also approved "$1.15 for cheese and soda biscuits for firemen at the recent fire and $1 for matches." Matches?

The owner of the first team of horses that took the fire engine to the fire and returned it to the fire hall received $5. In case the team was not required, the owner received $1.50. Later on, hose reels were hand drawn by companies of volunteers.

In 1806-7 underground tanks were built in various locations in the village for water storage in case of fire. They served until the waterworks was built in 1909. For many years, Burlington's tall water tower at Maria and John Streets was a well-known landmark. It was 80 feet high at the outset and later another 20 feet were added. A cover was placed over the top and a little fence and walkway built around it. The old water tower was torn down and in 1956 the property became the site of the office building of the Inter-Urban Area Water Board.

Old accounts tell of a fire at a local lumber yard when the fire brigade lost 100 feet of hose. Council billed the lumber company. A volunteer injured at the fire was unable to work for ten weeks and was granted $20 by council.

There were rumblings of trouble in 1898 (unfortunately not recorded in full) and the brigade was asked by council to resign en bloc. The village constable was given charge of the equipment until a new brigade could be formed. He was authorized to call on any citizens to assist at fires. At the same time, council was presented with a bill of $106.55 for repairs to the steam fire engine and the commissioner was advised to appoint a "responsible person who would manage the fire reels." This may be a hint as to the cause of the trouble.

Volunteer Fire Department Marching Band.   *– courtesy Joseph Brant Museum*

Every year, council had to deal with a long list of rebates on taxes charged for buildings that had burned. For example, in 1901 council approved a rebate to W. Kerns and Co. for a wharf and warehouse destroyed by fire.

Allan S. Nicholson served as chief in 1911 and as secretary-treasurer in 1914 when Charles Lyons was chief. The following year a deputation from the brigade asked council to help pay expenses for the trip to the Annual Firemen's Convention in Thorold and were given $75.

In March, 1916, volunteer firemen in the west end of town asked for money to furnish a building for No. 3 company and were granted $25 to equip a storehouse and meeting place.

The first motorized fire truck was bought in September, 1916, and it greatly increased the brigade's efficiency. It cost $4,855 and consisted of one motor combination chemical and hose truck of two-ton capacity. No longer would it be necessary to pay men "one dollar for drawing fire engine to wharf." By this time, the brigade was divided into three companies and had 36 men.

That fall, the firemen were permitted to display the new Denby truck at Oakville Fall Fair, provided they left a wagon with "hose loaded, and team harnessed for emergencies." The old hose reel was later given to the Peel-Halton House of Refuge in Brampton.

The new truck had a good workout on a windy night at the beach when 14 two-storey houses burned.

In 1918, the fire and light committee wished to install a signal siren fire alarm, but decided the one purchased "is absolutely unsatisfactory and we will not accept same." A local family continued to attend to the ringing of the fire bell, a telephone having been placed in their home to notify them of the location of fires.

It was shortly after this that a special meeting of council was "abruptly adjourned when fire broke out on Councillor Koenig's premises."

Through the years, the volunteer fire brigade has been active in town activities. In 1919, Tom Jocelyn, then secretary, was granted use of the unused town band instruments to form the Burlington Fire Brigade Band. For many years, the firemen supported a drill team which competed with other fancy drill squads at the annual conventions. Under Chief James Waumsley, the brigade raised funds and bought a $3,000 steel life-saving boat in 1947 and moored it close to Spencer Smith Park.

The Ontario Volunteer Firemen's Association convention was held in Burlington in the summer of 1923. Again in 1958, it was a gala five days with Tom Waumsley as host chairman.

Prior to 1900, hook and ladder companies were strictly voluntary. Members carried out their duties without remuneration, the social activities of the company being their reward. In some towns, the fire-fighters were exempt from the poll tax, from militia duty in peace time and from serving in the capacity of constable, juryman or in any other office.

There was a spirit of camaraderie in the volunteer organization and much wholesome rivalry between the companies of the brigade was the result. Burlington firemen were constantly kept busy with the town band and sponsoring sports activities. As fire fighting apparatus developed in efficiency and towns increased in size and population, more permanent arrangements became necessary.

Burlington's first fire station was an addition built on the town hall building on Elizabeth Street. The station at Elizabeth and Pine was built later as was the No. 2 station on Queensway Drive. The latter gave protection to Nelson Township and became part of the Burlington department after the 1958 amalgamation. The station in Aldershot was constructed on Waterdown Rd. in 1959.

A station built in 1966 on Guelph Line was the new headquarters building taking the place of the overcrowded Queensway Dr. station. Architect John Harkness won an award for his design. No longer in use, it has since become the second Burlington location of the Smith Funeral Home.

As the city grew, the number of fire stations grew to meet the need. No. 4 at 711 Appleby Line was opened in 1969; No. 5 on Kilbride Rd. in 1979; and in 1994, No. 2 (replacing Guelph Line) at Upper Middle Rd. and Mountain Grove Ave.; and No. 6 at Cumberland Ave. and New St. A new headquarters building, No. 1 Station, was erected on Fairview St.in 1983. The new building included a training tower; a year later a vehicle maintenance facility was added.

The 1966 fire chief Reg. Law was assisted by three district chiefs, Ian Olson at No. 1, W. Inglis at No. 2 and George Nesbit at No. 3 station. Each station had a brigade of 30 volunteers and the department also employed 27 firemen and four dispatchers.

The 1966 fleet included eight units ranging from a 1942 Ford which pumped 420 gallons per minute, to a 1964 model with a capacity of 840 gallons per minute. There were, in addition, panel trucks, a rescue van with underwater diving equipment, a station wagon used by the fire prevention department, a snorkel unit and approximately 20,000 feet of fire hose.

These statistics were dwarfed by those of 1995 when the department had a fleet of four pumper/rescue vehicles, two pumper aerial trucks, five pumpers, and a pumper tanker. In addition, there were a maintenance vehicle, a platoon chief's van, a utility van, a zodiac boat for water rescue, seven staff vehicles and a 32' mobile command trailer constructed by fire department staff.

By 1995, the Burlington department was the largest composite force in Ontario, one that used 140 volunteers along with 122 full-time personnel.

Fire chief Reg. Law, the first full-time chief, retired in 1975, succeeded by Warren Corp who retired in 1991. Terry Edwards took the top spot in June,1991.

Over the years the Burlington department became more pro-active in fire prevention and public education. Since 1978, home inspections have been carried out from May to October; commercial areas also have annual inspections. In 1987, a grade 5 fire safety program was instituted in schools. In 1994, a "Learn Not To Burn" curriculum was introduced at both the pre-school level and in the elementary schools from Kindergarten to grade 3.

The 1975 Ontario building code made smoke detectors mandatory in all new residential buildings and, in 1989, a Burlington bylaw mandated detectors in all residential buildings including high rise units.

In November, 1985, the 911 telephone emergency number was intro-duced. Ten years later, technology made possible an enhanced system which flashed the caller's address automatically. Since July 1990, a tiered response system sends fire department and ambulance vehicles to all life-threatening emergencies, and in 1996, fire fighters were trained in the heart defibrillation program.

But memories of the old days are not forgotten. Still used in parades and often in demand at fire fighters' weddings is a 1923 Reo fire truck, stored at the Aldershot station but no longer used in active service.

PART III - LAW AND ORDER: THE POLICE DEPARTMENT

As mounting statistics on road accidents accumulate at the police depart-ment, we may think that traffic laws are peculiar only to the age of the automobile. An early traffic law of Upper Canada, however, was passed March 6, 1812, "to prevent damage to travellers on the highways of this province."

There were no policemen as such in the early days, but the laws were upheld by Justices of the Peace such as Hiram Smith and William Chisholm who served the Wellington Square district from 1830 to 1852. It is not known who was in office here to enforce the 1812 traffic law which said in part: "Whereas evil disposed persons travelling the highways in this province with sleds or other carriages, frequently do injury to His Majesty's (George III) subjects whom they do meet on the highway, by not giving an equal half of the side of the road or beaten track, for the convenience of passing each other..."

To remedy "such evil practices" the Legislative Assembly of Upper Canada made it law for persons travelling in sleds or carriages to turn out to the right hand and give an equal half of the road to anyone they might meet coming the other way "for more easy passing by each other without doing damage to either party's team, sled or carriage."

The law further said that anyone driving a sleigh must have affixed two or more bells to the harness, and if he neglected to do so, could be convicted either by confessing the crime or by the oath of one creditable witness. He was then liable to a fine imposed by the Justice of the Peace, of ten shillings to be raised "by the sale of the offender's goods and chattels." Presumably the credible witness could have been the person who wasn't given his rightful half of the road, which surely must have led to some loud discussions in the courtroom.

Inability to pay one's debts was a serious crime. If an insolvent debtor, however, detained in prison, applied to the court and swore by oath that he was not worth five pounds, he could be discharged or else a dollar per week for his support was to be paid in advance by his creditor every Monday.

There is considerable evidence that liquor was blamed for lawlessness in the pioneer days. Small wonder that the taverns became popular, even though their privileges were often abused. A writer in 1836 moaned that the expense on books imported from England added at least one-third to their price, but there was no duty on whisky.

Small grocery stores also served as drinking houses, although a law existed which forbade the sale of spirituous liquors by any but licensed publicans.

A writer of the early times in Upper Canada, Robert Gourlay, considered the law-breaking practice of smuggling tobacco to be worse than the problem of liquor which he felt was declining.

Mr. Gourlay also noted that "another bad practice is declining, the vulgar practice of pugilism." He considered fighting to be "a transgression of the Law of God... which spreads animosities through whole neighbourhoods and townships."

In 1895, Joseph Anderson was the entire Burlington police department with a yearly salary of $365 for serving as village commissioner, constable and truant officer. Sometimes he served as lighter of the coal oil lamps installed in 1892. Occasionally he needed help to combat a crime wave in town. The 1895 council minutes read that "Reeve Richardson and

Councillors Cleaver and Allan were appointed as a committee to endeavour to capture and convict the party or parties who have been breaking into dwellings and committing robberies in the village and that an order be drawn on the treasury for the sum of $100, to be expended as they may deem best for the above purpose."

The lone constable was never idle with not only his nightly duties as lamplighter but also as a keeper of stray animals. Around the turn of the century, he also had to "prepare the town hall for use on all occasions, provide a competent man in his absence, keep good order of the village, prevent improper conduct and arrest guilty persons for disturbing the peace or being drunk and disorderly."

By 1898, there was a dog bylaw on the books and the police officer was instructed to enforce it by making certain that every dog owner buy a tag or be fined and have his dog destroyed.

There was one consolation in his job, however; Constable Anderson had an expense account. It is recorded that he received $1.25 for taking a woman prisoner to the Milton jail, and on another occasion he got $1.50 for keeping a prisoner overnight.

One bylaw which caused a good deal of bickering was passed in Burlington in 1898 and in the rest of Nelson Township in 1900. Any person "riding, driving or propelling a bicycle, carriage, wagon or sleigh, other than carriages for invalids or children, on the sidewalks of the village or township" was liable to a fine of not less than $1 or more than $20, or, if the fine was defaulted, a jail term of one to 20 days.

In 1904, Reeve Kerns was empowered to take such action as he thought best to abate the nuisance caused by rowdyism on the streets of the village. A reward of $10 was offered for information about vandals who were breaking the globes on the new street lights and shooting holes in the library's glass door. Public morals were also an issue and notices were posted around the village warning that "loafing on the sidewalks, spitting on the sidewalks, riding bicycles on the sidewalks and discharging crackers or any other fireworks are strictly prohibited by this council."

A newspaper account of 1905 reads, "The Village Council are to be commended upon securing the services of William Benns as extra constable to put down the loafing nuisance in front of business places and on the corners." 'Twas ever thus!

To make matters worse, the old plank sidewalks were falling apart and council had to contend with a series of lawsuits. Dr. Richardson was paid $1.50 for dressing a man's injured hand. Two councillors, after talking with the man, managed to settle the matter for $30.25. A Burlington woman received $50 for injuries after a loose board flew up and struck her. Another woman got $15 when she fell on a defective sidewalk. Council soon "found it necessary to appoint an assistant constable." A special meeting of council was called in 1903, "to consider the business of a woman who had fallen on a broken sidewalk while walking to church." She thought she was entitled to $30 but the final settlement was for $10.

Wooden bridges also caused troubles as they began to wear out.

In 1901, a Mr. Henderson was paid $2 for "damages to harness done by his horse breaking through Rambo Bridge on Water St." A cement bridge was built at that point in 1907.

In 1901, the village had a mild smallpox scare. Another duty was added to the one-man police department. Constable Sneath was ordered to see that a certain house was quarantined for two weeks. The family were to stop removing the placard from their door and to remain on their own premises. Sneath then had to watch the house to see that no one left or entered and also had to place a box in a convenient spot for provisions for the family. Finally he had to have the house disinfected to the satisfaction of the medical advisor.

It is not too surprising that there was a constant succession of constables. In 1911, Burlington hired and fired four of them in a space of a few months.

Some of the officers who served the village of Burlington before World War I were Wilson Henderson, William Armstrong, William Greene, John Troughton, Allan Mitchell Sr. and William Tufgar (whose salary was $800 a year). In 1914, Burlington became a town. Lee J. Smith was appointed constable in 1916 with a raise in salary to $17.50 a week, the same as the town's sanitary and liquor inspectors. He was Chief of Police for many years. The year 1916 witnessed the first telephone installed in the police office.

During the war, there was a food shortage and the Chief of Police was instructed, "to permit citizens to keep pigs within the town of Burlington providing they are kept in such a condition as not to be a nuisance."

Burlington in 1916 was a small residential town of 2,530 peaceable citizens, "not averaging one offender a week." Besides the police department, there were five duly qualified and capable justices of the peace, in addition to the mayor, all competent to dispose of any police cases requiring attention.

Special help was sometimes hired and, in 1917, "Bert Dunham was appointed special constable for the balance of the year at $2 for every other Sunday." Help in emergencies was also paid as when Allen Mitchell assisted police in connection with the Taylor store robbery and the shooting of the night constable, Allan Mitchell, Sr. The assailant proved to be a well-known local man about town.

A history of the town, written in 1927 about conditions in the pre-automobile era, stated wistfully: "Between Wellington Square and Hamilton, there were two toll gates, one at Aldershot and the other near the city... and no speed officers to issue blue papers." By 1920, the local magistrate had a full calendar of traffic violators and his request to council was granted, "that he be permitted to retain one-half of costs of all cases coming before him for breach of the Motor Vehicle Act."

Chief Lee Smith.

*Chief Ken Skerrett, Chief of Police
1962– 1981.*

One continuing problem in Burlington during the early years of the century was the presence of "knights of the road" who "rode the rods" on the railroad and stopped off for handouts. The bills for food or transportation would then show up in council accounts. One man put in a bill for $6 "for keeping tramp."

The town clerk was instructed in 1913, "to write the Grand Trunk Railway in reference to the tramp nuisance." If they were in town overnight, the weary willies slept in the 'lockup' behind the town hall.

Sympathy was felt by townspeople for these unfortunate men. Once Mrs. Dorothy Angus asked Chief Lee Smith why so many tramps just happened to come to her house and the chief replied that her address was written on the wall of the lockup as a good place to get a meal in Burlington.

By 1947, Chief Smith's department had grown from night and day constables to a four-man police force with one cruiser. Headquarters were still in the town hall on Elizabeth St. where there were sleeping quarters as well as four steel and concrete cells beneath the office. The department was handling between 400 and 500 cases a year.

Chief Lee Smith retired in 1956 and was succeeded by Deputy Chief Crawford. After amalgamation in 1958, Deputy Chiefs Fred Gaylord and Harvey Hunt from former East Flamborough and Nelson Township police departments aided in setting up the enlarged Burlington police force. Kenneth Skerrett became Chief in 1962.

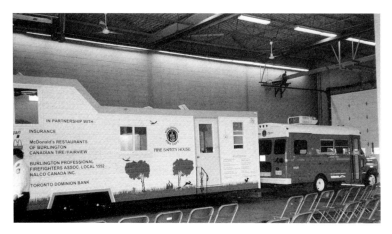

Fire Safety House for instruction of children in fire safety, Burlington Fire Department, 1997.

Police work in 1966 naturally was much different from the early days and Burlington had a force of 51, including civilian staff, two inspectors, a staff sergeant, five detectives, the uniform division and four cadets in training who served as radio dispatchers. Operating from the headquarters on Elgin St., the force was under the direction of Chief Kenneth Skerrett and Deputy Chief Lisle Crawford.

Well-known to all Burlington school children was Constable Peter Bromley, the safety officer. Detective George Moore was in charge of the Juvenile Division, Maria St.

In 1966, the department relied on a fleet of vehicles which included eight patrol cars, three plain vehicles, a paddy wagon and one motorcycle. The officers' duties no longer included street lighting or sweeping out the town hall!

In 1968, the federal Justice Department which shared the Elgin St. building needed more space, necessitating a move of half the police force to Maria Street. With the advent of regional government in 1974, police service became a regional responsibility, with headquarters at 1229 White Oaks Blvd., Oakville.

Kenneth Skerrett was the first Chief of Police for the Halton Regional Police Service. James Harding of Peel Region became Chief in 1979, followed by Peter J. Campbell of Oakville, appointed in 1994 after the retirement of Chief Harding. A new 85,000 square ft. headquarters facility was opened in 1991 at 1151 Bronte Rd. attached to the Regional complex.

The provincial court was at Burlington Square but was later moved to 2021 Plains Rd. near Brant St.

In April, 1983, the city of Burlington gave Halton Region a parking lot on Elgin St. in exchange for the Burlington police property. A new $1.389

million District No. 3 headquarters, built on Locust at Elgin, was opened May 12, 1983.

In February, 1975, the teletype telephone circuit (TTY) was installed to allow people with hearing disabilities to contact police headquarters. Some 1983 developments included the institution of Neighbourhood Watch for children's safety and the beginning of computerization. In November, 1985, the 911 telephone emergency number was introduced. Ten years later technology made possible an enhanced system which flashed the caller's address automatically.

Appropriate police, fire and ambulance services were immediately alerted.

The Children's Safety Village, which was opened in 1987 adjacent to the headquarters building, featured miniature cars and bicycles which travelled the paved streets. There were traffic signals, road signs, railway crossings and sidewalks. It was built with $300,000 in community donations and the project was spearheaded by Staff Inspector Kent Laidlaw of District No.3, Burlington. Continuing support comes from the companies which are featured in miniature stores and businesses. It was refurbished in the 1990s through collective efforts of the Region's Optimist Clubs.

Another important children's program is Drug Abuse Resistance Education (DARE) taught in all grade 6 classes.

In December, 1988, the Crime Stoppers program was begun. Its mission was to solve and deter crime by providing a means of citizen reporting of criminal activity with guaranteed anonymity through co-operation with police, the media and the community. Promotional material and rewards for this service are provided not with tax dollars but through fundraising by the staff of Crime Stoppers.

With the growth of specialized police work, policing became more remote in contrast to the well-known one-man force who patrolled a few village blocks on foot. To return to this more intimate relationship, "Community Policing" was devised, putting the police officer in closer communication with the public. It is a return to citizen participation with Community Consultation Committees in each of eight communities and villages in the Region. Village Constables assigned to the downtown core area and Warwick, a highly populated area in west Burlington, use bicycles for their daily patrols. "Project Visibility" serves north Burlington and Nelson, with Village Constables and a community donated office. The Community Policing model is being adopted across North America and around the world.

There is police participation in special community events such as blood donor clinics, Respect for Law camps for youth in conjunction with Optimist Clubs of Halton, charity sporting events, and the presenting of special charity functions. One of these is Cops Care, an annual project that includes a barbecue, Valentine Dance and Christmas visit, sponsored by Longo's Fruit

Market, all in aid of the Joseph Brant Hospital. All of these activities serve to raise the profile of the Halton Police Service.

Crime rates in 1995 were continuing to decline in Halton and Chief Campbell attributed some of this success to Community Policing initiatives. Indeed the Police Service Motto is "Progress Through Participation."

PART IV - ELECTRICITY, WATER AND GAS

Previous to the 1890s, Burlington streets were unlighted but about 1892 special coal oil lamps were purchased in Montreal and installed at a cost of $1.50 for each lamp and post. The lamps were erected on turned wooden posts and the first official village lamp lighter was Joseph Anderson. By 1897, Thomas Sneath had been hired to light the lamps each night for a yearly salary of $40. Charles Ladle assisted him in the west end. Lamps were located at the principal intersections and, in 1899, council moved "that lamps be placed on the corner of Pine and Martha Streets, at the school house crossing and at Rambo Bridge."

Although electricity came to the village in the late 1890s with the electric radial line, the first mention of it as an illuminator was at a council meeting in 1900: "Reeve and councillors to enquire into the cost of lighting the village by electricity and the best method of doing so." Within a short time, Messrs. Kilmer and Read, representing the Electric Light Company, asked for the privilege of installing a plant to "supply light and power to parties requiring the same". Council approved and a plant was constructed to generate electricity, beginning November 1, 1900. By November 15, the village clerk was selling the coal oil lamps and posts for $1 each. When the town hall was wired, one 16 candlepower lamp was suspended in the council chamber and all agreed that the new method of lighting was very satisfactory.

Now that the streets in the centre of the village were lighted by electricity, two additional lights were ordered for the west end of the village. The expense for street lighting from November 17 to December 31, 1900, was $50.

But the system had its problems. In January, 1901, the power company was asked for a rebate of $5.56, "on account of no lights for three nights." This became a common occurrence. Meanwhile council found it necessary to post a reward of $10 for "such information as will lead to the conviction of the party or parties found breaking the globes on electric lights."

Nelson Township at the same time had its first experience with electric lighting. On July 1, 1900, permission was granted to the Ontario Electric Light and Power Company of Hamilton (represented by Kilmer and Read) to erect poles and string wires in the township.

They were instructed not to "interfere with, obstruct or endanger the travelling public, or to be a nuisance to private property." Strict precautions were taken against any possible accidents or dangers, and if the poles were

Ontario Court of Justice Building.

not erected within six months, the township was to remove all the installations, sell the poles and charge the company for putting the roadway back in good condition. The power company contracted to "furnish free of charge, five electric street lights of 32 candlepower each, which would be maintained and kept lighted from one hour after sunset to one hour before sunrise," on condition that the township would have an employee turn the lights on and off, each street light having its own switch.

Nelson records fail to elaborate if there were the same mechanical headaches at Burlington. The village had to tell the supplier of electricity "that the lights, according to by-law, are not up to agreement and that if not remedied, this council will order in the inspector."

By the end of 1901, accounts were being paid to the Cataract Power Company and the charges remained constant at $55.64 a month. Gradually the entire village became lighted at night, usually following petitions by residents. A sheet of paper in the village's minute book is dated Burlington, March 19, 1906, and reads, "We the undersigned ratepayers of the village of Burlington do hereby petition the Council of the said village to continue electric lights on New Street to the Guelph Line so called." It had 11 signatures.

The Cataract Power and Traction Company which was supplying electricity to Burlington had been founded in 1896 by five Hamilton enterprisers. They had constructed a power plant near St. Catharines at the foot of the escarpment, approximately 35 miles from Hamilton. Within a decade, the company had built up a flourishing business in the peninsula and, in 1907, the Cataract Company was re-organized as the Dominion Power and Transmission Company. The company had absorbed the Hamilton Street Railway, the Hamilton and Dundas Railway and other radial electric lines. Ontario Hydro bought out the D.P.and T. in 1930.

In that year, Hydro indicated it would be interested in selling the distribution system within the municipality to the town corporation. In 1919, Burlington had turned down such a proposition because it was heavily in debt paying for schools and the extension of sewers and water-works. Council was

Burlington Hydro line crew, Joseph Brant Museum in background.   – courtesy Burlington Hydro

equally unresponsive in the depression times of the 1930s. Consequently the Hydro Electric Power Commission was the distributor locally until June 5, 1945, when the town took over.

By 1949, the town had set up its own organization and had become part of the Ontario H.E.P.C. When in January, 1958, Burlington annexed part of Nelson Township and part of East Flamborough, the Ontario Municipal Board ordered that "there shall be established a Public Utilities Commission for the Town of Burlington which shall consist of five members in accordance with the provisions of Section 42 of the Public Utilities Act, which said Public Utilities Commission shall be for the purpose of controlling and managing the Water Works and the Hydro Electric Power systems of the municipality." Members of the first commission were Norman Craig, chairman; Andrew Frame, Gerlacus Moes, Kenneth Morris and John Lockhart, Mayor.

It was decided that Hydro and waterworks should be under one roof to effect economy and efficient administrative handling. Headquarters were on Maria St. from May, 1958, until new quarters were completed at 1340 Brant St. in October, 1962. The staff employed by the P.U.C. at that time numbered 100 people including office employees and outside workers such as linemen, meter readers, testers and waterworks crewmen.

In 1968, it became mandatory that hydro lines be underground in new developments, the cost factored into the cost of homes.In September, 1975, citizens opposed the construction of six 120' high hydro transmission towers in the Sprucehill Ave. area. Later that year the towers were removed and the project cancelled.

The number of hydro consumers grew from 12,000 in 1958 to 46,124 in 1995 and water users from 8712 to 35,916 (apartment and town houses had individual hydro meters but in many cases a single bulk water meter). A plentiful supply of electrical energy is ensured by the grid system which connects all of Ontario Hydro's thermal-electric, thermo-nuclear and hydro electric generating stations.

WATERWORKS

Burlington established a waterworks system in 1909 and laid its first sewerage and storm conduits in 1915. By 1927, town statistics reported that Burlington possessed 11 miles of water mains, 16 miles of sewers and 12 miles of electric cables.

The original record book shows that the first meeting of the Water Commission was held on May 18, 1909. The following took the oath of office: Maxwell Charles Smith, Reeve; and J.S. Allen and W.J. Brush who had been elected by ratepayers on March 8, 1909. Their task was to install a waterworks in Burlington.

Wells had served homes and businesses until then. When water storage was needed for fire protection, a number of underground cement tanks were built at various places in 1896. In 1909, a water tower was built at Maria and John Streets.

A problem each summer was the watering of the dirt and gravelled streets in town to keep the dust down. In 1895, Edward Near got the job for 50 cents a week during the summer months and was told to discontinue after September 17. In 1897, A.H. Finnemore was hired at 50 cents a day to pump water into the tank of the watering truck.

Some thought street watering was a costly frill and the next summer council decided to take no action unless villagers demanded the service. By the next meeting, two petitions had been received, one with 45 names and the other with 11 names. The merits of buying an electric motor to facilitate pumping of water were debated with great vigour by the councillors. Petitions continued to pour in from people who wished their streets watered. Councillor Finnemore, whose pumping job may have been at stake, introduced one with 56 names asking for a bylaw on the matter. There was also much dissatisfaction over the route taken by the one-horse water cart, some residents feeling that certain streets were being watered more than others.

In 1899, council decided to mechanize its water pumping facilities. Once the electric pump was working, industries wanted to use the system. In 1900, Baxter and Galloway Milling Company was charged $5 per year for using corporation water. Any individual wanting water had to pay 10 cents a load. One summer, council was not at all satisfied with the street watering job being done. In line with a policy of concern for tax dollars, the individual doing it was told "that hereafter a percentage of his pay would be stopped for every day such service was not up to the agreement". In 1902, three men applied for the position which by then was paying $150 per season. Still with an eye to thrift, council was seriously considering engaging someone who could also haul gravel and help keep the roads in repair. The street watering problem was resolved by 1915 when the town was paying $140.82 annually to the British American Oil Company for oiling the roads.

The waterworks question had been debated, pro and con, year in and year out until, in 1907, council called for complete plans, specifications and costs of a water system. A special meeting was held on September 15, 1908, "to discuss proceedings to be taken should council decide to submit a by-law to a vote of the people regarding the establishment of a system of water-works for the use of the village". Several samples of water obtained from different sources were sent to Toronto for analysis, to ascertain the relative purity of the water for domestic and other uses.

A bylaw was subsequently passed, authorizing construction of the system and the issue of debentures to pay for it. In June, 1909, $47,200 received from the sale of debentures was paid to the Waterworks Commission. A further amount of $15,000 was raised in 1914 to extend and improve the system. Watermains were laid throughout the village and extended where needed as the community grew. The first sewer system and laying of storm conduits was begun in 1915. The filtration plant was completed in 1935 and an addition built in 1962 for the purification plant on Lakeshore Rd.

SEWERS

Dr. A.H. Speers, Medical Health Officer, was responsible for convincing council of the necessity of sewers. It was essential to install them on Water St. before the permanent Hamilton-Toronto highway was finished, so applica-tion was made to the Provincial Board of Health in 1915 requesting a mandatory order for the installation of a suitable system. A bylaw was passed in June, 1915, to borrow $24,700 to build storm sewers and $53,200 to build the sewage disposal works. Council offered Alex Bell $1,000 per acre for land behind Central Arena as the site for the works.

Alteration to this Drury Lane plant made it the first modern sewage treatment plant in Burlington followed by the Elizabeth Gardens plant in 1959. The Skyway plant on Beach Boulevard was one of the major achieve-ments of amalgamation. Opened in September, 1964, it was constructed under the aegis of the Ontario Water Resources Commission with a capacity of 3,000,000 gallons a day.

Development in the east end (town houses and apartment towers) created a need for expanded sewage treatment capability. In 1975, flows from Elizabeth Gardens and Drury Lane treatment centres were diverted to the Skyway plant where there was an expansion to 20 million gallons a day with phosphorus removal equipment. This allowed several large residential developments such as Brant Hills, Palmer Community and Headon Forest to go ahead. Developers were asked to contribute a portion of the cost of this expansion. Elizabeth Gardens and Drury Lane are still in use, but only as pumping stations to the Skyway plant. By 1995, Skyway was nearing capacity and an addition was planned for 1998. This was to include the removal of ammonia and nitrogen.

Developers must finance the cost of the installation of sewer and water lines. In 1980, sewer and water rates began on a user-pay system.

GAS

Home heating was no great problem for the pioneers as long as there was a plentiful supply of wood and strong arms to wield axes. The convenience of coal furnaces at the turn of the century kept coke and coal dealers busy for many years.

Today, home builders have three main choices for heating purposes: the newest concepts in electric heating, oil heating and gas service which dates back to the old lamplighters.

The Hamilton Gas Light Company was the sole distributor of gas here until 1904 when the new Ontario Pipe Line Company obtained a franchise covering the distribution of natural gas. A period of competition followed as gas heat grew in popularity, and, by 1929, Burlington and Oakville were obtaining gas from the United Suburban Gas Company Limited.

Gas for domestic heating was discontinued during World War II and manufactured gas in place of natural gas was used after 1947. By 1958, in the entire Hamilton-Burlington area, conversion to natural gas was completed on tie-up with Trans-Canada Pipe Line from western Canada.

A crisis in the oil industry gave rise in 1982 to a federal grant for homeowners switching from oil furnaces to alternate heating systems. By 1996, natural gas was the major energy source for homes and industry. It was also beginning to be used as a fuel in motor vehicles. Natural gas is available throughout the urban area, distributed by Union Gas Limited. The 1996 headquarters was at 4450 Paletta Court.

PART V - WASTE DISPOSAL

In the fall, Lakeshore Road used to be clouded with a fog of bonfire smoke, as residents burned leaves from their many large trees. Since this created a danger for traffic, in 1967 a bylaw was passed prohibiting bonfires on property adjacent to highways. Other areas with mounds of fallen leaves also had fires. With an increasing awareness of air pollution, in 1968, bonfires were prohibited unless permission was specifically granted. Eventually it was realized how valuable leaves could be as compost and they began to be collected by the city. In 1995, garden waste collection was implemented.

Garbage collection was put on a three day a week schedule in March, 1968. As in most other communities, it was eventually changed to once a week. Even with recycling, by 1983, the landfill site in Aldershot was nearing capacity and a search for a replacement was sought. West Burlington Citizens Group opposed suggested Aldershot sites. A landfill site at 5400 Highway 25 in Milton became the sole "dump" for the Region. The last one in Burlington on North Service Road was closed in 1987.

Memories of past landfill sites were ever-present in the form of methane gas and leaching from rotting garbage. The landfill site off Kerns Road closed in 1957, but by 1981, a check for leaching had to be made at Bayview Park which was on the old landfill site. Tests were commenced in the summer for leachate on a former landfill site off King Road above Highway 403, closed in 1972. Garbage remains an ongoing concern and landfill sites have had to become state-of-the-art operations, especially since so many products used are still non-biodegradable.

RECYCLING:

In 1970, Mrs. Roberta Golightly of Aldershot led a campaign for the collection of tin, glass and newspaper from garbage. A collection from 300 Aldershot homes proved this could be profitable. The following year, a recycling centre was opened at 891 Brant St., operated by the newly-formed Citizens Committee for Pollution Control (CCPC) and the province gave the town a $25,000 grant for a pilot recycling project.

George Kerr, the first Ontario Minister of the Environment, introduced, in the early 1970s, a program for a deposit on soft drink bottles to encourage their reuse.

In 1971, a glass crusher and newsprint baler were installed at the recycling centre. At first, the work was done by volunteers but, in 1978, two part-time paid employees were added. By 1981, the community-operated recycling project, having moved to the Guelph Line north of Highway 5, was one of the longest-running in the province. Curbside collecting began in March, 1982. Items were placed in grocery bags until 1985 when sturdy blue boxes were distributed to households after a successful pilot project in Aldershot. This concept originated in Kamloops, B.C.; in 1981 Kitchener was the first city in Ontario to use blue boxes.

Halton, in 1985, was the first region to co-ordinate a recycling program through the region, rather than by individual communities. That year, Burlington hosted the 6th annual Recycling Council of Ontario convention, and Halton was cited as the most progressive of all regional areas in Ontario. Billie Holgrave was recognized for 15 years of pioneer volunteer work with CCPC.

By 1995, recycling of paper was so profitable that in some communities thieves were making off with bundles set out at the curbs for collection, before they could be picked up by the municipality. Laidlaw Waste Systems has been responsible for the pick-up of recyclables for processing by a

254 FROM PATHWAY TO SKYWAY REVISITED
Burlington company, Halton Recycling Ltd. on Pioneer Drive.

By 1996, recycling was mandatory and recyclable material could not be accepted at the landfill site. An exception was good material for re-use, accepted at the Amity trailer.

PART VI - BELL TELEPHONE

In the late 1800s, the telephone was a miraculous new gadget. On September 24, 1877, a Mr. Black, a telegraph company official, came to the Ocean House at the beach to disconnect the telegraph wire for the winter. He brought a primitive telephone and connected it up with similar equipment set up at the Burlington telegraph office. Unfortunately the experiment produced a good deal of static.

Regular telephone service first came to Burlington in 1885. Agent for the Bell Telephone Company was T.A. "Tom" LePatourel and the switchboard was located in the dispensing room at the rear of his drug store on Brant St. near Pine Street. Business subscribers listed in 1886 were Mr. LePatourel and the stores of Baxter and Galloway, W. Kerns and Company and Freeman Brothers. The first residence telephone listed in 1889 was for Dr. F. DeW. Bates' home on Water St.

Until he built new premises for his drug store farther south, Mr. LePatourel himself handled all telephone calls and business for the company. Mrs. C. Smith (nee Pansy Anderson) became the first operator in the new store. Mr. LePatourel retained the managership in Burlington until 1914.

Previous to 1900, telephone service was furnished from 8 a.m. to 9 p.m. on weekdays and from 2 p.m. to 4 p.m. on Sundays. A petition was received from subscribers requesting 24-hour service. At that time, there were 80 subscribers but it was necessary to increase the number to 100 before additional service could be provided. E.J. LePatourel, brother of the Burlington agent, came out from the Hamilton office and soon signed up the needed twenty additional subscribers.

At that time, the rate was $15 a year, including three free calls to Hamilton a day. If the subscriber did not use these calls in one day, he might have five the next day.

Permission had to be obtained from the village council before the network of wires and poles could be erected. Poles were installed under the direction of the chairman of the village's roads and sidewalks committee and the roads commissioner.

An old telephone directory, circa 1905, listing all phones in western Ontario was owned by Mrs. W.P. Schultz and was originally used by the Schultz Manufacturing Company.

The first phone charges paid by Burlington council were 30 or 40 cents a month. In 1907, a bill of $2.63 for three months for the town hall office was approved.

In 1910, telephone poles were beginning to dot the landscape more and more. Nelson Township minutes recorded that "since complaint had been made that telephone companies have placed poles on the highway where they will be detrimental to the maintenance of the roads, a committee was appointed to investigate and remove poles where necessary".

Usually council didn't complain unless it was necessary since the township occasionally garnered some revenue from electric and telephone companies. When trees had to be cut down to make way for the poles, the township got the wood to sell or use.

Early telephone, about 1915.
– courtesy Les Armstrong

Demands for new phones were increasing by 1921. Change from the old magneto switchboard to a battery switchboard was made on March 19, 1927. In that same year, Burlington's one thousandth telephone was installed. This locality did not convert to the dial system until October, 1949, when Miss Marion LePatourel, daughter of the first telephone agent, made the first local call, and Mayor Norman R. Craig dialled the first long distance call. There were more than 2,500 phones in Burlington by then.

In 1948, all telephone numbers were changed to four digits. As this became insufficient to meet the demand, in 1953, two letter, five digit numbers were introduced and the exchange prefix NE(Nelson) 4 was assigned to the Burlington exchange. Five years later NE 7 was added. Changes were made as usage increased until the use of area codes, with three exchange numbers followed by four digits, were needed.

In 1957, an addition was added to the dial exchange building at the northeast corner of Caroline and Brant Streets enabling Bell to provide some 1,700 additional customers with dial service by the end of March, 1958.

In order to cope with the growing telephone needs of the area, in 1959 underground conduit pipe was laid throughout the town. By 1965, there were 20,370 phones serving the Town of Burlington. On October 30, 1966, the all-new "Touch Tone" dialling was introduced and on the same date direct distance dialling, without any contact with the operator, became a fact.

The building at 507 Brant St. remained, in 1996, the main switching centre. Another was on the Guelph Line north of the QEW. There was a work centre at 1171 Pioneer Rd. and a phone centre at Mapleview Mall. There were

77,000 lines of service with six charge-free exchanges, including Hamilton, Oakville and Milton.

By 1996 Bell Canada provided a complete range of services including telephone, teletype, TWX, data equipment and transmission, mobile radio, video conferencing and inter-communication equipment of all types. Bell Canada has continued to deploy fibre-optic cable within the Burlington commercial and industrial areas. November, 1994, marked the availability of the latest in fibre ring technology. ISDN, (Integrated Services Digital Network) is a telecommunications service that links the user directly to the digital network, making possible the simultaneous, high-speed transmission of voice, data, still image and video signals over a single telephone line. Applications include LAN bridging, group video conferencing, credit card verification, high-speed file transfer and Internet access. ISDN's multiple channels allow more than one application at a time.

Times have changed from the days of 1918 when town council ruled that "if the town engineer requires a telephone in his residence, he be requested to pay for same".

27
Communications: The Media

Newspapers have played an important role in this country since the early years of the 19th century. To the homesick and lonely pioneers who lacked dependable mail services, a copy of any newspaper or periodical was precious and it was passed from person to person in the community. The only newspaper published in the late 18th century was *The Upper Canada Gazette*. A popular newspaper around 1836 was *The New York Albion*, "an extensive double folio, compiled for the use of the British settlers in the United States and Canada." The paper contained extracts from the leading English journals.

A respected periodical was *The Genesee Farmer*, published monthly in Rochester, New York, and circulated in Upper Canada. Its writing was typical of the era's style in newspapers with flowery passages, long paragraphs and no photographs. The sometimes inaccurate drawings of animals were important to such publications and one letter to the editor complained of a sketch of a cow weighing about 1,000 pounds with legs like four slender candles.

As well as the most practical of farm news and price quotations, there were articles about the experiences of people trying to raise silkworms and handy household hints such as a formula for waterproofing boots by heating a mixture of beeswax, turpentine, oil tar and pitch, "taking care not to set the mass on fire."

An editorial tried to encourage women to grow large gardens by saying it was good for their health and a graceful accomplishment. A male reader wrote to say that he "would ride 20 miles to see one really healthy woman."

Does this editorial comment of years ago sound familiar? "The hundreds of young men scattered throughout the country and lounging about the towns, furnish indisputable evidence that many in the rising generation are contracting habits which in after life must cause a large amount of sorrow and wretchedness."

New settlers in Upper Canada often placed ads in the newspapers, inviting girls to join them in wedlock, promising to be the "most adoring and obedient of husbands."

One paper widely welcomed was *The London Illustrated News* which from 1862 published a special Canadian edition. Later, loading down the rural carriers' mailbags, were copies of *The Mail and Empire* (now *The Globe and Mail*).

There is evidence that a small newspaper was published about the time of Confederation at Nelson Village by the McCoy family. Called *The Little Wasp*, the weekly sheet had all the local news and gossip. For some reason its motto was, "Arrah! how hot his little feet is", supposedly the remark of a visiting Irishman after a wasp had landed on his hand.

The Halton Journal carried no real news at all, but invited subscribers to take *The Daily Globe*, *The Bi-Weekly* and *The Weekly Globe*, Toronto publications. From the files of Milton's *Canadian Champion* comes the following item in September, 1873: "The village known as Wellington Square was on Tuesday incorporated by the County Council under the name Burlington and is now a full blown village. The old name was inconvenient on account of the large percentage of letters being sent to Wellington".

In the 1870s, newspapers printed names of persons for whom mail was being held at the post offices and a Traveller's Guide listed stagecoach schedules leaving from Milton. "For Bronte station: Stage leaves every morning at 5:50 and every afternoon at 1:30. Fares 50c. For Hamilton: Stage leaves every morning at 5 o'clock, fare $1".

Scrapbooks were a family hobby, popular around the turn of the century when reading material was still scarce. Favourite articles, recipes, dramatic fiction, serialized love stories, and emotion-charged poems were cut from newspapers and pasted close together. Picture postcards were spaced for contrast while fillers and jokes were used in small spaces as they are in some newspapers today.

The first Burlington newspaper was *The Burlington Budget* published in the early 1890s. Editor and proprietor was J.A. Belt. In the issue of October 24, 1890, the following were advertisers: T.A. LePatourel, C.F. Coleman, the general store of J. Galloway and Son; W.H. Finnemore, rolling and flour mills; G. Nelles, general store; S. Cline, Burlington Marble and Granite Works; E. Williamson, undertaker; Geo. Allen, hardware; Geo. Knife, painter and decorator; J. N. Ogg, harness dealer,; L.J. Rusby, butcher; John Campbell, butcher; Geo. Noyes, tonsorial artist; T.A. Atkinson, groceries; and Dr. Richardson, medical surgeon.

Among the news items: "The Village Council are grading one of the streets in town and are certainly doing a fine piece of work. They are using a machine for the grading and from all appearances are making a splendid job. In a short time if the grading is continued, Burlington will have streets second to no village of its size in Ontario." Another item concerned the shutdown of the Baby Carriage Factory which was putting in new machinery to keep up with the strong demand for its product.

An early newspaper, *The Burlington Record*, published from 1896, faltered two years later. The equipment and a list of 300 subscribers were bought for $1,500 by Elgin A. Harris, an experienced printer on Petrolia, Wingham and Caledonia papers.

Gazette *newspaper office, about 1902.*
               – courtesy Joseph Brant Museum

Elgin Harris.
   – courtesy Joseph Brant Museum

For four years he published *The Gazette* in a building on Water St. opposite John St. and when the site was purchased for a canning factory, he moved the business to Elgin Street. This land was needed by the Toronto-Niagara power line and again *The Gazette* moved, this time to 370 Brant St.

Subscriptions in the early 1890s were often paid with eggs, butter, firewood, apples and chickens. Mr. Harris recalled that no charge was made for birth, death and marriage notices. They were considered news.

The Gazette soon had a good business operating job printing: tax notices, dog tag certificates, bicycle permits, ballots and pay sheets for the town. In 1900, Council authorized the clerk "to get minutes, bylaws and financial statement of last year printed as cheap as possible". Apparently Mr. Harris offered them a good price since thereafter the words, "Gazette Print, Burlington" appeared on all records.

Elgin Harris was *The Gazette* editor and publisher for 57 years, later being joined by his son, George. Elgin Harris retired in 1956 after selling the paper to a group of Burlington businessmen.

After his retirement he continued to take an active interest in town activities with daily visits to *The Gazette* and *The Hamilton Spectator* branch office.

In 1966, on the occasion of his 90th birthday, he recalled his active life in Burlington, not only as local newspaper editor but as Reeve, Mayor, County Warden, member of the Water Commission and the School Board!

In 1965, *The Gazette* was sold to PCO Publishing Co. Ltd., a subsidiary of

Examples from local 1997 newspapers.

The Toronto Star, later to Metrospan Publishing Ltd. and finally, in 1975, to Southam Press, publisher of *The Hamilton Spectator*.

This headline story on January 8, 1958, showed that other newspapers found that Burlington news made good copy the week of amalgamation: "'Birth of the New Burlington ... The Biggest Town in Canada' made headlines big and small in papers all over Ontario last week." By 1966, the *Gazette*'s circulation had climbed to 8,000.

In 1971, it went to a tabloid format, competing with another local tabloid, *The Burlington Post*. The following year yet another competitor was added, *Sports Burlington*. A wider range of news produced a name change to *News Burlington*. In July 1976 the name was again changed to *Saturday Morning News*, but the faltering publication folded later that year.

Weekly newspapers emphasize the good news of a community but sometimes a sad event occurs. One of the biggest stories, necessitating a special Friday *Gazette* edition, was the Halliday Homes fire of 1974.

After the turn of the century, Burlington had its own "column" in *The Hamilton Spectator* consisting mainly of "jottings" from residents in the lakeside community. One of Burlington's early contributors to *The Spectator* column was Nora Gilbert who combined this for 20 years with her regular job as Bell Telephone employee. Her devotion to journalism finally won her a full-time position on *The Spectator*'s staff as Burlington reporter.

As Burlington grew, so did *The Spectator*'s coverage. The paper maintained a bureau in the city with a staff of reporters and photographers and printed daily news and pictures transmitted to Hamilton by teletype printers.

Over the years *The Gazette*, its writers and photographers, won many Canadian Weekly Newspapers Association awards, one of the last for a Promising Artists Program showcasing local talent.

The final edition of *The Gazette* was September 2, 1986, after being named the best weekly newspaper in Canada the year before.

The coverage of Burlington news by *The Hamilton Spectator* made its melding with *The Burlington Gazette* as a daily, *The Burlington Spectator*, a natural evolution. Brent Lawson, last editor of *The Gazette*, became editor of the new paper at the new offices at 534 Brant St., former retail outlet for Union Gas. Due to cutbacks in the mid-1990s, *The Burlington Spectator* ceased to be a part of the newspaper which shortened its name to *The Spectator*. *The Spectator* continues to have a "Burlington News" section.

The Burlington Post began in a small office at the corner of Caroline and John Streets, the first edition on September 15, 1965. In 1967, the *Post* was purchased by Inland Publishing and, in 1970, Roy Singleton, the advertising manager, was named publisher. Ten years later a Saturday paper was added and by January, 1986, it was a Wednesday, Friday and Sunday paper, published from a location on Fairview Street. The *Post*, like *The Gazette*, was the recipient of many awards for excellence.

Roy Singleton left the Post in 1993 and founded *Burlington Journal*, another weekly tabloid. Located on Brant St., it was owned and operated by Singleton's company, Nelson Printing, Publishing and Distributing.

Cityscope, a monthly tabloid, published by Joncor Publishing, began in the spring of 1995. As well as *Cityscope*, Joncor published *Enterprise*, oriented towards business news, five times a year and *Heritage Burlington,* in February, heritage month. Dave De Jong, former *Post* editor, was founding publisher and editor.

OTHER MEDIA

In 1976, a group of 22 Burlington shareholders started radio station CING. A major shareholder was Douglas Cunningham who became station manager. The first broadcast was July 21 from an antenna at Kerns Rd.and Highway 5. The transmitter was strong and interfered with CHWO Oakville. The issue was taken to the Canadian Radio-Television and Telecommunications Commission which granted CING permission to go ahead, and on September 24 broadcasting resumed. In the 1990s, the station became known as Energy 108 directed to a youthful audience.

Citizens Cable TV began offering service January 21, 1972, after the local operating license was purchased from Famous Players the year before. President was lawyer Harry Zahoruk and vice-president was Mayor George Harrington. By 1976, cable channel converters were being sold, able to bring in 15 to 20 television channels. In 1980, Citizens Cable was sold to Agra Industries and operated as Cablenet. On February 11, 1983, Cablenet began offering Pay TV. Cablenet was sold in 1990 to Cogeco, a Quebec-based media conglomerate.

28
The Library

Library services began in Burlington in January, 1872, at a meeting of the public school trustees of S.S. No.1 Nelson, with William Bunton, Benjamin Eager and William Kerns in attendance. The question of establishing a library for the use of the school was discussed and a resolution passed that the trustees purchase a supply of suitable books from the Board of Education in Toronto.

In March, $56 was spent on books which were placed in the hallway at the school and the next year an additional $25 was appropriated. No further grants were made until 1883. The following year, a concert was given by the teachers and pupils and $50 was raised to buy more books. The trustees matched this amount and the library collection continued to grow.

It is interesting to note that, in 1872, the library was open to the public one hour a week on Friday afternoons between 4 and 5 o'clock. Later when the service proved popular, and more books were available, the school was opened for two hours on Tuesday evenings and for four hours on Saturdays from 5 p.m. to 9 p.m.

W.H. Finnemore was the first chairman of the library board. Later chairmen were Dr. William Richardson, W.F.W. Fisher, O.T. Springer, F.W. Galloway, Joseph Ackland, W.R. Gilbert, H.T. Foster, Harry Rowsome, V.H. Peart, B.S. Hicks, H. Goodwin and A. Boynton. This record is not complete and names are not necessarily in order of service, the list being made up from minutes of meetings from 1872 on. Others who gave outstanding service through the years include William Wiggins who served as secretary-treasurer for 47 consecutive years, Fred Blessinger, Edmond Holtby, J.A. Lockhart, Ivan Moxham, Gordon Berry and C.D. Bull.

Skipping to more recent times, Frank Rose was a member of the library board from 1965 and chairman from 1969 to 1972. Having worked for many years with the advertising firm of Russell T. Kelly he used his skill of persuasion to convince city council of the need for a new library to meet the needs of patrons in the coming years. At his death, his family donated to the library the 20-volume Oxford English Dictionary. Central Library's Board Room was named the Frank Rose Room in his memory.

Jack Simpson retired from the Board in 1983 after 15 years, all but two of them as chairman. Allan Ward was another long-time member who served for 24 years.

While library services in Burlington were provided from the early days

Post Office (left) and library on site of current city hall.

under various names, the institution as such always served as the cultural core of the community. The Mechanics Institute figured prominently in Upper Canada in the 1850s and '60s, the first one having been established in 1831 at York (Toronto). It relinquished its library facilities under the Free Libraries Act of 1882 while social and recreational activities were taken over first by the Canadian Institute and later by the Y.M.C.A.

In 1896, Henry Berry's small library in a house on lower Brant St. also served the literary needs of the village.

In 1906, Burlington's library board received an offer from John Waldie, Toronto, a respected former citizen of the community, Burlington's first reeve and Member of Parliament for Halton, to donate a building for library purposes, provided the village would furnish a suitable site. The village council submitted a bylaw to the people on April 6, 1906, and they voted 83 for the project, two against. The library board was given $1,000 to purchase a site and a lot on Brant St. was bought from Alex Riach, located adjacent to what was Dr. W.A. Weaver's home at 432 Brant St., occupied at that time by Dr. William Richardson.

Plans for the library were drawn by architect Charles Mills, a summer resident who lived in a house called Thayendanegea at Water St. (Lakeshore Rd.) and Brant Ave. (Brock Ave.). Various artisans and local firms helped construct the building under Mr. Mills' direction and on February 21, 1907, the Burlington Public Library was formally opened.

Space in the town hall on Elizabeth St. eventually became over-taxed by the police and fire departments' needs so the village clerk, O.T. Springer, was permitted to occupy space in the new library building, council paying rent to the board. Originally the library's book stacks were on the right hand side of the building and the left side was used for socials and later divided into two rooms. The front was used as a reading room, the back as the library when the courtroom was located on the premises. The reading section was used for classrooms for students in 1921 when Central High School was being constructed. It would seem that the necessity to shuffle civic offices from place to place to meet space demands was the same problem the town was grappling with before the new 1964 town hall was built.

An early librarian was Edward Webber who served for many years. He was a manufacturer of carriages and wagons in his business life. From 1908 to 1935 Miss Mary Detlor was librarian and after her death Miss May Holtby served for a short time. Mrs. Dorothy Angus became head librarian in 1935 and soon was "friend to thousands". She was named Citizen of the Year in 1957, the first woman to receive the award.

Ida Reddy joined the staff of the Elizabeth Street library in January, 1961, and when Dorothy Angus retired a year and a half later, she was made Chief Librarian. She saw the building become over-crowded and despite additions and alterations it was obvious it could no longer serve the community's needs.

Ida Reddy resigned in 1967, and Lucille Galloway came to Burlington as Chief Librarian in 1968, in time to become closely involved in the move to the new Central Library on New Street. During her tenure, the collections grew along with the budget, branches moved to expanded quarters, new branches opened and the library began its first automation programs. On her retirement, in March 1985, the local history room was named the Galloway Room.

Wendy Schick joined the staff in 1968 and was appointed Chief Librarian in 1985.

Duties of today's library staff are much different from those of town clerk Springer when he combined his work as a town employee with that of part-time librarian. He agreed to keep the library open while he was working as clerk, so the library was open longer than it would have been otherwise. There was a wicket at the back of the town office where borrowers were given a list of available books. No one was allowed to touch the books, and only the librarian could take them from the shelves for borrowers who paid a rental fee on each one.

The income and town grants soon proved inadequate and town council agreed to finance the care and upkeep of the library building in place of the annual grant, in return for the use of the space it occupied. This helped ease the burden considerably and the library board carried on until 1946. A study was made of the library situation and it was decided that its activities should be brought under the Public Libraries Act which then made it a free library to Burlington readers. The first chairman under the new arrangement was Judge C.D. Harkness and the board consisted of eight members appointed by the municipality and the public and separate school boards.

Under the new regulations, the town took over the property on Brant St. and within three years library requirements had outgrown these premises. Council placed before the ratepayers a bylaw to authorize an expenditure of some $200,000 to build a new municipal office but the ratepayers turned down the proposal. The library board then approached council with the suggestion that the late Dr.A.H. Speers' residence on Elizabeth St. be bought and the Brant St. property turned over to the town for its own offices.

The Speers property was subsequently bought and remodelled for about $36,000 of which amount the province paid $12,000; then it underwent several renovations designed to give better library service.

Volunteers through the years aided the library's work, among them, during the 1950s Mrs. Nick Findlater who conducted a children's story hour each week with 40-60 youngsters attending. Mrs. Dorothy Taylor delivered books of their choice weekly to shut-ins. The library also provided accommodation for pre-natal classes in conjunction with the Halton County Health Unit.

An unusual library service in Burlington was for young English war brides who, after 1945, came to the library looking for advice on Canadian housekeeping. Librarian Dorothy Angus befriended many of these girls and helped them with their shopping problems created by the difference in weights, measures and currency. A lecturer from MacDonald Institute in Guelph came to give the girls lessons in planning and cooking meals, a service that was never forgotten.

As Burlington grew, the Elizabeth St. main library became overcrowded, despite additions made to the building. The opening of branch libraries in Aldershot and east Burlington did not alleviate the problems completely. Two professional librarians, Ida Reddy and Janis Lewis, children's librarian, carried on as best they could. William Loosely was chairman of the board for several years during this time in the mid-1960s as plans were being discussed for a new main building.

In March, 1967, city council offered the library board a site in Central Park for the long-needed new building. The architect of the $532,000 edifice was Philip Brook of the firm of Brook-Carruthers-Grierson-Shaw. The library was opened by Governor General Roland Michener on November 15, 1970. The old town bell had been installed at the front entrance of the new building and was struck at 4:30 p.m. by the Governor General to officially open the building. An original painting "White Pines" by Robert Bateman, commissioned by the library board was presented to Governor General and Mrs. Michener.

The following year the National Design Council and the Department of Industry, Trade and Commerce awarded Central Library an Award of Excellence in the Concrete Awards Program, attesting to the fact that the building was the most impressive of its type in Canada.

Central Library was designed to be built in two stages. Accordingly, with circulation increasing, the second stage was constructed and opened May 24, 1975. The three-storey addition provided additional space for both reference and circulating collections and included an audio-visual area and an elevator.

Tansley Woods Centre which includes a branch library, opened 1996.

The year 1972 marked the 100th anniversary of library service in Burlington. To celebrate this milestone, a centennial dinner was held on January 16. Mayor George Harrington declared the name of the 'multi-purpose' room, Centennial Hall.

In January, 1978, Information Burlington was relocated to Central Library. Established in 1971, it was subsidized by a town grant and had been operated by the Chamber of Commerce in its offices. In 1992, it became a department of the library.

For Central Library's 10th anniversary celebration in 1980, *Toronto Star* columnist, Gary Lautens, and his wife Jackie, who lived in Burlington, were guests at a special celebration. Lautens assisted Lucille Galloway in cutting a birthday cake.

In 1981, designated "Year of the Disabled" by The United Nations, a wheelchair ramp was installed at Central Library along with enhanced service to the blind and partially sighted. In 1986, an automatic door opener was installed, adding to the accessibility. Talking and large print books, books on tape and print enhancers were all available by the early 1980s.

Aldershot Branch began in 1960 in the basement of the Dominion Store (later Super Fresh) in Aldershot. Four years later it rose above ground to a location in the same plaza. It was moved to Maplehurst Plaza in 1979 and then, in 1989, to Downsview Plaza, both on Plains Rd.

Skyway Branch, opened in 1965 in the Skyway Plaza on Lakeshore Rd.in east Burlington, was moved in 1971 to Appleby Mall at Appleby Line and New St. and appropriately renamed New Appleby Branch. In 1983, it was moved to Appleview Square at Appleby Line and Fairview.

Mountain Gardens Branch was opened in 1968 at Mount Royal Plaza on Brant St., north of the Q.E.W. In 1978, it was moved to Upper Middle Rd. and Brant St. and renamed Tyandaga Branch.

Storytime, Central Library.
– John Bauld, photographer

A book deposit centre was opened in Kilbride School in 1969 to serve the rural areas. This service was established in partnership with the Halton Board of Eduction.

In November, 1994, a new Burlington community centre and library began to be constructed in the northeast area of the city. A joint project with the City of Burlington, the library was not a leased facility as other branches. The facility encompassed a recreation leisure pool, the library, a double gymnasium, meeting and all-purpose rooms. In 1996 the facility was named Tansley Woods Centre.

Automation allowed the library to improve its delivery of services over the years. Beginning in 1977, computer terminals were linked by telecommunication to computers at the University of Toronto. This system provided cataloguing data and printed the catalogue cards. Microfiche readers replaced the card catalogues in 1979. A few years later, the GEAC Integrated Library System for circulation control, including holds, fines, overdues, etc., was installed.

With the beginning of the home computer era, small micro-computers were made available for borrowing in 1983 and '84, the first public library in Canada to provide this service. Computer courses were also taught at Central Library, beginning in 1983 and continuing for five years.

On-line public access to the catalogue, yet another step in the library board's automation plan, was introduced in the late 1980s. Two years later dial-up access to the library data base was made available to home and office computers.

The library established electronic links in 1993 with collections of the other Halton public libraries and those of Halton school boards and Sheridan College. A new automated library system was also established that year.

Lucille Galloway was a strong supporter of library programs. With her guidance and the ability of program co-ordinator Marilyn Branch, celebrities were enticed to Centennial Hall. Well-known Canadians in the fields of literature, music, the media, the political scene, the stage, radio and televison came to educate and entertain. For the town's Centennial in 1973, a gala concert evening in June featured pianist Oscar Peterson. From its inception, the walls of Centennial Hall have held ongoing exhibits of art, giving new and established artists a venue for their work.

From 1970 to 1996, library activity more than tripled as the population grew and services at Central Library expanded. In 1983, circulation passed the one million mark.

The 1990s brought increased needs from job seekers, those training for second and third careers, early retirees and students with more sophisticated demands. All this with decreased provincial funding!

The Burlington libraries are people-places. The logo, designed in 1972 by Ross McJannett, a senior design student at Sheridan College, stretches arms out to the community. The library, attempting within restricted budgets to keep up with the rapid advance of technology and the new and varying needs of the people of Burlington, will, above all, still be the welcoming place it has been over the years.

29
Leisure Pursuits: Sports and Culture

The history of recreation and sports in this area goes back to the days of the Mohawk Indians, some of whom competed in such contests as lacrosse, swimming, canoeing and archery, while others among them turned their talents to crafts. Examples of their ceramics, weaving and bead work have been preserved and can be seen at Joseph Brant Museum. When the United Empire Loyalists and other white settlers came to the head of the lake, they often combined work and recreation, so barn raisings or quilting bees were occasions to anticipate. Settlers on widely-separated acres got together in summer for picnics, boating and log-rolling while, in winter, dances and sleigh rides were favoured. As churches were constructed in the township and village, they became the centres of community activities. People gathered in them, and in the homes, for suppers, singing and story-telling.

At the time of Confederation, the Bachelors' Ball was a social affair held once a year, eagerly awaited by young ladies and by bachelors, as well. After 1873, the newly-incorporated village of Burlington became a popular vacation place. Summer cottages sprang up along the lake front and on the beach strip. Rambo Flats was a favourite picnic spot and boat trips on the bay and on the lake brought visitors back year after year.

Lawn bowling was first organized in 1904 on the green between Trinity Methodist Church and the parsonage and later on a private green at the Brant Hotel. From 1910, local bowlers owned their own green on Elgin Street on property enlarged by a purchase from Ontario Hydro in 1938. The green was moved to Central Park in later years. At one time, there was a green on Shadeland Ave. in Aldershot. Bowling enthusiasts may also use the city's modern indoor five and ten-pin bowling alleys.

Although few records have been found of their activities, there was a Burlington Athletic Club in the early 1900s and Burlington had a championship hockey team in 1912. One of the town's great all-round athletes was Howard "Hud" Sheppard whose memories of bygone contests were legion.

There were individual champs, too, such as Eddie Cotter, famous long-distance runner. At his home in Guelph in 1966, Mr. Cotter recalled winning his first long distance race Christmas Day, 1904, in Burlington. The distance was 11 miles. Holder of the record for this annual race, he was a member of Canada's Olympic team in England in 1908, and the following year won the Brantford to Hamilton marathon of 26 miles, 176 yards. *The Hamilton Spectator*, sponsor of this race, sent Eddie to England for another marathon

Eddie Cotter.

Burlington Hockey team, 1911– 1912. Back row: Percy Thorpe, Lee Filman, A.L. Craven, Howard Sheppard, Stan Coates. Front row: George Muirson, Delos Cole, H.T. Blair, Russell Sheppard, Gordon Colton. Centre: Hartley Allan.   *– courtesy Joseph Brant Museum*

event which was cancelled due to the death of King Edward VII in 1910. When the *Herald* (a Hamilton newspaper) road race around the bay was an annual event, Eddie Cotter was a frequent entrant and invariably was among the leaders. Of historical interest, a black granite 15-mile marker for the *Herald* Road Race still stands in 1997 on the north side of Plains Rd. near West Plains United Church. The City of Burlington 15-mile road race began in 1974. The May, 1978, race attracted more than 900 runners, a 50% increase over 1977. With the rebuilding of Plains Rd., the Burlington race ended and runners reverted to the Around the Bay marathon which celebrated 102 years in 1996.

In 1980, Terry Fox, a young British Columbia man suffering from cancer, ran through Burlington on a proposed cross-Canada run to raise money for cancer research. Although the disease claimed him before he could finish, his run initiated annual Terry Fox runs beginning in 1981, proceeds continuing to be directed to cancer research. The Miles for Millions was another marathon based in Hamilton which attracted many Burlington runners.

Skating and hockey were popular then as now. Bert Allen recalled that boys used to skate on the bay starting at the old inlet near the Brant Hotel and ending at James St. wharf in Hamilton, always careful to skirt the open water near the canal. The first outdoor skating rink was opened in 1904 and a covered rink was built in 1914 at a cost of $10,000. This was a Quonset-hut type of building on Elgin Street where the Works Department had its building. (With the change to Regional government, Public Works headquarters moved to Oakville). Hockey games attracted many spectators and on one occasion there were 1,200 in attendance at a home game. Later that night, it snowed heavily and the weight of the snow caved in the roof, fortunately with no one in the building at the time. The damage was repaired and the building continued in use. Newspaperman Elgin Harris recalled trainloads of Burlington fans going to Milton to support the local team.

Town council aided local sports programs whenever possible. In 1919, the Council minutes recorded a request by Dr.Tom Peart for a donation and use of a team of horses and a grader to help lay out grounds for the Burlington Baseball Club. He was given $25, enough to get started on the project. In 1922, a motion was passed for "a grant of $150 to the Burlington Skating Rink Company".

The Lions Club, organized in 1925, bought the old car barn site between Martha and Pearl Streets in 1929 and converted it to a children's playground with swings, slides, a wading pool and a softball diamond. Later they turned an old barn on the property into the Lions Club Hall. It was used for many community activities and at one time for headquarters of groups such as the Scottish Country Dancing Society. A new building was erected in 1992 at the James and Martha Streets corner. The Lions share some of the building with Children's Assessment and Treatment Centre relocated from Lakeshore School.

Before the formation of a town recreation committee, service clubs financed league sports while library and church groups taught arts and crafts. The police department sponsored judo and wrestling groups and the volunteer fire department in 1933 operated a park bounded by Hager Ave. and Caroline St. featuring playground facilities and a full softball schedule. In the same year, the Freeman Athletic Association was organized to promote hockey, lacrosse and softball in the area north of town.

Burlington Central High School spirit was given a real lift in the 1930-31 season. The track and field team won the Halton County and East Flamborough inter-scholastic field championship for the fourth year in succession; the senior boys' rugby team, winners of the Niagara district championship, went undefeated in the series; the boys of the senior hockey team were district champs, and the girls' senior basketball team went all the way to win the COSSA championship. The high schools have had many successes but 1930-31 was a tremendous year for a school which had just begun to put emphasis on sports. Burlington Central High had won a place in the sun!

Until the mid-1940s, the town, financially assisted by the fire department, promoted lacrosse and hockey at the covered ice rink. The need for a larger arena had grown apparent and a committee composed of Dr .and

Mrs.W.A.Weaver, co-chairmen; Harry M. Saunders, A.S. Nicholson, E.R. Macklin, N.R. Vinton and Earl Swift, was formed. After much discussion, it was decided to build on New St. on a 12-acre site. Funds were raised by public subscription, and a sod-turning ceremony was held on May 23, 1951.

When completed, the large arena was equipped to handle hockey teams and skating clubs on its 80 by 185 foot surface. The Circus Room auditorium was built upstairs to accommodate meetings and craft classes. The town's first recreation commission had been formed in 1950 and took up headquarters in the new arena. In 1952, the committee took over the maintenance of town parks from the Burlington Horticultural Society and became known as the Recreation and Parks committee with Ted Lambert and later, Earl Davis, as director. Davis was assisted by Bob Ballantyne and, in 1962, by Tony Dojcak. After the 1958 amalgamation, Central Park was purchased and the recreation office was moved to a small house on New St. in front of the bandshell. Nearby was the Lankester farm residence, one of Burlington's fine old homes, later used as the centre for the Senior Citizens Club. Central Library was erected on this site.

In April, 1968, the 1951 arena was closed with a hockey special and a few months later a new arena opened in Central Park. The ice surface was larger than Maple Leaf Gardens, so went a report of the time, and the building included a seniors' wing and an auditorium. In October, 1979, a new seniors centre was opened in Central Park. Designed by Burlington architect, Michael Torsney, it included a hall for dances and banquets, kitchen, sitting room, pottery workshop, woodworking shop, crafts room and a billiard room.

Shortly afterwards, a hockey arena was built in Mountainside Park with funding assistance from the Lions Club. Other arenas include Nelson (1964) with an outdoor pool and wading pool as well, Kiwanis Park Arena in Aldershot and Skyway. Mainway (twin-pad) was built in the mid-1980s with financial assistance by Burlington Lions, Optimist Minor Hockey League, Burlington Oldtimers Hockey Club, Burlington Figure Skating Club and city, federal and provincial (Wintario lottery) governments.

Indoor skating in the form of roller skating has had enduring popularity, becoming extremely popular in the late 1970s and 1980s. Construction on the Burlington Sports Centre, a roller skating rink on Harvester Road, began in April, 1978, the sod turned by Laurie Branch on behalf of developer Rudy Reimer. It later became known as Roller Gardens of Burlington.

Swimming in Lake Ontario and the Bay was a popular pastime and nude bathing was sometimes encountered at LaSalle Park but frowned upon. Even the wearing of bathing suits, cumbersome garments in the early days, made necessary the 1933 Town of Burlington bylaw No. 763: "No person shall wear a bathing suit or costume on any of the streets or in any of the public places ... without also wearing an overcoat, cloak or kimono ... no person shall roll down his or her bathing suit below the arms".

Eventually the public clamoured for public swimming pools. The first publicly-owned indoor pool in Burlington was opened in 1972 attached to M.M. Robinson High School. It was named for Angela Coughlan, a swimmer who won four gold medals at the Canadian Open Swimming Championship in Winnipeg and a bronze medal in the 1968 Olympics in Mexico. Centennial Pool, built in conjunction with Lord Elgin High School, was opened in 1974. That same year, Tyandaga outdoor pool was opened to the public. It was part of the clubhouse complex of Tyandaga Golf Club when it was constructed as a private facility. Another indoor pool was opened at a secondary school, this time, Aldershot High School. As well, there were outdoor pools spaced in the three areas defined by the city's Parks and Recreation Department. In the mid-1990s, however, some outdoor pools were closed due to economic restraints (Tyandaga, Hidden Valley and Optimist.)

Plans for the Burlington Family YMCA got under way in 1964 under Jaycees' sponsorship. The building was constructed adjacent to Central Park on Drury Lane and officially opened in April, 1970, (the pool opened in February). In September, 1981, the official opening of an addition to the "Y" meant a second gym, four racquetball courts, and new and expanded facilities.

With the increase in leisure time, more people have turned to golf, and, for many years, the Burlington Golf and Country Club on North Shore Blvd. was the only one in the area. Opened in 1922, the original clubhouse was replaced by a new building in 1970. Tyandaga Golf Club opened in 1962 but was bankrupt by 1969. In 1973, the town of Burlington purchased the course and made it public. In the late 1960s, Medad Heights at Lake Medad and Burlington Springs on Cedar Springs Rd. were established. Other clubs followed: Hidden Lake Golf and Country Club on No.1 Side Rd.; Indian Wells Golf Club on Walkers Line; Lowville Heights Golf Club at Britannia Rd. and Guelph Line; Camisle, on Cedar Springs Road at No.2 Side Road; and the newest, Millcroft Golf Club adjacent to the Millcroft subdivision on Country Club Drive.

Burlington Yacht Club was active until disbanding in the 1960s when many members helped to form the Bronte Harbour Yacht Club. The Mohawk Canoe Club, founded in 1957 on Lakeshore Rd., was a growing influence in canoeing circles. The Burlington Sailing and Boating Club was organized in 1975 and about that time a LaSalle Park marina was set up. A larger marina was established in the early 1980s. In 1977, the club dedicated its first permanent clubhouse, perched on a bluff in the park, with a sail-past of 138 boats. Tragedy struck in June, 1980, when fire destroyed the building. A new larger two storey clubhouse on the same site was built two years later.

LaSalle Park pavilion was built in 1917 and was in use for many years. The upper level was once used for summer theatre, but much of the pavilion fell into disuse and was boarded up in 1991. The main floor was rebuilt in 1994 with a grand reopening in June, 1995. A few months later, in May, fire

La Salle Marina.
– courtesy City of Burlington

destroyed most of the building. By 1996, plans were complete to rebuild the pavilion, financed by insurance money. It was re-opened in 1997.

Burlington young people may participate in nearly every sport imaginable. Tri-County Hockey teams are co-sponsored by the Lions and Optimist Clubs. At the BLOMHA's annual city "Rep Teams" banquets well-known sports figures address the minor hockey players and help distribute trophies. In the summer, the Burlington Eskimos play football in the Hamilton Old Timers' League and the Burlington Braves in the Ontario Junior Football conference. 1971 was a good year for sports. Burlington Braves won their second straight Eastern Canada Junior Football title. The same year, Nelson Lords won the all-Ontario Junior basketball championship. And in that year, Doug Mundell recovered from a broken leg to win the 6000 meter event at the Canadian Cross Country championships in Halifax. Was it something in the water?

In 1985, Tony Gabriel of the Hamilton Tiger Cats, who began his football career at Burlington Central High School, was inducted into the Football Hall of Fame in Hamilton. At age 36, he was the youngest to be so honoured.

Soccer enthusiasts of any age may play, from minor soccer to adult and senior leagues. In 1977, Wintario lottery funds helped the city build a multi-purpose indoor sports facility at Sherwood Park on Fairview Street. This allowed soccer to be played indoors. The facility holds up to 400 people.

There are minor baseball and softball associations with a Ladies' Softball League. One of the most popular leagues from a spectator point of view is the Burlington Senior Fastball League. Sports activity runs the gamut from basketball to cricket and from martial arts to volleyball. In 1975, the new Central Park Tennis Club building won an award for its design from the Ontario Association of Architects. Indoor tennis is played in an inflated "bubble" on Gallagher Rd. in Aldershot Park and one on Longmoor Dr. in Nelson Park, which are taken down in the summer for outdoor play. The list of sports should also include the many house leagues sponsored by the city.

In 1968, Burlington International Games (BIG) were initiated and the first competition was held in Burlington, Vermont. Succeeding games are held alternately in the American and Canadian "Burlingtons", in competition for the Rotary International Goodwill Trophy.

1981 was designated the Year of the Disabled. That year, Burlington hosted the Ontario Games for the Physically Handicapped, first held in 1975, and later named the Special Olympics. More than 650 volunteers helped with the event which featured 275 athletes competing in categories for the blind, those with cerebral palsy, and wheelchair and amputee athletes. More than 180 records were broken.

Another special event hosted by the city was the Labatt Tankard in 1983, the 46th annual competition for the provincial men's curling championship. The winning team, Ed Werenick's Toronto Avonlea rink, proceeded to the Labatt Briar in Sudbury. The Burlington Curling Club, whose home is the 1951 arena on New St., was much involved in the Tankard. (There is curling also at the Burlington Golf and Country Club.)

A Wintario grant assisted, in 1980, with the building of Burlington Gymnastics Club Inc. on Maple Ave., in Maple Park. The facility is co-educational for children up to the age of six and for girls over that age. The Burlington Boys Gymnastics Inc., the largest such club in Canada at that time, opened a new facility in Maple Park in 1985, next to the girls' club. A joint venture with the City of Burlington, the activities of the club include a special program for the disabled.

The A.J. Dunn award for Sportsman of the Year was established for amateurs in 1970. In 1977, the first woman to win the award was Patti Simmons, a blind athlete. Aged 18, she competed in the Ontario Games for the Handicapped and won three gold medals in swimming and a silver in track and field. In 1984, the Rotary Club of Burlington Lakeshore established the Rotary Athletic Assistance Awards to finance training or assistance for athletes entering national or international competition.

The town's major Centennial project, in 1967, was the development of Spencer Smith Park at the foot of Brant Street. J. Austin Floyd, landscape architect, drew up plans for this beauty spot.

The breakwater, once the domain of the federal government, became the responsibility of the city. More than once, wild water coming in over the breakwater had destroyed the beauty of Spencer Park, as it was once known. To prevent water washing over the wall and freezing spray damaging plant material, trees, sod and walkways, the breakwater was topped with a parapet of concrete four feet high. With this, the seawall altogether is about eight feet above the high water level. The water area behind the wall was then completely filled in. (This area had been used for boat mooring and swim instruction.)

Combined in the Centennial project, was the raising of the park to gently slope up to Lakeshore Rd. eliminating long stairways. At the entrance to the park, at the foot of Brant St., a cedar planked Confederation Terrace was built, with a fountain donated by Sovereign Chapter IODE, flags and flowers. Two-thirds of the cost came from federal and provincial Centennial grants. Winged Man, a $1,500, 27" sculpture by Louis Archambault, was installed there, a gift of the University Women's Club. A few months afterwards, it was found in a flowerbed, thrown there by vandals. It was removed to the City Hall lobby and then given a place of honour inside the front entrance of Central Library. In the 1970s, The Lady of the Lake sculpture fountain was installed.

A railing facing Lakeshore Rd. bears the inscription, "Commemorating 100 Years of Nationhood 1867-1967". Spencer Smith Park has continued to be expanded and improved. It stretches behind Venture Inn and, to the west, to Brock Ave., including space for parking. A boat launching facility was included in a new section of the park.

Elsewhere on the lakeshore, a Halton-Wentworth Waterfront Study was released in 1974 proposing that the entire Lake Ontario waterfront from east Oakville to Grimsby be open to the public. There would be community parks and parkettes every half mile with connecting walkways.

A Waterfront Trail, not quite as far to the west as the study envisioned, but magnificent nevertheless, was completed in May, 1995. The 325 kilometre trail stretched from the Royal Botanical Gardens to the Trent River at the Bay of Quinte. Two days of activities marked the official opening, starting at the Valley Inn Bridge, Sunday, May 14, 1995. Mayor Walter Mulkewich, accompanied by David Crombie (former Mayor of Toronto), Chair of the Waterfront Regeneration Trust, walked and biked through Burlington to Burloak Park. From here, David Crombie continued to hike the trail to its end. In Burlington, the trail crosses several Lakeshore Rd. parkettes, called Windows to the Lake, including Port Nelson Park, Sioux Lookout, and the former McNichol estate at Shoreacres.

By 1996, there were 87 parks in Burlington, encompassing about 435 hectares. There were six community centres. Most were affiliated with schools but Brant Hills Community Centre for the Duncaster Park area opened in 1982 as the first detached building. The new Burlington community centre and Library opened in 1996 on Upper Middle Road east of Walkers Line. Named Tansley Woods Centre, it included a public library branch, a pool, a double gym and space for seniors, pre-schoolers and community groups. Funding assistance came from the JobsOntario Community Action program with the remaining 90% collected from subdivision development charges.

Burlington Parks and Recreation Department sponsored, in recent years, Harvest Fallfest, Christmas Parade, Winter Carnival, Multicultural Festival and The Sound of Music Festival.

In 1967, Laurie Branch came to Burlington as Director of Recreation

Services. Under his guidance, recreation became one of the busiest and most exciting of Burlington's departments. The city's recreation program has often been cited by residents as one of the important reasons Burlington is such a great place to live. Laurie Branch retired in 1988 after 21 years' service. In his honour, the auditorium in Mainway Arena at Mainway and Walkers Line was named Laurie G. Branch Auditorium. Assistant Director, James Olmstead, was appointed director in 1989.

Burlington residents may also avail themselves of recreation spots such as Rattlesnake Point Conservation area, property of the Halton Region Conservation Authority, and the Royal Botanical Gardens land. A short trip to the north near Campbellville is Crawford Lake Conservation Area, with a reconstructed Iroquois village. Skiing is nearby at Cedar Springs Ski Club and Glen Eden at Milton.

Church bulletins and newspapers publicize the myriad of interests offered Burlington residents, ranging from ballroom dancing to craft guilds and from the Arts and Letters Club, established in 1948, to Toastmasters International. Indeed, in the 1960s, statistics showed Burlington led Halton and Peel in arts and crafts participation. Service clubs abound, quietly aiding worthy causes such as crippled children, those who are developmentally challenged, and the underprivileged.

The Junior League of Hamilton/Burlington Inc. began in 1935, the first Burlington Rotary Club in 1951, University Women's Club in 1957, Zonta in 1963, Newcomers Club in 1967, Volunteer Bureau and Canadian Club in 1972. There is also a French language organization, Club Alouette-Laval, Inc. The list could go on...

On the cultural scene, the Burlington Little Theatre, founded in 1951, has, over the years, distinguished itself. A high point in its life was in the summer of 1977 when it represented Canada in the International Theatre Festival in Ireland. It won three nominations and one individual award, more than any other competitor. The theatre's home is in the Drama Centre in Central Park, next to the Music Centre.

Important in the town's recreational programs are the well-attended evening classes in every category from rug hooking to high school credits. About 1933, a group of new Canadians requested classes in basic English and Miss Emma Eby was hired to teach them. After World War II, the Department of Education again established English classes for new Canadians, and IODE chapters assisted with Christmas parties and presentations at graduation ceremonies.

Today, Burlington offers classes and recreational facilities for everyone including its large teen population which has special programs geared to its interests. In 1984, the Burlington Youth Centre, a project of the Burlington Rotary Club, opened on Guelph Line in Central Park. A two-storey $500,000 building which included two large meeting rooms and a public washroom, was to be used by Scouts, Junior Achievement, Big Brothers, Guides and Burlington Minor Baseball Association. The province paid half the cost, with the remainder split between the Rotary Club and the City. The new centre, linked to the Pines Recreation Centre by a pathway, replaced the scout building on the same site.

ART CENTRE

In the 1960s, Burlington had an active art scene with many of the local artists owning studios. Workshop areas, however, were scattered throughout the city, often in less than ideal locations.

Early in 1969, a meeting of members from five guilds - Weavers, Rug Hooking, Potters, Fine Arts and Guild of Arts - met with city representatives to determine the needs of the arts in the community. A committee of three, Doris Hyde, Gery Puley and Jeanette Edwards made a presentation to the city council on behalf of all groups, requesting a centre for working artists and crafts persons. After two presentations, the groups were advised to form an arts council of all groups which was to become Arts Burlington.

To represent the art of the community, a three-day exhibition and sale, "Kaleidoscope", was held at the Burlington Arena in the spring of 1972 to demonstrate to the public the high degree of artwork that prevailed in the community. More than 300 Burlington painters and crafts persons contributed their work to what was to become an annual event.

A city fund-raising project was sponsored by Arts Burlington. It not only received funds from the city's recreation budget but also applied to Wintario for a grant, matching funds raised from the community. The City of Burlington provided Brock Park north of Lakeshore Rd. between Brock and Nelson Avenues as the site. Architect John Harkness drew up plans based on requests from the various groups, and with funds from the city, the province, a public campaign and Wintario, the $1.5 million dream became a reality.

On June 6, 1978, the Burlington Cultural Centre (Burlington Art Centre since 1993) was officially opened by Kay Cardiff, first president of Arts Burlington. Two weeks later, Kaleidoscope was held in the new building. To complete the picture, that summer an orange aluminum sculpture, 24 feet high, was installed outside on the lawn. Created by sculptor Hayden Davies, it was entitled "Space Composition for Rebecca" (Davies' niece). Grants came from Kaiser Aluminum and Wintario as well as 10% mandated by law for public sculpture.

In July, 1980, the Guild Gallery was renamed R.K.Perry Gallery in honour of a local man who was chair of the Centre's research committee beginning in the mid-1970s, the chair of the steering committee and the first president of the Centre's board.

On November 29, 1991, a 3,000 square foot extension, adding studio workspace, was officially opened.

Art in the Park.
  – Bob Chambers,
    photographer

Pottery Guild, Burlington
Art Centre.
  – courtesy W.R. Warren

The annual major fundraiser, the Art Auction, began before the centre opened. Many talented artists are represented, including world renowned wildlife artist Robert Bateman who has donated an original work of art for each of the Art Centre's annual auctions.

Other annual Arts Burlington fund-raisers include the Art Market in Spencer Smith Park begun in 1978; Art in the Park, a juried show, held in September; Monte Carlo Night and a fashion show.

Since the beginning, other guilds have, at different times, become part of the centre - Latow Photographers Guild, Woodcarvers Guild, Sculptors Guild and Quilters Guild.

In 1995, the Latow Photographers Guild initiated a week-end juried show following Kaleidoscope and, in 1995 and '96, studio tours were added to the Kaleidoscope event.

The various areas of the Art Centre are put to good use with artist exhibitions and displays. Docents are available for tours of the many visiting groups. The centre collects ceramic sculpture as its permanent collection.

MUSIC

Music schools and churches give distinguished service in the fields of choral and instrumental music, but it is not every community that has kept a town band in existence for many years. Before the turn of the century, villagers used to gather for impromptu concerts in the town hall. Council minutes for 1895 record that the Burlington Amateur Minstrels were granted the use of the town hall free for one evening. Travelling "Tom" shows used the hall, and Little Eva was hoisted heavenwards by block and tackle while audiences wept.

Records of June, 1909, read "that $50 be granted to the Burlington Band on the following conditions: first that they give ten weekly concerts in the Gore Park; second, that they deliver to the keeping of the village property committee, all instruments purchased by public subscription."

Pleasant evening concerts were held on summer nights in the park on Water St. between Elizabeth and Pearl Streets. Council voted the bandsmen $6.70 on October 31, 1914, for escorting volunteer soldiers to the railroad station at Freeman.

The following year, the band asked council for a grant to erect a bandstand in order that they might give open air concerts. Council instructed that the stand be erected "in Gore Park on Water Street for the present."

Members of the uniformed Citizens' Band at this time included W.H.Copeland, Alex Land, Jesse Dorland, H.K. Copeland, Harry Morse, Murray Green, Everett Shapland, Tom Fleetham, Bert Baker and Bandmaster Herbert Tufford.

The band continued to be subsidized by the town until the summer of 1919 when it was decided that "council take over all band instruments mentioned in the list received from Mr. Herbert Tufford, bandmaster, as requested." The musicians sent a letter of appreciation and the Fire Department thenceforth assumed responsibility under the name of the Burlington Firemen's Band. Among returning veterans of the World War I was a young bugler, Tom Waumsley, who became bandmaster, succeeding Mr. Tufford. The Dorland brothers, Fred and Jesse, and Fred Johnson were other bandsmen. The Fire Department supported the band until the late 1920s when the Canadian Legion took over. Lively sessions were held at the Legion Hall on Elizabeth St.

Another World War saw the band's ranks drastically reduced but the Legion carried on until peace came.

When the Chamber of Commerce, sparked by Frank Ellerbeck, invited Elgin Corlett to organize a boys and girls band in 1947, a whole new generation was ready to learn the march music. More than 200 young musicians signed up for instruction and soon the new band was rehearsing in the Lions Club Hall and marching in the adjacent park. Majorettes were trained, parents joined to help raise funds to buy band uniforms and shortly the band was playing out-of-town engagements and bringing home awards.

In 1949, a bylaw for a band tax of one half mill was approved by the ratepayers, the purpose being to maintain in future a community instrumental musical organization

Members of the Burlington Light Opera Society, now Drury Lane Theatrical Productions

under the guidance of the Burlington Musical Society. In 1957, the Burlington Concert Band, directed by Elgin Corlett, gave its first concert at the arena.

In 1963, the Musical Society found a permanent home - the modernistic headquarters in Central Park, with an addition built in the early 1980s. Elgin Corlett continued to direct the Musical Society until February 1, 1968, when it came under the town's Parks and Recreation department. In 1985, a plaque honouring Corlett was placed at the Music Centre. Eric Ford was conductor of the Teen Tour Band until 1977. When he was 11, Bob Webb began playing percussion in the Boys and Girls Band, going on to become band manager and marching director of the Teen Tour Band until 1980. Bob Webb was named Outstanding Young Man by the Jaycees in 1971.

American parades beckoned the band - the Rose Bowl, the Orange Bowl, the Windsor-Detroit Freedom Festival, Disney World. The band was the first to earn outstanding marks in all categories at Philadelphia's 9th annual Parade of Champions in 1974. Overseas tours and appearances at celebrations throughout Canada and the United States have kept the 'redcoats' in the forefront of marching bands. In 1996, Don Allen directs the musical destinies of an organization which includes the Junior Redcoats Band, Teen Tour Band and an adult concert band under Cliff Hunt.

The first of the city's annual Sound of Music Festivals, initiated by Laurie Branch, was held in June, 1980. It commenced with a Grand Festival Parade of Bands, in the rain, led by the Teen Tour Band and parade marshall, entertainer Dinah Christie. This was followed by concerts in several locations in the core area, Nelson stadium and the bandshell at Central Park. Another of the city's important annual events is Music in the Park - at Central, Spencer Smith and LaSalle Parks.

There is no dearth of musical performing groups in Burlington. In 1982, Eric Ford and Bob Webb formed the Top Hat Marching Band whose members perform in top hats and tails. Independent of the city, the group in 1996 is now headed by Bob Webb, manager and marching director. There are the Burlington Choral Society, barbershop groups for men and women, Senior Citizens' Choir and Burlington Light Opera Society. The latter, founded in 1971 as part of the Inter-City Opera Company (Hamilton, Kitchener, and Galt were included), the Burlington Light Opera Society found a permanent home in 1984, adjacent to the Burlington Curling Club on New St. in the remaining front portion of the 1914 arena. Its name was changed in 1995 to Drury Lane Theatrical Productions Inc.

The Mozart Chamber Orchestra got off to a rocky start. Founded in 1979 by lawyer Ted Luchak and Seigfried Tupper, music director, it was composed of professional musicians. The 1981-82 season was suspended for financial reasons but the orchestra gave a benefit concert in January, 1982, at the Royal Botanical Gardens. Subsequent successful years established the group as an important part of the city's music scene.

The Burlington Commanders Senior Drum and Bugle Corps was established under the city's music program in 1969. Formerly the Canadian Commanders in Toronto, under Metro Toronto's police, they won the Canadian Senior A championship in 1971 but ceased operations about 1972.

SCOUTING AND GUIDING

Burlington Boy Scout Association traces its organization back to 1909 when the town's population was about 1,000. Sir Robert Baden-Powell had advanced the idea of scouting in 1908 so Burlington was one of the first towns to take up the new idea. The first local Scoutmaster was Archie McGibbon, who remained in his position for more than a year, after which there was a succession of leaders including Hughes Cleaver and William Gilbert. The original enrolment of 25 boys was considered excellent for the small population of Burlington.

At first, some residents complained about the scouts marching through the streets with bugles blaring and drums beating, but for the most part people favoured the new movement and merchants generously subscribed to their appeals, as they continue to do. It was the merchants of 1909 who bought the band instruments at a cost of several hundred dollars and stood beaming their approval in the doorways of their shops as the troop marched past in the dust of unpaved Brant Street. The meeting place in those days was the basement of the former public library on Brant Street (the site of the present Civic Administration Building).

In 1912, His Royal Highness the Duke of Connaught, Governor-General of Canada, took the salute at the march past of thousands of boy scouts at the Ontario Jamboree held at Exhibition Park in Toronto. Burlington's scouts

1st Burlington Boy Scouts, 1950.   *– courtesy Les Armstrong*

proudly brought home first prize for the best marching and best-equipped troop.

When the first World War broke out, many former scouts enlisted and a great many of them were either wounded or killed overseas.

About 1918, Rev. George W. Tebbs took over the troop. It was in the 1920s when scoutmaster Tebbs and the local troop met Lord Baden-Powell in Burlington. The founder was motoring to Toronto and broke his trip for a short while when he saw the scouts lined up at Gore Park on the waterfront.

For many years, Rev. Tebbs led the boys as they marched out of town, hauling the trek cart to some distant camping place. It wasn't until 1958 that the scouts' combined group committees were able to buy the 90 acre camping grounds in North Burlington at Camp Manitou and in 1966 a $13,000 swimming pool was added.

At the outbreak of the second World War, the organization faltered as enlistments took a heavy toll of the leaders.

At that time, Stanley Craze was appointed chairman of the group committee and began the work of reconstruction; by 1953, there were about 200 cubs and scouts in three troops and three packs with a waiting list.

The Burlington Boy Scouts Local Association was formed in 1952 under president W.G. Gowing. The headquarters on Elizabeth St. was acquired from the town when it vacated the building as a town hall. Later, when the police and fire departments built new quarters, the entire premises were taken over by the cubs and scouts.

Trinity United Church (later Wellington Square United Church) needed extra space and, in 1959, they purchased the scout hall which was next door

Laurie Branch, Director of Recreation Services, 1967-1988.

and renamed it Trinity Annex. Cubs and scouts then began meeting in various schools and churches.

For many years, boys in the Strathcona district had their own scout hall on Belvenia Rd. constructed originally by area residents for community gatherings.

In 1966, a new district headquarters in Burlington was obtained at 450 John St. and a new group called the Venturers was formed for high school boys. District Commissioner Peter Bromley headed an organization of 250 leaders, 50 cub packs, 25 scout troops and 9 Rover crews for a total of about 1680 Burlington boys active in scouting.

When the Rotary Youth Centre was built on Guelph Line, Scout headquarters was relocated there. In 1996, there were 60 Venturers, (for 14-16 year-olds) and 18 Rovers (for youths 16 and over). The younger boys, 425 of them, aged 5-7 years, enjoyed Beavers; there were 388 Cubs, aged 8-10; and 209 Scouts, 11-13 years.

Guiding was started in Burlington in November, 1929, by Division Commissioner Mrs. Allan Scott and this area was then part of the Wentworth Guide Division. They were registered as the 1st Burlington Guide Company and the 1st Burlington Brownie Pack and were later sponsored by Thayendanegea Chapter I.O.D.E. as the 64th I.O.D.E. Company.

During the first year, the company flags were dedicated in St. Luke's Church by Rev. G.W. Tebbs. Past district commissioners include Florence Richardson, Phyllis Donkin, Mrs. Lionel Millen, Mrs. Douglas Fisken, Mrs. A.P. Cadeau, Mrs. Wade Townsend, Mrs. Phillip Gage, Mrs. A.R. Douglas and Mrs. D. W. Best. Jean Burns (Mrs. A.R.) Douglas who retired in 1953, devoted 21 years to the guiding movement and served in many capacities including commandant for several summer camps.

In 1943, the membership dropped drastically but during the next five years grew to 50 guides and 50 brownies in two companies and two packs. By 1948, the Local Association Committee found that a permanent home was needed for the fast-growing organization. Despite many setbacks, by September 16, 1951, the new guide home, Trefoil Lodge, was ready. Built by volunteers, the wood used was donated by Nicholson Lumber. The grounds belonged to the city.

Located next to the present Brant Plaza, the lodge was officially opened by A.S. Nicholson using gold keys which were accepted for the district by brownie Anne Ireland and guide Sally Duke. Rev. H.G. Lowry from Knox Presbyterian Church led the dedication ceremony. Eventually, when the building rotted and the floor became unsafe, it was taken down.

By 1953, there were five brownie packs, three guide companies, a Land Ranger company, the Local Association Committee, the Guiders' Council and a new group, the Parents Auxiliary of both mothers and fathers. Amalgamation of the town made administration more complex and, in 1961, guilding was split into Burlington East under Division Commissioner Mrs. R.J. Johnston and Burlington West under Mrs. A.L. Hurst. In 1966, Mrs. Hurst headed the East Division and Commissioner to Burlington West was Mrs. Ross Proctor.

By 1966, the movement had grown to 23 companies and 32 packs with five companies of Land Rangers and one Sea Ranger group called S.R.S. Skeena. Since then, the Sea Rangers have disbanded.

Statistics for 1996 reveal there are 2,024 girls in the guiding movement, a figure which includes Carlisle, Millgrove, Freelton, Waterdown, Lowville, Campbellville and Kilbride as well as Burlington.

30
"In Sickness and in Health"

In the early 1800s, immigrants were being encouraged to come to Upper Canada but no provision was made for their medical care. The high death rate was due to negligence, ignorance and unsanitary conditions, and to the unscrupulous quack medical men who capitalized on the needs of the pioneers. As Gwen Clarke said in *Halton's Pages of the Past*, diphtheria, smallpox, typhoid, cholera and other infectious diseases took a heavy toll of lives. Many young folk died of 'consumption' and isolation of infectious diseases was unheard of. It actually became a time of 'survival of the fittest'.

In the early years of the 19th century, there were only three qualified doctors between Toronto and Hamilton: Dr. Adamson of Port Credit, Dr. James Cobban of Milton and Dr. Nathaniel Bell of Nelson Township, who was born in New Jersey in 1790 and moved to Canada at the age of two. He later became Halton County's first doctor. Dr. Anson Buck, a veteran of the American Civil War, also practised in this area about the same time and led the hectic, sleepless life of typical country doctor.

An optimistic note on the health scene in 1817 was written by Robert Gourlay in *Sketches of Upper Canada* in which he said, "The climate of Upper Canada is favourable to health and longevity ... This opinion is founded upon the information of medical gentlemen and others, confirmed by observation and my own personal experience. I have found travelling and residing in it to be salutary and restorative to a feeble constitution." This statement must have encouraged a number of possible immigrants, since the book was written to promote, among the British, the advantages of living in Canada.

A letter, written in 1834 by Mrs. Dickson, an ancestor of W.D. Ham of Burlington, has been preserved. In it, Mrs. Dickson told her father in Scotland that her sister and the latter's husband, Dr. John Swan "intended to settle in a place named Wellington Square somewhere between York and Hamilton." Mentioning some of the hardships endured by the pioneers in the 1830s, the letter continues: "That dreaded pestilence, cholera, has been awfully prevalent in this country, but is now on the decrease. In the course of a few weeks, Montreal lost 1,100 of its inhabitants. My dread of it was so great that I dared not go to see the burying ground of St. Ann's as I intended."

She speaks of the discomfort of a boat trip up the St. Lawrence River: "We were exposed to a burning sun through the day and dews so rank through the night that I could almost have wrung our outer clothes in the morning, together with the thunder and rain, and a boat without any edge to prevent the children from falling over. It was no small relief to me when we boarded a steamer which we had all the way from Brockville to Hamilton and thence we were brought in wagons which took us three days and we had no other covering at night save the shelter of an open barn or shed, so afraid were the people of the cholera that they would not permit us to enter their houses in many places."

A common sickness which struck homes in the winter was called 'ague'. This was described in an 1837 book as lake or cold fever with chills and fever. Cinchona bark from which quinine was extracted was the general and 'unfailing' remedy of the day for ague.

Smallpox was the big scare of the 1840s and one of the Jane Van Norman-Aaron Emery letters said, "The smallpox is raging in the city (Hamilton) and two of our day scholars have it. I don't, however, apprehend any danger of its getting in the school simply for this reason, that I believe we are under the direct protection of a wise and all-powerful Providence."

With the absence of our modern miracle drugs, people depended on quack remedies and patent medicines with complete trust. Smith's *Canadian Gazetteer* of 1846 (which listed one physician and surgeon for Wellington Square) also contained commercial advertisements. Bristol's Sarsaparilla claimed to be a safe and certain remedy for every complaint from pimples to leprosy, while Dr. Rush's Infallible Health Pills were "very superior to all ages, sexes, seasons, constitutions and climates." Circassian Balm was not only good for chilblains, preserving the teeth and barber's itch, but for removing paint from cloth. No home should be without it! Wild Cherry Bitters was prescribed for nervous weakness and general debility and was especially recommended for drowsiness caused by spring fever.

Later in the 19th century, the local government set up a Board of Health to supervise contagious diseases and try to control unsanitary practices. In 1888, for example, John Harris, David Hartley and C.G.Davis were appointed members of the Nelson Township Board under Medical Health Officer A.C.Jones, M.D. A directory of Burlington for the next year lists the following physicians: Dr. Anderson, Dr. Bates, Dr. Arthur Carter and Dr. William Richardson, as well as E. Thomas who was a dentist. Supplies were available at the Burlington Drug Company.

Dr. A.C.Jones' annual report in 1887 said, "The low rate of mortality and the scarcity of malarial and contagious diseases, are the best indications that the township (Nelson) may congratulate itself upon a good sanitary condition during the year." He attributed the good showing to a plentiful supply of pure water, general absence of poverty or overcrowding of citizens, and the great efficiency of the Provincial Board of Health in enforcing quarantine against cholera and smallpox.

He recommended an annual sanitary inspection of public schools, dairies and slaughter houses "in preference to the present system of waiting

Burlington's first new ambulance, 1957, operated by Jack Harris and son Jim. — *courtesy Frank Armstrong*

for a complaint to be made," and said vaccination of all school children should be considered.

Meanwhile, Burlington's Board of Health was hiring a sanitary inspector to check stables, water closets and privy pits. Three hundred copies of health notices were distributed around the village, notifying residents to have all outside nuisances cleaned up by May 15 to avoid the occasional complaints that drainage from Mr. N's yard was tainting the water in Mr. D's well.

In 1901, a smallpox scare hit the village, and Burlington council authorized Dr. Richardson to vaccinate all persons desiring it. All those not able to pay the fee charged (25 cents) were to be vaccinated at the village expense.

When someone did catch the dread disease, families were quarantined for six weeks. Sheets were hung all over the house and the doctor poured formaldehyde over the sheets to disinfect the premises. If the patient was cared for at home, a quarantine card was placed on the door and a constable was sometimes hired to see that no one entered or left the house. A box was placed at the far end of the yard for local merchants to deposit milk and groceries, and someone ran out for them after the delivery boy had left. No money changed hands and the bills were paid by council, which presumably collected from the family when the danger was past.

Sometimes more drastic measures were taken to control smallpox. In July, 1901, a Mr. Pettigrew from Nelson Township became ill with smallpox while visiting in the village. Dr. Watson was sent in a rig to notify Reeve Richardson of Nelson to meet with the Burlington Board of Health the next morning. It was agreed that Mr. Pettigrew's care would be a joint expense and tents were placed in the middle of a large field belonging to Wood Freeman. The village clerk arranged for a bed and other supplies while a constable and attendants were hired to care for the patient and keep the place isolated.

This type of quarantine was expensive for the local council who paid all the resulting bills. Expenses in another smallpox case in the township were detailed in the minute book: "$5 for vaccine points and $40 for smallpox isolation tents; $10 for moving E. General and family to and from the isolation tents, removing and storing tents, lumber, etc.; $20 to Mr. Freeman for use of his field and for wood burned by patients; J.S. Allen $4.50 for stove pipe and other items; E. Williamson $5.75 for furniture (he was the undertaker as well as furniture dealer but this bill was likely for renting tables and chairs, since the patient recovered); T. LePatourel $1.95 for disinfectants; J. Galloway $1 for one tub; Freeman Bros. $21.75 for provisions; G.Renton $2.75 for milk; carrying food to tent $14; E. General and wife, care of patient $29 and Dr. Richardson's account for $140."

At the end of that year, Dr. Jones was paid $17.50 for vaccinating in seven Nelson school sections and his annual report said that, although the province-wide smallpox epidemic had touched the municipality, it was of a mild nature here with no fatalities. He also complained that everyone had not been vaccinated, although the service was free.

In 1910, there were only four cases of scarlet fever and seven cases of infantile paralysis, with a scarcity of malaria, typhoid fever and smallpox. Township residents considered it had been a good year healthwise and they were congratulated by their Medical Health Officer for "the sanitary condition of the township during the year." Board of Health members in 1910 were Chairman J.P. Griffin of Nelson, J.F. Richardson of Milton, A.C. Pettit of Freeman, George Erwin of Kilbride, John Sheppard of Nelson and George Forth, sanitary inspector from Lowville.

Meanwhile, a man in Burlington was ill with scarlet fever and the Board ruled that neither he nor his family could leave the farm, but he would be allowed to harvest his fruit crop, provided someone else took it to the shipping point. Dr. W.R. Watson said that the few cases of diphtheria and mild typhoid cases were probably due to drinking water from polluted wells and added, "This shows the people how dangerous it is to use doubtful well water when there is an abundant supply of absolutely pure water to be had through the water works supply source." Burlington's new water works had just been installed that year.

Town council took the responsibility of sending tuberculosis patients to the Hamilton sanitarium or the Muskoka Free Hospital for Consumptives and paid large bills each year to other Hamilton hospitals for the care of indigent citizens. There is this item from 1917: an account of $7 paid to Mr. Copeland for "taking the children who were bitten by the mad dog to Toronto for treatment." The Pasteur treatment at the Hospital for Sick Children cost the town $75.

Of course, most patients were able to pay their own expenses but the nearest hospitals were in Hamilton and when Burlington did get a hospital during World War I it was only for returned soldiers.

The large hotel known as Brant House was bought by the government and it became Brant Military Hospital. The open verandahs were closed in to make wards in the former luxury hotel and a new wing was added later.

A second wing was built in 1919, mostly for wounded soldiers who were brought there after the war as convalescents. When most of the men had recovered and returned to their home towns, the remaining patients were transferred to other hospitals and Brant Military Hospital was torn down.

A general hospital for the Burlington area was discussed informally for years before any action was taken. In times past, most adults were born at home - or had their tonsils removed by the family doctor on a scrubbed kitchen table. Following World War II, when this district was beginning to grow in all directions, the need for a local hospital became more urgent.

The first public steps were taken in 1955 when a meeting was called and a steering committee was set up under the chairmanship of M.M. Robinson. Members called on every organization, commercial and industrial business in the area, asking each to appoint representatives. From these, along with representatives of the town's doctors (about 15 at that time), grew a committee of 100 which recommended that a hospital board be established. Plans for a hospital then began to be considered in earnest.

Election of the first Board of Governors swiftly followed town amalgamation in January, 1958, and the members who served under chairman A.S. Nicholson were Rev. H. Lowry, Mrs. B. Bates, Mrs. V. Vallance, Dr. W. J. Deadman, Rev. J. Warren, R.H. Shannon, F.P. Gallagher, B. Coleman, W.E. Breckon, Eric Gudgeon, H.Tier, Leonard Eames, L. Campbell, A. Leishman, Hughes Cleaver, W.N. Smith and Paul Fisher, vice-chairman.

With 668 in favour and 254 against, members of the Burlington Nelson Hospital Association declared themselves in favour of the Brant Museum Park as the site for the new hospital which was appropriately named Joseph Brant Memorial Hospital. Sod turning was held in May, 1959. The money to build the $3,700,000 building came from municipal, county and provincial grants, plus public subscription. The L-shaped building consisted of six-storey nursing wings joined by a 100-foot elevator tower. When the hospital opened its doors in February, 1961, the first patient was a mother-to-be; it wasn't long before the Brant was operating at nearly full capacity.

Almost at the time the hospital was planned, the Women's Hospital Auxiliary was formed with Mrs. Kenneth Brown as its first president. Many thousands of dollars of equipment have been donated to the hospital as a result of the auxiliary's work.

Architects Prack and Prack, who designed the original building, were engaged in 1966 to draw up plans for a needed hospital addition.

This would double the size and include psychiatric facilities. By 1968, there were nearly 1,000 people waiting for admission as Board members contemplated placing beds in the basement. In July, 1970, the new $9.5 million wing was officially opened by George Kerr of Burlington, Minister of Energy and Resources Management.

The hospital underwent a massive renovation and systems overhaul in 1994-95, known as the JBMH Renewal Project. It produced among other

Joseph Brant Memorial Hospital, opened 1961.

– courtesy Joseph Brant Museum

things, new Emergency, Intensive Care and Outpatient Procedures Units. The hospital then had 304 beds, more than 90% occupied.

The hospital began renting space for a Community Health Services Centre at Mohawk School in 1981, to provide rehabilitation and support for elderly, frail and physically challenged clients. A move from the school became necessary and a separate building for this program was deemed desirable. A name, the Joseph Brant Wellness House was chosen. A successful fundraising campaign was undertaken for a specially-designed low-profile building. In 1996, its location to be in McNichol Park was confirmed but later overturned.

In 1976, the Joseph Brant Memorial Hospital Foundation was developed to provide support for new equipment and to improve facilities. In 1995, the hospital served a population of more than 250,000 people including residents of Milton, Waterdown, Flamborough Township, Stoney Creek and east-end Hamilton. In 1995, 220 physicians had hospital privileges, and there were more than 1100 full-time, part-time and relief staff.

In 1974, another health program, the Children's Assessment and Treatment Centre, was established at Lakeshore School. In 1992, CATS moved to space in a new building on Pearl St. in Lions Club Park.

With regional government, health care became a regional responsibility under the Halton Regional Health Unit. Some of the unit's programs include communicable disease control, tuberculosis control, immunization clinics, counselling, and the Home Care Program. There are programs for parents and children, and seniors. Health counselling is carried out in public schools

Red Cross Offices, originally the Wesleyan Methodist Chapel, built 1862, Port Nelson, Guelph Line.

for staff and students. In addition, there are programs in day care facilities and nursery schools. The prevention of mental illness through counselling and guidance is another important concern.

A recent development in health care has been the establishment, in the community, of X-ray clinics and emergency clinics to relieve stress at the hospital. Cuts in provincial funding to hospitals is prompting further innovations to meet the needs of a population that is not only growing but growing older.

Maple Villa, a long term care centre.

31
"Do Unto Others": Welfare Practices

Back in the 1800s, there was no Family Service Bureau, no Department of Welfare or any government-sponsored help for the poor and sick. Each village and township took care of its own. Public sympathy was felt for widows with young children to support or for the infirm and elderly who could no longer work. In those times when there were no public institutions to speak of, and homes were larger than they are today, there was no trouble absorbing another person into the family group, especially if the local council paid for his support.

Accounts of Nelson Township council, in the latter years of the century, indicate that much deliberation was given to charity cases. In 1888, council approved names of several people as "being indigent and fit subjects for public charity".. to be paid $4 monthly. One woman was paid this sum "for keeping imbecile child until suitable place can be procured for her."

The following year a male infant was found abandoned at the door of a local resident and was later placed in an infants' home in Hamilton at a cost a $1.50 a week. The baby was appropriately named Percy Nelson after the township in which he was found, and he became the responsibility of Nelson council. Thereafter, regular bills appeared on the agenda "for board and nursing of the child Percy Nelson in the Home of the Friendless and Infants" in Hamilton amounting to $24.

In 1894, the matron of the home wrote to council to state that the child was then over five years old and they only cared for children under five. The reeve and clerk were authorized to make other provisions for the boy and he was soon placed in a home for boys in Hamilton. The last mention of Percy in the township accounts was a bill for $13 paying in full for his care at the orphanage at the time when he was finally placed for adoption.

Paying of charity accounts was a part of each council meeting. Money was appropriated for treatment of the sick in Hamilton hospitals, for the care of such persons as "a helpless old woman having no means of support," payment to a doctor for "certifying male person was a lunatic," and care of an "invalid who can be looked after in a home" (it was later reported that she had been placed in a private home in Kilbride for $2 a week and was slowly regaining her health).

Sometimes people applied to council for aid and occasionally their names were referred to the reeve. There was no secrecy involved in protecting the names of those who were paid from the Poor Fund. In the township's

293

Carey House, independent living for the physically challenged, Ontario Street.

accounts for 1871, for example, are two full pages of names of people and the money paid to each, amounting to $520. Cost of death was low in 1864, when this item showed up on the accounts: "On motion of Mr. Halstead, the treasurer was ordered to pay Thos. Boden $2 for digging two graves for indigent persons, and also $3 to Joseph Date for a coffin for Bradley."

The Village of Burlington had its own Poor Fund and its own problems in distributing the money. One woman, getting $4 monthly was turned down in her request for more, it being noted another widow got along on $2 a month! By 1895, Burlington had a Charity Committee which determined the actual need in each case. One elderly woman, "Mrs. D." was looked after by a different family each month for $6, until a place was found for her in the House of Providence at Dundas for the same price. The village bought her a few supplies she would need in the home. When she died six years later, council handled the funeral arrangements.

Before the turn of the century, there was a negro widow, Mrs. Virginia who ran a small variety shop on Brant St., near the lakeshore, as long as she was able to work. When she did apply for charity, it was only for the winter months. Mrs. Virginia died July, 1900, and the outstanding accounts of $22, incurred by her death, were paid out of the village fund.

In 1898, the United Charities of the Village of Burlington was established. The chairman was Reeve E.H. Cleaver and members were Councillor James S. Allen, Messrs. C. Murphy and P.C. Patriarche from the Catholic church; Messrs J. Morrine and James Davidson from the Presbyterian church; Dr. A.H. Speers from the Methodist church; Messrs. E. Weber, and F. Ackland from the Episcopal church and James Anderson from the Baptist church. They investigated all names that came before them for charitable donations, and discussed the need for a poor house in the county.

Reeve William Kerns, in 1903, suggested that no charity should be given to anyone unless by written order of the chairman, lest the situation get out of hand.

Gradually, responsibility for the aged, sick and indigent was taken under government and charitable organization supervision and in recent years, functional buildings such as Halton Centennial Manor in Milton for senior citizens have been constructed. First mention of the Children's Aid Society was in 1917. When World War I ended, "Council endorsed the resolution of the Galt city council petitioning the government to take up the problem of child welfare and widows' pensions and that the clerk be instructed to forward copies of this resolution to Prime Minister Borden and to Dr. Anderson, the member for the county of Halton in the Dominion Parliament."

The lists of people dependent on the Poor Fund disappeared and any further references to aid were in connections with donations to charitable or health organizations such as the Victorian Order of Nurses, the Canadian Red Cross and the Salvation Army which did invaluable work during the first World War, continuing to minister to the sick and needy in peacetime.

By now, Burlington had a relief committee, consisting of three town councillors. Any doubtful cases were referred to Chief of Police Smith who investigated a family's need for assistance. An advertisement appeared in *The Gazette*: "Commissioner Betzner has a number of unemployed cutting down and trimming trees throughout the town. As a result the town is securing a large quantity of wood which will be distributed by the Welfare Board." The next week, a report said, "About 25 cords of wood have been obtained by cutting down trees. Several large ones estimated to be at least 130 years old were cut down in Lakeside Park. All of them were rotten in the centre and it would only have been a short time before they would have toppled over anyway."

Another notice read, "Relief boxes have been placed in all the local grocery stores, and already a good amount of supplies has been collected and turned over to the Welfare Board."

In September, 1933, the *Burlington Gazette* reported on dire problems elsewhere. "Free transportation from Ontario to the west has been granted for carloads of fruit, vegetables, and other relief foodstuffs and clothing being sent in aid of those whose gardens and crops have been ruined by drought and grasshoppers. United Churches of Halton County are making arrangements to ship the carloads to the stricken areas."

In 1935, Police Chief Lee Smith of Burlington and Chief Harvey Hunt, Nelson Township police, collected funds from various clubs and organizations which they used to buy food baskets for the needy. In 1955, a public meeting was held and a Christmas Welfare Committee was formed under the joint chairmanship of Chief Smith and Inspector Hunt. A central registry was set up to provide better distribution to needy families.

By 1962, the Halton Christmas Bureau was formed and town organizations gave the project whole-hearted support. The following year the Bureau was re-formed as the Burlington Christmas Bureau under the sponsorship of the Inter-Service Clubs. From the early days of the program George Johnson's house on Wellington St. was the headquarters for toy repairing and distributing. Mr. Johnson was chosen as Burlington's Citizen of the Year in 1963.

Pilkey House, youth residence, Elizabeth Street.

Wellington Terrace, geared to income housing, John Street.

The list of volunteer charity helpers throughout the year includes church and school groups, sororities, auxiliaries and service clubs. Some groups have been organized for a specific purpose, such as the Joseph Brant Memorial Hospital's Women's Auxiliary, the Margaret McKindley Auxiliary for the Blind and the Burlington Association for the Mentally Retarded (Association for Community Living). Lending a hand to local, as well as national projects, are such societies as the University Women's Club and the three I.O.D.E. chapters, Thayendanegea, Wellington Square and Sovereign.

Service Clubs in the Burlington area embrace a great many of our citizens including women's auxiliaries. The Inter-Service Council includes representatives from service clubs along with a representative from the city. The Inter-Service Club's "Citizen to be Remembered" award was begun in 1955. With the name change to 'Council' came the change to the award's name, * "Citizen of the Year". The Zonta Club (Burlington's first women's service club) began to designate its Women of Achievement in 1984. The Jaycees also established an award, Outstanding Young Man.

In 1996, welfare is a responsibility of Halton Department of Social and Family services. Programs include Income Maintenance, Family Counselling and Day Care. In 1994, it was estimated more than 25,000 children aged up to l2 years needed child care. In April 1995, there were 7,050 social assistance cases in Halton, a 132 per cent increase from April, 1989. In September, 1994, there were 1,224 households on Halton Housing Authority's waiting list for subsidized housing, a 76 per cent increase over 1989. The recession of the 1990s, unemployment caused by bankruptcies and downsizing by business and industry, and deficit fighting resulting in grant reductions by both federal and provincial governments, have made welfare an important concern for our area and communities across the country.

Service Clubs of Burlington sign.

* These citizens whom we must remember are listed in the order of the year of their designation from 1955: Lee J. Smith, Charles Parsons, Dorothy Angus, A.S. Nicholson, M. M. Robinson, Mrs. Earl Swift, Dr. W.A. Weaver, Dr. James MacFarlane Bates, George Johnson, Mrs. J. Gordon Blair, Mrs. J.D. Mills, J.H. Parker, K.L. Dingledine, G.M. Schottlander, Marie Hudson, Harold R. McGrath, Bonnie Duke, Del Roth, Sally Ferguson, Frances Day, Mr. H. B. Monaghan, Robert Carey (posthumously), Kenneth Skerrett, Tom Tonelli, Louise Hebb, Leo Podetz, Cecil McFadden, G.W. (Bud) Gordon, Mary Fraser, Alex G. Robb, Phyllis Hawkins, Ernie Francis, Florence Meares, Douglas Horsley, Fred Bucknam, Sue Irmisch, Michele Wood, Katie Kidd, Jean Galloway, Linda Cupido and Cheryl Harrison in 1995.

32
Homes and Subdivisions

The first early land sales at what became Wellington Square were made by Joseph Brant who had been deeded Brant's Block in 1798. These sales were made to Loyalists, some of whom were friends of Brant before and during the War of American Independence. In 1803, Brant sold 200 acres to Nicholas Kerns and 211 acres to Robert Wilson.

The Robert Wilson land was sold in 1808 to Benjamin Mallory, then to John Heigh for 300 pounds and, later in the same year, back to Mallory. In 1815, the sheriff of the Home district gave a deed for the same land to Augustus Bates for 50 pounds, 10 shillings, apparently a mortgage sale. This is typical of the back and forth transfer of many of the early realty transactions.

The earliest white settler on the land of Wellington Square is believed to have been Augustus Bates who came here in 1800. His farm ran west from Brant St. over to the middle line of the present St. Luke's graveyard. Augustus was the brother of the William Bates who had operated the King's Head Inn at the south end of the beach. His 1806 licence to sell spirituous liquors by retail indicated that Augustus Bates, too, ran some type of hostelry.

James Gage of Stoney Creek laid the foundation for the village of Wellington Square by making the first survey of Brant's Block and buying 338 1/2 acres for 232 pounds, 14 shillings, 4 pence. This was a rectangle fronting on the lake between Rambo Creek and Brant Street. Gage put up mills and commercial establishments. There is a possibility that James, Maria and Martha Streets could have been named after members of the Gage family. In 1805, Brant mortgaged 1,000 acres to Mather Elliot and in 1812, after Brant's death, the land was deeded to Elliot.

Other early sales were made to John Davis, 240 acres; Ralph Morden, 161 3/4 acres; Michael Groat, 140 acres; John Dawson, 106 acres; and Peter Desjardins, 125 acres. George Chisholm settled at the old outlet between the lake and bay. John Chisholm was another early landowner nearby.

In 1805, Thomas Ghent bought 205 1/2 acres from Brant and in 1806 Asahel Davis bought 240 acres. The Davis-Ghent story is the saga of two U.E.L. families. Originally from Wales, they had emigrated to North Carolina where plantations had brought them wealth and position. In 1792, loyal to the British Crown, they fled north to the mouth of the Genesee River, the site of the city of Rochester. They remained there until an old friend, Governor Simcoe, hearing of their plight, had them transported by gunboat to Fort Niagara.

Here they spent the next winter before going on in the spring to settle on Crown lands at Mount Albion in the township of Saltfleet. A few years later, they bought land from Joseph Brant and settled their families on Brant's Block. With them they carried, by canoe across the bay, small apple trees they had raised in Saltfleet from seeds brought from the Carolinas. They cleared their land and planted the seedlings which prospered and formed the nucleus of the orchards which made this area noted for apples. Thomas Ghent built his homestead near what is now Maple Ave. and Ontario Street. The second Davis homestead site is, in 1996, occupied by L.H. Schwindt and Co. Ltd. east of Maple Ave. at 1134 Plains Rd. E.

The families joined hands with the marriage of Thomas Ghent's son to Elizabeth Davis. Their son, George, born in 1806, and Augustus Bates Jr., born January 4, 1805, were the first two white children native to this area. These families were also linked in 1831 when George Ghent married Catherine Bates, a second cousin of Augustus Jr.

These families and others of the first settlers went through many hardships, only the fittest surviving. Log cabins were erected after a clearing had been made in the forest. Rather smugly, a writer in The Genesee Farmer said in 1841, "A log house in a newly settled country has always struck me as exceedingly good taste and first rate domestic economy". Frame houses of sawn logs came later after barns were built. Anna Jameson, travelling through Wellington Square in 1837, said of the settlement, "It has been recently laid out and contains about 20 wooden houses."

After the Loyalist settlers had arrived, the next newcomers were mostly immigrants from the British Isles. They found it a lonely life in Upper Canada, especially the women. "There are many pining and discontented women in Canada," observed Mrs. Jameson who said of the inhabitants, "Their love, their pride, are not for poor Canada but for high and happy England; but a few more generations must change all this."

Life here was, indeed, a far cry from what these people had been used to. "It was flax, the pedlar's pack and buckskins that the early settlers had to depend on for clothing when their first supply ran out," said Egerton Ryerson, an itinerant preacher who visited locally. With the help and advice of the Indians, deerskins were preserved, dressed and made into coats and trousers for the men. The government encouraged the growth of flax for linen and every farmhouse had a loom.

The everyday menu would include slices of dried venison, hot cakes of Indian corn, eggs, a bowl of milk and perhaps radishes or pieces of sassafras root. The occasional visitor might be given venison steaks, fried fish, coffee, cheese, whisky punch and tea brewed on special occasions and tasting like mouldy hay.

Farm work was hard and labour scarce. In November, 1817, when there were 16 houses in Wellington Square, John Brant, Augustus Bates,

Port Nelson, Guelph Line and Lakeshore Road, about 1912.
– courtesy Joseph Brant Museum

Asahel Davis, Thomas Ghent, Ralph and James Morden and Nicholas Kern reported, "The reason the province has not improved more is in part, owing to the inhabitants wanting the means of assisting themselves more than they were capable of doing by manual labour."

There was little cash available and horses cost 15 pounds at Wellington Square when any were for sale. A hired man, if one could be found, would work for 25 pounds a year or 5 shillings a day at harvest time. Farm implements were of the most primitive kind.

The sad plight of many settlers is described in the 1817 Trafalgar Township report, "The greater number of our farmers, when they first settled in the wild woods have little more property than a cow, a yoke of oxen, a log chain and an axe... The family generally consists of a man and his wife and a number of young children and is unable to hire hands. The whole of the labour devolves upon the man until the eldest of his children grows up to help him. His toil is incessant. Four or five acres is all that he is able to clear and sow in a season. Often he has to work out for a part of his bread."

"By the time he gets his farm in such a state of improvement as might permit him to live comfortably, he is frequently obliged to sell it, in order to pay off his debt. Those who weather out the first ten years without sinking are generally able to spend the remainder of their days in comfort."

Conditions had improved by 1845 when there were about 400 inhabitants in Wellington Square. Smith's *Canadian Gazetteer* of that year noted the village had been settled about 20 years. There was just about every type of store as well as a doctor, tavern and churches. Transportation by steamer to Hamilton was available.

Meanwhile, at Port Nelson, there had been a settlement probably earlier than at Wellington Square. This community was just outside Brant's

Block at the Guelph Line and before Brant was ready to sell off lots, Crown land could be had in Port Nelson.

One of the first substantial homes at Port Nelson was that of Dr. Thomas Greene, first rector of St. Luke's Anglican Church who came here from Ireland and settled on a 200 acre farm in 1832. His home was at what is now the corner of First St. and Hart Avenue. Great pines, acacias and honeysuckle lined the drive leading from the lake. Mrs. Greene's roses from her native land gave the place the name of "Roseland".

The community at the foot of Guelph Line originally had been called Cape Paradise but in 1839 the name Port Nelson appeared on a provincial map. The population eventually reached 250 but in 1846 there were 60 inhabitants, a store, tavern and shoemaker. Five years later a carpenter and shipbuilder had settled there.

By 1869, the population was 150. The centre of the village was at the corner of the Guelph Line and Water St., extending for a distance on both sides of the Guelph Line. A portion was south of Water St. but where it stood is now under water, the shoreline having eroded with the action of the waves. Market St. appeared on an early map of Port Nelson. It may have symbolized the port's anticipation of a commercial area which never materialized.

Farther north, Harman Fisher of the Philadelphia region, who had settled near Vineland, bought 200 acres on what is now Guelph Line from Catharine Brant for his son, Peter. Peter Fisher settled there with his bride in 1825 in a log cabin. The Fisher home at 801 Guelph Line was built in 1837. The Fisher farms became a part of a busy commercial area and the location of Burlington Mall.

In 1873, the part of Port Nelson west of the Guelph Line joined with Wellington Square to become the incorporated village of Burlington. The shipping activities of the port declined as the lumber and grain shipments fell off. By the end of the 19th century it had become a residential and farming community.

The names of Port Nelson and Roseland were retained and have become attached to the area easterly from the Guelph Line and between the lake and New St.

The first developer of Roseland was W.D. Flatt, a lumber merchant who had built a "suburban" home in 1910 at 3074 Lakeshore Road. He and his wife were "so delighted with our environment... that we decided to purchase other properties on the Lakeshore and to develop a suburban community."

In a 1912 brochure, Mr. Flatt, a salesman par excellence, describes the "invigorating" breezes, the rich garden soil and the magnificent shore line. He did not remain in this beautiful setting too long, selling his home in 1914 to John Moodie, of the Hamilton Knitting Mills family, whose daughter, Mrs. Victor Vallance, lived there for many years. The home was sold in 1992 and

The Fisher home (Shady Cottage), built 1837, now the location of the Burlington Mall.
– courtesy Joseph Brant Museum

due to the cost of renovations and repairs, was torn down to make way for smaller but upscale residences.

Mr. Flatt, by 1912, had laid out what he called Pine Cove Survey stretching from the Guelph Line to Pomona Ave. on both sides of the highway (Lakeshore Rd.). Along to the east were Pine Cove Addition and Pine Cove Extension. In Pine Cove, he had set aside a six acre recreation park and at the lake shore another 600 foot frontage with a pier. Lots in Pine Cove were going for $1,000 to $1,500 in 1912, while those farther east in the extension were from $250 to as high as $1,500.

Still farther to the east, at Walkers Line, was Flatt's Crystal Beach subdivision. Each lot had a 50 foot lake frontage extending back as far as 425 feet. These lots were listed from $800 up. Shore Acres was the most expensive survey with wooded lots going for $1,500 to $3,000. These were from two to five acres in size with a pier and good harbour for small boats.

Unfortunately, as far as the lakeshore was concerned, Flatt was ahead of his time. Some large homes were built along the highway but most of his land remained empty.

In 1922, Ross Hart, for whom Rossmore Blvd. and Hart Ave. are named, laid out Chestnut Park which extended on both sides of First St. from the Guelph Line to Rossmore Boulevard. In 1924, the Cleavers began the developing of Roseland as it is today.

The Roseland Park Survey took in Balmoral Ave., Hart Ave., Princess Dr., South Dr. and Woodland Park Drive. In the early 1930s, Hughes Cleaver developed Roseland Court Survey, Rossmore and a continuation of Princess. Mr. Cleaver recalled the area was open fields before he planted the trees which add so much to the district's charm. What is said to be Burlington's earliest sporting association was Roseland Park Country Club, founded in 1929.

In the late 1950s, Mr. Cleaver opened up Roseland Heights, northeast of the filtration plant and later, Shore Acres Heights. In these surveys, he continued his policy of tree planting, putting a Schwedler maple on each lot.

In the mid-19th century, a settlement was started on Brant Street. Joshua Freeman, formerly of Nova Scotia, divided equally his 400 acre farm with his son, Joseph, and each worked his holdings on the northern corners of Brant St. and Plains Road. One of the district's oldest homes, the Joseph Freeman farmhouse, was torn down when Holland Motors was built on Plains Rd., just west of Brant Street. Joseph's son, a president of the Burlington Horticultural Society, lived at another Freeman home at 906 Brant St. until 1988. Then, carefully restored and renovated, it became the location of Henry Sieders Funeral Home, now Ward Funeral Home. The building won a Heritage award in 1990.

Freeman train station encouraged the establishment of several industries around the railroad and a few houses were built there. Edwin and Wesley Freeman, sons of Joseph, operated a general store and post office on the east side of Brant St., north of the C.N.R. tracks. This was run by a Mr. Armstrong and then by William Cannom whose wife was related to the Freeman and the Ghent families. South of the tracks, on the west side of Brant St., was the "Freeman House", a boarding house operated by George Renton. It was believed to have been a hotel before Renton's time. It became a barber shop and store in later years.

After the turn of the century, when Brant St. was a dirt road and the Q.E.W. was a nine foot wide strip of gravel, the Lewis's, Sherwoods, Klodts, Kerns, Pearts, Bells and Malcolmsons lived at Freeman.

After 1900, A.B. Coleman built the Brant Hotel and developed Indian Point as a residential area. The six-hole golf course there was the first in Burlington. Mr. Coleman died in 1939. For many years the streets were without names but in 1951, with the advice and help of Brant Coleman, son of the founder, the streets of Indian Point were given names such as Iroquois, Algonquin, Mohawk and Indian to perpetuate the memory of the nations of warriors who were the original residents. Several of the old "cottages" remained in the 1990s, some retaining the original exterior appearance but renovated inside.

W.D. Flatt helped to develop the shores of the bay. Buena Vista survey was opened on the King property and, to the west, Brighton Beach became a close-knit little community. Brighton Beach had been owned by Daniel Harrison who sold 22 1/2 acres of his farm on the north shore of the bay in 1912 to Mr. Flatt for $20,000. This acreage lay between Woodland and Holy Sepulchre Cemeteries.

A pumping system was installed by residents for their water supply, electric lighting installed on the main streets, streets widened and their names posted, baseball teams organized, a tennis club started, and postal

W.D. Flatt's Lakehurst Villa, built 1910, now demolished.
– courtesy The Burlington News, *a publication of* The Hamilton Spectator

delivery and pick-up instituted. The survey attained the status of an electoral subdivision and residents had places on the township council and high school and elementary school boards.

Burlington was sprouting its wings with the dawn of the 20th century. Wooden sidewalks such as those in front of the Roderick home on Water St., west of Brant St., would disappear. The Roderick house was built and owned by Capt. Sharp and was said to have had parquet hardwood floors, the first in town.

In 1892, Caroline St. from the limits of the village of Burlington to Lorne St., and a part of Lorne St., were accepted by Nelson Township as public roads. John Gray had laid out streets in this survey extending between Caroline and Lorne. In the same year, Addison Hager laid out a street extending from Ontario St. to the Hurd farm and named it Hager Avenue. It was accepted as a public road and was a portion of the town boundary at the time.

Bits and pieces of Nelson Township were annexed by Burlington from time to time and, in 1909, the boundary was extended to Maple Avenue. This relatively large chunk of expropriated land went across Birch, southward along the C.N.R. property, across to Maple Ave. and down to the beach.

By 1911, Ghent's survey had been opened with the township accepting Ghent Ave. as a public road. Roads and housing went hand in hand and the creation of Bayshore Dr. (North Shore Blvd.) in Aldershot opened up the Inglehaven and Glenhaven surveys.

From the turn of the century right up to the 1930s, Burlington was the kind of small town in which every child should live, in the judgement of residents who remembered those days. Caroline St. was the boundary of the town proper and, west of Brant St., Hurd's farm stretched north. The Bell and Blair orchards extended north on the east side of Brant Street. Along Brant to Freeman there were a few homes. Beyond Freeman was the "country". In the late 1930s, Emerald Cres. was being developed and from there to Freeman the view was green countryside for the most part. The atmosphere was peaceful with the only sound the occasional whistle of a locomotive or the pealing of the town bell. There was no clangor of industry or traffic to shatter the peace and calm. Everybody knew everybody else. Families intermarried and business was done on a more personal basis with a man's word as good as his bond. But change, or as some say, "progress", was just around the corner.

Inglewood survey, reminiscent in a modest way of Indian Point, was begun in 1925 by Irwin Proctor who owned a farm east of the present Strathcona Drive. As a pioneer aviator he had a hangar and an aeroplane located on the property. Proctor's father, a prominent Hamilton settler after whom Proctor Blvd. was named, had owned the lakeshore property and willed it to his son.

Originally the lakeshore road had curved to follow the shore line of the lake. When the No.2 highway was paved and straightened after World War I, Proctor had found himself with land running on either side of the highway. He opened up Belvenia Ave. in the middle of his farm, north of the highway. The land remained idle for some time until, about 1925, he opened a survey and offered lots, south of the highway, for sale. Inglewood Dr., curving around from the highway to the lake and back, was constructed. Two lots were sold and then the depression set in. One of the houses is the stucco home on the southeast corner of Inglewood and Lakeshore built by Mr. Proctor on speculation.

Many beautiful, substantial homes were built in the 1920s and 30s and are an indication of the lives of the wealthy in that era. The mansion in McNichol Park, Shoreacres Estate, is one of them, built by Cyrus Birge in 1929 or 30. In 1996, recently purchased by the city, and standing empty and boarded up, its future is still in doubt.

Another example is Northgate Manor on North Shore Blvd. which has been carefully maintained. Built in 1928, it was the home of the Carses, then the Hendries and the Coopers. Developer John Rosart is the 1996 owner.

Toward the end of the depression, the town found itself with a great number of vacant properties acquired by tax sale. In the latter part of 1938, a program of selling lots for $25 to $50 each was started with the provision that the purchaser, within a year, begin construction of a home worth not less than $3,500. Home building was stimulated and the growth of the town has never faltered since then.

One of the "deals" made at this pre-World War II period was a trade between the town and M.C. Smith. The corporation had 11 lots on Smith Ave. and Mr. Smith had 12 1/4 acres adjoining Central School, the last open land

Shoreacres Estate home, built by Cyrus Birge about 1929.
– courtesy Cityscope, *a publication of Joncor Publishing Inc.*

within Burlington. The town and the ex-mayor, for a token dollar, bought each other's land. The farm property was developed as a park and a section was later given to Central School as a football field and for future expansion. It is reasonably sure that Central could not have continued at its present location or have grown to its present size without Mr. Smith's land.

It was after World War II when Burlington began to mushroom. W. Frank Utter had, just prior to the war, developed the Glenwood survey, west of the Guelph Line. After the war, parcels of Veterans' Land Act property were sold farther west on the Clarence Wood farm, and the Queensway survey was opened. More V.L.A. lots were sold to veterans on Pomona Ave., north of Roseland, and in other sections in Nelson Township and Aldershot.

In the centre of town, A.S. Nicholson sold land to C.F. Hewitt who developed, after the war, Eden and Halifax Places, Baldwin Ave. and Hurd Avenue. He also opened up Harris Cres. from Torrance Street. The Blair farm was subdivided by John and Stanley Blair in 1952. The former Ogg farm on Brant St. north of Blairholme Ave. had been bought by George Blair whose substantial farmhouse across from St. John's Church, Blairholme, built in 1896, was the home of Blairs until the death of Stanley, many years later.

The former Bell property on Brant St., where the Brant Plaza is located, was originally the Springer and later the Koenig farm. The Springer home of Gothic design with a fountain in front stood about where No Frills (previously Loblaws) stands in 1996. As well as operating successful orchards, Mr. Bell built a large cold storage plant which was torn down to

Habourview, Lakeshore commercial and residential accommodation.

make way for the Brant St. commercial development. Some of the streets in the adjacent subdivision, Courtland, Wagner and Tallman are named after species of Bell apples and Bellwood commemorates the family name.

North of the Q.E.W, west of the Guelph Line, George Fisher had a farm. His son-in-law, Ira Clark, who had married Nellie Fisher, was a Quaker mathematics teacher in Orillia. At George Fisher's death, the Clarks came down to Nelson and settled on the Fisher farm. Ira Clark was a good farmer and the farm continued to prosper under his management. About 1949 when he died, the survey of Clarksdale was opened up for residential development. Fisher Ave. runs through the centre of the original survey. Later homes in Clarksdale are on what was the Peart farm.

Just about the time Clarksdale was being developed, some houses were built adjacent to the Q.E.W. west of Guelph Line. The Department of Highways ruled that they be moved back from the highway and they were taken up to the Clarksdale property to the north.

Mountain Gardens survey is on the former Eaton farm and Rolling Meadows takes in the upper part of the Eaton farm and land owned by the Kerns brothers. West of the Guelph Line and Clarksdale School, the subdivision Maryvale was opened by Arrigo Bros. Ltd., the company which also built townhouses and multiple housing south of Maryvale off Mountainside Dr.

Tyandaga Estates was opened north of the Q.E.W. in the 1960s, a 600 acre complex built around the golf course, consisting of garden apartments, townhouses and fine residences developed by the Rampart Company. Brant Hills Estates, comprising hundreds of acres north of M.M. Robinson High School was a project of Western Heritage. Long Pines, a townhouse complex, was developed east of Guelph Line, north of New St. by Gerald Stark who

Unsworth Green, 1995-1997 residential development.

also opened Cranston Court in Aldershot and Rothesay Place, west of Walkers Line and New St.

In Aldershot, after World War II, Hughes Cleaver acquired the Long farm and opened up Long Acres subdivision. Jacob Cooke developed "Birdland" on the Filman farm in the early 1950s and later Glen Acres and adjacent surveys. John Cowan, in 1952, developed 35 acres in North Shore Gardens, west of the Burlington Golf Course. It was in Aldershot that Jacob Cooke opened up Harbour Heights overlooking the bay. Mr. Cooke developed Marley Park, east of Francis Rd. and Fairwood Acres behind Aldershot Plaza's Super Fresh supermarket (formerly Dominion Store).

Elizabeth Gardens in the far east end below New St., stretching from Hampton Heath Road, was developed before amalgamation. After 1958, Burlington found itself with a subdivision in which roads were unfinished or not up to standard. Crews were despatched to finish the job and the costs were charged to the developer.

West of Elizabeth Gardens, a partially wooded area was opened up by Verhoeven Construction Limited. White Pines became a charming subdivision of split level homes. Guildwood subdivision, another Verhoeven project, south of New St., west of Walkers Line, was developed about 1964.

Strathcona Gardens, Pineland South, east of Appleby Line, and Ravenswood were developed between 1955 and 1962. Ravenswood was a 100 acre farm owned by Colin Smith, west of Walkers Line. The homestead, called "Ravenswood" is back from Lakeshore Rd. on a winding driveway, the former home of R.A. Carlton whose wife was a Smith. The Smith line traces back to Hiram Smith, one of the town's first businessmen who is mentioned elsewhere in the chapter dealing with education.

While it is not possible to list all the subdivisions, the population figures tell the story. Between 1947 and 1960, the growth rate for Burlington was 228 per cent while that of Ontario was only 33 per cent.

A development of the 1960s was the high rise apartment of six or more storeys. As the federal government made available more mortgage money for multiple housing, builders began the construction of several tall structures. Understandably, people who had moved to Burlington attracted by the "small town" atmosphere and its close proximity to bucolic rural areas, were concerned about the rapid growth. Some thought of multiple dwellings as slum cubicles in mass human warehouses, according to a newspaper report, and they were strongly opposed. Citizens in residential areas protested the intrusion of high rises on their privacy. The municipal elections of December, 1965, were stormy and an almost completely new council was voted in, committed to halt or at least slow down the apartment building in predominantly residential, low density areas.

Torrance Terrace, the first of the "cliff dwellings" at Torrance St. and Lakeshore Rd. is set in landscaped grounds. Other high rise buildings have sprouted here and there across the city.

One of the housing concerns was high rise buildings being constructed on the lakefront. In May 1971, the newly-formed Save the Lakeshore Committee, asked that all lakeshore development be frozen while an overall plan could be designed. In the east end the Lakeshore Park Motel and Top Hat Motel properties were frozen. In January, 1972, a Lakeshore Land Use Plan was initiated by Hamilton and Halton Region Conservation Authorities, and the Lakeshore Citizens Council for a Waterfront Study was formed by people from lakefront towns between Port Credit and Grimsby.

Eventually town houses were erected on the Lakeshore Park Motel property and Admirals Walk condominiums were built on the lakeshore site of the Top Hat Motel in 1977. The same year, the Ontario Municipal Board (OMB) approved the construction of high rise buildings on Lakeshore Rd. at the foot of Smith Avenue. The Anchorage mixed-use project at the foot of Brant St. met strong opposition until a set-back bylaw was passed. By then, loss of financing by the developer dictated the sale of the property and the erection of a hotel instead.

With the advent of rent control in 1976, fewer apartments were constructed, builders preferring condominiums. By 1996, condos were appearing throughout the city, in high rise and townhouse styles. The Brownstones, across from Mapleview Mall are one of the largest of the townhouse developments. Other examples are Roseland Green on New St. and Monarch Construction's Millcroft on Upper Middle Road. The cost of shoreline protection against erosion, increasing taxes and the cost of maintenance resulted in many of the old lakeshore estates being subdivided for the construction of multiple buildings and luxury homes. The beautiful old Victor Vallance home was torn down in 1992. The former Max Smith home, at Lakeshore and Stratheden, was moved forward 100 feet and converted to two apartments. Behind it, a condominium apartment complex, Brant's Landing, with a view

Appleby Place, retirement apartments.

of the lake, was built.

With interest rates soaring in 1979, housing starts in Burlington were down 51% and by 1981 interest rates had skyrocketed to 22 per cent. Plans continued, however, for several mega-projects. Headon Community plans were approved by the OMB in 1978, despite opposition by the city which felt it was premature since land was still available within the established urban area, and 500 new houses were unsold. The site was between Walkers and Guelph Lines, Upper Middle Road, and No.5 Highway. Developers Costain Ltd. (later Coscan Development Corp.) and Wimpey Construction Ltd. together owned 600 acres of the area's 800 acres.

The Maple Community of more than 120 acres east of the QEW along Maple Ave. north from Lakeshore Rd. was to be residential with a huge adjacent mall of 500,000 square feet. Monarch Construction's Rose Community was proposed in 1982 for 1000 acres defined by Highway 5, Upper Middle Road, Walkers Line and Appleby Line. To the west, the Palmer Community, another 1000 acre site of the oldest farmland in Burlington, predicted a doubling of the area's population when completed in 1984. All of these plans were delayed several years by the economy and the need for infrastructure to be provided by the city.

One of the developments of the 1990s was The Orchard, begun in 1996 by Mattamy Homes. The community stretches from Upper Middle Rd. to Highway 5, bounded by Appleby Line to the west and Burloak to the east.

Some of the names of specific areas in 1996 are: West Aldershot, Birdland, Highview up Cedar Spring Rd.,Maples, Freeman, Roseland, Ravenswood, Strathcona Gardens, Shoreacres, Pineland, Elizabeth Gardens, Burloak Estates, Tyandaga, Tyandaga Highland, Brant Hills, Mountainside, Longmoor, Dynes, Wellington Square, Headon Forest, Palmer, Rose and Millcroft.

A crisis in the oil industry gave rise in 1982 to a federal grant for home-owners switching from oil furnaces to alternate heating systems. In the same year grants were requested by homeowners (and later given to them) for removal of Urea Formaldehyde Foam Insulation from their homes.

Seniors were not forgotten in the housing race. To Rotary's Bonnie Place near Guelph Line and New St., was added an 11 storey apartment building in 1969. The next year, the first Ontario Housing seniors' complex was constructed at Pineland Ave. and Wedgewood Drive. Maranatha on New St. was opened in September, 1976, half of the units geared-to-income. Woodward Park, another subsidized seniors residence, opened in 1979 on Woodward Ave. near Central Park and the Seniors Centre. Christopher Terrace Retirement Home on New St. opened in 1984 modelled after Christopher Court on Pearl St.

In 1976, two special homes were opened, Pilkey House and Carey House. Halton Cheshire Homes purchased, with funding by the Maycourt Club, a house on Ontario St. as a home for people with disabilities. In 1977, it was named Carey House after Robert Carey who suffered for 15 years with Multiple Sclerosis and died late in 1976. He was named Citizen to be Remembered for 1976 for his work with the Social Planning Council's Services to the Handicapped Committee. In 1984, again with funding from the Maycourt Club and also from the Lakeshore Rotary Club, a 200 square foot extension was added to accommodate seven wheelchair residents.

Pilkey House Burlington Youth Residence was opened in an old home at the corner of Elizabeth and Maria Streets, renovated to accommodate 12 beds for troubled, disadvantaged teens aged 13-19. The house was donated by the Pilkey family. In 1996, it was under the aegis of Halton Adolescent Support Services. The Children's Aid Society, based in Oakville, also maintains group homes in the area. Subsidized housing had also begun to be built in the city – Driftwood Village in north Burlington and Wellington Square Housing Co-operative on Plains Rd., both in 1983. Social housing, including co-operative, non-profit and geared-to-income in the mid-1990s accounted for about 3 per cent of the total number of housing units according to Burlington Profile, published by the city's Office of Business Development. Sixty per cent were single family homes, townhouses and apartments, each 20 per cent. 'Affordable' housing has been built in several areas, not without protests by neighbouring residents. Population projected for 1996 was 137,500, awaiting the results of the more accurate 1996 census.

Burlington has pioneered in the field of town planning, council agreeing back in 1921 that preparations should be made for the years ahead. In was in 1949 when the district was made a planning area under the Ontario Planning Act of 1946, and the Burlington and Suburban Area Planning Board was set up by the Chamber of Commerce. Members have included men such as Edmond Holtby, Allan S. Nicholson, Gordon Schottlander, Gordon Gallagher and Robert Serena. The board consisted of eight Burlington

Aerial view looking north on Brant Street, 1946.

members appointed by council, two from Waterdown and two from East Flamborough.

The town's official plan, approved in 1962, made Burlington one of the first municipalities in the area to have an official master plan. The planning department was established in 1961, directed by Roger Roberts. His successor was Robert Serena, followed by Gary Goodman. Burlington's New Official Plan, approved by council in June, 1994, sets out growth for the next 20 years.

The Halton County Planning Association was formed in 1964 to coordinate planning throughout the county. As Robert Serena stated in 1966,"The uses of land are no longer confined to a single municipality; they tend to spill over from one municipality to another". Also, he later recalled that town planners and some councillors were realizing that a uniform tax base throughout the county would provide for non-residential and residential development with municipalities as partners in a regional organization rather than competing against one another. When definite steps were taken for the formation of regional government, the Halton County Planning Association ceased to function.

The Provincial Planning Act set out certain requirements for developers. After 1959 the act was broadened to allow municipalities to set their own standards. Developers in Burlington must put in hydro facilities, storm and sanitary sewers, satisfactory streets and street signs. The city and developer work together in deciding what refinements should go in. Some main roads leading to schools, for instance, call for curbs, boulevards and sidewalks while other short streets need only curbs and sidewalks.

In the 1970s, a zoning by-law set standards for aesthetics relating to neighbourhood appearance such as landscaping, and outdoor storage. Nor was industry exempt from standards. After Robert Serena retired as planning commissioner he became supervisor of site plan approval for industry seeking permits.

The education development charges bylaw was passed in 1992, under which builders were required to pay $1160 for each new residential unit. Commercial and industrial buildings were also assessed.

Burlington has run the gamut from log cabins to luxury penthouses. Little evidence remains of the town once described as the "Brighton of Canada", a watering place and summer resort without peer. The new Burlington meets the needs of a different age.

33
CELEBRATIONS

If there's one thing the people of Burlington know how to do, it's to celebrate auspicious historic occasions. One such was the coronation of King George VI, May 12, 1937. The celebration in Burlington was described in *The Gazette*: "Under a glorious May sky Burlington last Wednesday paid joyous tribute to our newly crowned monarch, George the Sixth".

On Brant St., businessmen decorated their stores with red, white and blue bunting and streamers, and flew the Union Jack. Strings of coloured lights were strung across the street. The Citizens' Band led a parade of school children from Central School down Brant St. and over to Lions Park. Prizes were given for the best bicycles, 'teddy waggons', doll buggies and tricycles. There was an address in the park by Hughes Cleaver MP, a maypole dance and the presentation of 500 coronation medals. To top it all off, there was a coronation dance that evening in the Legion Hall.

A more sombre occasion was the death of King George VI, February 5, 1952. There was a special memorial service at Trinity United Church on Thursday, February 14, arranged by Rev. H.G. Lowry and Rev. Keith Love. The speaker was Rev. Harold Carnegy of Hamilton; Lloyd D. Dingle, Q.C., Crown Attorney for Halton, read the oath of allegiance. The next day was proclaimed an official day of mourning with municipal offices, schools and the post office closed. At 11:00 a.m there were two minutes of silence. St. Luke's Church had held a special service that morning. King George VI was well-loved and widely mourned.

The coronation of Queen Elizabeth II was cause for celebration in June, 1953. A Burlington Coronation Committee had been organized with chairman, A.D. Pellerin. Special services were held at several churches: St. Luke's Anglican, Trinity United, Knox Presbyterian, Calvary Baptist, Burlington Baptist, St. John's Anglican, Gospel Tabernacle and Port Nelson United.

The Boy Scouts marked the occasion by organizing a Coronation Camp Site at Hydro Park from May 29 to June 2. On the evening of June 1, they hosted a bonfire on the Roy McKeon farm at the corner of Brant St. and Highway 5.

On the actual Coronation day, Tuesday, June 2, 1953, a community worship service was held at the arena with ministers from several area churches taking part. After the service, the Girl Guides marched along New Street. Another parade was organized in the afternoon, proceeding from Central School to Lions Park. Coronation Park was dedicated that day and a tree was planted there and at Spencer Smith Park.

The ceremony at Westminster Abbey was televised but for the many who had no sets, the Community Centre had a screen. Later in the day, there were softball games, a dance at the arena and fireworks at dusk.

CONFEDERATION CENTENNIAL

We do not know how people celebrated July 1, 1867. Were there parades and fireworks, or did many, without today's media coverage, not realize the significance of that date? Certainly in Burlington 100 years later, we knew.

In 1963, M.M.Robinson was made chairman of the Burlington Confederation Centennial Committee and preparations began.

Since federal money was available for approved projects to mark the Centennial year, Mr. Robinson quickly put in a request. With financing ensured and major projects in place, Mr. Robinson turned the chairmanship over to James Parker.

One of the major projects was the book *From Pathway to Skyway, A History of Burlington*. It was released Wednesday, March 22, 1967, with Mr. Parker presenting a copy to Mayor Lloyd Berryman. The winner of a contest for the book's name was Mrs. Ed. Parsons. Photographer Jim Fish took a shot of the new centennial tartan in his jacket and designed the cover. Ryerson Press of Toronto was the printer.

A second major project was the redevelopment of Spencer Smith Park. A redwood deck, Centennial Terrace was erected. The dedication ceremony of the $165,000 structure took place July 1 with M.M. Robinson and Robert Sones raising the flag. A Centennial Tea, organized by the Jaycettes, was held there on August 7, 1967. Ceremonies included the dedication of a tree given by the Horticultural Society, a drinking fountain from the I.O.D.E. and a bench from the Zonta Club. The University Women's Club donated a sculpture, "Winged Man" by Louis Archambault which had a short-lived stay in the park and eventually found a home at Central Library. In the park, clubs and organizations demonstrated the type of work in which they had been involved over the years.

Over the next few years, the breakwater was raised with the addition of a 4-foot parapet and a cement walkway, and further landscaping was undertaken.

To culminate the Canada Day celebrations, a Jaycees-sponsored street dance, with five bands playing, attracted 10,000 residents to downtown Brant St.

The Burlington newspapers were much involved with publicizing the many events and in assisting with programs. In 1966, a Centennial dress pattern appeared in *The Gazette* to enable seamstresses to begin making costumes for several events. A special section of *The Gazette* featured businesses of 1967 and a map pinpointing 28 Burlington farms which were held in uninterrupted possession by the same family for at least 100 years.

Mayor George W. Harrington
and
Members of Council of the Town of Burlington
-- in cooperation with --
The Archaeological and Historic Sites
Board of Ontario
respectfully request your presence
at the unveiling of
an historical plaque
commemorating the founding of Burlington
Sunday, September 9th, 1973
at 2:30 P.M.
Civic Administration Building
Brant Street
Burlington, Ontario

R.S.V.P.
Regrets only
Mrs. Strang   637-3851

Invitation from the Mayor's Office issued during the Burlington Centennial year 1973.

Winged Man, centennial gift to the city by the University Women's Club of Burlington.

The Centennial Committee sponsored many events such as Twelfth Night Ceremonies, Lowville Winter Carnival and Youth Day celebrations. The latter event, on May 22, included a parade of 3000 children and 12 bands marching to Central Park where CHML's Paul Hanover was MC for a variety show. Parade Marshall was Constable Peter Bromley of the Police Department. Of course there were fireworks at night, ending with a display depicting the Canadian flag.

The social event of the year was the Grand Centennial Ball held on June 16. Members of the Little Theatre made 1200 paper roses to decorate Nelson Recreation Centre. Evergreens enhanced the walls and there were flowers floating in the pool. Guest of honour was Premier John Robarts who, with other special guests, attended a civic dinner at the Estaminet before returning to dance to John Hood's 'society' orchestra. The Petite Club demonstrated period dances at intermission.

As often happens, the weather did not cooperate. Amid the showers, Burlington Band members, holding beach umbrellas, escorted guests from their cars to the arena.

A contest was held for home decorations and lighting, sponsored appropriately by the Public Utilities Commission. Many of the men of the town put away razors and joined the beard growing contest.

The federal government provided a Centennial Caravan of eight giant tractor trailers travelling across Canada, housing displays showing the development of Canada with an emphasis on the people of all walks of life who contributed to the country's history. The caravan came to Burlington and was set up in Central Park for six days from August 22.

Some of the other special events included a seniors' Centennial picnic at LaSalle Park in September, an arts and creative crafts exhibition at Royal Botanical Gardens in October, and Pioneer Days which attracted more than 5000 to Lowville Park for "old time" activities including a costume contest.

Nelson Township pioneers were not forgotten. A giant red granite rock from a No. 5 Sideroad farm was placed in front of the Board of Education offices on Guelph Line with a plaque to mark the occasion. The Burlington Historical Society sponsored the move as a Centennial project.

Chairs of the sub-committees of the Centennial Committee were: Mrs. K.R. Feldkamp, Centennial Ball; Roy Freckleton and Robert Sones, Pageantry and Special Events; Frank Dana, Caravan; Don Malpass, Sports; D. Kemp and E. Lavender, Education. Centennial Chairman, James Parker, one of the winners in the beard-growing contest, was chosen Citizen of the Year for 1967, in part for his efforts on behalf of the Centennial Committee.

Space does not allow a listing of all the events which were held on a Centennial theme. Suffice it to say, Burlington took the year to heart and did it up proud.

100 YEARS YOUNG

In 1973, Burlington celebrated its own Centennial. According to the lighthouse keeper's diary, the inaugural date was September 26, 1873. One hundred years later, just about every organization had a special event to mark the year. In fact, there were so many activities that the town published a calendar, distributed to every home.

At the end of July, 1972, as prelude to the celebrations, Burlington's Centennial flag was presented to Mayor George Harrington by Centennial chairman, Leo Podetz. It was later carried at the front of the Teen Tour Band as the band marched with the Commanders Drum and Bugle Corps to the mid-western band competition at Nelson Arena.

The Centennial Committee produced a kit of historical information for the schools. The Historical Society and the Joseph Brant Museum cooperated in the reprinting of *The Garden of Canada*, originally published in 1902.

Burlington became a garden once more in 1973 with many beautification projects. In the summer of 1972, the Garden Club planted, in the grounds of Joseph Brant Museum, flowers and shrubs that had been popular in 1873. A Centennial project of the Horticultural Society was a donation of funds to the city for a rose arbour. The arbour was to be built in front of Central Library and was erected in 1974. The Junior League of Hamilton-

Burlington contributed funds to assist the town's recreation department in the development of a Centennial Bikeway and Park along the Hydro right-of-way from Smith Avenue to Seneca Ave., including flowers and a play area. Yet another horticultural display was the town's Centennial emblem planted by Cornelius Van Staalduinen, a nursery operator, in front of Central Library. The parks department had built a sloping bed making the Indian head emblem visible to the street.

In November, 1972, a film was commissioned by the town, "Eyes of Memory" to be produced by George Thompson, grandson of the old light-house keeper. The 32-minute film was premiered in January, 1973.

On January 1, 1973, James Snow MPP and Mayor George Harrington opened the town's Centennial Year in front of the town hall.

During the year, concerts abounded, including Oscar Peterson's perfor-mance at Central Library, a rock concert with The Stampeders and another featuring Guy Lombardo and his Royal Canadians at Central Arena. The week of June 17-24 was set aside as Centennial Fun and Games Week. Events included a Town and Country Fair at the Shell property near Burloak Dr., Optimist Fun Fair at Optimist Park, Legion Highland Games and a St. John Ambulance pageant.

The first week of September was proclaimed Centennial Week. Special anniversary coins were to be accepted as cash but merchants had until September 14 to redeem them from the city. A Centennial medallion was presented to citizens who had made a significant contribution to the town.

Labour Day week-end featured such events as a family picnic, a youth parade and old fashioned contests including a swim suit contest with intro-ductions of past beauty show winners, and an evening concert by the Burlington Pops Orchestra and Choir. Because Labour Day was very hot with an off-shore breeze giving no relief, the Can-Am Catamaran Championships attracted only a handful of spectators to the lake.

Other waterside events included the Great Burlington Seaplane Race on Tuesday, September 11. Sixty aircraft taxied out of Burlington Bay for a five-day adventure, the first such race held in North America. Other events planned to follow the seaplane race were some spectacular air displays. On Saturday afternoon, September 15, the Burlington Belvedere Air Show was held at Spencer Smith Park and included a water-ski show.

On September 8, The Grand Centennial Ball was held at Burlington Mall. Women were encouraged to dress in costume; Ruby Hamilton had researched styles of the 1870s to design a simplified pattern for sewers. The centre of the mall became a dance floor with the Glen Miller Orchestra and Metro Stompers providing music. Tables and seats were arranged in the side aisles for the 2,000 attenders.

The Burlington Naval Association arranged for the HMCS Margaree, a Canadian Forces helicopter destroyer to be open to the public at Canada

Centre for Inland Waters, September 28. The sail training brigantine *S.T.V. Pathfinder* welcomed visitors. Finally, on September 29, there was a Grand Naval Ball at Central Recreation Centre with a parade the next day.

The grand finale to the year was New Year's Eve celebrations - fireworks and a giant bonfire at Central Park. Hot cider was served in cups to be kept as souvenirs. There was also a public dance at Tyandaga Golf Club. On New Year's Day, all recreation facilities were open for children with free skating and swimming, and there was a public reception at "CITY" hall.

Scottish dancers at Joseph Brant Day Celebration, 1990.   – courtesy The Burlington Post

The New Year celebrations also marked the status change from town to city and the inauguration of regional government in Halton.

ONTARIO BICENTENNIAL

Joyce Savoline and Walter Mulkewich were co-chairs for the Ontario Bicentennial celebrations in 1984, aided by a $10,000 grant from the city to assist with their programs. The big event was Canada Day week-end in July. The opening ceremonies for the fifth year of the Sound of Music Festival June 27 - July 1 featured the unveiling of Burlington's official flag designed by Canon Ralph Spence of St. Luke's Church. Four Ontario Centennial flags were presented to the Teen Tour Band. Parade Marshall of The Grand Festival Parade on Saturday morning was Billy O'Connor, television personality. Leading the parade was the Teen Tour Band, and other bands from as far away as Saskatchewan, the United States and Denmark were featured. Stages were set up for entertainment at Sims Square, Village Square, Brant St. Plaza, and at the foot of Brant St.

Other events were the visit of the tall ships to Burlington Bay for three days from July 27; Joseph Brant Day August 6 at LaSalle Park organized by Joseph Brant Jaycees and Joseph Brant Museum, and featuring an historical re-enactment and Indian dancers; and a Country Fair September 9 at Central

Sound of Music annual festival parade.   *– courtesy City of Burlington*

Park with a kissing booth, home baking and hot air balloon rides, among other amusements.

John Lawrence Reynolds was commissioned to produce a local history booklet, which was distributed to every home.

Bicentennial medals were given to 14 citizens for outstanding volunteer service.

The development of municipal patriotism and the bonding together of Burlington residents are just some of the benefits of such celebrations as these. Amid the fun, and sometimes the pathos, we share with each other feelings of warmth, and our love for this city.

34
Preserving the Past

HISTORICAL SOCIETY

There was an Historical Society in Burlington about 1914 with H.T. Foster, William Fisher and Arthur Peart among its active members. This group disbanded but, in 1959, an attempt was made to reactivate the society. Ruth Blair, Eva Blair, Dorothy Angus, Dorothy Spence, Jessie Small and Florence Peart met regularly for nearly a year before calling a public meeting in 1960. Leaders elected at that time included Grant Johnston, Florence Peart, Bob Rannie, Mrs. John Blair, Mrs. Eric Gudgeon, John McCallum and Jessie Small.

The society was instrumental in the formation of the Save Old Burlington Committee to protect the residential part of the core area from development. A House Survey Committee was formed in the early 1970s to identify and photograph all historic buildings.

The society had Provincial historical plaques placed at City Hall, LaSalle Park and Joseph Brant Museum. A plaque recognized the former Township of Nelson and another, W.E. Breckon as World Wheat King.

Since Burlington's l00th birthday in 1973, buildings which are more than 100 years old are being marked with Historical Society plaques. These consist of the Centennial logo on a wooden background with the year built and the name of the first owner of the building and his profession. The Royal Bank provided financial assistance as its contribution to Burlington's Centennial celebrations.

In 1976, the Historical Society persuaded the city to form a Local Architectural Conservation Advisory Committee. In 1977, the society was given the Award of Excellence by the Ontario Historical Society "for its outstanding contribution in the field of local history".

In 1989, the Society published *Burlington: Memories of Pioneer Days* and in 1992, *Burlington: The Growing Years*, both by Dorothy Turcotte.

This volume, the republication of *From Pathway to Skyway* with revisions and update to the mid-1990s, is an attempt to preserve some of the events and flavour of the past.

LACAC

The first meeting of Burlington's Local Architectural Conservation Advisory Committee was held on March 28, 1977. Attending were Mary Fraser, Chairman; Paul Smith, Vice Chairman; Helen Langford, R.S. Carter,

Historical Society plaque to pioneers, at Halton Board of Education Office.

Pioneer basement kitchen with open fireplace for cooking, Ireland House. – courtesy Ireland House Museum

J. Blums and J. Roberts. Matt Shuster of the Ontario Heritage Foundation outlined the responsibilities of this committee in the designation, under the Ontario Heritage Act, of buildings of architectural and historical significance. LACAC can advise city council of such buildings but council has the final decision on their designation. Once designated, a building has some protection against demolition and damaging alterations. Cast bronze plaques in blue and gold are placed on the buildings.

By 1994, a total of 27 buildings had been designated. The first was Ireland House. Most are in the old core area of the city but included are Lowville Mill, Lowville Church and parsonage, the Wood home at Q.E.W. and Guelph Line, the old Kilbride School converted to a private home, and Breckon House on Century Drive. This latter building was on land which became an industrial park and was saved from demolition by the Historical Society. It was eventually used for commercial purposes. The Hendrie Gates at Royal Botanical Gardens were also designated.

For Burlington LACAC's Inventory of Heritage Resources, members compiled evaluation records, photographs and information sources. Included are buildings more than 70 years of age and some newer ones of historical significance. In the first year of its existence, LACAC members made a list of 40 historic buildings. In 1978, a list was prepared of buildings in the core area which were being used for commercial purposes. In 1981, legal titles of 46 buildings in north Burlington were searched. These are examples of the accomplishments of LACAC; work such as this is continuing.

Every year since 1981, Heritage Building Awards, along with an artist's sketch of the home, have been given to owners for compatible maintenance, restorations or renovations of their homes. To educate people of the signifi-

Locust Lodge (built about 1839), Glenwood School Drive, designated under The Heritage Act.

LaSalle Park Pavilion, reopened 1997.
– courtesy LaSalle Park Pavilion Committee

cance of local architecture, a driving tour of the rural area and a walking tour of the core area were devised and flyers published for use on the tours.

Fortunately, with the work of the Historical Society and LACAC, the beauty of the early buildings of the city are being preserved. Businesses are discovering the value of locating offices in charming, restored homes. The tearing away of our history for a condo or a parking lot has been prevented or at least the pace slowed. Hopefully lovers of history will prevail over those who think only of today.

35
The Way Ahead

There was a time when residents of Burlington could walk down Brant St. and recognize everyone. Brant was THE main business street. Today it is merely one of many. Burlington has grown from the rural village of 1873 with a population of something over 750, to a town of 1914 with 2100 inhabitants, to a sprawling community of 1966 with population of 65,507, to a big city encompassing nearly 68 square miles, with a population of more than 137,000 in 1996. By 2011 population is projected to be 173,800.

Growth pressure coming from the west, and especially from the Greater Toronto Area to the east, has made it difficult for planners to keep some semblance of the city's rural heritage. Housing is filling just about every vacant area, and is marching up to Highway 5 apace.

Credit must be given to town departments for keeping up with the growth, ensuring services such as fire, police, and recreation meet the needs of the citizens. Financial constraints, especially on schools, libraries and hospitals, make the job tough. Yet driving though the city, one can still observe the care people take in their homes and gardens. The many trees, the clean streets, the fine public buildings, the bustling shopping areas, the successful industries, the many lovely parks, these are what make Burlington a vibrant and attractive place to live.

Did we mention air pollution, or traffic congestion? Big City woes that are hard to avoid!

It would appear then, that if present growth continues, Burlington may eventually become a part of a larger complex stretching either to the west or the east. More exact predictions are only likely to produce a chuckle for future readers just as Rev.G.W. Tebbs' forecast of 1927 did. "Is it too much to hope that by the time Burlington celebrates the centenary of Confederation, 40 years hence, it may be known as one of the beautiful cities of the Province?" Mr. Tebbs asked, and added with pride, "Surely Burlington stands a town 'nearest to Heaven and most like it'."

Perhaps this celestial comparison is less valid with the urban development of the past number of years than it was in 1927. Yet there grows among new residents the same pride in the town felt by past generations, a pride not only in the physical beauty of the town's location but in its achievements in keeping pace with a modern age.

Our children are Burlington's future.   *– courtesy City of Burlington*

Bibliography

Aldershot Historical Society, Tweedsmuir History Volumes

Booklets including *Burlington Lodge 1861-1964; The Garden of Canada; Souvenir Booklet of Burlington, 1927; Coronation Booklet, 1953*

The Burlington Gazette from 1966 to 1986 on microfilm, at Burlington Central Library

Burlington Central Library, microfilm and clippings

Burlington Historical Society files including copies of speeches given by guests at meetings, and research done by members

Burlington Office of Business Development, various publications

Burlington Women's Institute, Tweedsmuir scrapbook

Campbell, Marjorie Freeman, *Niagara: Hinge of the Golden Arc*, Ryerson Press, 1958

Canada's Story in Song, W.J. Gage Co., Toronto, 1965

Canadian Parliamentary Guides, published by P.G. Normandin, Ottawa, various years

Caniff, William, *The History of the Province of Ontario*, published by A. Hovey, Toronto, 1872

Chalmers, Harvey and Monture, Ethel Brant; *Joseph Brant: Mohawk*, Ryerson Press, 1955

Chapman, L.J. and Putnam, D.F., *The Physiography of Southern Ontario*, published for The Ontario Research Foundation by University of Toronto Press, 1966

Clarke, Gwen, *Halton's Pages of the Past*, published by Dills Printing and Publishing, Acton, 1955

Diaries of George Thomson from 1854 to 1875

Economic Survey of Ontario, 1956

Flatt, W.D., *A Brief Description of Lake Shore Surveys*, c.1900

Gernsheim, Alison, *Fashion and Reality*, published by Faber and Faber, London

Gourlay, Robert, *Sketches of Upper Canada*, London, 1822

Guillet, Edwin, *Early Life in Upper Canada*, University of Toronto Press, 1963

Halton County Atlas of 1877

Historical Sketch of the County of Haldimand

Jameson, Anna, *Winter Studies and Summer Rambles in Canada*, McClelland and Stewart, 1965

Johnson, Charles M., *Head of the Lake*, Wentworth County Council, 1958

Johnson Charles M., *Valley of the Six Nations*, University of Toronto Press, 1964

Kilbourn, William, *The Firebrand*, Clarke Irwin Co., 1956

Loverseed, Helga V., *Burlington, An Illustrated History*, Windsor Publications (Canada) Ltd., Burlington, 1988

Lower, A.R.M., *Colony to Nation*, Longmans Canada Ltd., 1964

The Mail Monopoly - Analyzing the Canadian Postal Service, Fraser Institute, Vancouver 1990

Mason, Philip P., *After Tippecanoe, Some Aspects of the War of 1812*, East Lansing: Michigan State University, 1963

McCallum, John, thesis: *Burlington: An Urban Study*, 1957

Minutes of Burlington Council

Minutes of Burlington Public Utilities Commission

Minutes of Halton Reform Association from 1860

Minutes of Nelson Township Council from 1836

New Genesee Farmer, published monthly in Rochester, N.Y., copies dated 1841

Newspaper clippings

Ryerson, Egerton, *The Loyalists of America and Their Times, Vol.II*, Briggs, Toronto, 1880

Smith's Canadian Gazetteer, 1846

Turcotte, Dorothy, *Burlington, Memories of Pioneer Days*, Burlington Historical Society, 1989

Turcotte, Dorothy, *Burlington The Growing Years*, Burlington Historical Society, 1992

Weaver, Emily P., *The Story of The Counties of Ontario*, Bell & Cockburn, 1913

Wentworth Historical Society booklets

Woodhouse, Roy, *History of the Town of Dundas, Part I*, Dundas Historical Society, 1965

Colour Illustrations

Black & White Illustrations

Index

The Burlington Centennial committee luncheon at the Estaminet Restaurant yesterday saw a preview of the book, Pathway to Skyway, by Mrs. David Ford, centre, and Mrs. Glenn Emery, right. Mrs. Edwin Parsons, who gave the book its title, is at the left.

From Pathway To Skyway

First Copy Goes To Mayor

BURLINGTON — F r o m Pathway to Skyway, the town's centennial book, made its first appearance here yesterday.

The first copy, a special leather - bound volume, was presented to Mayor Lloyd Berryman by James Parker, chairman of Burlington's centennial committee.

Barbara Ford and Claire Emery, co - authors of the work, were guests at a special "book introductory" luncheon at the Estaminet Restaurant.

The authors, both Burlington housewives, spent 22 months researching material used i n the book.

From Pathway to Skyway

traces the history of Burlington all the way from the ice age to the present day.

IT IS BELIEVED to be one of the finest books of its type yet produced.

"This is a monumental and historical day for the community," Mayor Berryman told Mrs. Ford and Mrs. Emery.

"This is more than just another book — you have given us a rich heritage."

Mr. Parker said the book is a most complete history of Burlington, one that every citizen in town now, and in the future, would find most informative and interesting.

"All residents of Burlington can be proud of this work. The board of education already has ordered copies for all school libraries," Mr. Parker said.

William J. McCulloch, local historian and editor of the book, paid tribute to the authors.

"TO MY GREAT satisfaction the two ladies did a lot of digging and brought out a lot of facts that had been hidden for a long time."

The 250 - page volume contains 33 chapters and close to 60 illustrations. First edition printing was 3,000 books.

It will be on sale at book st es and the centennial offi the town administra ing. The pri

$7,000 Budget Boost

BURLINGTON — budget for the tow development dep recommended by executive comm

This is $7,00

The com ended that given per two of i the Al

TF ne c

THE BURLINGTON GA

VOL. 70   NO. 7   BURLINGTON, ONTARIO, THURSDAY, MARCH 23, 1967

'PATHWAY TO SKYWAY' RELEASED YESTERDAY

To mark the release of "From Pathway to Skyway," the history of Burlington, a civic reception was held Wednesday afternoon at the Estaminet.

Special maroon leather bound editions of the book were presented to Mayor Lloyd Berryman, Mrs. E. Parsons of Cayuga who suggested the title and to the authors, Claire Emery and Barbara Ford. The special edition copies were also received by W. J. McCulloch who edited the book, M. M. Robinson, who was instrumental in having the project undertaken.

Those attending the luncheon included members of the Confederation Centennial Committee of Burlington and members of council.

"From Pathway to Skyway" was begun in May 1965, one of the town's Centennial projects. Free-lance writers Emery and Ford spent 15 months in research and writing and the technical production of the book was spread over 16 months.

The volume is well illustrated, with many of the pictures supplied from old family photograph albums. Burlington photographer James Fish and Ed Stewart's Toronto engraving firm have done a fine job of photograph and reproducing.

"From Pathway to Skyway" will be available next week in area book stores and at the Centennial office in the Public Administration Building for $4.95.

FROM PATHWAY TO SKYWAY . . . The first edition of Burlington's history is presented to Mayor Lloyd Berryman as the 260-page book, almost two years in the making, was released yesterday. Authors Claire Emery and Barbara Ford, right, make the presentation along with the town's Centennial committee chairman James Parker. The book is priced at $4.95 and has been highly praised by prominent local historian William McCulloch.

LIBRARY WANTS BUILDING

Asks money now

A presentation to council last week by Burlington library officials has left the board far from satisfied.

At that meeting council sympathized with library needs but said it was a matter of priority and that other requirements had left town coffers extremely low. It was added, however, that a sum of $400,000 was in the 1968 capital budget for a new main library building and a site selection committe had been established.

The library board requested $400,000 this year and $350,000 the following year as well as the

commitment for a definite site.

"We were glad to hear that a committee had been formed to recommend a site," library board chairman W. E. Loosley commented. He said however that the library needs not only an official offer of a suitable site, but that the allocation THIS YEAR of $450,000 so that construction of a main library building could begin this summer.

"Putting an item in the capital budget for 1968 is no assurance of a start on the building, not only because the life of the present council ends

in 1967, but because the capital budget is always subject to considerable revision," he said.

"The sum of $400,000 in 1968, even if it remains in the budget for that year, is far short of the $750,000 needed to build the first stage of the new main library building," Mr. Loosley added.

B.C. industry buys local firm

Glulam Products Ltd. of New Westminster, B.C., one of Canada's leading producers of laminated structural beams,

Barbara Ford and Claire Emery were on the staff of *The Burlington Gazette* when they were asked to write a history of Burlington. A happy collaboration produced *From Pathway to Skyway* in 1967. When Barbara moved with her family back to her native Windsor she became, for many years, a columnist with *The Windsor Star*.

Claire Emery, the former Claire Dickson, was born in Hamilton and is a graduate of McMaster University. After the death of her husband, Claire married Glen Machan and moved to Waterloo. While employed with the Kitchener-Waterloo Symphony she authored *The First 40 Years*, a history of the symphony. She also contributed editorially to two cookbooks. A request from the Burlington Historical Society to revise and update the original *From Pathway to Skyway* brought her back to the Burlington scene, and a city that is much changed from the community she left.

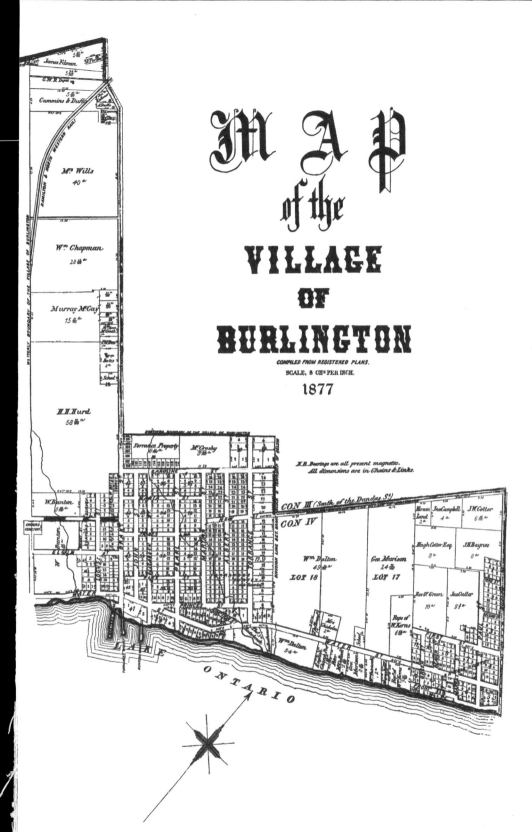

M A P

of the

VILLAGE

OF

BURLINGTON

COMPILED FROM REGISTERED PLANS.

SCALE, 8 CHS PER INCH.

1877

N.B. Bearings are all present magnetic.
All dimensions are in Chains & Links.

LAND FOR SALE
AT
WELLINGTON SQUAR

That beautiful property, the residence of
CAPT. JOSEPH BRANT, with 53 acres of choi
The property is delightfully situated, adjoining the
and overlooking the Lake, Bay and Canal. It
suited for a Gentleman's Home or Summer Resort
TERMS reasonable, immediate possession give
ALSO seven acres of Land with a Comfortabl
FRAME HOUSE.

Address BENJ. EAGER Wellington